Young
Children
in
ACTION

The Cognitively Oriented Preschool Curriculum

HIGH/SCOPE
EDUCATIONAL RESEARCH
FOUNDATION   Ypsilanti, Michigan

Young Children in ACTION

A Manual for Preschool Educators

by Mary Hohmann, Bernard Banet & David P. Weikart

THE HIGH/SCOPE PRESS

Published by
THE HIGH/SCOPE PRESS
High/Scope Educational Research Foundation
600 North River Street
Ypsilanti, Michigan 48197
(313) 485-2000

Library of Congress Cataloging in Publication Data

Hohmann, Mary.
    Young children in action.

    Bibliography: p.
    Includes index.
    1. Education, Preschool—Handbooks, manuals, etc. I. Banet, Bernard, joint author. II. Weikart, David P., joint author. III. Title.

LB1140.2.H59   372.21   78-22013

ISBN 0-931114-05-5

SECOND PRINTING, SEPTEMBER 1979

Preface

Nearly a decade has gone by since the publication of *The Cognitively Oriented Curriculum—A Framework for Preschool Teachers* (ERIC-NAEYC). During that time the program described in that volume has undergone many changes, been influenced by many people, young and old, and come into its own, we believe, as an exemplar of a fruitful direction for early childhood education. We have been fortunate in being able to work with a diverse group of adults over the years, women and men representing many different backgrounds, kinds of teaching experience, concerns and talents. Each teaching team that has used the curriculum framework has interpreted it in new ways, and in so doing has contributed to our practical knowledge. One clear trend that has emerged from this variety of interpretations is the increasing use of the small-group format for children's planning and for other group activities in which close attention by adults to what children are doing and saying is likely to make a difference in their development. That is only one example of the many evolutionary changes in the program that readers of the earlier volume will note in *Young Children in Action*.

The children, from whom we have learned so much as curriculum developers, have been another marvelously diverse group. As our program became known in communities throughout the U.S., Latin America and Australia, the curriculum framework had to stretch in order to be of use to all those children and the adults who worked with and cared for them. The curriculum no longer serves only the mildly handicapped or economically disadvantaged. In cognitively oriented preschools there are and have been gifted children, middle-class children, moderately and severely handicapped children, rural children, urban children, children of migrant field workers, children of extreme poverty in Latin America, bilingual children, Native American children, and so on. Some strategies which worked well with the original "target population" of disadvantaged children are not universally appropriate. For example, the emphasis in the original program on stimulus limitation and narrowness of instructional purpose in each activity is clearly inappropriate if applied to the full developmental spectrum of preschoolers. On the other hand, in working with developmentally delayed children, we have learned (or perhaps re-learned) that there are preschoolers still functioning at the sensorimotor level who require teaching strategies more akin to traditional infant/toddler activities than to activities designed for "preoperational" children.

As demands for behavioral objectives, accountability, basic skills and competency based teacher training were made by sources external to the classroom, we attempted to help teachers and teacher educators translate the Cognitively Oriented Curriculum into terms that could be comprehended by administrators and parents. The movement from a local demonstration project to national and international replication of the curriculum, which began in 1968, also brought home to us the necessity of describing our program in terms that would be clearer to practitioners. We substituted the terms "action" and "language" for "motoric level" and "verbalization", to give just one small but telling example. We also found that some of the ways of summarizing the framework were too condensed to be helpful in all cases, so we attempted to be more explicit; the diagram used throughout the earlier book led to the teaching strategies and "key experiences" that form the core of the present book.

We learned too that films, videotapes, slides and photographs often conveyed our ideas more clearly than a book could, so we developed audio-visual presentations on some of the topics that would eventually be covered in this book. In so doing we clarified our thinking, simplified concepts and produced an extensive pictorial record of young children (and adults) in action. Checklists such as the Child Observation Record and Preschool Teacher Training Profile were developed as aids to communication with the outside world as well as for use by the classroom teams. The key experiences concept was designed to convey more precisely the kind of purposefulness on the part of adults that we are after.

Over the years our interpretation of child development theory has undergone changes, often influenced by other English-speaking interpreters of Piaget such as Lawrence Kohlberg, John Flavell, Burton White, David Elkind, J. McV. Hunt, Hans Furth and Irving Sigel. We hope that the spirit in which we have used developmental theory and research comes through as respectful but not reverent. We feel that the theory base from which educators can work is far too inadequate for deductively derived educational practices to be of much use. We present the reader, then, with a framework derived from both theory and practice. This framework, in keeping with Piagetian assumptions, stresses the importance of the child's initiative, of active learning; both teacher and child have important roles in defining learning experiences. We urge that this not be viewed as a narrowly Piagetian curriculum but rather as a general framework for an approach to education that stresses problem-solving and decision-making by both child and adult.

The program, of course, is not complete; it can never be, because the society in which our children grow is constantly changing and education must respond to change, and because each "cognitively oriented" teacher is in effect applying the general principles of the curriculum to a set of circumstances that for all practical purposes are unique. This is of the essence: the curriculum is not a package developed by an elite corps of "experts" and applied mechanically by a mass of pedagogical technicians; it is composed, rather, of ideas and attitudes that all who are seriously involved in it use as the basis for their own thinking and development. It is not easy to put into practice. Every adult who works within it must spend several years developing the right combination of personal style and "cognitive" style, making it his or her own through use and study. Such an undertaking represents a major commitment to improve the future of children. The work involved is great, but the stakes are high.

Many individuals have made important specific contributions to the development and production of this book. Charles Silverman had the major responsibility for overall editorial supervision. His contribution to the consistency and flow of the volume is a vital one. Assisting him over the years were Ellen Ilfeld, Nancy Altman and Paul Phillips. Gwen Coppersmith had a major role in the creation of the draft edition from which this volume has evolved. Marilyn Adams, working from materials outlined by

Chavela Flores and Dennis Vigil, has contributed the statement on bilingual/bicultural applications. Chavela Flores is largely responsible for the chapter on working with parents.

High/Scope field consultants and teachers have had an important role in the development of the curriculum, especially Carole Thomson, Patricia Nederveld, Betsy McIntosh, Linda Rogers, Susan Shipstead, Joanna Phinney, Sara Jane Adler, Bettye McDonald, Ruth Grochowski, Thelma Valenstein, Donna McClelland, Sharon Bixby, William Fabricius, Sheila Mainwaring and Alice Hudson.

Jan Diamondstone, our instructional systems specialist, has had a key role in developing the total training system, of which this book is one part. Many of her audiovisual productions and those coordinated by Dennis Ackley predated these chapters and were extremely helpful in writing this edition.

Research Associates Robert Matz, Jean Ispa and James (Terry) Bond contributed their expertise in instrument design to the creation of the assessment tools contained in this book, in addition to adding importantly to the ongoing discussion of the applications of developmental theory to educational practice.

Gary Easter documented our classrooms on film for many years and produced the photographs that grace these pages. Patrick Mullaly, our graphic designer, spent many long and thoughtful hours turning all the words and photographs into a lively and attractive book. Typing of the manuscript was coordinated by Nancy Brussolo and carried out through its several stages by Carolyn Ofiara, Sarah Prueter, Sylvia Jenkins, Sheryl Vigmostad and Susan Miller.

We cannot list all of the teachers, curriculum assistants, scholars, Head Start directors, education coordinators, federal and local project officers, teacher preparation instructors, inservice trainers, consultants, school and daycare administrators, parents and children who have aided High/Scope staff in developing this approach to preschool education. We would like, however, to explicitly acknowledge those individuals not directly associated with High/Scope who took the trouble to give us specific suggestions after reviewing the field draft of this book. Of course, they do not bear any responsibility for the book's defects. These reviewers are Courtney B. Cazden, Leonard Sealey, Judith Ramirez, Angelo Angelocci, Leah Adams, Judith Williston, Samuel Meisels, Gerald R. Levin, Josue Cruz, Jane Teleki, Zina Steinberg and Shirley Willard. Useful in-house suggestions were received from Dolores Lambie and Lawrence Schweinhart.

We wish also to thank those organizations and agencies that have given us the financial resources with which to accomplish some of the work of curriculum documentation, manuscript preparation and project evaluation: The Bureau of Education for the Handicapped, the Office of Child Development, the Lilly Endowment, the Spencer Foundation and the Carnegie Corporation of New York.

And finally we wish to acknowledge the help and support of our families: Lucy Norton, an understanding mother and grandmother who spent many hours with Susanna and Tommy Hohmann while their mother wrote; Charles Hohmann, who along with his unremitting support gave his wife many personal guided tours through the labyrinthian writings of Piaget; Barbara Banet, who contributed substantively as well as affectively from her experience as a preschool teacher and author; Phyllis Weikart, who was encouraging in all her capacities as wife, High/Scope Board member, educator, author and friend; and most especially our own children—Susanna and Tommy Hohmann, Jeffrey Banet and Cindy, Cathy, Jenny and Gretchen Weikart—whose growth and development have been and continue to be our greatest treasure and inspiration.

Ypsilanti, Michigan   M.H.
December 1978   B.B.
                                        D.P.W.

Contents

Foreword

In the late 1950s a rapid expansion of special education services was undertaken in the State of Michigan in response to a growing awareness of the need for the public schools to provide more services to children traditionally served poorly or only in specialized institutions. Classes for the handicapped were encouraged through liberal state financing. Citizens could initiate special tax levies to support additional services in special education. In addition to classroom programs, specialists in school social work, school psychology and speech therapy, and professionals in the various disciplines specializing in education for the handicapped, were consulted. The Ypsilanti, Michigan school district, correctly identifying a massive need within the district for additional services to children, rapidly expanded special services from two full-time staff members in 1957 to more than 40 in 1962. Expansion of special services occurred throughout the state, making Michigan a national leader in programs for handicapped children.

By 1960 it had become apparent to the special services staff in Ypsilanti that the lower-socio-economic groups within the district were almost categorically eligible for special services. This was pointed up in the finding that 50 percent of the children in one working-class school had been retained in grade by fourth grade while only 8 percent in a middle-class school had been retained. The majority of the so-called mentally retarded students, discipline cases and referrals to outside agencies were from the lower-socio-economic population of the community, both black and southern white. When these patterns of service needs became obvious and predictable, various proposals were generated to effect some changes in the outlook of the school system toward these groups, an outlook shaped by the desire to "adjust" the children to the demands of the educational system.

Recommendations to adjust the educational system to the needs of the children were not well received. It was in this context that our focus on preschool education evolved. The special services staff and several principals from the school system started a planning group to discuss possible courses of action. From these discussions it was determined that the potential of preschool intervention should be explored, not because anything was known about the effects of such efforts, but, first, because preschool could be offered before entry into the regular schools and was therefore outside the normal channels of educational control, and second, because it was felt that disadvantaged young children could be taught how to wrest an education from the school system as middle-class children did. Our long-range prediction, actually our hope, was that through preschool education we could reduce retention in grade and related symptoms of alienation such as juvenile delinquency. Thus the Ypsilanti Perry Preschool Project was born, a project which is still in long-term follow-up. The Cognitively Oriented Curriculum, however, was still in the wings, for we had little idea of what should constitute an educational preschool program for disadvantaged children.*

Two issues shaped our initial thinking about curriculum. First, we were determined that it should not be a "manners and morals" approach. We visited a nearby metropolitan school district where a principal had established an after-school preschool project for the brothers and sisters of children who attended the school. The class was run by an elementary teacher with firm ideas of discipline and correct behavior. The program included a snack time during which each child was required to say "excuse me" after he had finished and before he could leave the table. Each child complied, some in voices so soft that the teacher requested a repeat in a louder tone. Things went relatively well until the last child was required to intone the proper response before leaving the now empty table. Looking around at the empty chairs, he steadfastly refused to comply. The teacher finally relented, after a prolonged period of demanding compliance with the "rule." So much for the manners and morals approach; it did not offer the type of student development we envisioned.

The second issue that shaped our thinking was whether to accept the prevalent notion that a preschool program ought to be limited to general social-emotional support for the child. This was a more difficult decision. From a review of the literature it appeared to us that typical preschool

programs did in fact pay little attention to intellectual development in young children, which seemed to us a serious lack given the prognosis for the children we were to serve. Those few programs that concentrated on intellectual development tended to restrict themselves to training in specific skills, focusing on rote learning and memorization; this seemed to us both short-sighted and inappropriate. We chose, finally, to focus on the general cognitive growth of the child, more from a reaction against the alternatives than from a sound knowledge of what the curriculum should be. The major early commitment was to a teacher-planned program that avoided rigid structure while helping children acquire the intellectual strengths they would need in school.

At this early stage there was also a strong (though ambivalent) commitment to a group process, wherein teachers and researchers worked together to build the curriculum. This ethical bias toward a collaborative effort narrowed the range of forms the curriculum could assume. It would have been impossible for such a group to produce either a direct-instruction model or a free-play model. Thus the preferred operating style of the staff helped shape the style of the program, just as the scholastic needs of the children contributed a sense of realism regarding the proper focus of the educational content.

It is difficult in the 1970s to imagine the dearth of information about preschool curriculum that the Perry Project faced. In 1960, when the first planning for the project began, there were few clear guidelines on how to operate a nursery school. A review of the literature turned up philosophical treatments of curriculum but little else. The university laboratory schools had their master teachers and "open" programs, and

---

*At this early stage the program was directed toward disadvantaged children only. While the staff wished to include a wider socio-economic grouping, this was not possible, because the only funding available was for children with special needs from low-income families. Use of the Cognitively Oriented Curriculum for all socio-economic groups and all ability levels did not occur until after 1970.

the cooperative nursery schools flourished in free play. Published discussions of curriculum that the staff turned up stressed group dynamics and physical, social and emotional development, but programs specifically aimed at school success and/or cognitive development were not accessible to us if they were in fact available.

The preschool program was launched, then, without benefit of much information about preschool programming. Drawing from their formal teaching experience, the classroom staff decided to have daily plans and to outline long-term goals for the program to guide the short-term planning. They organized themselves into a teaching team, with each staff member assuming responsibility for six or seven students—a responsibility that included weekly educational home visits. Regular meetings with the research and administrative staffs provided points of reference for content discussions, and consultants who could advise us in specific areas were identified.

Though there was much excitement and good spirit among the staff at this time, a certain ambivalence about collaboration was clearly evident in the early planning meetings. All staff agreed on the need to provide adequate "content"—number activities, reading readiness and other identifiable school subjects. When the teaching staff met to carry out these decisions, however, there were major problems. The four teachers had taken to playing Scrabble during their planning meetings, hardly a device to focus attention on the children but certainly a means to reduce the burden of interaction on the issues. One teacher would suggest a particular activity or strategy and another would shrug a shoulder or lift an eyebrow. The whole process seemed to be a reflection of a tacit agreement that each teacher would "do her own thing," with no central planning. There seemed to be no way to get

the creative interaction necessary to produce a truly effective program. They seemed to be saying to their inexperienced project director, "You have your ideas and we have ours, and we're simply not going to be pushed into anything." The situation appeared to have the makings of an ironic melodrama, with the teachers re-enacting the roles that had blocked change in the public schools and led to the new project in the first place.

We had forgotten the children, and they in turn provided the solution, or at least the motivation for a solution. About six rather frustrating weeks into the project a four-year-old boy threw a folding chair across the classroom in defiance and boredom. A hurried telephone call brought the project director, and a planning conference was convened. Out of this grew a serious and truly cooperative plan by the teaching staff, with genuine support from the research staff. The project was underway at last, with everyone fully committed. Of course there were other incidents and other issues, but from here on in it was all done professionally. Teachers, researchers and support staff learned to function together and resolve differences.

During that first year the program was distinctly directive without being specifically didactic, more the flavor of an organized kindergarten than a free-play co-op nursery. The teacher had specific goals drawn from a fairly traditional view of curriculum content. When not engaged in a specific teaching task, she had general goals, such as "to surround the child with language" (later called "verbal bombardment") and "to guide activities." In spite of our rejection of the idea that general social and emotional goals should be the major focus of a preschool program, these goals were also very much present in the thinking and planning of the staff.

The theoretical position of the staff was one of acceptance of developmental goals but on a rather limited basis. For example, while there was an understanding that children learn through discovery, there was also a commitment to highly organized and sequenced teaching; the teaching task was defined as preparing the children for school, and that required teaching specific information and skills.

In the fall of 1963, *Contemporary Psychology*, a journal of book reviews published by the American Psychological Association, carried a review of J. McVicker Hunt's major new book, *Intelligence and Experience*. This book cracked the myth of fixed intelligence and opened the door to debate regarding the role of education in helping all children develop their true potential. While it was the old nature-nurture controversy unleashed at gale strength, Hunt placed the issues within a broad intellectual framework that caught the imagination of many educators and psychologists. The reviewer commented that Hunt presented a good description of the work of a little known Swiss psychologist, Jean Piaget. Some of us on the Perry Project staff read Hunt's book, and it was immediately clear to us that Piaget's theories were concerned with the very same issues of cognitive development that were coming up in our own staff discussions. We had to find out more.

The next step was to establish a seminar for the staff in Piagetian theory so that we could see whether the theory could be translated into operational principles for the curriculum. Six two-hour seminars were arranged to introduce the work of Piaget to the staff, most of whom had not heard of Piaget before. The staff then began the slow, difficult, but ultimately rewarding process of organizing the classroom program around Piagetian developmental theory and learning to work within and around the limits of the theory.

Another event of major importance in the development of the curriculum was a day of consultation provided by Sara Smilansky, an Israeli psychologist who was studying the socio-dramatic play behavior of Israeli disadvantaged youngsters. This took place in the fall of 1964. Smilansky showed us how to integrate our new ways of working with children with some of the best in traditional early childhood education which we, perhaps rather smugly, had overlooked.

The full statement of the curriculum of this period appears in the book, *The Cognitively Oriented Curriculum*, by Weikart, Rogers, Adcock, and McClelland, published in 1971. Piagetian theory was important in determining the content of this program. The format of the day and the general method of teacher-child interaction, however, were rooted in the suggestions of Smilansky and traditional nursery-school programming. Smilansky's three-part sequence of planning, working and evaluating by children became the organizing principle for the daily routine, and has remained so—with some modifications—to the present time.

The Piagetian influence led to some important changes in the curriculum during the period 1964-69. The emphasis on pre-academic activities was replaced by an emphasis on the strengths of each child, viewed from the perspective of the child's developmental level. This was a decisive reorientation—away from a preoccupation with deficits and toward a focus on the child's assets. And the idea of representation, so critical in Piagetian theory, served as a basis for building the links to traditional academic exercises in reading and mathematics.

The most significant change, however, was

yet to come: the devolution of responsibility for initiating learning experiences from the teacher alone to the child and teacher together. The transition to this position of increased initiative for the child, precipitated by the new emphasis on children's planning, took years to complete—for at this stage the teaching staff still looked upon the child as one who is chiefly on the receiving end of the teaching-learning continuum.

During this period the teachers were "teaching" specific Piagetian tasks related to developmental stages. Given what we know now, teaching developmentally based tasks is hardly a realistic educational goal, for both theoretical and practical reasons. But as Bernard Banet has pointed out, all Piagetian programs seem to have gone through this stage of direct teaching, either to accelerate children's development or to strengthen particular abilities that would help in school. Some programs have even gone so far as to create kits to "teach" classification, etc., or to diagnose children by means of Piagetian developmental tests so that remedial teaching could be undertaken. The Cognitively Oriented Curriculum, partly because of its tie to traditional nursery education, didn't stumble into that blind alley. However, the staff did aspire to "teach" basic Piagetian skills, and it wasn't until the next phase of curriculum development that the role of the child as "constructor" of knowledge became paramount.

The early 1970s saw a major step forward in the development of the Cognitively Oriented Curriculum with the organization of the classroom program around a set of key experiences derived from developmental theory and the practical knowledge gained by the staff during a decade of work with young children. With these key experiences at their disposal, the teachers stopped asking questions of the children to which they (the teachers) knew the answers and began asking children to talk about what they were doing, thinking, intending. The purpose was to explore the dimensions of the child's thinking instead of asking "test" questions for a predetermined list of goals. The conversations became real. Gone was the "verbal bombardment" of the early period where the teacher "surrounds the child with language." The new focus was on helping children use the preschool and home environment for their own activities and goals. The teacher fit his or her developmental knowledge to the purposes of the child. In a sense the program became less overtly Piagetian by becoming more committed to the fundamental theme of Piaget. As Banet has written, "The point of Piaget's epistemology is that children abstract underlying truths through active encounters with reality, not through active encounters with genetic epistemologists."

By way of a summary of the complex process that led to the preschool program described in these pages, we should like now to portray the essential features of the adult's role at each stage in the development of the program.

In stage 1, the teacher instructs the children in a fairly relaxed but organized manner in those skills he or she deems important in respect to preparation for school. The teacher uses "verbal bombardment" to surround the children with language and plans sequential experiences in pre-math, pre-science, pre-reading, etc., encouraging graduated learning by each child. The child *receives* education through adult instruction.

In stage 2, the teacher accepts the idea that children are at different developmental stages and attempts to teach children the skills that typify their stage so they can "progress" to the next stage. While Piagetian terminology is employed and the class is organized around developmental goals, the teacher still instructs primarily by asking questions to which the answer is already known; she constantly tests the children with her questions. The child is more free to interact with the environment than before but is not granted the time or the latitude to truly take the initiative, or more properly, *share* the initiative, in the learning process.

In stage 3, the teacher helps the children consolidate their abilities in developmentally appropriate ways, through direct and representational experience, without trying to accelerate their development or push them along to the next level. The teacher asks questions of the children about their plans, intentions, experiences and observations. When the teacher "tests" the children, the purpose is to gather information, so that the children will have maximum support for independent learning. Each child is recognized as an individual who builds his or her own knowledge through initiatives shared with supportive adults. Which is to say, each child is *active*. And so we arrive at the present volume, *Young Children in Action*.

Introduction:
A curriculum framework

The overarching goal of our work at the High/ Scope Foundation is to produce a framework for *developmentally valid education*. The concept of developmental validity makes the assumption that human beings develop capacities in predictable sequences throughout the life span. At each developmental stage new capabilities emerge. Good environments for learning exercise and challenge the developing potentials. Poor environments for learning do not permit newly developing skills to be used, or demand that these skills be employed at a level of competence too far beyond the learner's reach.

Despite the predictability of developmental sequences, human development of course does not produce uniform, predictable outcomes. All people have individual characteristics from birth which progressively differentiate into unique personalities. Learning always occurs in the context of the learner's unique characteristics. Educational procedures which ignore or attempt to eliminate these characteristics obviously do so with unfortunate consequences.

If there is predictability in the process of growth and change from infancy through old age, that is, if there are developmental stages, then it is likely that there are times during the life cycle when certain kinds of things are learned best or most efficiently, and that there are pedagogical methods that are more appropriate at certain times in the developmental sequence than at others.

Given that developmental change is a basic fact of human existence, but that each person is also developmentally unique, and that there are optimal times for particular kinds of learning, developmentally valid education can be defined by way of three criteria: An educational experience, procedure or method is developmentally valid if it 1) exercises and challenges the capacities of the learner that are emerging at a given developmental stage; 2) encourages and helps the learner to develop his or her unique pattern of interests, talents and long-term goals; and 3) presents the learning experience when the learner is developmentally best able to master, generalize and retain that which is learned and relate it to previous experiences and future expectations.

High/Scope's Cognitively Oriented Preschool Curriculum represents an attempt to construct a developmentally valid educational framework for children who are functioning in what Piaget calls the "preoperational" period of development.

We have utilized developmental theory and research to identify the nature of the developmental changes occurring during the preschool years—the characteristics of the young child, his emerging abilities and developmental limitations. We have also reviewed the developmental-psychological literature in order to better understand the processes that account for developmental change.

A word about social and emotional development

Many adults, noting the term "cognitively oriented," have assumed that there is little concern in this program for the social and emotional development of young children. They fear that the program may be insensitive to critical problems and landmarks of children's growth. In fact, the program is highly sensitive to these issues but deals with them through indirect means. The reasoning, based on much experience, is that it's easier and more productive to focus directly on, say, children's planning than on group dynamics, on classifying objects and events than on interpreting fantasies—the one is concrete and intelligible, the other abstract and esoteric. The following are some of those "indirect means" by which social and emotional growth are promoted in a cognitively oriented program:

One of the chief concerns of the curriculum is that adults accept children (and their parents) as they are—linguistically, culturally and developmentally. Such acceptance means that adults do not try to maneuver children into preconceived roles ordained by the methods or objectives of the program but view them instead as participants, contributing members, so to speak, who help to *create* the program. This results almost invariably in a positive and supportive relationship between teachers and children, which of course is crucial to social and emotional growth.

Children in this program have control over what happens to them. The emphasis on planning, working and evaluating establishes personal responsibility in the child. The adult is asked to risk allowing the child to be in charge of his or her own activities; the reward, when adults are wise enough to know how to guide the process, is that children's sense of self-worth and of independence are strengthened—a sure sign of social and emotional growth.

Because the curriculum is attuned to the cognitive development of the individual child, children have ample opportunity to explore and experiment at their own level of knowledge. Children's activities are both interesting and satisfying to them because adults are aware of their need for challenge and success, for the right developmental fit and for room to grow. Full involvement in and satisfaction from one's work is of course of prime importance for social and emotional growth.

Developmental theory: useful but incomplete

Scientific knowledge of the processes of development is still primitive, and on many points there is no agreement among researchers and theorists. Given this state of affairs we have chosen to take the following path: 1) utilize the most complete and coherent theory available: that of Jean Piaget; 2) base curriculum strategies and goals on the most widely accepted principles in Piaget's work rather than on the esoteric, controversial fine-points.

Piaget has called attention to the importance of changes in the underlying structure of the thought processes for an understanding of human development. We accept as a useful starting point Piaget's assumption that developmental change is based both on biological processes of maturation and on the experiences of an active subject who gains knowledge by acting upon the world and by utilizing feedback from his actions to construct increasingly useful hypotheses about reality. New experiences are interpreted by the subject in light of the hypotheses, assumptions and theories—the cognitive "structures"—that constitute his intellect at a given moment in his development; at the same time, these experiences serve to change the cognitive structures and thus to effect a further development. Our "map" of developing systems within a child has been profoundly affected by the theories of Piaget and the investigations of researchers working within the Piagetian frame of reference. The set of psychological systems of interest to developmental psychologists at the present time includes sensorimotor processes, perception, memory, nonverbal representation, language, cognitive structures and operations (systems of mental transformations) and affective processes. These systems are seen as interacting with each other, and as being influenced by the biological systems that define the human organism's characteristics, including those that determine growth, maturation and aging. Of course psychological systems are also influenced by a person's experiences with the environment; one of Piaget's contributions has been to help us see that experience is initiated by an active subject and thus that learning and development are more than the conditioning of reflexes.

How these psychological systems interact has become one of the central issues in contemporary psychology. It would be convenient for curriculum developers if issues such as the relation between language and logical operations or between sensorimotor processes, mental images and memory systems were resolved. But this is not the case. Even more frustrating for the curriculum developer is the absence of a clear theoretical picture, let alone supporting data, concerning the relation between experience or specific maturational processes on the one hand and any of these developing systems on the other. We have better ways of *describing* development, thanks to the work of such scholars as Piaget, Bruner and Chomsky, but remarkably little information on the specific determinants of developmental change of the sort that can be translated into educational practice. This becomes painfully evident when teachers interact with children who are not making "normal" developmental progress. What we can do at best is to take a theory such as Piaget's and use it to generate hypotheses about the kinds of experiences that would be most relevant to the goal of supporting the rapidly growing cognitive systems of the normal child (and infer from these how a handicapped child might best be helped).

Implications of Piaget's theory for early childhood education

Piaget has been most interested in the development of the logic implicit in a child's thought and actions. He has shown that logical truths, such as the principle of transitivity (if A is greater than B and B is greater than C, then A must be greater than C), are comprehended without formal teaching, but neither is their comprehension something innate; logical-mathematical knowledge is constructed by the child out of many specific actions and experiences. Logical insights such as number conservation, transitivity, the class-inclusion relation and the conservation of physical properties despite apparent transformations (transformations of mass, weight, volume, etc.) emerge in predictable developmental sequences that resist acceleration through adult intervention.

For educators it should be stressed that logical-mathematical knowledge is the least "teachable" kind of knowledge there is. This knowledge is *inevitably* mastered by organically intact human beings, at least through the "concrete operations" level. Acceleration of development through didactic teaching does not seem to be a developmentally valid course since children construct their *own* models of reality, which develop over time in response to new experiences and exposure to other viewpoints.

To us, the overriding implication of Piaget's work for educators is that *the teacher is a supporter of development*, and as such his or her prime goal is to promote *active learning* on the part of the child. Active learning—the direct and immediate experiencing of objects, people and events—is a necessary condition for cognitive restructuring and hence for development; put simply, young children learn concepts through self-initiated activity. Such activity, carried on in a social context in which an alert and sensitive teacher is a participant-observer, makes it possible for the child to be involved in experiences which produce the optimal degree of cognitive disequilibrium and hence the impetus for cognitive restructuring. The interests and talents of the child are most readily enlisted when learning is conceived as an interplay of physical and mental action initiated by the learner.

Learning is decisive and lasting to the degree that it is active and direct, because active and direct experiences engage the senses and the motoric system; they provide the child with the core understandings around which new knowledge can be built through less direct means when the child is developmentally more mature.

It could be said that Piaget is not alone in this view, that this philosophy is wholly consistent with Dewey or Montessori or Socrates. We agree, enthusiastically, and feel that this consensus among philosophers of education represents a firm base from which to proceed.

Characteristics of the preschool child

Let us make *active learning* the central assumption of the "process" side of our curriculum framework. What of the *content* of a child's development? What is it about preschoolers that differentiates them developmentally from infants on the one hand and school-age children on the other? What are the most important developing systems to support in three- and four-year-olds?

After a couple of years of hard work as an infant and toddler, the developmentally normal

Key experiences in active learning
• Exploring actively with all the senses.
• Discovering relations through direct experience.
• Manipulating, transforming and combining materials.
• Choosing materials, activities, purposes.
• Acquiring skills with tools and equipment.
• Using the large muscles.
• Taking care of one's own needs.

Key experiences in using language
• Talking with others about personally meaningful experiences.
• Describing objects, events and relations.
• Expressing feelings in words.
• Having one's own spoken language written down by an adult and read back.
• Having fun with language: rhyming, making up stories, listening to poems and stories.

Key experiences in representing experiences and ideas
• Recognizing objects by sound, touch, taste, and smell.
• Imitating actions.
• Relating pictures, photographs, and models to real places and things.
• Role playing, pretending.

- Making models out of clay, blocks, etc.
- Drawing and painting.

Key experiences in developing logical reasoning

CLASSIFICATION

- Investigating and labeling the attributes of things.
- Noticing and describing how things are the same and how they are different. Sorting and matching.
- Using and describing something in several different ways.
- Describing what characteristics something does *not* possess or what class it does not belong to.
- Holding more than one attribute in mind at a time. (Example: Can you find something that is red and made of wood?)
- Distinguishing between "some" and "all."

SERIATION

- Comparing: Which one is bigger (smaller), heavier (lighter), rougher (smoother), louder (softer), harder (softer), longer (shorter), taller (shorter), wider (narrower), sharper, darker, etc.
- Arranging several things in order along some dimension and describing the relations (the longest one, the shortest one, etc).

child has substantially achieved the ability to *mentally represent* and direct his or her actions and experiences, and to communicate verbally with others. These are enormous accomplishments; at three years, the human being is already a more competent problem solver than the adult members of any other animal species on earth. The preschooler is becoming able to *reflect on his or her own actions*, to *recall* past experience, to *predict* consequences in familiar cause-and-effect sequences, to *solve* everyday kinds of problems mentally without relying exclusively on physical trial and error, and to think about places and times other than the here and now.

Symbolic representation, the utilization of so-called "figurative knowledge" in the form of mental images and imitation, has developed out of the actions of the sensorimotor period (the first year and a half to two years of life). Preschoolers are powerfully motivated to exercise these symbolic processes, just as they are obviously "programmed" by inherited patterns to exercise their language-using and language-learning capabilities. Preschool children enjoy *imitating, pretending, drawing pictures, making "models"* of real things out of blocks or clay, because through these activities they are able to exercise their ability to represent the world. They are *learning to distinguish symbols or representations from the things they stand for*, although sometimes fantasy, magic, dreams, and make-believe are difficult for them to distinguish from reality.

The unconscious *operative mental structures* which guide the young child's thinking processes are, however, *not yet organized into systems* of mental transformations as they will be in the next period of development, the period of concrete operations. This lack of organization results in an *inability to mentally reverse* a process

or transformation, to separate mentally that which has been combined or to reverse a temporal sequence. While preschool children can mentally represent a given state, they *cannot depict* in their minds the sequence of steps which occur in *a transformation*, whether that transformation represents motion from one point to another or change due to physical processes such as melting and freezing. They have *difficulty focusing on more than one aspect of a relation or process at a time*, and they have not yet achieved an understanding of "class inclusion," "transitivity" of relations, or "conservation."

Preoperational thinking is also characterized by *egocentrism*—centering on one's own viewpoint. A young child's conception of space and time is egocentric, i.e., not objective, hence his or her understanding of causality and measurement cannot be the same as an adult's.

Language is another mode of representation which is emerging during the preoperational years. Cognitive-developmentalists and most psycholinguists agree that intellectual understandings are mastered *before* the appropriate use of linguistic forms which indicate comprehension of these understandings. Children master, for example, the acts of comparing and ordering *before* the syntactical forms of the comparative and superlative appear in their speech. Once children have mastered a concept, it is possible to teach them a verbal label for that concept, but teaching a verbal label does not teach the concept. Language, in other words, is not the primary means by which logical and physical relations are mastered. Action is. However, language and other forms of representation (such as mental images and motor encoding) do seem to be involved in the problem-solving process. Language is also a medium for communication between individuals, making possible the corrective feedback necessary to reduce ego-centrism and facilitating social transmission of knowledge.

Key experiences

From the assumption that active learning is at the heart of the developmental process, and with the description, outlined above from Piaget's theory, of the most important cognitive characteristics of "preoperational" children, we have derived approximately fifty "key experiences" to serve as guideposts for planning and evaluating developmentally valid programs for young children. These key experiences are admittedly an arbitrary list, but one modified and extended by many preschool teachers over the past 16 years (1962-1978). They form the basis for the High/Scope Cognitively Oriented Curriculum and for the organization of this book.

Interrelation of the key experiences

The key experiences are not intended to create fragmented teaching/learning situations organized around specific concepts. Rather they are designed to give teachers an awareness of the basic intellectual processes and contents with which any activity can be enriched and extended. Taken together they are the framework for supporting child development. We believe such experiences should be included in some form in any preschool program.

It should be apparent that the key experiences are interrelated and should be integrated in any actual learning activity rather than occur independently of each other. The relationship between key experiences can be described this way:

All preschool learning activities should be built upon active experiences with objects. These active experiences can be extended through language and through nonverbal representation (Bruner's "iconic" and "enactive" representation, Piaget's "index" and "symbolic" modes of representation). Concrete, active experience is examined and elaborated through language and nonverbal representation; it is not replaced by symbolic modes.

It follows that experiences associated with spatial, temporal and logical concepts must be built on an active, concrete core, and that language and nonverbal representation can be used to reflect upon and elaborate these experiences. For example, an activity in which children are given different grades of sandpaper (differing textures) is active if the children feel or use the sandpaper. The ongoing conversation during the activity would reflect the children's desire to talk about the textures, and it would also reflect the key experiences in classification, seriation, spatial relations or temporal relations that the teacher wanted to emphasize for this group of children. The children might represent their thoughts about the experience nonverbally by, say, pretending to be sanding a piece of wood.

The key experiences are listed in prescribed sequence, either across or within the various categories. *Each experience can be realized through an infinite number of activities across a range of developmental levels. These activities can be initiated both by adults and children.*

To sequence activities over the year, either for the class as a whole or for individual children, or to extend any given activity, think of starting at the left side of each of the following dimensions and moving to the right:

concrete ────────→ abstract
simple ────────→ complex
here and now ────→ remote in time and space

NUMBER CONCEPTS
• Comparing number and amount: more/less, same amount; more/fewer, same number.
• Comparing the number of items in two sets by matching them up in one-to-one correspondence. (Example: are there as many crackers as there are children?)
• Enumerating (counting) objects, as well as counting by rote.

Key experiences in understanding time and space
SPATIAL RELATIONS
• Fitting things together and taking them apart.
• Rearranging a set of objects or one object in space (folding twisting, stretching, stacking, tying) and observing the spatial transformations.
• Observing things and places from different spatial viewpoints.
• Experiencing and describing the positions of things in relation to each other (e.g., in the middle, on the side of; on, off, on top of, over, above).
• Experiencing and describing the direction of movement of things and people (to, from, into, out of, toward, away from).
• Experiencing and describing relative distances among things and locations (close, near, far, next to, apart, together).

• Experiencing and representing one's own body: how it is structured, what various body parts can do.

• Learning to locate things in the classroom, school, and neighborhood.

• Interpreting representations of spatial relations in drawings and pictures.

• Distinguishing and describing shapes.

TIME

• Planning and completing what one has planned.

• Describing and representing past events.

• Anticipating future events verbally and by making appropriate preparations.

• Starting and stopping an action on signal.

• Noticing, describing, and representing the order of events.

• Experiencing and describing different rates of movement.

• Using conventional time units when talking about past and future events (morning, yesterday, hour, etc.).

• Comparing time periods (short, long; new, old; young, old; a little while, a long time).

• Observing that clocks and calendars are used to mark the passage of time.

• Observing seasonal changes.

The key experiences should each appear many times—they are not goals to "attain" and check off but are more like vitamins and other nutrients: their repeated presence in many different forms is important for good "intellectual nutrition." Thus they should be embedded in a wide variety of activities. The Cognitively Oriented Curriculum is a framework from which teachers can extend and broaden the interests of children rather than an agenda of lessons or a "cookbook" of specific activities.

The adult's role

The adult's role in the Cognitively Oriented Curriculum is perhaps best described as that of an instigator of problem-solving activities. The adult can instigate or stimulate problem-solving by—

• Providing a rich array of materials and activities from which children are invited to select.

• Explicitly asking children to plan, in some way, what they are going to do and how they are going to do it. This permits children to begin to set goals for themselves and to generate and evaluate alternative solutions to problems en route to achieving the goals.

• Asking questions and making suggestions in order to set the stage for key experiences that stimulate the child's thinking processes, language development and social development. (A summary of teaching methods is presented in appendix 1.)

A balance between adult initiation and child initiation is vital to this approach. Using the Cognitively Oriented Curriculum is a process of constantly asking the question, How can the teaching staff provide the key experiences most supportive of learning and development for each child while acknowledging the child's own interests?

A curriculum that provides goals and strategies rather than specific classroom materials has certain obvious difficulties. It cannot be learned quickly; nor can it be mastered in preservice training, before the teacher has actually encountered children in the classroom. A corollary is that teacher training in this program is a long-term continuous process, so much more than a workshop here, a seminar there or a sprinkling of discrete concepts that remain unrooted in a practical vision.

The most successful inservice training the High/Scope Foundation has conducted combines several kinds of learning experiences for those in training: feedback from a "curriculum assistant" based on classroom observation, workshops, use of multimedia modules, observing a demonstration classroom or teaching in the High/Scope preschool, working alongside a "master teacher," teaching with someone who is also learning the program. This book, then, is only a part of High/Scope's comprehensive training program for early childhood educators and others concerned with the growth and development of young children. It can be used as an introduction to an integral educational philosophy and method, whose contours and interrelations have here been briefly sketched.

Related films and publications from the High/Scope Foundation

Films—

(For a complete description of each film and instructions for ordering, see appendix 4.)

The Cognitively Oriented Curriculum: A Framework for Education

El Curriculum Cognitivo (Spanish)

Key Experiences for Intellectual Development During the Preschool Years

Thinking and Reasoning in Preschool Children

This Is the Way We Go to School

Infant Development series: 1. *Early Learning: An Introduction to the Stages of Development in Infancy;* 2. *Learning to Talk: An Introduction to Language;* 3. *Visual Pursuit and Object Permanence;* 4. *Toot 'n Tub—Object Concepts During Sensory-Motor Stage 3;* 5. *Development of Means for Achieving Desired Ends;* 6. *Causing Events to Occur—Development of Causality*

Publications—

The Cognitively Oriented Curriculum: A Framework for Preschool Teachers (book, 182 pp.) by D.P. Weikart, L. Rogers, C. Adcock, D. McClelland. Urbana, Illinois: NAEYC, 1971.

This book is the first comprehensive description of the High/Scope Cognitively Oriented Preschool Curriculum. *Young Children in Action* expands and builds upon the curriculum originally outlined here.

An Introduction to the Cognitively Oriented Curriculum for Elementary Grades (booklet, 70 pp.) [Supplement: *A Classroom Handbook (booklet, 56 pp.)*] by Richard Lalli, 1979.

As a starting point for venturing into a cognitively oriented elementary program, this introduction invites adults to clarify their educational goals for children. Educational philosophies and practices are contrasted. Chapters on the child's role, the adult's role, and the principles of child development compose the body of this curriculum overview. The curriculum framework is sketched. Appendixes include a complete list of key experiences for children, definitions of terms, an index to other guides, and suggested reading lists on child development and educational philosophy and practice. The "Classroom Handbook," which contains the program goals, key experiences and Child Observation Record, is a supplement to this guide.

High/Scope Foundation Annual Report

This yearly publication reports on the activities of the Foundation in early childhood and elementary education, teacher training, longitudinal research on the effects of educational programs, and other areas, in a readable magazine format. The report is mailed, free of charge, to interested educators.

Bulletin of the High/Scope Foundation

Published annually, the Bulletin reports on the educational activities of the Foundation, with an emphasis on research. The Bulletin is mailed, free of charge, to interested educators.

Home Teaching with Mothers & Infants: The Ypsilanti-Carnegie Infant Education Project—An Experiment (book, 129 pp.) by D.Z. Lambie, J.T. Bond, D.P. Weikart, 1975.

An account of a High/Scope experiment in home-based parent-infant education. Chapters on the project's philosophy of infant education, the families selected for the project, the implementation of the program, the experimental design, and the results of the research.

Related reading on child development

Short Introductions to Piaget's Theory

Elkind, David. "Giant in the Nursery," *New York Times Magazine,* May 26, 1968.

Hall, Elizabeth. "A Conversation with Jean Piaget and Barbel Inhelder," *Psychology Today,* May, 1970. pp. 25-32, 54-56.

Piaget's Summaries of His Work

Piaget, Jean and Barbel Inhelder. *The Psychology of the Child.* New York: Basic Books, 1969.

Piaget, Jean. "Piaget's Theory," in *Carmichael's Manual of Child Psychology,* Paul Mussen, ed. New York: John Wiley and Sons, 1970. Chapter 9, pp. 703-732.

Summaries of Piaget's Theory by Other Authors

Almy, M.; Chittenden, E. and P. Miller. *Young Children's Thinking.* New York: Teachers College Press, 1966. Chapters 1 and 2.

Elkind, D. *Children and Adolescents.* New York: Oxford University Press, 1974.

Flavell, John H. *The Developmental Psychology of Jean Piaget.* Princeton, New Jersey: Van Nostrand, 1963.

Furth, H. *Piaget and Knowledge*. Englewood Cliffs, New Jersey: Prentice-Hall, 1969.

Ginsburg, Herbert and Sylvia Opper. *Piaget's Theory of Intellectual Development, An Introduction*. Englewood Cliffs, New Jersey: Prentice-Hall, 1969.

Hunt, J. McV. "The Impact and Limitations of the Giant of Developmental Psychology," in *Studies in Cognitive Development, Essays in Honor of Jean Piaget*, David Elkind and John H. Flavell, eds. New York: Oxford University Press, 1969.

Phillips, John H., Jr. *The Origins of Intellect: Piaget's Theory*. San Francisco: W.H. Freeman and Co., 1969.

Rohwer, W.D., Jr.; Ammon, P.R. and P. Cramer. *Understanding Intellectual Development*. Hinsdale, Illinois: The Dryden Press, 1974. Chapters 8-13.

Sensorimotor Period

Brazelton, T. Berry. *Infants and Mothers: Differences in Development*. New York: Dell, 1969.

Brazelton, T. Berry. *Toddlers and Parents: A Declaration of Independence*. New York: Dell, 1974.

Caplan, Frank, ed. *The First Twelve Months of Life*. New York: Grosset and Dunlap, 1977.

Caplan, Frank and Theresa. *The Second Twelve Months of Life: A Kaleidoscope of Growth*. New York: Grosset and Dunlap, 1977.

Flavell, John H. *The Developmental Psychology of Jean Piaget*. Princeton, New Jersey: Van Nostrand, 1963. Chapters 3 and 4.

Ginsburg, Herbert and Sylvia Opper. *Piaget's Theory of Intellectual Development, An Introduction*. Englewood Cliffs, New Jersey: Prentice-Hall, 1969. Chapter 2.

Kessen, Harth and Salapatek. "Human Infancy: A Bibliography and Guide," in *Carmichael's Manual of Child Psychology, Volume I*, Paul H. Mussen, ed. New York: John Wiley and Sons, Inc., 1970.

Langer, Jonas. *Theories of Development*. New York: Holt, Rinehart and Winston, Inc., 1969. pp. 112-129.

Leach, Penelope. *Babyhood: Infant Development from Birth to Two Years*. New York, Knopf, 1976.

Lewis, Michael. *Origins of Intelligence: Infancy and Early Childhood*. Princeton, New Jersey: Plenum Press, 1976.

Phillips, John H., Jr. *The Origins of Intellect: Piaget's Theory*. San Francisco: W.H. Freeman and Co., 1969. Chapter II.

Piaget, Jean. *The Origins of Intelligence in Children*. New York: International Universities Press, 1952.

Piaget, Jean. *The Construction of Reality in the Child*. New York: Basic Books, Inc., 1954.

Piaget, Jean. *Intelligence and Affectivity in Early Childhood*. New York: International Universities Press, Inc., 1965.

Piaget, Jean and Barbel Inhelder. *The Psychology of the Child*. New York: Basic Books, 1969. Chapter 1.

Stone, Joseph L.; Smith, Henrietta T. and Lois B. Murphy. *The Competent Infant: Research and Commentary*. New York: Basic Books, Inc., 1973.

Werner, Emmy E. "Infants Around the World: Cross Cultural Studies of Psychomotor Development from Birth to Two Years," in *Annual Progress in Child Psychiatry and Child Development*, Stella Chess and Alexander Thomas, eds. New York: Brunner/Mazel, Inc., 1974.

White, Burton. "The Initial Coordination of Sensorimotor Schemas in Human Infants: Piaget's Ideas and the Role of Experiences," in *Cognitive Studies*, Vol. I, Jerome Hellmuth, ed. New York: Brunner/Mazel, Inc., 1970. page 25.

White, Burton. *The First Three Years of Life*. Englewood Cliffs, New Jersey: Prentice-Hall, Inc., 1975.

Preoperational Subperiod and Concrete Operations

Flavell, John H. *The Developmental Psychology of Jean Piaget*. Princeton, New Jersey: Van Nostrand, 1963. Chapters 4 and 5.

Ginsburg, Herbert and Sylvia Opper. *Piaget's Theory of Intellectual Development, An Introduction*. Englewood Cliffs, New Jersey: Prentice-Hall, 1969. Chapters 3 and 4.

Phillips, John H., Jr. *The Origins of Intellect: Piaget's Theory*. San Francisco: W.H. Freeman and Co., 1969.

Piaget, Jean. *The Psychology of Intelligence*. New York: Harcourt Brace, 1950.

Piaget, Jean and Barbel Inhelder. *The Psychology of the Child*. New York: Basic Books, 1969. Chapter 4.

Wohlwill, Joachin. "The Mystery of the Pre-logical Child," *Psychology Today*, July, 1967.

Wohlwill, Joachin. "The Place of Structured Experience in Early Cognitive Development," in *Revisiting Early Childhood Education*, J.L. Frost, ed. New York: Holt, Rinehart, and Winston, 1973.

Formal Operations Period

Flavell, John H. *The Developmental Psychology of Jean Piaget*. Princeton, New Jersey: Van Nostrand, 1963. Chapter 6.

Ginsburg, Herbert and Sylvia Opper. *Piaget's Theory of Intellectual Development, An Introduction.* Englewood Cliffs, New Jersey: Prentice-Hall, 1969. Chapter 5.

Neimark, E.D. "Intellectual Development During Adolescence," in *Review of Child Development Research*, Vol. 4., F.D. Horowitz, ed. Chicago: The University of Chicago Press, 1975.

Piaget, Jean and Barbel Inhelder. *The Psychology of the Child.* New York: Basic Books, 1969. Chapter 5.

The Stage Concept

Case, R. "Gearing the Demands of Instruction to the Developmental Capacities of the Learner," *Review of Educational Research*, Winter, 1975. pp. 59-89.

Flavell, John H. *The Developmental Psychology of Jean Piaget.* Princeton, New Jersey: Van Nostrand, 1963. pp. 15-24.

Piaget, Jean. "The Stages of the Intellectual Development of the Child," in *Readings in Child Development and Personality*, John Conger, Paul Mussen and Jerome Kagen, eds. 2nd edition. New York: Harper and Row, 1970.

Pinard, Adrien and Monique Laurendeau. "'Stage' in Piaget's Cognitive-Developmental Theory: Exegesis of a Concept," in *Studies in Cognitive Development, Essays in Honor of Jean Piaget*, David Elkind and John H. Flavell, eds. New York: Oxford University Press, 1969. pp. 121-170.

Implications of Piaget's Theory for Education

Almy, M. and Associates. *Logical Thinking in Second Grade.* New York: Teachers College Press, 1970.

Almy M. "Piaget in Action," *Young Children*, January, 1976. pp. 93-96.

Athey, I. and D. Rubadeau. *Educational Implications of Piaget's Theory.* Waltham, Mass.: Ginn & Blaisdell, 1970.

Chittenden, Edward A. "What is Learned and What is Taught?" *Young Children*, October, 1969. pp. 12-19.

Duckworth, Eleanor. "The Having of Wonderful Ideas," *Harvard Educational Review*, Vol. 42, No.2, May, 1972. pp. 217-231.

Elkind, David. "The Educational Implications of Piaget's Work," *The Open Classroom Reader*, Charles E. Silberman, ed. New York: Random House, 1973. Chapter 7, pp. 182-208.

Elkind, David. *Children and Adolescents.* New York: Oxford University Press, 1974. Chapter 8.

Flavell, John H. *The Developmental Psychology of Jean Piaget.* Princeton, New Jersey: Van Nostrand, 1963. pp. 365-369.

Ginsburg, Herbert and Sylvia Opper. *Piaget's Theory of Intellectual Development.* Englewood Cliffs, New Jersey: Prentice-Hall, 1969. Chapter 6. "Genetic Epistemology and the Implications of Piaget's Findings for Education," pp. 218-232.

Hunt, J. McV. "The Psychological Basis for Using Preschool Enrichment as an Antidote for Cultural Deprivation," *Merrill-Palmer Quarterly of Behavior and Development*, Vol. 10, No. 3. pp. 257-299.

Kohlberg, Lawrence. "Early Education: A Cognitive Developmental View," *Child Development*, 1968, Vol. 39. pp. 1013-1062.

Kohlberg, Lawrence and Rochelle Mayer. "Development as the Aim of Education," *Harvard Educational Review*, Vol. 42, No. 4, 1972. p. 449.

Piaget, Jean. "Educational Principles and Psychological Data," in *Science of Education and Psychology of the Child.* New York: Grossman, 1970. Chapter 2, pp. 151-180.

Raph, Jane and Milton Schwebel. *Piaget in the Classroom.* New York: Basic Books, 1973.

Rohwer, W.D., Jr.; Ammon, R.P. and P. Cramer. *Understanding Intellectual Development.* Hinsdale, Illinois: The Dryden Press, 1974. Chapter 13.

Sigel, Irving E. "The Piagetian System and the World of Education," in *Studies in Cognitive Development: Essays in Honor of Jean Piaget*, David Elkind and John H. Flavell, eds. New York: Oxford University Press, 1969. pp. 465-489.

Related Developmental Theories and Approaches to Education

Dennis, Lawrence. "Play in Dewey's Theory of Education," *Young Children*, March, 1970. pp. 230-235.

Dewey, John. "The Child and the Curriculum," in *John Dewey on Education, Selected Writings*, Reginald D. Archambault, ed. Chicago: University of Chicago Press, 1964. pp. 339-358.

Dewey, John. "My Pedagogic Creed," in *John Dewey on Education, Selected Writings*, Reginald D. Archambault, ed. Chicago: University of Chicago Press, 1964. pp. 426-439.

Ebbeck, Frederick N. and Marjory A. *Now We Are Four.* Columbus, Ohio: Charles E. Merrill, 1974.

Flavell, John H. *Cognitive Development.* Englewood Cliffs, New Jersey: Prentice-Hall, Inc., 1977.

Fleiss, Bernice H. "A Beginner's Bibliography," *Young Children*, July, 1976. pp. 394-401.

Hess, Robert D. and Doreen J. Croft. *Teachers of Young Children*. Boston: Houghton Mifflin, 1975.

Hom, Harry L., Jr. and Paul A. Robinson, eds. *Psychological Processes in Early Education*. New York: Academic Press, 1977.

Leeper, Sarah H.; Dales, Ruth J.; Skipper, Dora S. and Ralph L. Witherspoon. *Good Schools for Young Children*. New York: Macmillan Co., 1968.

Nimnicht, Glen; McAfee, Oralie and John Meier. *The New Nursery School*. Morristown, New Jersey: General Learning Press, 1969.

Postman, Neil and Charles Weingartner. *The School Book*. New York: Delacorte Press, 1973. pp. 112-157.

Read, Katherine H. *The Nursery School, A Human Relations Laboratory*. Philadelphia, Pennsylvania: W. B. Saunders Co., 1966.

Silberman, Charles. *Crisis in the Classroom*. New York: Random House, 1970. Chapter 4, pp. 112-157.

Spodek, Bernard. *Teaching in the Early Years*. Englewood Cliffs, New Jersey: Prentice-Hall, Inc., 1972.

Spodek, Bernard. "What are the Sources of Early Childhood Curriculum?" *Young Children*, October, 1970. pp. 48-56.

Adaptations of the curriculum

An approach to bilingual/ bicultural preschool education

Because the Cognitively Oriented Curriculum is a framework for teachers and not a set of prescribed activities or lessons to do with children, it is adaptable in a wide variety of settings. Aspects of the curriculum have been applied to preschool "plaza" or outdoor situations in Latin America, where teenagers supervised by a professional have been the primary educators of young children; in isolated rural areas of the high Andean plains with community volunteers as teachers; in full-day and half-day programs; in mainstreamed and self-contained classrooms for handicapped children; and in bilingual/bicultural preschool programs.

The Cognitively Oriented Curriculum shares with many other bilingual/bicultural approaches the following basic assumptions:

• Educational programs for children must support the child's self-esteem and pride in family, community, ethnic heritage and linguistic heritage. Too often, school programs have been destructive of such pride.

• Educational programs should encourage children to utilize their mother tongue as well as learn the dominant or "official" language. A dual-language heritage should be a rich treasure, not the burden that some schools in the United States have historically sought to make it.

According to this outlook, a bilingual program is *not* a melting pot (or pressure cooker) wherein children assimilate the dominant culture as quickly as possible. A bilingual/bicultural program should be geared to help children learn to function successfully in both the dominant culture and their "minority" culture, and to become fluent in two languages (at least) by the time they have finished school. And the monolingual English-speaking child should be given the same right to acquire a second language and to learn about other cultures.

If one were to observe a "regular" cognitively oriented preschool classroom and then a bilingual/bicultural one, he would find that the children in both classrooms were dealing with the *same* concepts or "key experiences" although the cultural artifacts and the languages used would be different. The crucial fact in either classroom would be that the teaching team builds upon—rather than directs or controls—the thoughts and actions of the children. Children learn because they become intensely involved in activities or projects of their own design. The adult's role is to structure the environment to maximize opportunities for natural learning. The teaching strategies to support cognitive development discussed in this book are of equal value and importance whether the group of children is linguistically and culturally homogeneous or diverse.

⌒

Given an open and supportive environment, with opportunities for children to interact with peers and adults and with a wide variety of materials, the need to communicate will arise naturally. Children will want to talk about their needs, feelings and ideas in relation to their actions.

In an "open framework" classroom, *language* is integrated with the entire preschool experience; it is not given primary attention as something the adults have to teach. Where this approach is used in a bilingual setting, both languages are spoken throughout the day by children and adults. Children are not expected to please adults by answering questions correctly or by repeating a sentence pattern that has little to do with their present interests. Language is directly related to their ongoing activity.

When both languages are used concurrently (with simultaneous translation and code switching*), the children are in a secure environment where they know both languages are equally accepted and respected. Their learning doesn't have to be postponed until they gain control of the second language. Their frustration in learning a new language is reduced because language learning is in the context of work and play rather than in the context of a "lesson." When children hear both languages routinely, they begin to pick up the second language naturally, and

*Simultaneous translation: restating the meaning in the other language. Code switching: changing and mixing the two languages without restating.

they're motivated to try out their new skills because of the supportive environment and the variety of language abilities present in the classroom. For the teacher, working with different language abilities is like working with different developmental ranges.

For this naturalistic approach to work most effectively, it's important to use approximately equal proportions of each language in the classroom. If one language is used more than the other, the program will become transitional rather than supportive of development in the child's first and second language.

It's not expected that a monolingual preschooler will become fluent in a second language by the end of one year. Full bilingualism is a long-range goal. It is reasonable, however, to expect a child to demonstrate a positive attitude toward both languages (interacting spontaneously with peers and adults from both language backgrounds), to be able to use some words and phrases in the second language and to understand significantly more than he or she can say. Children's progress will vary according to their starting point and the language patterns and support given at home and in the community. A bilingual/bicultural preschool experience gives the child a solid base for continued participation in a bilingual/bicultural primary-school setting.

⌒

When we speak of the *culture* of a group of people, we're talking about the whole range of values, customs, traditions and social institutions that distinguish the way of life of a community. Culture comprises everything from tools, dress, shelter and modes of transportation, to a people's history, artistic productions, social organization, family structures, marriage customs, religion and language or dialect. Culture is the broad context within which all education takes place. This is why it's mistaken to think of "adding culture" to a school curriculum. School should be a part of the culture, not culture a part of the school.

Since culture is the bedrock of education, the cultural appropriateness of a curriculum is crucial. A curriculum must be responsive to the particular needs of the children for whom it's intended. If a school's curriculum and methods produce feelings of inferiority and inadequacy in the child; if they create a conflict of values, making the child feel that what he or she represents is shameful or bad; and if they make it difficult for a child to adjust to the environment—then that curriculum and those methods aren't culturally appropriate and aren't meeting the needs of the children.

Children's self-concept is largely shaped by the way others react to them. Children who feel unaccepted develop not only a poor self-concept but also negative attitudes towards others. By placing the child's culture at the center of the program, a culturally relevant curriculum allows the child to feel accepted and enhances the development of positive attitudes towards learning and towards other people and cultures.

The Cognitively Oriented Preschool Curriculum is actually a multicultural framework, rather than a bicultural one, in that it focuses on each child's background of experience. These backgrounds differ in many ways, even in a relatively homogeneous ethnic community. Family patterns (single parent, nuclear or extended family), migration patterns (rural to urban, urban to suburban, region to region), home life-styles, child-rearing practices, language usage—all of these factors combine in unique ways for different children. Multiculturalism means understanding and appreciating more than one

cultural heritage and functioning comfortably within more than one cultural context; it begins in the preschool with everyday experiences and the representation of these experiences in play, language, art, music, etc.—not "lessons" about people and places remote from the child's experience. Adults focus on what is contemporary about a child's culture (i.e., *present* for the child) rather than what is only of historical interest.

Adults must be sensitive to and aware of the values, attitudes and interests of the community at large and of the individual families if they are to support the culture the child brings into the classroom and broaden the child's experience. In the past, many culture-oriented programs seem to have ignored the fact that because of geographical, regional and historical factors, there are few attributes that can be considered general characteristics of any cultural group. One Chicano community, for example, may include chile caribe or atole in its diet, while another Chicano community may not. Or one group of Native Americans may observe its traditional laws and rites while another may not. Though we tend to think of Chicanos, Native Americans, Chinese Americans, etc. as homogeneous groups, the fact is they aren't. Consequently, if each community's and each individual's cultural patterns are to be respected and fostered, we must be careful not to impose stereotypic cultural settings in the schools. Before considering the general attributes of cultural groups, schools must attend to the cultural patterns of their own immediate communities. One way to assure continuity between home and school and to avoid cultural stereotyping is to have parents and other community members work in the classroom.

In an open framework classroom, adults are resource people for children—they help children solve problems, and they serve as *linguistic and cultural models.* What does being a "language model" mean in a bilingual program using a naturalistic approach to language learning, and how does this role affect the composition of the teaching team? Ideally, all the adults in such a program will be bilingual, but this isn't always possible. Some bilingual programs assign one adult the role of the English speaker and another that of the Spanish,* each adult addressing the children in only one language. Traditionally this has meant the teacher speaks English and a paraprofessional Spanish. The paraprofessional usually performs "lower level" duties than the teacher (supervising free play while the teacher takes a break, taking children to the bathroom, preparing materials for the teacher, and so on). Children are aware of this uneven distribution of power and responsibility. In this situation the English speaker represents a dominant position and the Spanish speaker a less powerful position. This can easily imply to children that neither Spanish nor the culture associated with Spanish-speaking people is respected.

Adults in a cognitively oriented program, regardless of language or heritage, are equal planners and doers in the program. Adults depend on one another to observe and interact with children throughout the day. Because the whole team participates in inservice training and works together with the trainer, each team member shares a common curriculum framework. Because all adults share in the teaching responsibilities and classroom chores, all represent equally respected roles for the children.

While monolingual adults with a positive attitude towards both languages can play an im-

portant role as linguistic models, it's vital to include team members who can easily switch back and forth between Spanish and English. If all members of a team are not bilingual, every effort should be made to have at least a *balance* of Spanish- and English-speaking adults working with the children. In a classroom where more team members speak English than Spanish (or the reverse), the tendency will be to use that language more often, thus giving it more importance. *In an open framework program, both languages must be equally valued and used.*

⌒

Adults are not the only resource people in the classroom—children are resource people for each other. They help each other solve problems, they share ideas in play, and they serve as linguistic and cultural models. *Mixed age and ability grouping* are important because children learn from each other. In a bilingual preschool this is true for mixed language grouping as well. A wide range of language abilities should be represented: from monolingual English to monolingual Spanish with different degrees of bilingualism in between. Again, to use this approach most effectively, it's important to maintain a balance of Spanish- and English-dominant children, or the tendency will be to use one language more than the other and thus give it more importance.

With heterogeneous grouping, a child's native language will continue to develop while he or she begins to learn a second language through interaction with classmates and adults. When the teaching team divides the children into small groups for planning, recall and group time, there should be a balanced cross-section of developmental and linguistic levels represented in each group. If there's a monolingual adult on the teaching team, he or she should make sure there

*Examples here deal with Spanish/English programs, but the principles apply equally to other bilingual programs.

are bilingual children in the group to act as interpreters.

⌒

No matter what their linguistic and ethnic background, all children need the opportunities for active learning which form the basis for the development of mental, physical and social abilities. The teaching team plans developmentally appropriate activities around the key experiences discussed throughout this book. The key experiences are constant for preschoolers; it's the cultural and linguistic context that varies. There's probably no such thing as a monolingual/monocultural environment; even in the most homogeneous classroom there are individual differences in experiences, interests, learning styles and developmental levels. For this reason the teacher must be flexible, a keen observer, and must know how to deal with each child as an individual; the open framework provides the structure within which the teacher can plan to meet the needs of individual children.

Along with an emphasis on what's the *same* for all preschool classrooms implementing the Cognitively Oriented Curriculum, issues specific to bilingual/bicultural application have been addressed in this statement: a naturalistic approach to language learning, culture as direct experience, the role of the adult, the grouping of children. A supplementary manual for bilingual/bicultural application of the curriculum and training materials to be used with teachers and parents are being produced by the High/Scope Foundation. These materials will provide more detailed discussion of teaching strategies and examples taken from real classroom situations.

A developmental approach for preschool children with special needs

There are two basic approaches to the design of individualized educational programs for young handicapped children, each incorporating a different pedagogical logic—either the logic of *developmental validity* or the logic of *diagnosis and correction*.

Programs based on a diagnostic/corrective perspective assume that the major purpose of early education intervention is to identify areas in which children show deficits in relation to their age peers, or a lack of consistency in their own performance. Testing often provides the data for educational prescriptions in the diagnostic/corrective mode. From information about a child's deficits, specific objectives can be developed which represent steps toward remediation. Sometimes information about the etiology of a particular handicapping condition is used in making educational plans or prescriptions. Or the technology of behavior modification may be used by the special education interventionist. Incentives or "reinforcers" may be systematically used to motivate attainment of objectives.

Diagnostic/corrective interventions are typified, in our observations, by assuming not only that the child must be motivated by adults (therapist, teacher, parents) but that he or she must be "taught" new skills in a direct, didactic way. Often the teaching is done in clinical sessions where a particular skill is persistently and patiently drilled by the special educator. In contrast, programs based on the logic of "developmental validity" attempt primarily to promote learning that exercises and extends developmentally emerging abilities, develops the learners' interests and long-term plans and is optimally timed for ease of learning and retention.

A developmental approach, as we conceive it, has elements that are analogous to diagnosis and prescription, but the individualized programs that evolve do not start with an analysis of a child's deficits. Rather, educators seeking developmentally valid programs for handicapped children identify the child's status on a developmental continuum and provide experiences which permit the child to exercise emerging abilities that in most cases he or she will be strongly motivated to use. A developmentalist identifies the experiences which challenge and help the child to practice broadly generalizable skills that are typical for children at that particular developmental period. Thus we assume, at least as an initial strategy, that children can take a very active role in defining the appropriate developmental "match" between their skills and the learning activities they engage in. In other words, a developmental approach need not substitute highly specific developmental-sequential information for highly specific behavioral-deficit information. The child as well as the adult should have a role in planning and selecting activities. In the High/Scope approach, the child makes an explicit plan each day, and the adult helps the child first to formulate and then to carry out that plan.

Our work with handicapped preschoolers is an outgrowth of universally applicable developmental principles. The view that certain handicapping conditions are *developmental delays* may provide one very effective general strategy within a framework that looks for developmental universals. Perhaps the best way to promote growth in a four-year-old child who is two years behind his or her age peers in intellectual and verbal development is to provide the rich variety of concrete experience and accompanying language that one provides for a nonhandicapped two-year-old. Attempts to narrowly target certain behaviors that appear more age-appropriate for a four-year-old may only result in very narrow learning, not generalizable to other skills, and not matching the child's motivational inclinations.

For a child who is not neurologically impaired but shows developmental lags because of sensory or motor limitations, the educator's task is to mobilize the child's existing resources toward achieving developmentally appropriate intellectual and social competencies. These skills may be channeled in different ways and through different media—for example, communication for a deaf child may include experiences with signing rather than exclusively with oral language—but the experiential base that provides interesting things to talk about, a reason and an invitation to communicate, must be present, and this set of active experiences should be basically the same for the deaf child and hearing child, or for the language-impaired child and the child with "normal" language ability.

Teachers in a cognitively oriented program focus on experiences pertaining to developmental processes rather than on behavioral outcomes. We label them "key experiences." These are the classes of active experience that cognitive-developmental theory suggests are involved in mastery of the developmental tasks of the preschool-age child. These key experiences are used to plan activities for groups of children as well to provide a way of thinking about individual children. We call them "experiences" rather than goals because we want teachers to think about the many different ways each key experience can occur in the life of a child. This is more useful than thinking of experiences as "attainable" concepts that can be checked off on a checklist and never returned to.

We encourage adults to develop general strategies in order to provide an optimum match between a child's classroom activities and the appropriate key experiences. These strategies are exactly the same for handicapped and non-handicapped children.

∾

We begin a cycle of experiences with concrete materials and physical involvement—both sensory and motoric—on the part of children. For very young children or for children who are still functioning primarily at the sensorimotor level, we may stay at this concrete level. For those who are able to use more abstract mental abilities, we extend the active, concrete experience via representations in a variety of modes and, of course, through language. We try, always, to tie representational activity to some concrete event or experience, even when children are able to deal with the concept or event on a more symbolic level. Representational activity may be channeled by the teacher, but the specific content and style of the representation is not dictated by the adult.

We have found the key experiences and the general strategy of building on active learning with real materials to be highly effective with special-needs children. Some special-needs chil-

dren are still functioning at the sensorimotor level when they are three years old or older. For these children, as well as for others with less severe delays, the basic manipulative/exploratory activities are the developmentally appropriate ones; there is no attempt immediately to extend these activities into ones that require high-level (i.e., more abstract) symbolic or representational processes. Thus, for an educably or trainably retarded preschool child, we provide readily transformable materials such as water, sand and finger paint. Of course, these materials are used by all preschool children, but the activities the special-needs child engages in with the materials may be different, and the teacher's responses and questions are based on the way the child interacts with the materials. A good learning environment encourages children to interact with materials in diverse ways, according to their developmental level.

EXAMPLE: A normally developing four-year-old child will use sand to make "roads" for toy cars. A child still functioning at the sensorimotor level will be interested in filling and emptying containers of sand, but not in using the sand to stand for something else.

EXAMPLE: A four- or five-year-old can make playdough from a picture-recipe chart, measuring the flour, water, salt and oil with measuring cups and spoons. A child who is developmentally two years old, however, will enjoy exploring the gooey product of the older child's labors, but won't be able to participate except by observation in decoding the chart, counting the scoops, etc. In the same work/play group, a child with a hearing impairment might assist with some of the activities requiring fine-motor coordination such as pouring or mixing.

For children with language delays or impairments, the active, concrete experiences provide a context and a reason to talk with others. In the course of such experiences, peers can act both as models and sources of reinforcement. Asking other children for materials or equipment or describing to the teacher what one has accomplished are ideal ways to exercise the language a child is learning. This is language that is purposeful, social and generalizable outside the classroom. Too often, language in the speech clinic is removed from real experiences, from the need and joy of communication, and therefore it may generalize disappointingly to home and school situations. Encouraging children to represent in a variety of modes, not just verbally, also means that children whose language lags behind their general cognitive development have a number of ways to make their feelings about and understanding of the world clearer: through art media, role play and pantomime, dance and movement and construction with blocks or with real carpentry tools and wood. This richness of materials and diversity of possibilities means also that a child with sensory or perceptual deficits has alternative means of initiating active transactions with the environment and with peers. The hearing-impaired or visually impaired child is given incentives to interact with materials and with people; these children are invited by the environment to use *both* their impaired sensory channels and their normally functioning ones.

◇

Another basic strategy, which complements active-concrete learning and extension through language and representation, is to *help children define goals, discover problems* in the process of trying to attain goals and *explore and evaluate alternative solutions* to a problem, whether it's a "thing" problem or a "people" problem. It's exciting for teachers and parents to see this problem-solving orientation developing in young

children. It's all the more exciting when one sees it "work" for children with special needs.

Children experience a daily routine in the Cognitively Oriented Curriculum that asks them to make plans and choices. They learn from this that they can accomplish something if they first make a plan, and that they have explicit choices and alternatives. We've seen this approach generalize from the classroom to the home. We create environments in which teachers and parents learn that it is their job to help children encounter interesting (and solvable) problems.

EXAMPLE: An emotionally disturbed boy, labeled "hyperactive" by some, exhibits long periods of focused attention and purposeful activity as he makes an airplane out of wood at the workbench. He chose to go to the workbench, *he* decided that *he wanted to make an airplane. The teacher helped him think about the materials, tools and procedures he would need. Later at recall time, he may draw the airplane, dictate a story about it or tell the others about what he did when the glue wasn't strong enough to hold it together.*

By providing *choices* and a *rich variety of materials* we seem to be doing the opposite of what is prescribed by the conventional wisdom in special education, which says that many children with special needs require stimulus-lean environments and highly structured tasks and expectations. Where developmentally appropriate materials and activities are available for children, we have typically *not* found it necessary to engage in this kind of environmental restriction for handicapped children. We fear that environmental restriction may be a strategy that's used to get children to attend to tasks that are not developmentally appropriate and not very interesting. In such cases it's easy to see why children get "distracted" by other "stimuli." The same may hold for the notion that special-needs children require extrinsic reinforcers for participating in learning activities. This may be true when the activities are not developmentally appropriate. For most children who are intact enough to participate in a group preschool program, we have found that there is no problem in finding sufficient "developmental pull" toward activities chosen and planned by both child and teacher that are intrinsically motivating for the child and do not require tangible rewards. Even systematic use of "social reinforcers" seems unnecessary; these rewards operate efficiently given the natural contingencies of an "open" preschool environment and do not seem to require systematic record keeping and scheduling by the teachers. We want children to feel that they're doing things *they've* planned to do, rather than things to please the teacher.

❧

An approach which stresses active learning and choices must help teachers support intellectual growth in many ways. Clearly representation and conversation are ways to stretch young minds. Another basic strategy teachers use in the Cognitively Oriented Curriculum is to move conversation and representational activities from the here and now to more remote events and places, as children become more able to deal with the past and future and with spatially distant realities. This is part of an expansion of learning from things to relationships, comparisons, quantifications.

When special education programs attempt to teach school skills (e.g., alphabet recognition, clock or calendar reading, simple arithmetic) before children have mastered the underlying spatial or temporal concepts on which these skills are based, the result can only be frustration for the children. Often academic skills are introduced to developmentally delayed children with the thought that the children will "look" normal if they can write their names, appear to understand the calendar, know right from left, and so forth. There is so much that can be done at the preschool level to build up the basic concepts a child will need later on in school that it seems to us a misallocation of resources to drill concepts which are not grasped by the developmentally younger child and can only be mastered in rote, parrot-like fashion. Building up expectations about the flow of time in the daily routine (planning time, work time, clean-up time, recall time, etc.) is a useful step toward mastery of clocks, calendars and the like. We have also found that an organized (structured, if you will) daily routine and classroom environment can provide the predictability and stability that all children need if they are to be comfortable in an environment that invites choices and creativity. For emotionally disturbed, retarded and "hyperactive" children, knowing where to find the things they need and knowing what comes next are especially important.

❧

The general strategies and key experiences described in this manual are used with all children, not just handicapped children. This makes the Cognitively Oriented Curriculum a framework that can serve as the basic tool for teachers working with integrated groups of handicapped and nonhandicapped children. We believe, on the basis of our experience at the High/Scope Preschool and with programs around the country using our model, that a program which strives for developmental validity rather than remediation of deficits and attainment of specific objectives through didactic teaching can best help to create learning environments that are both "least restrictive" and "most facilitative."

There is certainly a need for research to shed more light on the applicability of developmental vs. diagnostic/corrective models and on issues relating to the structure of environments for young handicapped children. It's our strong hunch that good learning environments for "normal" and for "special" children will turn out to be remarkably similar.

Working with parents

The purposes of this section are to alert classroom staff to the many ways parents can act as classroom resources and to provide strategies for supporting and encouraging parent-staff rapport. These strategies are organized under the following *key experiences for parents:*
  • Discovering that parenting is teaching—home visits
  • Contributing to the classroom program
  • Planning and participating in parent-staff meetings
  • Learning about child development and classroom curriculum
  It is our hope that in providing these key experiences for parents, classroom staff will learn to view parents as key contributors to any educational undertaking.

* * *

Key Experience for Parents:
Discovering that parenting is teaching—home visits

Parents are children's first teachers. Before children start preschool, they have taken in and processed an unbelievable amount of information and mastered a wide variety of complex skills. Largely through the efforts and care of their parents, they have changed from relatively helpless infants to very able young children. With the help and support of their parents they have learned and mastered an array of physical skills; they have learned how to communicate their thoughts, feelings, ideas and desires; and they have collected a great many notions and impressions about the events and values of their family's culture—birthdays, festivals, holidays, what to do in the grocery store, the difference between playing and fighting.

Many parents don't regard themselves as teachers, however. They're very proud of their children's accomplishments but often fail to recognize their own contributory role. They believe, instead, that classroom teachers are the only ones who teach; it's when their children start preschool that they expect them to start "learning." The teaching team, therefore, can help parents realize that 1) parenting *is* teaching, 2) they already know a lot about child development in general and about their own children in particular, and 3) teachers are not purveyors of knowledge but rather people who wish to support and extend the learning that's already going on at home. A major way classroom staff can convey these ideas is through home visits.

It's not unusual for both parents and classroom staff to resist the idea of home visits initially. Parents may fear ridicule and criticism from classroom staff while classroom staff may fear rejection and resistance from parents; rather than risk intruding on the other's domain, they would rather avoid all but the most necessary contact. And even when both parties are willing, it's not always easy to find time to make regular home visits. Some parents may not want what they see as an intrusion, and they may have limited time to spend at home with their children. In some areas it may be difficult to get to remote places where children live. But in spite of these initial problems, once the ice is broken most parents welcome classroom staff into their home. Once parents realize that classroom staff respect and wish to learn from them, home visits become a significant part of the educational program.

Following are ways classsroom staff can initiate and capitalize on the home visit process.

Suggestions for classroom staff

Prepare parents for home visits

Make sure that parents know from the outset that home visits are part of the program. As soon as school starts, talk with all parents about home visits—on the phone, as they observe in the classroom, through notes and newsletters, as they enroll their children. Use part of an early parent meeting to discuss home visits. Explain to parents what regular home visits are and why they're important: so that parents and classroom staff can support one another in the education of the child. Assure parents that you want to find out about them and their children and that you want them to find out about you, so that together you can design and carry out the best possible edu-

cational program in school and at home. Be sure they understand that home visits involve an exchange; they supplement and support what the child is learning in school, while at the same time they provide classroom staff with ideas and activities they can include in school.

Ask parents to work together with classroom staff to pool all that they know about children's language, culture, interests and abilities, so that the sum of a child's educational experience is greater than either parents or classroom staff alone could provide.

Use the initial home visit to establish rapport and share information

The first home visit should be spent in casual conversation to help the parents feel comfortable having a classroom staff member in their home and to help the staff member feel comfortable outside the school environment.

The initial home visit may not even take place at home but rather in more "neutral" territory, like a restaurant, over a cup of coffee. Wherever the first home visit takes place, use it to establish and build rapport. Tell parents what their child has been doing in school, what the child enjoys doing, who the child likes to play with, the things the child does well. Ask for advice about immediate concerns you may have about the child. Invite and answer questions parents have about any aspect of the program that puzzles or troubles them. Ask parents what they aspire to for their children, what kinds of things they would like to see their children doing. Many teaching teams use an initial-home-visit interview form, like the one presented in appendix 6, to assure that they come away with the appropriate information. Often this form, by providing enough structure and formality to the initial visit, actually works to relax both parties and serves as a springboard for related but more casual discussion.

Plan each subsequent home visit according to what you know about the child and parents

Because each home visit is tailored to the needs of a particular child in a particular family setting, it isn't possible to dip into a stack of preplanned home visit activities and come up with one that's exactly right for the family you're about to visit. Instead, before each visit generate a plan based on everything you know so far about all the people involved. Here are some things to consider at this juncture: the cognitive and social abilities of the child; the particular interests of the child; materials to bring and materials in the home which might also be used; activities that can be continued until the next home visit; activities in which the child can be successful; developmentally appropriate ways of focusing on parental educational concerns (for example, building one-to-one correspondence into the activity if the parents are anxious about having the child learn to count).

Information obtained during the first home visit will be helpful in planning future visits. For example, a staff member might learn that the parents are concerned about their child's limited use of language and so might plan to use and discuss some of the language strategies during future home visits.

Carry out home visit plans, but be flexible

If, for example, the plan you've devised calls for exploring ways in which parents can work on number relations with their children using both classroom objects and household objects, carry out this plan as well as you are able but be prepared to make adjustments. For instance, a younger sibling may become involved in rolling and building with the beads, the mother may be reluctant to allow this child to use household items for anything but their intended purpose, and she may also be more concerned at the moment with the older child's negative behavior toward the younger than about number concepts. Rather than plug away at number concepts, the home visitor would be better advised to discuss the issues at hand with the mother, and then return to the original plan with appropriate modifications. The parent and home visitor could discuss the educational value of the younger child's activity with the beads. The home visitor could ask the mother to describe how she has been dealing with the aggressiveness between the two children, and the home visitor could describe the ways the classroom staff deal with similar problems in the classroom. The home visitor could also talk with the mother about "throwaway" household items like empty boxes, cans and junk mail that children can use for their own projects.

Leave time during each home visit for discussion with the parents

During the "activity" part of home visits, parents, children and classroom staff are all working together with materials to explore and learn about anything from counting to creating books and songs. When the activity is finished and the child has turned to something else or begun using the materials in another way, spend time sharing observations about the child, planning ways to work with the child in both settings, laying the groundwork for the next home visit and discussing any other issues you or the parent may wish to raise concerning the child or the program.

*   *   *

Evaluate, record and follow up home visits

After each home visit, record in some way what happened, ideas about what might work better in the future, insights about the child and strategies to try in the classroom. Be sure to share these insights and strategies with the rest of the teaching team.

Be supportive of parents

Begin any conversation with a parent with a positive statement about the child. Far more can be gained for the child if classroom staff concentrate on supporting and working together with parents than if they criticize and try to "retrain" them.

Key Experience for Parents: Contributing to the classroom program

The classroom is another setting in which parents and classroom staff can work together and serve as mutual resources. Not only can parents see their children in action, they can also try out ways of interacting with their children in the more neutral setting the classroom provides. The spilled juice of a child who is learning to pour is far less unsettling to a parent when it's the preschool floor rather than the kitchen floor that has to be cleaned. A preschool classroom is designed for exploration and provides an environment in which children and parents alike are freed from the constraints imposed by parents' natural desire for order at home.

When parents spend time in the classroom, they have the chance to learn how other people's children are doing. In this sense the classroom can serve as a child development laboratory where parents can discover, for example, that theirs isn't the only child who has difficulty sharing, but that many other preschoolers need the same kind of assistance in finding alternatives to aggressive behavior. Such discoveries help many parents feel less guilty about their child's normal behavior and enable them to turn their energies from guilt to constructive work with their child.

Classroom contact also gives parents the opportunity to shape the classroom environment, to directly affect classroom goals and activities and share their knowledge with classroom staff.

Suggestions for classroom staff

Make parents feel welcome and needed in the classroom

In order for parents to contribute to the classroom program, they need to know that their contributions are wanted and needed. Many parents want to be involved in the classroom program in some specific way but won't indicate their interest until it's solicited or until they feel it will be well received. Other parents have never even thought of being involved and need to be made aware of opportunities. Here are some ways a teaching team can make parents feel welcome and needed:

• Plan a parent visiting day or a family potluck supper before school begins. Children and parents can tour the classroom, meet classroom and administrative personnel and have a chance to meet and talk with each other.

• Encourage parents to stop in the classroom and observe. Make it a practice to speak to parents as they drop off or pick up their children and invite them to stay a few minutes or as long as possible. Post a sign on the door inviting parents in and, somewhere nearby, post a short description of the daily routine in which times for questions and discussion with staff are indicated.

• A newsletter is a good way to let parents know what their children are doing in school. This is a way to reach all parents, especially those with little time to attend meetings or visit the classroom.

• Keeping an informal log of parents' interests, comments, concerns and observations can help classroom staff plan home visits and strategies for particular children.

Encourage parents to work as classroom volunteers

When parents work in the classroom as volunteers, be sure to include them as part of the team during the daily evaluation and planning session. This provides an important opportunity for exchange of information.

Remember too that many parents prefer to volunteer other kinds of classroom services. In one classroom, for example, aside from the parents who worked in the classroom with the teaching team on a regular basis, there were also parents who helped serve lunch, gave the classroom a thorough cleaning periodically, made labels for classroom equipment, called and organized parents for meetings and outings, made special classroom materials and accompanied the group on field trips.

Encourage parents to share their special interests with children

Classroom staff can enrich the classroom environment by asking parents to share hobbies, songs, games, stories, holiday customs, foods and dances they know. A mother in one classroom, for example, knew several Spanish dances, so she often came to work in the music area with the children, bringing records of Spanish dance

music, castanets and *rebozos*. The children became so involved in dancing that a group of mothers got together and made holiday costumes for the children to wear in the classroom as they danced.

Key Experience for Parents: Planning and participating in parent-staff meetings

Parent-staff meetings can be an exciting and valuable forum for the exchange of information and ideas and for mutual support if parents and staff jointly assume responsibility for planning, organizing, selecting topics and leading the meetings. The more parents contribute, the more meaningful the meetings will be to them.

Suggestions for classroom staff

Conduct a parent survey

During the first two weeks of school, ask parents about issues or concerns they would like to discuss with other parents and classroom staff.

Plan and evaluate parent-staff meetings

A group of parents and classroom staff were meeting to discuss the selection of gifts for the children's Christmas party, the money for which they had raised by holding several cake sales. At the meeting the parents decided to get guns for the boys and little glass animals for the girls. After the meeting the classroom staff agreed among themselves that the gifts seemed inappropriate, and that it was apparent that a previous meeting on child development and active learning had not been sufficient to influence the parents in this situation. However, the staff didn't interfere, hoping that the children themselves would help the parents see some of the problems of guns and glass animals. On the day of the party the children received their gifts. As one small girl opened her gift she announced to all: "I don't want this because if it falls, it will break, and I'll cut myself." The parents listened and decided they had bought the wrong toys. They decided that the next parent-staff meeting would focus on buying and making toys for young children, and with classroom staff they made plans to have a speaker who would lead a discussion and demonstrate some sample toys and materials.

Here are some pointers for classroom staff to keep in mind as they work with parents to plan and evaluate parent-staff meetings:

• Plan meetings around topics selected by parents.

• Ask one or two parents from the previous year to help plan and lead the first parent-staff meeting. Thereafter, ask for volunteers at each meeting to work on the next meeting.

• Plan around available community resources when possible—printed materials from local agencies, local "experts" (including parents), films from the local library, visits to related programs and institutions.

• Encourage experienced parent planners and leaders to share their skills and experience with parents who are planning and leading meetings for the first time.

• As you plan the format for each meeting, consider how to provide time for people to talk together before the meeting starts, how to introduce the topic, how to present related media and materials, how to open a discussion and keep it going, how to wrap up the session so that people can pull together what they've learned.

• Plan active meetings so that participants don't just listen or talk but have a chance to do something related to the topic.

• Evaluate each meeting soon after it occurs and make recommendations to the next group.

• Remember also to 1) send notices to all parents before each parent-staff meeting to inform them of the time, place and topic of the meeting; 2) provide baby-sitting services for each meeting; and 3) tell all parents who are unable to attend what happened at the meeting, perhaps through a newsletter produced by parents and staff.

Key Experience for Parents: Learning about child development and classroom curriculum

All parents have concerns and questions about their child's preschool program. What will my child learn? Why? How does the staff handle behavior problems? How will the program ready my child for kindergarten? In order to help parents share their ideas and concerns, staff can provide information on child development at parent-staff meetings; they can encourage parents to observe and participate in the classroom to gain an understanding of the curriculum; and they can discuss issues during home visits and at meetings with parent volunteers.

Suggestions for classroom staff

Provide parents with child-development and curriculum materials

Obtain relevant materials from all possible sources. Head Start offices and health clinics, for example, acquire many pamphlets in the areas of child care and child development. Distribute them to parents as they drop off and pick up their children, at parent-staff meetings and on home visits.

Help parents learn about the arrangement of the classroom

Here are some ways classroom staff can acquaint parents with the room arrangement:

• Introduce the work areas of the room using photographs or slides, a videotape or the classroom itself.

• Indicate other areas to be opened as the year progresses.

• Give parents a list of the materials used in the classroom.

• Suggest that parents draw a map of the room arrangement at home with their children.

• Give reasons for the present room arrangement.

• Ask parents to evaluate the room using the room arrangement checklist (see appendix 2).

Help parents learn about the daily routine

• Introduce the principles of the daily routine, providing a rationale for each component.

• Plan a parent meeting in which the parents actually participate in the planning-working-reviewing sequence.

• Ask parents to give personal accounts of the different elements of the routine their children may have talked about.

• Explain the child planning process.

• View and discuss the *Daily Routine* film (see appendix 4).

• Distribute, and encourage parents to use, the daily routine checklist (appendix 2) as an aid to classroom observation.

Involve parents in planning and evaluating

Have parent volunteers participate in team planning and evaluation sessions on the days they work in the classroom. Encourage them to contribute their observations, insights and ideas to the team's formulation of the next day's plan.

Help parents learn about child development

All parents need information on how their children develop physically and mentally. For most parents, discussion with classroom staff and, perhaps, written materials on child development will be sufficient. Some parents, however, such as abusive parents and parents of unusually active or handicapped children, will need special attention.

Teaching teams working with a physically abused or a neglected child or one whom they suspect is being physically abused or neglected should seek assistance immediately from a community social worker. Unless they are specifically trained in this area, classroom staff should work with the parents through supportive services. Find out from the case worker how the classroom team can best help the parents and child in school and on home visits.

Working with parents of unusually active or handicapped children.   Again, work together with support services, parents and children to establish a consistent way of dealing with the particular issues involved. It often helps to arrange a meeting with support workers and parents at which the parents describe issues they face with their child, and all the adults work together to devise strategies to try at school and at home.

Related films and publications from the High/Scope Foundation

BILINGUAL/BICULTURAL EDUCATION

Films—

(For a complete description of each film and instructions for ordering, see appendix 4.)

El Curriculum Cognitivo (Spanish)

Parents as Volunteers (Spanish and English)

Publications—

An Exploratory Bilingual Program (article) by Dennis Vigil, *High/Scope Foundation Annual Report, 1975-76.*

An informal look at the High/Scope experimental bilingual preschool classroom during several months in 1975. Illustrated with many lively examples from observations of the classroom in action, the article shows how a preschool which supports growth in two languages can provide an enriching experience for both Spanish- and English-speaking children.

A Perspective for Bilingual/Bicultural Education (article) by Dennis Vigil and Donal Moore, *High/Scope Foundation Annual Report, 1974-75.*

This article is an argument for an open framework perspective on bilingual/bicultural education. It holds that what bilingual education needs is what education in general needs, and that it is therefore misleading to speak of a bilingual "curriculum" or even a bilingual "component." Instead, it asks that we speak of a "new education" for children of all cultures.

Un Marco Abierto by High/Scope Bilingual/Bicultural Preschool Curriculum Project Staff.

In development at this writing, this is a complete set of curriculum materials for the High/Scope open framework model for bilingual/bicultural programs. It includes a teacher's manual, a guide for teacher trainers, and a set of booklets for parents.

Young Children in Action (Spanish-language version).

The Spanish-language edition of this volume is in development at this writing.

CHILDREN WITH SPECIAL NEEDS

Films—

(For a complete description of each film and instructions for ordering, see appendix 4.)

Integration of Handicapped and Nonhandicapped Preschool Children—Parents' Perspectives

Publications—

Bulletin of the High/Scope First Chance Outreach Project (newsletter)

Published several times yearly, this newsletter reports progress throughout the replication network for the High/Scope First Chance Outreach Project, a program providing training and technical assistance to sites using the Cognitively Oriented Curriculum in preschools serving handicapped children. It includes suggestions for classroom activities, firsthand stories from teachers about their experiences, comments from High/Scope staff, and other features of interest to preschool teachers and teacher trainers.

Serving Young Children with Special Needs (article) by Sara Jane Adler, *Bulletin of the High/Scope Foundation,* fall, 1977.

This is an informal account of the successful use of the Cognitively Oriented Curriculum in an integrated classroom of nonhandicapped and mild to moderately handicapped preschoolers. The setting is the High/Scope First Chance Demonstration Preschool, which operated from 1974 to 1977.

That New Room (article) by Mary Fleck, *Bulletin of the High/Scope First Chance Outreach Project,* winter, 1978.

This brief account by a teacher in a preschool early intervention program describes how she prepared the older children in an elementary school for the addition of a classroom of handicapped preschoolers to the school. The author describes how she designed an active learning experience which sensitized the older children to what it means to be handicapped, while introducing them to the new teacher and classroom.

WORKING WITH PARENTS

Films—

(For a complete description of each film and instructions for ordering, see appendix 4.)

Parents as Volunteers (Spanish and English)

Working with Teachers and Parents: Leading Group Discussions

Working with Teachers and Parents: Inservice Training

Home Visitor Training series: *1. The Role of the Home Visitor;*

2. Building a Relationship with Mother & Child; 3. Building a Relationship with Family Members; 4. Focusing on the Baby's Actions and Development; 5. Problems Encountered by the Home Visitor; 6. A Home Visit with Julie–12 Weeks Old. (Parent-infant education)

Publications—

Parents and Educators: Experts and Equals (article) by Dolores Z. Lambie, *High/Scope Foundation Annual Report, 1975-76.*

After briefly describing the evolution of High/Scope's "Parents as Equals" approach to home visiting, this article demonstrates, with specific examples, how home visitors can help parents feel that their views are important, that they can learn to observe their children, and that they can rely on their own informed judgment in raising them.

Mothers as Teachers (article) by Dolores Z. Lambie, *High/Scope Foundation Annual Report, 1973.*

A primary goal of High/Scope's programs in parent-infant education has been to support parents as the primary teachers of their children. This article explains what High/Scope means by "mothers as teachers" and why this principle is central to High/Scope's home visit programs. It goes on to describe the kinds of behavior and attitudes which make mothers effective as teachers of their infants.

Home Teaching with Mothers & Infants: The Ypsilanti-Carnegie Infant Education Project–An Experiment, (book, 129 pp.) by D.Z. Lambie, J.T. Bond, D.P. Weikart, 1975.

An account of a High/Scope experiment in home-based parent-infant education. Chapters on the project's philosophy of infant education, the families selected for the project, the implementation of the program, the experimental design, and the results of the research.

Home Visits (chapter in book) from *The Cognitively Oriented Curriculum: A Framework for Preschool Teachers* by D.P. Weikart, L. Rogers, C. Adcock, D. McClelland. Urbana, Illinois: NAEYC, 1971.

This chapter describes the home visit component of the preschool program in which High/Scope staff first developed the Cognitively Oriented Curriculum.

Related reading on adaptations of the curriculum

BILINGUAL/BICULTURAL EDUCATION

Sources of Information—

DACBE: Dissemination and Assessment Center
  for Bilingual Education
6504 Tracor Lane
Austin, Texas 78721

ERIC Clearinghouse on Early Childhood Education
University of Illinois
805 West Pennsylvania Ave.
Urbana, Illinois 61801

National Clearinghouse for Bilingual Education
1500 Wilson Blvd.
Suite 802
Rosslyn, Virginia 22209

Publications —

Bilingual Education for Children: An ERIC Abstract Bibliography. Urbana, Illinois: ERIC/ECE, Catalog No. 163, June, 1977.

Cartel: Annotated Bibliography of Bilingual Bicultural Materials. Austin, Texas: DACBE.

Castillo, Max and Josué Cruz, Jr. "Special Competencies for Teachers of Preschool Chicano Children: Rationale, Content, and Assessment Process," *Young Children*, September, 1974. pp. 341-347.

Cazden, Courtney; Cancino, M.; Robansky, F. and J. Schumann. "Second Language Acquisition Sequences in Children, Adolescents and Adults." Final Report Project No. 730744, Grant No. NE-6-00-3-0014, U.S. Department of Health, Education and Welfare, National Institute of Education Office of Research Grants, August, 1975.

De Avila, Edward A. and Barbara Havassy. "Piagetian Alternative to IQ: Mexican-American Study," in *Issues in the Classification of Exceptional Children,* Nicholas Hobbs, ed. San Francisco: Jossey-Bass Publishers, 1975. pp. 246-265.

De Avila, Edward A. and Barbara Havassy. "The Testing of Minority Children: A Neo-Piagetian Approach," *Today's Education,* November-December, 1974. pp. 72-75.

Dulay, Heidi C. and Marina K. Burt. "Natural Sequences in Child Second Language Acquisition," paper presented at annual TESOL convention, Denver, Colorado, March, 1974. (TESOL, 451 Nevils Bldg., Georgetown University, Washington, D.C. 20057.)

Ervin-Tripp, Susan. *Language Acquisition and Communicative Choice*. Stanford, California: Stanford University Press, 1973.

Epstein, Noel. *Language, Ethnicity and the Schools: Policy Alternatives for Bilingual-Bicultural Education*. Washington, D.C.: The George Washington University Institute for Educational Leadership, 1977.

Fishman, Joshua A. "Bilingual Education—A Perspective," IRCD Bulletin, Teachers College, Columbia University, Vol. 12, No. 2, spring, 1977.

Hollomon, John W. "A Conceptual Approach to Assessing Bilingualism in Children Entering School," *TESOL Quarterly*, Vol. 2, No. 4, December, 1977.

Hyland, Ann. *A Mexican American Bibliography: A Collection of Print and Non-Print Materials*. Toledo, Ohio: The Mexican American Curriculum Office, Toledo Public Schools, 1974.

John, Vera. *Early Childhood Bilingual Education*. New York: Modern Language Association, 1971.

Laosa, Luis M. "Socialization, Education and Continuity: The Importance of the Sociocultural Context," *Young Children*, July, 1977. pp. 21-27.

Michigan Department of Education. *A Position Statement on Bilingual Instruction in Michigan*. Lansing, Michigan: March, 1976.

Ravem, Roar. "Language Acquisition in a Second Language Environment," *International Review of Applied Linguistics*, Vol. 6, No. 2, 1968. pp. 165-185.

Saville-Troike, Muriel. *Bilingual Children: A Resource Document*. Arlington, Virginia: Center for Applied Linguistics, 1973.

Simoēs, A., Jr., ed. *The Bilingual Child: Research and Analysis of Existing Educational Themes*. New York: Academic Press, 1976.

Trix, Frances. "Some Issues of Language and Cognitive Development in Bilingual/Bicultural Education," TESOL (ED 515), fall, 1976. pp. 1-11.

CHILDREN WITH SPECIAL NEEDS

Sources of Information—

BEH Technical Assistance Centers
    University of Washington
    E.E.V.W.J.—10
    Seattle, Washington 98195

    Technical Assistance Development System
    University of North Carolina
    500 NCNB Plaza
    Chapel Hill, North Carolina 27514

CEC/ERIC Clearinghouse on Handicapped
  and Gifted Children
The Council for Exceptional Children
1920 Association Drive
Reston, Virginia 22091

CEC: Council for Exceptional Children
1920 Association Drive
Reston, Virginia 22091

Publications—

A Selected Guide to Government Agencies Concerned with Exceptional Children. Reston, Virginia: CEC, 1972.

A Selected Guide to Public Agencies Concerned with Exceptional Children. Reston, Virginia: CEC, 1972.

Cross, Lee and Kenneth Goin, eds. *Identifying Handicapped Children: A Guide to Casefinding, Screening, Diagnosis, Assessment and Evaluation*. New York: Walker and Company, 1977.

Cruickshank, W. M. and G. Orville Johnson. *Education of Exceptional Children*. Englewood Cliffs, New Jersey: Prentice-Hall, 1975.

Furth, Hans G. *Thinking Without Language: Psychological Implications of Deafness*. New York: Free Press, 1966.

Hewett, Frank M. with Steven R. Forness. *Education of Exceptional Learners*. Boston: Allyn and Bacon, Inc., 1974.

Ispa, J. and R. D. Matz. "Integrating Handicapped Preschool Children within a Cognitively Oriented Program," in *Early Intervention and the Integration of Handicapped and Non-handicapped Children*, M. J. Guralnick, ed. Baltimore: University Park Press, 1978. pp. 167-190.

Klein, J. "Mainstreaming the Preschooler," *Young Children*, July, 1975. pp. 317-326.

Levitt, E. and S. Cohen. "Educating Parents of Children with Special Needs—Approaches and Issues," in *Young Children*, May, 1976. pp. 263-272.

Meisels, Samuel. *First Steps in Mainstreaming: Some Questions and Answers*. Medford, Massachusetts: Tufts University, 1977.

Meisels, Samuel. *Special Education and Development: Perspectives on Young Children with Special Needs*. Baltimore, Maryland: University Park Press, 1979.

WORKING WITH PARENTS

Sources of Information—

PMIC: Parenting Materials Information Center
Southwest Educational Development Lab
211 East 7th St.
Austin, Texas 78701

ERIC Clearinghouse on Early Childhood Education
University of Illinois
805 West Pennsylvania Ave.
Urbana, Illinois 61801

Publications—

Bell, Terrell H. *Active Parent Concern.* Englewood Cliffs, New Jersey: Prentice-Hall, Inc., 1976.

A Bibliography of Home-Based Child Development Resources. Washington, D.C.: ACYF, DHEW Publication No. HEW-391, March, 1973.

Brazelton, T. Berry. *Infants and Mothers: Differences in Development.* New York: Delta, Dell, Delacorte Press, Seymour Lawrence, 1969.

Bronfenbrenner, U. *Is Early Intervention Effective?: A Report on Longitudinal Evaluations of Preschool Programs* (Vol. 2). Washington, D.C.: Department of Health, Education and Welfare, Office of Child Development, 1974.

Bronfenbrenner, U. "Who Needs Parent Education?", paper presented at the Working Conference on Parent Education, Charles Stewart Mott Foundation, Flint, Michigan, September, 1977.

Chess, Stella; Thomas, Alexander and Herbert G. Birch. *Your Child Is a Person.* New York: Viking Press, 1965.

Clarke-Stewart, Alison. *Child Care in the Family: A Review of Research and Some Propositions for Policy.* New York: Academic Press, 1977.

Clarke-Stewart, Alison. *Interactions Between Mothers and Their Young Children: Characteristics and Consequences,* Monographs of the Society for Research in Child Development, 38 (6-7, Serial No. 153). Chicago: University of Chicago Press, 1973.

Dodson, Fitzhugh. *How to Father.* Los Angeles: Nash, 1974.

Dodson, Fitzhugh. *How to Parent.* New York: Signet Books, 1970.

Fraiberg, Selma. *Every Child's Birthright: In Defense of Mothering.* New York: Basic books, 1977.

Goodson, B. D. and R. D. Hess. *Parents as Teachers of Young Children: An Evaluative Review of Some Contemporary Concepts and Programs.* Urbana, Illinois: ERIC, ED 136 967, 1975.

Gordon, Ira and Win Brievagel, eds. *Building Effective Home-School Relationships.* Englewood Cliffs, New Jersey: Prentice-Hall, 1974.

Guinagh, B. J. and I. J. Gordon. "School Performance as a Function of Early Stimulation." Final Report to Office of Child Development, University of Florida, Gainesville, Florida, 1976.

Hahn, Joyce and Virginia Dunstan. "The Child's Whole World: A Bilingual Preschool that Includes Parent Training in the Home," *Young Children,* May, 1975.

Hanes, Michael L. and Dunn, Sandra K. "Maternal Attitudes: and the Development of Mothers and children," in *Mother/Child, Father/Child Relationships,* J. Stevens *et al,* eds. Washington, D.C.: NAEYC, 1978.

Hewett, Kathryn D.; Grogan, Marian; Rubin, Ann D.; Nauta, Marrit and Mona Stein. *Partners with Parents: The Home Start Experience with Preschoolers and their Families.* Washington, D.C.: ACYF, DHEW Publication No. DHEW (OHDS) 78-31106, 1978.

Honig, Alice S. *Parent Involvement in Early Childhood Education.* Washington, D.C.: NAEYC, 1975.

Keniston, Kenneth and the Carnegie Council on Children. *All Our Children: The American Family Under Pressure.* New York: Harcourt Brace Jovanovich, 1977.

Lamb, Michael E. *The Role of the Father in Child Development.* New York: John Wiley & Sons, 1976.

Lambie, D. Z.; Bond, J. T. and D. P. Weikart. "Framework for Infant Education," in *Exceptional Infant,* Vol. 3, B. Friedlander and G. Sterritt, eds. New York: Brunner/Mazel, 1974.

Lane, Mary B. *Education for Parenting.* Washington, D.C.: NAEYC, 1975.

Love, John M.; Nauta, Marrit; Coelen, Craig G.; Hewett, Kathryn and Richard R. Ruopp. "National Home Start Evaluation: Final Report, Findings and Implications." Washington, D.C.: Home Start, ACYF, ED 134 314, March, 1976.

Lundberg, Christina and Beatrice Miller. *Parent Involvement Staff Handbook.* Washington, D.C.: DCCDCA, 1971.

Madden, J.; Levenstein, P. and S. Levenstein. "Longitudinal I.Q. Outcomes of the Mother-Child Home Program," *Child Development,* No. 47, 1976. pp. 1015-1025.

McBride, Angela Barron. *The Growth and Development of Mothers.* New York: Harper and Row, 1973.

The Midwest Teacher Corps Network. "Planning and Implementing Parent/Community Involvement into the Instructional Delivery System." Proceedings from a

Parent/Community Involvement Conference, Michigan State University Teacher Corps Project, Erickson Hall, East Lansing, Michigan 48824, 1978.

Morrison, George S. *Parent Involvement in the Home, School and Community*. Columbus, Ohio: Charles E. Merrill Publishing Co., 1978.

Palmer, F. H. "The Effects of Minimal Early Intervention on Subsequent I.Q. Scores and Reading Achievement." Final Report for Education Commission of the States, State University of New York, Stony Brook, New York, 1976.

Parent Education: An ERIC Bibliography. Urbana, Illinois: ERIC, Catalog No. 175, January, 1978.

Parenting. Washington, D.C.: ACEI, 1974.

Rheingold, H. "To Rear a Child," *American Psychologist*, No. 28, 1973. pp. 42-46.

Rozdilsky, Mary Lou and Barbara Banet. *What Now: A Handbook for New Parents*. New York: Charles Scribner's Sons, 1975.

Schaffer, Rudolph. *Mothering*. Cambridge, Massachusetts: Harvard University Press, 1977.

Seitz, V.; Apfel, N.H. and C. Efron. *Long-term Effects of Intervention: A Longitudinal Investigation*. Hamden, Connecticut: Hamden-New Haven Cooperative Education Center, 1976.

Stevens, J. *et al*, eds. *Mother/Child, Father/Child Relationships*. Washington, D.C.: NAEYC, 1978.

U.S. Department of Health, Education and Welfare, Office of Child Development, Children's Bureau. *Your Child From 1 to 6*. Washington, D.C.: Superintendent of Documents, U.S. Government Printing Office, DHEW Publication No. (OCD) 73-26, 1962.

Weikart, D.P. "Learning Through Parents: Lessons for Teachers," *Childhood Education*, No. 11, 1971. pp. 119-236.

White, Burton. *The First Three Years of Life*. Englewood Cliffs, New Jersey: Prentice-Hall, 1975.

Part One

The Classroom

The Day

The Staff

1/ *Arranging & equipping the classroom*

A cognitively oriented classroom needs space—space for active children and space for a wide variety of materials and equipment. The classroom needs storage space that is visible and accessible to the children. Children need space in which to learn through their own actions, space in which they can move, build, sort, create, spread out, construct, experiment, pretend, work with friends, store belongings, display their work, work by themselves and in small and large groups. The arrangement of this space is important because it affects everything the children do. It affects the degree to which they can be active and to which they can talk about their work. It affects the choices they can make and the ease with which they can carry out their plans. It affects their relationships with other people and the ways in which they use materials.

Many kinds of structures can be converted to cognitively oriented preschool classrooms—houses, church basements, gymnasiums, classrooms, house basements, barns, gas stations, one-room schoolhouses, trailers, mobile classroom annexes, picnic pavilions—as long as there is enough space for each child. Space is essential for active learning.

Room arrangement reflects the educational beliefs of the adults responsible for the classroom. Imagine, for example, what a preschool classroom would look like if the responsible adults believed that young children learn best by listening to teachers, watching demonstrations, looking at pictures, following directions and engaging in quiet activities like looking at books, coloring, stringing beads and reproducing numbers and letters. The room would not need to be large. It would probably be filled with tables and chairs, and the teacher would sit at the front of the classroom directing and correcting the children's work.

The arrangement of a cognitively oriented classroom reflects the belief that children learn best in a stimulating but ordered environment in which they can make choices and act on them. The classroom is divided into well defined work areas, and the materials in each area are logically organized and clearly labeled, which enables the children to act independently and with as much control over the classroom environment as possible.

Classroom space works best for children who make their own choices when it is divided into distinct *work areas*. These work areas help children to see what their choices are, because each area provides a unique set of materials and work opportunities. A block area, for example, has building materials as well as toy people and vehicles the children can use with the structures they build. When children plan to work in this area, they know which materials are available and what can be done with them; so their plans can be thoughtful, purposeful decisions rather than offhand spurts of energy.

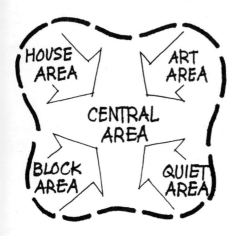

Whenever possible, work areas should be located around the perimeter of the room, with a central space left for moving from one area to another and for group meetings and action games. In classrooms that can't have a central area, one of the work areas should be big enough for group meetings.

Each classroom also needs space for the storage of children's personal belongings; each child can be given a wooden or metal locker, a carton or a plastic dishtub.

Where weather permits, the outdoors can become part of the classroom. The art, music, sand-and-water and construction areas, for example, will thrive outside as long as they are clearly defined, well organized and well equipped.

There are as many imaginative ways to arrange classroom space as there are imaginative adults and children to think of them. For people who have the opportunity to design and build their own preschool facilities, here are some suggestions:

• Space—the number of square feet per child as determined by local licensing requirements
• A bathroom (with child-level fixtures) opening directly off the classroom
• A sink, preferably in the art area
• Floor tiling in the art area
• Electrical outlets above children's reach
• The first 4½ feet of each wall covered with bulletin-board material on which children can display their own work
• Carpeting throughout the classroom except in the art area
• Ample closet storage space away from children's sight and reach, for materials and supplies not intended for immediate classroom use
• A door from each classroom to the outside
• A covered area immediately outside the door

for outdoor play in inclement weather
• A protected outdoor storage area for riding toys, balls, etc.

Once teaching teams have arranged their classrooms in clearly defined work areas with a variety of materials stored visibly and within reach, their next task is to help the children become familiar and comfortable with the room so that they will know what their choices are and where they can find the materials they wish to use. Some suggestions for helping children learn the areas of the room and what's available in them are given in chapter 2.

The areas of the room that will be considered in detail in the following sections are the core areas for a cognitively oriented program—the block area, the house area, the art area, the quiet area, the construction area, the music and movement area, the sand and water area, the animal and plant area and the outdoor play area. Adults, of course, can add other areas during the year as the children's interests become known to them.

Arranging and equipping a block area

A preschool classroom needs a spacious and well equipped block area not only because block building fascinates and challenges many three- and four-year-old children but also because blocks can be used in so many different ways for so many different purposes. Preschool children use blocks to build structures that go up, out or around and in the process deal with the spatial and structural problems of balance and enclosure. They also deal with similarities and differences and create patterns in their structures. Preschoolers also use blocks, little people, animals, furniture and vehicles in make-believe play.

Block play provides opportunities for adults to observe children exploring, building cooperatively or independently, sorting, grouping, comparing and arranging objects, representing experiences and role playing. A classroom without an amply supplied block area deprives children of these important cognitive and social experiences.

A block area requires space for structures as well as freedom from people passing through to another area who may inadvertently topple a building or tower. Space away from the general traffic flow can usually be found in a door-free corner. A block area that opens into the center of the room can accommodate many large structures on days when more than the usual number of children plan to work there.

Since role play often extends from the house area to the block area, locating the block area

next to or across from the house area encourages this process with a minimum of disruption to children working elsewhere. Blocks can become beds, walls, telephones, dishes and cars in the house area, and house area equipment can add realistic details to houses, stores, offices and fire stations built in the block area.

A block area, like any other area, needs to be bounded so that children have a sense of being *in* the area and at the same time can see out into the rest of the room. This can be accomplished by placing low block-storage shelves along the unwalled boundaries of the area. Low boundaries can also be improvised from cinder blocks and a board or from cardboard or plastic storage cartons (milk crates, for example).

Many teaching teams prefer a carpeted block area to cut down on the noise of block play. A carpet or rug also helps to define the limits of the area. It need not be expensive and should be as tightly woven and flat as possible so that struc-

Building materials

large hollow blocks, ramps and boards

unit blocks (as many shapes and sizes as possible)

small playskool blocks

cardboard blocks

cloth- or contact-paper-covered blocks made from shoeboxes or milk cartons

carpet pieces, boards, cardboard pieces, old sheets, blankets, bedspreads, plexiglass pieces, styrofoam packing pieces

boxes, large and small

homemade unit blocks made from scraps of 2x4's or 1x2's

tubes

string, rope and pulleys

photographs of children's buildings

Materials to take apart and put together

plastic or wooden "take apart" trucks and cars (some that snap and some that screw)

large plastic or wooden tinkertoys

interlocking blocks and boards

clip-on wheels and blocks

interlocking wooden train tracks

Materials for filling and emptying

dump trucks	small blocks
pickup trucks	stones
barn	chestnuts
dollhouse	small cars, people,
boxes, cartons	animals
baskets, cans	dollhouse furniture
buckets, crates	shells
spools	

Materials for pretending

cars and trucks of all sorts and sizes

construction and farm vehicles

planes, helicopters, boats, trains, buses
(scaled to blocks available)

traffic sign set

dollhouse people

dollhouse furniture

rubber, wooden and/or plastic animals

photographs of field trip sites

**Kitchen equipment for manipulating,
sorting, filling and emptying**

child-size* "stove"

child-size "refrigerator"

child-size "sink"

adult-size** silverware

adult-size pots and pans

adult-size cooking utensils
  large and small spoons
  large and small slotted spoons
  large and small spatulas
  eggbeater
  food mill
  egg timer (sand or wind-up)
  teapot, coffee pots
  ladle
  colander
  ice-cube trays
  cookie press and cutters

*Child-size refers to any height that can be comfortably reached and used by young children. A "stove," "refrigerator" and "sink" can be purchased from many preschool supply firms, or they can be constructed from wood scraps or heavy cardboard packing boxes.

**Adult-size refers to real kitchen equipment. It is generally much more durable than the kitchen equipment manufactured for children. Children also seem to prefer the "real things" to their smaller toy counterparts.

tures balance evenly on it. Parents or carpet stores often willingly donate carpets or remnants.

Block area equipment needs to be placed where children can see it and easily reach it. Big heavy blocks and bulky items like boxes, carpet pieces, large wooden vehicles and large tinkertoys can be stored on the floor as long as a space for each kind of material is clearly designated by a label or picture. Labeling* helps keep sets of blocks separated into distinct groups based on shape and size, and this gives the children a chance to exercise their ability to order and classify materials. Labeling and storing similar block area materials together also hastens clean-up time.

Block area equipment includes things to build with, to put together and take apart, to fill and empty, to pretend with. Much of it can be scavenged, donated, or made by parents, grandparents or older children. It's not necessary to

have a lot of commercial equipment as long as adults are willing to find and make their own materials.

Remember, a block area needs *space* for children to use all these materials. Therefore, omit riding toys, a workbench, a sand table, tables and chairs. Because they take up so much room and invite collisions into carefully constructed edifices, riding toys are best saved for use outside or during a time of day set aside just for large-motor activities. A workbench and a sand table should have their own areas rather than interfere and be interfered with in a block area. Tables and chairs serve no purpose in a block area and might better be included in a house or art area.

*"Labeling" refers to the process of marking where materials go. Since written labels have no meaning to most preschoolers, labels are constructed from tracings, catalog pictures or photographs of materials.

Arranging and equipping a house area

A house area inevitably becomes a center for make-believe and role play. Here young children have the opportunity to put together and act out all the things they know about the people and events they've observed and experienced—moms, dads, babies, siblings, uncles, aunts, grandparents, firemen, store clerks, babysitters, pets; going to the dentist and the doctor; moving to a new house; going to a funeral or a wedding; attending church or a family reunion; doing the grocery shopping; calling a neighbor on the phone; having a party. Pretending to be people in situations they've experienced helps children make sense of the adult world. It gives them

opportunities to work together, express their feelings and ideas and use language to communicate their roles and respond to others' needs and requests. For these reasons, having a house area in the room is especially important.

Not all children use the house area as a place for cooperative dramatic play. Many children use it instead as a place to explore, figure things out and use the tools, utensils and articles of clothing contained there. Rather than in role play, they spend their time stirring, filling, emptying, pouring, shaking, mixing, rolling, folding, zipping, buttoning, snapping, brushing, putting on and taking off. These children may become involved in a pretend sequence that includes only themselves and the dolls, animals or other materials they've been working with; they

hamburger or tortilla press
sieves
can opener
adult-size baking equipment
    large and small cake tins
    large and small loaf pans
    mixing bowls and lids (3 sizes)
    measuring cups and spoons
    cannister set
    rolling pin
    sifter
adult-size dishes—plates, cups, saucers, bowls
    sponges, dishcloths, towels, potholders, napkins, placemats, tablecloths
things to cook with
    plastic fruits and vegetables
    poker chips, bottlecaps
    styrofoam bits, buttons
    chestnuts, small pinecones, acorns, pumpkin seeds
empty food containers—boxes, cans, cartons, jars, bags

Materials to have on hand for real cooking activities*

hotplate
toaster oven
electric frying pan
popcorn popper with see-through lid
blender

Materials for dramatic play

dolls, stuffed animals
doll beds
baby rattles, bibs, bottles, clothes, diapers
child-size ironing board, iron
small table and chairs
broom, dustpan

*These cooking materials should be stored out of children's reach and used *only* under the supervision of an adult for a special work time or small-group-time project.

wooden or de-electrified toaster

mirror

two telephones

old clocks (de-electrified or wind-up)

small step ladder

dress-up clothes—hats, shoes, purses, dresses, scarves, jewelry, neckties, vests, boots, watches, wallets

briefcases, lunch box, picnic basket

play money, canceled stamps, Christmas and Easter Seals

old blankets, sheets, tablecloths, bedspreads (or large material scraps), beach towels

TV (just the case and the knobs)

sturdy cardboard boxes

low, movable partitions (cardboard or pegboard)

plants (real and plastic), watering can

prop boxes, assembled after field trips by adults and children—pictures on the outside of the box help children distinguish one prop box from another as they look for a particular set of props and as they clean up

Types of prop boxes

grocery store box:

   outside—pictures or photos of a check-out clerk, packer, meat cutter, customers

   inside—toy cash register, empty food containers, play money, paper bags

carpenter's box:

   outside—pictures or photos of carpenters at work and their tools and equipment

   inside—carpenter's apron and hat, ruler, some tools, empty paint cans and brushes, sandpaper

plumber's box:

   outside—pictures or photos of plumber at work and his tools

may play alongside other children but not include or acknowledge them.

   Since role play and block play often support and complement one another, it makes sense to locate the house area as close to the block area as possible. The boundaries of a house area can be defined by low storage shelves, child-size furniture, storage boxes, a low, versatile blocks-and-board shelf or a free-standing mirror.

   The storage of dress-up clothes presents a problem unique to a house area. One way to keep clothes sorted out, visible and accessible to children is to hang them on hooks inserted in the back of a shelf-unit facing another work area. Some teaching teams devise a "closet" from a sturdy packing box with a rod across it for hangers. Since not all young children can manipulate hangers, hooks should also be available. Labeled boxes or dressers can also store dress-up items, but don't expect three- and four-year-olds to be able to keep clothing folded.

   As in all work areas, identical and similar materials need to be stored together where chil-

dren can see and reach them, and storage places for materials need to be clearly labeled with samples of the materials or with pictures, photographs or outlines. Since many household utensils come in three or more sizes, these items can be hung or stored on shelves in series to help children become aware of their graduated sizes.

   Leaving part of a house area open and not defined as a kitchen or any other part of a house leaves room for other kinds of role play. Using blocks from the block area, or low, lightweight cardboard partitions, children can turn this space into a backyard, garage, workshop, doctor's office, store, fire station or whatever setting they need for their particular play.

   In equipping a house area, take into account the experiences and backgrounds of the children. In order to pretend to be the people they've seen, children need props and materials they've seen as well. The list of house area equipment includes many things that can be donated or purchased at low cost at garage sales, second-hand stores and discount stores. Prop boxes (any cardboard or wooden box containing a collection of materials relating to a particular role), added to the area after field trips, can be equipped in part by materials gathered at the field trip site. Many doctors, for example, gladly donate tongue depressors, gauze strips and bandaids.

   Unlike the block area, the house area can and should include a table, where classroom space permits. A regular round table rather than a child-size tea table can accommodate both real and pretend cooking episodes and "family meals" as well as small-group activities. Placing a table and chairs in the house area is a natural way to include them in a preschool classroom; it's better to have them there than to have them occupy valuable work and play space outside a work area.

inside—coveralls, wrench, faucets, plastic and metal pipes and pipe fittings

post-office box:

outside—pictures or photos of mail carriers driving trucks, emptying mailboxes, delivering mail from house to house; people inside a post office

inside—old shoulderstrap purses or paper bags with shoulder straps stapled on, canceled stamps or seals, envelopes, paper, postage scale, rubber stamp and ink pad

doctor's office box:

outside—pictures or photos of doctors and nurses

inside—white shirts for uniforms, nurses' caps (can be made from paper), band-aids, gauze, tape, tongue depressers, pill bottles, small suitcase or purse for doctor's bag, stethoscope, plastic syringes with needles removed

farm box:

outside—pictures or photos of animals, barns, farmers, farm machinery

inside—overalls, rubber boots, hat (whatever kind local farmers wear), pail, straw, calf feeding bottle and nipple, oat bag, bridle, saddle

gas station box:

outside—pictures or photos of gas stations, gas station personnel, gas pumps, cars being filled, washed and repaired

inside—workclothes, hats, empty oil can, hose or tubing (for gas pump), paper towels, plastic spray bottles, car jack and lug wrench

fire station box:

outside—pictures or photos of a fire station, fire trucks, firemen in the station, on the trucks and fighting fires

inside—firemen's hats, a child's rubber raincoat, a pair of boots, rubber hosing *hamburger shop box:*

> *outside*—pictures or photos of hamburger places, people working in them, customers, hamburgers, French fries, soft drinks
>
> *inside*—chef's hat, apron, cups, napkins, straws, plastic ketchup and mustard containers, French fries (cut from foam rubber or styrofoam), hamburgers (cardboard or clay), cash register, play money

shoe store box:

> *outside*—pictures or photos of shoes (child, adult, male and female shoes), people having their feet measured, people trying on shoes
>
> *inside*—a variety of shoes, ruler (or something to measure feet with), shoe boxes, shoe horns

Paper of different sizes, textures and colors

construction paper, many colors

white drawing paper

newsprint

fingerpaint paper

large roll of wrapping, butcher or shelving paper

computer paper (used only on one side; comes in rolls or sheets)

tissue paper

wrapping-paper scraps

foil

contact paper scraps

paper plates

cardboard pieces

wallpaper samples

Arranging and equipping an art area

With paint, crayons, playdough, paste, paper, scissors, boxes and string children can represent things they've done, seen and imagined. As they mix, stir, roll, cut, punch, twist, bend and fold materials, preschoolers learn to generate and observe changes: to fit things together, take them apart, arrange, combine and transform them.

Not all three- and four-year-olds will use art area materials the same way. Some will be more interested in exploring them, in learning how they work and what can be done with them. Their main interest is in the *process* of experimentation rather than in the results of their experimentation, which may be bits of cut paper, or paper covered with tape and glue or a wad of wheat-paste-covered newspaper. Other children already familiar with some art media may concentrate more on using them to make something. These children may be interested in dictating stories and descriptions of their models and pictures once they've completed them.

In thinking about where to locate an art area, consider the convenience of a nearby water sup-

ply and some kind of easily cleaned floor surface. If there's a low sink in the art area, children won't have to walk through other parts of the room spreading paint, paste and papier maché. If there's no running water in the classroom and it isn't possible to have a sink installed, set aside space for a couple of large buckets which children or adults can fill each day before work time begins. Some teaching teams have also used containers with spigots to supply water. Hang a roll of paper towels or a towel dispenser near the water supply as well as sponges or rags so that children can clean the work surfaces.

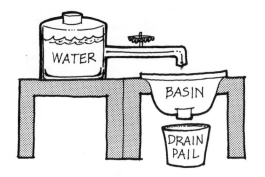

Since children are likely to spill art materials, choose an area of the classroom with a floor that's easy to clean. If part of the room isn't already tiled, and tiling or covering the art area space with a washable surface isn't immediately possible, cover the area with a plastic sheet or an old rug or plan to put newspaper down each day. If you are fortunate enough to have tiling for the area, remember that a smooth floor makes a better work surface than one with decorative ridges and hollows.

An art area needs plenty of work surfaces— a smooth floor, a low, large, sturdy table, counter-tops—as well as space for hanging smocks, drying painting, storing projects in progress and hanging and displaying completed ones. Smocks can be hung on hooks mounted on the back or end of a storage shelf or on a board attached to the wall. Some teaching teams use small clothes trees for smock storage. Pictures can be dried on clotheslines or on clothes racks that can be folded up out of the way when not in use. A clothesline on pulleys allows children to lower the line to hang their own pictures and raise the line out of the way for drying.

Materials for mixing and painting

tempera paint
liquid starch for fingerpaint
soap flakes
watercolor paints
easels
plastic squeeze bottles
jars with lids for storing paints
muffin tins, frozen food tins, saucers for
    painting and printing
newspaper
brushes of different sizes
sponges
paper towels
smocks or paintshirts
toothbrushes
screening

**Materials for holding things
together and taking them apart**

heavy-duty staplers
and staples
paper punch
paste
white glue
 ubber cement
masking tape
Scotch tape
paper clips
rubber bands
elastic
string
shoestrings
yarn
wire
needles and thread
scissors, sharp and blunt

Materials for making three-dimensional representations

moist clay (store in airtight containers)

modeling clay

playdough (store in airtight containers)

playdough accessories—rolling pins, cookie cutters, hamburger or tortilla press, plastic knives, potato masher

cardboard tubes

cloth, felt, rug, fur, vinyl scraps

old stockings and socks

food coloring

plaster of Paris

feathers

styrofoam bits and pieces, golf tees

macaroni (different shapes)

fringe

cotton balls

buttons

straws

egg cartons, shoeboxes, ice-cream tubs

pipe cleaners, wire

empty thread spools

clothespins

bits of wood and balsa

sequins

paper bags

Materials for making two-dimensional representations

pencils

colored pencils

crayons

pastel chalk, chalkboard

marking pens

magic markers (water soluble)

ink pads and stamps

magazines and catalogs

tracing forms

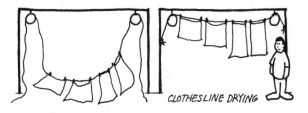

CLOTHESLINE DRYING

Similar art materials need to be stored together so that children can see them and easily reach them. Paper is best stored in a rack where it takes up little space and can be reached easily.

Small loose items like crayons, pencils, chalk, scissors, markers, paper clips, macaroni and toothpicks can be stored in clear plastic containers, clear plastic glasses, lidless cigar boxes or plastic shoe pockets.

Label storage areas and containers with samples of the materials or with pictures, photos or outlines so that children can find and return their own materials. Art area boundaries can be defined by low storage shelves, drying racks, paper racks, easels, smock trees and storage boxes or bins.*

*Joan Dean's book, *A Place to Paint* (1972), contains many well illustrated ideas for art area work surfaces, water facilities, shelving, storage facilities, display areas and easels as well as sources for materials and equipment. It is available from the Citation Press, Library and Trade Division, Scholastic Magazines, Inc., 50 West 44th Street, New York, NY 10036.

Introduce materials gradually at the beginning of the year so that children can learn how to use and care for them. Keep the supply of expendable materials constant, periodically checking and refilling glue bottles, paint jars, tape dispensers, staplers, paper racks, etc.

Arranging and equipping a quiet area

The term "quiet" is a relative one. A group of three- and four-year-olds are unlikely to remain quiet for any length of time, nor should they be expected to, but their activities in the quiet area are usually quieter than block building, role playing, hammering, instrument playing and playdough pounding. Some teaching teams prefer to call it the game area or the game and book area. This area is filled with books, puzzles and small manipulative games and materials; here children have the opportunity to work by themselves or with friends. They play simple games and make up their own games in which they take things apart, rearrange them, fit them together, sort, match, compare, make patterns. Here they can also look at books, listen to stories and make up their own stories as they interpret the illustrations in books.

Some children like to spend time in the quiet area mastering and repeating new fine-motor skills. A child who has figured out how a four- or five-piece puzzle goes together, for example, will often spend time doing that puzzle over and over before moving on to another challenge. Others may vary the activity of doing a puzzle by putting the pieces together outside the frame, doing it upside down or tracing all the pieces. Still other children may make their own puzzles.

Some children will use materials such as picture dominoes and nesting blocks to build with while other children will use them as they were probably intended to be used, or will make up their own games with them. Quiet area materials may also serve as resources for activities in other areas: beads as toy money in role play, inch cubes to add fine detail to a block structure, pegs for playdough cake candles.

In deciding where to locate a quiet area, consider putting it as far as possible from the noisy areas of the room. Many children don't mind noise, but almost all children need a quiet place to go to when they choose. Low storage shelves can help define a quiet area, but some of the shelves should also face into the room or be placed so their contents can be seen easily by children from where they make their plans. When a quiet area is so well bounded and enclosed that children can't see at least some of the materials as they make their plans, they may overlook the quiet area as a place to work and favor instead areas with larger, more visible materials.

A quiet area needs space for children to spread out with their puzzles, beads and lego blocks. A small table and a couple of chairs could be included as an alternative work space, but since most children prefer to spread out on the floor, a regular-sized table should be included only in a very large quiet area. A rug or carpet squares make working on the floor especially inviting.

Some teaching teams have made the book nook cozy and inviting by including a small covered crib mattress, pillows or beanbag chairs. If it's firm enough (and fireproof), some children may also enjoy using a mattress as a puzzle-making or building surface. Books stored on racks which allow the books to face forward help chil-

Materials to sort and build with

large beads and strings
small beads and strings
wooden cubes
plastic cubes
design cubes
parquetry blocks
small texture blocks
wooden picture dominoes
smell bottles (baby food jars with smell-saturated gauze pads made by children)
sound boxes (made from film cans or contact-covered baby cereal boxes)
attribute blocks
buttons, stones, shells, marbles
texture dominoes (using varying textures of cloth, sandpaper, leather, plastic)

Materials to order and build with

nesting boxes
nesting cups
nesting rings
contact-covered coffee can set with lids (large, medium, small)
cuisinaire rods
washers, nuts, and bolts (large, medium, small)
plastic pipe fittings (large, medium, small)

Materials to fit together and take apart

large pegs and pegboards
small pegs and pegboards
stacking roundabout rings
small tinkertoys
large lego blocks
interlocking plastic squares (play plax)
interlocking octagons
plastic nuts, bolts, screws and board set
wooden puzzles (simple four-piece puzzles and more complex puzzles)

magnets

shape sorters and shapes

constructo straws

scales, balances

sewing boards (children can make their
own from pegboard scraps)

georello gears

Materials for decoding and pretending

lotto games

matching card
games   } children and adults
               can make their own
puppets

magnifying glasses

Playskool village

photographs taken of the children
throughout the year (cover each with
clear contact)

picture books, including books the children
make

In selecting books for preschoolers,
consider the following:
- Most young children can say more about
  realistic pictures than about very
  abstract ones. They especially enjoy
  books illustrated with photographs.
- Children relate best to pictures and
  photographs of things they've
  experienced themselves.
- Even though pictures may be very
  complex (like Richard Scarry's
  illustrations), children enjoy and relate
  to them as long as they are realistic and
  recognizable.
- Look for simple story lines related to
  children's own experiences.
- Children enjoy *repetition* in a story
  because they can anticipate and thus
  participate in the story.

dren see what is available more readily than the
conventional way of storing books with only
their spines visible between bookends. In buying or building a forward-facing bookrack, however, make sure there is some provision for
securing the books so they don't fall out every
time someone knocks into the rack. One such
forward-facing bookrack would not hold a whole
preschool book supply, so books need to be
changed periodically.

Also arrange a place in the quiet area for a
sturdy puzzle rack that won't spill all the puzzle
frames and puzzle pieces every time a child goes
hunting for a puzzle. Puzzle racks, like art-area
paper racks, can be built into existing storage
shelves or can be free-standing and act as low
area-dividers.

Similar quiet area materials should be stored
together or in close proximity, and storage containers or areas should be clearly labeled with
outlines, pictures, photographs or actual objects.
Clear plastic shoeboxes, refrigerator dishes,
plastic disposable cups and divided plastic silverware trays make good storage containers for
the many small items in the quiet area children
enjoy using and then sorting back into their containers at clean-up time. Note that many quiet
area items can be found, donated or made. Also,
in selecting quiet area materials, look for things
that can be used in a number of different ways—
things with stackable or sortable pieces, moving
parts that can be taken apart. Avoid elaborate
battery-powered toys that children watch rather
than work with.

Arranging and equipping a construction area

In a construction area children can use real wood and tools to learn new skills, solve problems and make sturdy representations that can later be painted and used in other work areas or at home. Some children who find art area materials too small and demanding feel much more at home pounding and gluing wood chunks and scraps.

The major needs of a construction area are space away from the general traffic flow, a sturdy work surface that will accommodate up to four children and a place for tool and wood storage.

Workbenches can be purchased from many preschool supply catalogs, but they tend to be quite expensive. Here are some suggestions for building workbenches at much less expense:

Two 2 × 12's bolted onto two 25-inch sawhorses

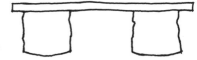

Two 2 × 12's bolted onto two 25-inch tree stumps

Two or three tree stumps around 25 inches high

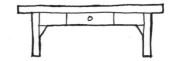

An old child-size wooden table or desk

Tools can be hung on a pegboard labeled with outlines and stored on low, open shelving where space permits or under the workbench in a large, well organized and labeled toolbox.

In equipping a construction area, be sure to have as many hammers as there are work spaces. If four children can work at the workbench, have four hammers so that no one has to wait until someone else decides to switch to another tool.

Wood scraps and wooden crates gathered on periodic trips to local lumber yards, toy makers, cabinet and furniture makers, ladder factories and supermarkets or donated by parents and staff can be stored in cardboard cartons, ice-cream tubs, dishpans, sturdy wastecans or a laundry basket.

In addition to basic tools, children may use art materials like glue, wire, pipe cleaners and rubber bands in their construction work.

Annotated lists of books for preschool children

Books in Preschool. Compiled by Louise Griffen. NAEYC,* 1970.
Children's Books Too Good to Miss. Arbuthnot, Clark and Long. Western Reserve University Press, 1966.
Children's Catalog. Thirteenth edition, 1976. Edited by Barbara Dill. The H. W. Wilson Company, New York, 1976. (See also the yearly supplements for 1977, 1978.)
Multi-Ethnic Books for Young Children: An Annotated Bibliography for Parents and Teachers. NAEYC, 1970.
Starting Out Right: Choosing Books About Black People for Young Children. Edited by Betty I.Latimer. DCCDCA.**

Construction area equipment

sturdy workbench	16-inch saw
vises	screwdrivers
C-clamps	pliers
hammers	
hand drill and/or brace and bit	
sandpaper (coarse and fine)	
nails (different sizes)	
screws (to fit drill or brace bits)	
nuts, bolts and washers	
wood scraps	
bottlecaps and jar lids	

*National Association for the Education of Young Children, 1834 Connecticut Avenue N.W., Washington, D.C. 20009.

**Day Care and Child Development Council of America, 1401 K Street N.W., Washington, D.C. 20005.

Equipment for music and movement area

record player	triangles (three
records	sizes)
tape recorder and	bells
tapes (both pre-	sand blocks
recorded and	maracas
blank)	wooden xylophone
microphone	tambourines (three
earphones	sizes)
	drums (three sizes)
	clavés

Addresses of instrument distributors

Music Education Group (MEG)
Box 1301
Union, New Jersey 07083
(201) 964-3610
(This group works on a bid basis; prices are negotiable.)

Peripole, Inc.
P.O. Box 146
Lewistown Road
Brown Mills, New Jersey 08015
(609) 893-9111
(This company has kits for making instruments and exploring sound.)

Magnamusic-Baton, Inc.
6390 Delmar Boulevard
St. Louis, Missouri 63130
(314) 721-3944
(314) 721-0991
(This is the original U.S. manufacturer of the xylophones designed for children by Carl Orff.)

Kitching Educational
Division of Ludwig Industries
1728 North Damen Avenue
Chicago, Illinois 60647

Arranging and equipping a music and movement area

Activities in a music and movement area give preschoolers a chance to experiment with and enjoy the rhythmic and musical skills that are the basis for later, more complex musical and rhythmical expressions. In this area children generate their own ensembles, mixtures of sounds, rhythms and movements. They explore and compare sounds and sound qualities and movements that can go with them, and they work with such ideas as "fast" and "slow," "first" and "next."

This area needs floor space for playing and moving as well as safe, clearly labeled pegboard or shelf space for storing instruments. Records should be stored in a forward-facing rack (see quiet area bookrack) if space permits or upright in a sturdy wire rack since horizontal piling of records often causes warping. (Check records periodically for scratches and sound quality. Badly scratched records can be very frustrating.) A simple record player children can learn to operate and care for by themselves can be stored

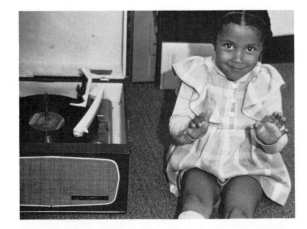

near an electrical outlet on the floor or on a low storage shelf. Keep electrical outlets covered when not in use, or better yet, have all low outlets moved up above children's reach. A sturdy cassette tape recorder is in some respects easier for young children to use, and cassettes last much longer than records. Also, battery-operated cassette recorders don't require an outlet, although batteries need to be checked and replaced frequently. Recorded cassettes need to be labeled with pictures so that children can find the particular cassette they want without having to hunt up an adult to read through all the titles for them. It also helps to label record jackets and the center of each record with identical labels so children can return each record to its own jacket.

Arranging and equipping a sand and water area

Most three- and four-year-olds enjoy sand and water play. Through mixing, stirring, heaping, dumping, digging, filling, emptying, pouring, patting, sifting and molding they experiment with and find out about textures, quantities and attributes. Sand and water can also be used for representation and role play—making cakes and pizzas and hamburgers, making roads and houses, acting out make-believe situations. And what better place than a sand and water table for trying out a car or boat just constructed at the workbench?

The sand and water area usually centers around a large, wheeled sand and water table built of wood and lined with metal or plastic with a stoppered hole for drainage. When the table is not in use a wooden cover keeps the sand moist and also permits the table to be used as a sturdy work surface. If classroom space does not permit a large sand and water table, a smaller one can be improvised from a baby bathtub with a hole cut in the bottom and stoppered.

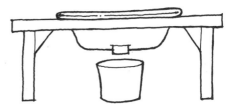

Plywood tabletop with hole cut for baby bathtub

Since sand and water get on the floor, plan to have a supply of newspapers or a roll of plastic handy to protect the floor and make clean-up easy, or locate the area on a tile surface, perhaps at the outskirts of the art area. This location would also allow the area to be near the water supply, so that children wouldn't have to walk back and forth across the room with dripping containers of water. If the sand and water area can't be near running water, plan to include a large, sturdy, covered bucket for water that can be stored under or near the table. Sand and water play equipment can be stored in pictorially labeled boxes under the table, on low shelving, or it can be hung on a labeled pegboard. One teaching team devised this efficient way of storing sand and water equipment:

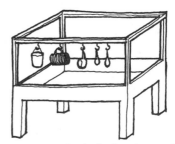

Frame of 1 × 1's with hooks for hanging sand and water toys

Some pets to consider

earthworms:
House in jars with holes punched in the lids. Fill jars with moist soil.

ants:
Ant farms—in which a colony of ants can be viewed through a see-through case—can be purchased at pet stores or through supply catalogs.

caterpillars:
Be sure to keep some of the grass or leaves on which they were found. House in a jar or a bug house of plastic screening stapled or stretched into a cylindrical shape with plastic lids for roof and floor.

tadpoles:
It's fascinating to watch tadpoles over a period of time as they grow limbs and change into frogs. Scoop them out of a pond in spring and keep them in a fish-tank full of pond water.

fish:
Goldfish are easily cared for and fairly hardy. Pairs of guppies are fast breeders and multiply rapidly.

guinea pigs:
Perhaps one of the best mammals for pre-school classrooms, guinea pigs freeze (hold still) when frightened rather than attack and can be kept in a terrarium or small cage. They do well on a diet of animal food pellets, water and fresh greens each day. They are easily handled by young children and do not run away.

cats, dogs, rabbits:
Cats, dogs and rabbits that join the class as baby animals and remain throughout the year provide children with concrete examples of growth and change over time. All three can be paper trained and require dry food daily (large quantities can be bought economically at the local farm bureau) and a supply of fresh water. They should also see a veterinarian for worming, rabies and distemper shots.

A sand and water table can be used for water alone, for sand alone and for sand and water together. In winter, snow can be added. Some teaching teams have filled their tables with small, smooth beach pebbles the children gathered on field trips. Other teams have used beans and styrofoam bits for variety.

In warm climates or seasons, a sand and water table can be wheeled outside, freeing classroom space for other materials and making clean-up simpler.

Arranging and equipping an animal and plant area

In an animal and plant area young children can observe growth and change and can learn to feed, water and care for living things. The amount of space needed for an animal and plant area depends entirely on the number and size of the animals and plants included. Some teaching teams include small animals and plants in the quiet area, while other teams prefer to have larger animals like rabbits and cats free to roam about the room with the children. Wherever plants and animals are kept, be sure to have cages and feeding materials together where children can get to them easily.

Include plants that are easy to grow (philodendron, succulents, geraniums), plants children can start themselves (sweet potatoes, beans, grass, marigolds) and indigenous plants. Keep a supply of pots, clear plastic tumblers and potting soil on hand. Remember that some plants and animals need to be kept separate. One teaching team arrived one morning, for example, to find all their plants eaten away to stubs by their resident rabbit who had spent the night out of his cage.

Setting up an outdoor play area

Many of the room arrangement principles already discussed apply in setting up an outdoor play area. First of all, space is needed—for action, and for the equipment that encourages action. The entire outdoor space needs to be bounded—by trees, shrubs, fencing, boulders, buildings, logs, hills—so that the children understand the limits and adults don't have to spend time disciplining or worry about children running off.

Once the entire playground space has been clearly defined, areas within it need to be designated for both permanent pieces of equipment and open, unstructured activities, with an eye to traffic patterns, safety and design.

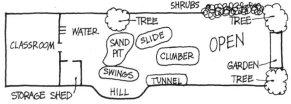

A CHILD HEADS FOR THE SLIDE AND CLIMBER, *running through the sand pit and disturbing sand play. How can he get from the water to the garden or storage area to open space without interfering with somebody?*

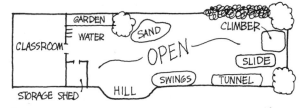

THIS ARRANGEMENT DISPENSES WITH THESE PROBLEMS *by placing the major pieces of equipment around the perimeter of the area and leaving the middle space open.*

Things to climb and balance on

permanent climbers or jungle gyms
take-apart climbers with movable pieces children can add and rearrange by themselves
sturdy wooden crates or barrels
railroad ties
tree trunks and stumps
balance beam
large rocks
net climber

Things to swing on

commercial swing set
rope swing from tree
tire swing
low canvas or nylon net hammock

Things to slide on

commercial slide
hill slide
low ramp (good for wheel toys, too)

Things to get into and under

concrete drainage pipes
hill tunnels (can be combined with hill slide)
sturdy packing boxes
sheet or blanket tents
play house
tree with low hanging branches like a willow
stump and board tunnels
fiber drums

Things to jump on and over

inner tubes	ropes
inner tube trampolines	low boxes
old mattress	
pile of leaves (in autumn)	

It's important to provide equipment out-doors that promotes a wide variety of active physical experience for children. Consider the categories listed in the margins and select pieces of equipment from each category.

Things to push, pull and ride on

tricycles
wheelbarrow
wagons
scooters
Swedish variplay take-apart car
variplay triangle set
rocking boat
dollies
pull cart

Things to kick, throw and aim for

balls, large and small
bean bags
low hung basketball hoop and net
tires
pails, buckets, boxes
bull's-eye painted large and low on a
    fenceboard

Things for sand and water play

See list of materials under *Arranging and equipping a sand and water area.*

Things to build with

boards of varying lengths
tree stumps
boxes
sheets, blankets
tires and inner tubes

Changing the room during the year

No matter how carefully a teaching team arranges and equips their classroom before the children arrive in the beginning of the year, they'll probably make numerous changes as they watch how their children actually use space and materials. A teaching team may decide to change the room for a number of reasons. Some children may not be using an area as much as others, so the team might try rearranging it, relocating it, or adding new materials; one area may be used a lot and need more space; the teaching team may want to add new areas as the children become familiar with the original ones; children and adults may become habituated to a room and need a change for its own sake; after field trips new materials may be added to certain areas so that children can represent or reenact their experiences—after a trip to a local grocery store, for example, the teaching team may rearrange the house area so that the kitchen area takes up less room, allowing more room for the construction of checkout counters and shelves of food; new materials may be added to suit the needs and interests of certain children—a child may have filled and emptied all the containers in the room, for example, and need new containers to investigate and experiment with.

Children can help decide where new materials and equipment should go, and they can make and attach labels.

Be sure to use the opportunity room changes create to talk with children about the differences they observe in the room and the comparisons they can make between the way the room used to be and the way it is now.

A teaching team should also keep a "want list" of all the things they'd like to add to their classroom by purchasing, making or "scavenging." Send lists home to parents, who are often glad to get rid of things they no longer need around the house. Keep a complete set of catalogs on hand, too, for ideas. Many of the materials pictured in them can be made by adults and by the children themselves.

Accommodating children with special needs

The same basic notions of room arrangement and equipment already discussed apply to children with special needs. All children do best in an environment in which there is a wide choice of materials they can work with and space for them to be active in their involvement with both materials and people. The purpose of modifications for children with special needs is to make space and materials more accessible to them.

Visually impaired children

Since visually impaired children encounter their environment through touch and sound, it is particularly important for them to know that the locations of equipment and materials are consistent from day to day. If the rubber animals in the block area are put back on one shelf one day and another the next, visually impaired children looking for them will be frustrated and confused rather than aided by their environment. When new work areas or equipment are added to the room, they should be added gradually rather than suddenly, and adults should acquaint visually impaired children with any change right away so they can reorient themselves with a minimum of anxiety and loss of control over their surroundings.

Labels for objects and equipment can be made of outlines cut from textured materials like sandpaper or felt, and paper outlines can be made of string so these children can *feel* where things belong.

Traffic patterns need to remain clear and constant and bounded by stable pieces of equipment rather than by things that are easily toppled. When changes in the traffic pattern are made, help the children reorient themselves right away. Go over the new routes with them, helping them recognize what's the same and what's different. If the floor is not fully carpeted, any scatter or area rugs of carpet pieces should be firmly anchored to the floor with double-faced tape to prevent tripping.

A music area and a sand and water area should be included in a room with visually impaired children, since these areas are geared to hearing and to touching rather than seeing.

Hearing-impaired children

For hearing-impaired children, extraneous classroom sounds interfere with vocal sounds, making it difficult for them to distinguish speech from the overall din of young children in action. Since all children need to be able to sort out and hear speech in order to communicate and understand, it is especially important for a teaching team with hearing-impaired children to make their classroom as sound-absorbent as possible. Carpeting, drapes and accoustical ceiling tile go a long way toward absorbing classroom noise. Covering a workbench surface with carpet scraps and fitting record players and tape recorders with earphones also helps.

Cinderblock walls and tile floors make a particularly difficult environment for hearing-im-

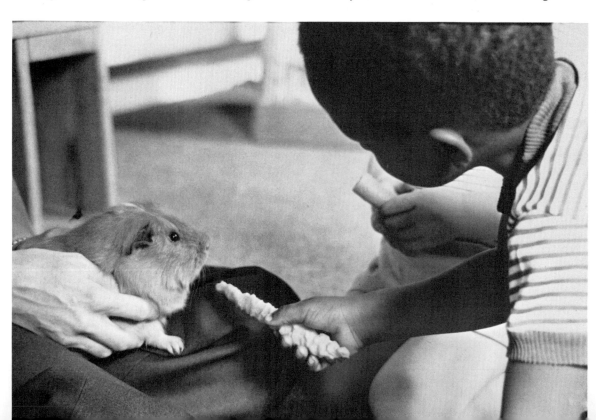

paired children because sounds ricochet from one hard surface to another. Tile floors should be carpeted and cinderblock walls either paneled or covered with bulletin boards, burlap or even egg cartons to absorb the sound.

Physically impaired children

Since all physically impaired children present their own unique needs and abilities, a teaching team must look at each child to see what specific modifications he needs in the room arrangement in order for the room to work for him. Work surfaces in each area, for example, need to be within each child's reach. For some physically impaired children this may mean including standing tables or low legless chairs they can be strapped into so they can play with their friends on the floor. For children in wheelchairs, the space between areas needs to be wide enough for them to maneuver through.

Physically handicapped children should be allowed to be as self-sufficient as possible. One teaching team, for example, had equipment stored within the reach of children in wheelchairs but found that some of these children were too weak to carry what they needed from the shelf to the work surface; rather than have adults carry the materials for the children, however, these teachers decided to fit each wheelchair with a carrying tray.

Mentally impaired children

Adults should be aware of the toys and materials a mentally impaired child in their classroom particularly enjoys and should add a variety of similar materials to the work areas. Watch each child to see what his or her abilities and needs are. Some mentally impaired children may just take longer than other children to learn the names of the areas and where the materials belong. For

these children it's best to use samples of real objects to identify the areas and the storage places. Other, more severely impaired children may need simpler, one-part toys and fewer choices to begin with.

Some mentally impaired children find changes difficult to deal with, so adults should make room arrangement and equipment changes gradually rather than all at once. Before making the changes, help the children anticipate them by talking about what's going to happen and how things will be different. Involve them in making the changes whenever possible, be prepared to accept their reactions positively and give them some ways of coping with changes.

Related films and publications from the High/Scope Foundation

Films—

(For a complete description of each film and instructions for ordering, see appendix 4.)

Classroom Structure and Equipment

Arranging the Classroom: Case Study of the High/Scope Preschool

The Block Area series: 1.*Setting up a Block Area*; 2. *A Place to Explore New Materials*; 3. *A Place to Build All Kinds of Structures*; 4. *A Place to Represent Things*; 5. *Observing a Child in the Block Area*

A Good Classroom is a Classroom Full of Choices from **Helping Children Make Choices and Decisions** series

Exploring the Possibilities of the Room from **Helping Children Make Choices and Decisions** series

Publications—

The Cognitively Oriented Curriculum–Room Arrangement and Materials (No. 3) (booklet, 44 pp.) by Sheila Mainwaring, 1978. (Elementary grades)

The High/Scope Cognitively Oriented Elementary Curriculum requires an environment in which children can test and express their ideas, make decisions, solve problems, apply their own reasoning to diverse situations, and share their experiences with others. The teacher's desk is no longer the focal point, and a wide variety of materials must be accessible to the children. This booklet describes the kinds of planning and strategic thinking that the teaching staff should exercise in order to produce such a learning environment for elementary-age children. A lengthy appendix lists equipment, supplies and resources for 15 interest areas.

Related reading on room arrangement and facility design

The major sources of the following pamphlets and articles are:

ACEI: Association for Childhood Education
International
3615 Wisconsin Avenue, N.W.
Washington, D.C. 20016

DCCDCA: Day Care and Child Development Council of America
1401 K Street, N.W.
Washington, D.C. 20005

EDC: Educational Development Center
55 Chapel Street
Newton, Massachusetts 02160

NAEYC: National Association for the Education of Young Children
1834 Connecticut Avenue, N.W.
Washington, D.C. 20009

Superintendent of Documents
U.S. Government Printing Office
Washington, D.C. 20402

Pamphlets and Articles

Baker, K.R. *Let's Play Outdoors.* Washington, D.C.: NAEYC, 1966.

Environmental Criteria: Mr. Preschool Day Care Facilities. (Conducted by Research Center, College of Architecture and Environmental Design, Texas A & M), HEW Social and Rehabilitation Service, Division of Mental Retardation.

Equipment and Supplies #9. Washington, D.C.: Project Head Start Series, Office of Economic Opportunity.

Friedberg, M. Paul. *Playgrounds for City Children.* Washington, D.C.: ACEI, 1969.

Friedman, David Belais; Colodny, Dorothy; Burnett, Mary and T.D. Cutsforth. *Water, Sand and Mud as Play Materials.* Washington, D.C.: NAEYC, 1959.

Hein, George and Jean Piaget. "Materials and Open Education," *EDC News,* Winter, 1973.

Housing for Early Childhood Education—Centers for Growing and Learning. Washington, D.C.: DCCDCA.

Kritchevsky, Sybil; Prescott, Elizabeth and Lee Walling. *Planning Environments for Young Children: Physical Space.* Washington, D.C.: NAEYC, 1969.

Materials: A Useful List of Classroom Items that Can Be Scrounged or Purchased, (Early Childhood Education Study Series). Newton, Massachusetts: EDC.

Murphy, Lois B. and Ethel M. Lepper. *A Setting for Growth,* (Caring for Children Series #6). DHEW Publication Number (OCD) 74-1031, Washington, D.C.: Superintendent of Documents.

Osmon, Fred Linn. *Patterns for Designing Children's Centers.* Washington, D.C.: DCCDCA.

Passantino, R.J. "Swedish Preschools: Environments of Sensitivity," *Childhood Education,* May, 1971. pp. 406-411.

Playgrounds for City Children. Washington, D.C.: DCCDCA.

Playscapes. Washington, D.C.: ACEI, 1973.

Safe Toys for Your Child, How to Select Them, How to Use them Safely, (Children's Bureau Publication 473). Washington, D.C.: Superintendent of Documents, 1971.

A Small World of Play and Learning. Washington, D.C.: DCCDCA.

Space for Learning—A Preschool Environment for Very Little Money. HEW OCD, Bureau of Head Start and Child Service Programs, 1972.

Zimmerman, L. and G. Calovini. "Toys as Learning Materials for Preschool Children," *Exceptional Children,* May, 1971, 37. pp. 642-54.

Books

Aaron, David and B.P. Winawer. *Child's Play: A Creative Approach to Playspaces for Today's Children.* New York: Harper and Row, 1965.

Blacklow, Julie, ed. *Environmental Design: New Relevance for Special Education.* Arlington, Virginia: Council for Exceptional Children, 1971.

Dattner, Richard. *Design for Play*. New York: Van Nostrand Reinhold, Co., 1969.

Early Childhood Education: How to Select and Evaluate Materials. Washington, D.C.: DCCDCA (Educational Products Information Exchange Institute), 1972.

Hamlin, Ruth; Mukeiji, Rose and Margaret Yonimura. *Schools for Young Disadvantaged Children*. New York: Teacher's College Press, 1967.

Hogan, Elizabeth. *Children's Rooms and Play Yards*. Menlo Park, California: Lane Books, 1970.

Hole, W. Vere. *Children's Play on Housing Estates*. London: Her Majesty's Stationery Office, 1966.

Lady Allen of Hurtwood. *Planning for Play*. Cambridge, Massachusetts: MIT Press, 1968.

Lady Allen of Hurtwood. *New Playgrounds*. London: The Housing Center Trust, 1964.

Ledermann, Alfred and Alfred Truchsel. *Creative Playgrounds and Recreation Centers*. New York: Frederick A. Praeger, 1967.

Leeper, Sarah, *et al. Good Schools for Young Children*. New York: Macmillan, 1971. pp. 407-421.

Matterson, E.M. *Play and Playthings for the Preschool Child*. Baltimore, Maryland: Penguin Books, 1967.

Monahan, Robert. *Free and Inexpensive Materials for Preschool and Early Childhood*. Belmont, California: Lear Siegler, Inc./Feuron Publishers, 1973.

Sarnoff, Henry; Sarnoff, Joan and Hensley Anderson. *Learning Environments for Children*. Raleigh, North Carolina: Learning Environments, 1972.

Utzinger, Robert. *Some European Nursery Schools and Playgrounds*. Ann Arbor, Michigan: University of Michigan Press, Educational Facilities Laboratories, 1970.

2/ Establishing a daily routine

By the time children reach the age of three or four, they're often concerned with time and the sequence of events. "When is mommy coming home?" "Can we go now?" "Is it my birthday yet?" A classroom routine that's consistent from day to day gives three- and four-year-olds a specific way to understand time. "First I take off my coat. Then I go over to Ms. Rainbow and tell her what I want to do. Then I go to the block area . . ." Once a child has participated in the sequence of the daily routine a number of times and has a name for each part, he can begin to understand classroom time as a predictable series of events. He doesn't have to depend on an adult to tell him what's going to happen next.

A consistent routine is a framework. It frees children and adults alike from worrying about or having to decide what comes next, and enables them to use their creative energies on the tasks at hand. Once the routine is established so the children feel comfortable, it becomes more flexible. A good work time occasionally gets extended, for example, or the routine is changed to accommodate a field trip or a visit by a local fireman. The daily routine is designed to accomplish three major goals: First, it provides a sequence of plan-do-review which gives children a process to help them explore, design and carry out projects, and make decisions in their learning. Second, it provides for many types of interaction—small and large group, adult to child, child to child, and adult teamwork—and times when activities are child-initiated and adult-initiated. Third, it provides time to work in a variety of environments—inside, outside, on field trips, in various work areas. When the daily routine is well implemented it can provide a many-faceted structure through which children and adults can be active and creative.

Helping children learn the daily routine

Children need to be aware of the daily routine and know the names of its parts so that they don't go through the day wondering what's going to happen next or worrying that they won't get a chance to go outside and play on the swings. Here are some ways to help children learn the daily routine from the very first day of school:

• Follow all the parts of the routine each day in the same order.

• Make a point of using the name of each time period conversationally with the children throughout the day: "I'm putting my coat on now because it's outside time and I want to be ready." "That's right, it's clean-up time, Tracy, and you're putting away all the square blocks." "There's still a lot of time left in work time, Kevin, so I think you and Andrea have time to finish your car before clean-up."

• Establish and use a signal to mark the end of time periods. For example, a child could go around the room playing the tambourine and say, "Clean-up time, clean-up time."

• Alert the children a few minutes before each time period is over so they'll be able to anticipate what's next and not get caught in the middle of a

Planning time △

Recall time △

Work time △   Clean-up time ▽

Snack time △   Small-group time ▽

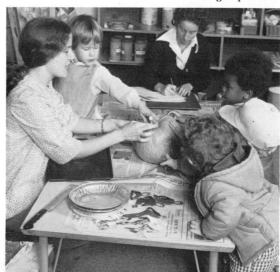

Elements of a daily routine

Each segment of a daily routine should provide a different kind of experience for children. These are the major elements in the routine of the Cognitively Oriented Curriculum:

PLANNING TIME—Children decide for themselves what they're going to do during work time. They indicate their plans to the adults, who help them think through and elaborate their ideas and also record the plans for them and help them get started.

WORK TIME—Children carry out the projects and activities they've planned. Adults move among them, assisting and supporting them and helping them extend their ideas. Children who complete their initial plan make and work on another.

CLEAN-UP TIME—Children store their unfinished projects and sort, order and put away materials they've used during work time.

RECALL, SNACK AND SMALL-GROUP TIME—These three segments of the daily routine are often grouped together. Recall time is the third element of the plan-do-review cycle. Small groups of five to eight children meet together with an adult to recall and represent their work time activities; often this is done while the children are having their snack. During small-group time the children work with materials, usually chosen by the adult, in an activity designed to allow the adult to observe and assess children in terms of a particular key experience. A small-group activity might, for example, involve each child making his own batch of playdough and observing changes that occur, or each child building with boxes and blocks to explore the different ways objects can be arranged.

OUTSIDE TIME—Children and adults are involved in vigorous physical activity—running, throwing, swinging, climbing, rolling. As in all activities, adults encourage the children to talk about what they're doing.

CIRCLE TIME—All the children and adults meet together as a large group to sing and make up action songs, play musical instruments, move to music, play games and sometimes discuss an upcoming special event.

It's up to each teaching team to arrange these elements into a daily routine that suits their particular time and scheduling constraints. Some programs, for example, work around meals, naps and playground schedules; other programs run all day and have both morning and afternoon work times. Some teams prefer to start the day with circle time; others plan with children for work time as they finish breakfast. The particular arrangement is not important as long as each element is included. However, *planning time, work time, clean-up and recall* should always follow one right after the other, and work time should be the longest single time period.

project. An adult might say, for example, "Work time's almost over. Then it will be clean-up time."

• At the end of each time period talk with children about what's coming next: "Now that we've cleaned up and finished small-group time we need to go to the circle for circle time." Be sure to inform the children at planning time if there's to be a change in the routine, so they can incorporate it into their thinking about the day's events.

• Take photographs of activities during each time period of the day. At small-group time have the children talk about what's happening in the photographs and help them connect the name of the time period to each activity. Later on, some

Outside time △   Circle time ▽

children may be able to sequence the photos in the order of the daily routine.

• After the children have talked about photos of the daily routine, some of them may be interested in helping construct a schedule of the daily routine to be hung where all children can see and refer to it. It might look like this:

We get on the bus.

We hang up our coats.

We make our plans.

etc.

• At circle time make up a song with the children about the daily routine. As they sing about each time period, the children could pantomime some of the things they do during that period. One preschool class made up this song to the tune of "The Farmer in the Dell":

Verse 1—We ride on the bus.
         We ride on the bus.
         Heigh-ho the derry-o
         We ride on the bus.
Verse 2—We hang up our coats . . .
Verse 3—Then we make our plans . . .
Verse 4—Then we have work time . . .
         etc.

Planning

At planning time adults and children meet together to talk about what each child wants to do, and how the child might go about it. Children decide for themselves how they'll use their work time. The adult encourages the child to say or demonstrate what he or she would like to do, helping the child get a better picture of it in mind. Instead of imposing choices on children, the adult helps them learn to identify choices themselves: "Well, Billy, I see you want to go to the block area. What are you going to use there?" "Could you bring me some things you might use?" "Let's go together and see what we can find to work with." "I see you've found the big blocks and the small blocks, is that what you're going to work with today?"

Usually the child can't make a single plan for the entire work time, so he or she indicates a starting activity and then makes another plan during work time when finished with the first

Sample daily routine for a half-day program

8:30- 8:50 a.m.	PLANNING TIME
8:50- 9:45 a.m.	WORK TIME
9:45-10:00 a.m.	CLEAN-UP TIME
10:00-10:30 a.m.	RECALL, SNACK AND SMALL-GROUP TIME
10:30-10:50 a.m.	OUTSIDE TIME
10:50-11:10 a.m.	CIRCLE TIME
11:10-11:20 a.m.	DISMISSAL

Sample daily routine for a full-day program

7:30- 8:30 a.m.	As children arrive, adults plan with them and get them started on a short work time.
8:30- 9:00 a.m.	Breakfast and brush teeth
9:00- 9:20	PLANNING TIME
9:20-10:30 a.m.	WORK TIME AND CLEAN-UP
10:30-10:50 a.m.	RECALL TIME
10:50-11:20 a.m.	OUTSIDE TIME
11:20-11:45 a.m.	CIRCLE TIME and preparation for lunch
11:45-12:30 p.m.	Lunch
12:30- 1:30 p.m.	Nap time. Children either sleep or lie quietly with a book
1:30- 2:15 p.m.	SMALL-GROUP AND SNACK TIME
2:15- 4:00 p.m.	Some children leave. Adults plan with the remaining children, who then work until they leave.

also gives children a chance to recognize and respond to their own moods in a constructive way. If a child is feeling quiet, or cranky, or excited, he or she can plan activities that channel these feelings. An adult can help the child to recognize moods and plan appropriate activities.

It's important for a child to talk over a plan before he or she carries it out. This helps the child form a mental picture of his or her idea and get a notion of how to proceed, or at least where to start. For adults, talking over the plan provides an opportunity not only to encourage and respond to children's ideas, but also to help children carry them out. This process gives both the child and the adult a good point of departure: the child feels reinforced and ready to start his or her plan; the adult has ideas of what to look for— what difficulties the child might have and where help may be needed.

Not all children can come up with something they want to do, especially when they're just beginning to learn about planning. An adult might need to offer some choices to such children, to help them learn a few of the possibilities of the room. These suggestions would be different for each child, depending on what the adult knew of his or her interests. Sometimes an adult might choose to go to an area with a child, or have the child find another child to work with. The planning process takes time to learn. It takes experience to know what's right for the situation. The following pages focus on how to make the planning process a positive, useful activity.

Getting ready to plan

Children new to the planning process do not start planning for work time on the first day of school. They begin by exploring the people, materials and choices that make up their environment. Once the children are familiar with the

project. In this way, although planning time is a designated time, the planning *process* continues throughout work time as children complete their activity and plan again. As the year progresses, some children learn to make more complete initial plans that they carry through the entire work time.

Children who plan for themselves see that they can make things happen. Children begin to view themselves as people who can decide and who can *act* on their own decisions; they have some control over their own activities. Planning possibilities available to them, they'll also need time to learn the planning process itself: how it takes place, where, when and with whom. The teaching team can help them by breaking this process down into separate steps:

HELP CHILDREN LEARN WHICH MATERIALS ARE AVAILABLE, so they understand what the possibilities are. By the time the children arrive in the fall, the room should be arranged in work areas equipped with materials children can see and reach. It should be well organized so their choices are easy to find and clearly visible. Before the children arrive in the morning, adults can set a few materials out on the floor in each area to help children who may find the array of materials in the classroom overwhelming. They can talk about materials as the children use them: "You're stringing the round beads, Wendy. What other beads on the shelf could you try stringing?" Adults can also use materials the children aren't familiar with during small-group time or circle time.

HELP CHILDREN LEARN THE NAMES OF THE WORK AREAS, so they'll have a way of indicating where they want to carry out their ideas. The best way to help children do this is to use the names of work areas when talking with the children throughout the day: "Joannie, you've sure made a great big tower here in the block area." "You've done a good job cleaning up the art area, Terry and Stacey." "I see one of your shoes in the quiet area, Jeannie." Children also enjoy circle-time games using the names of the work areas.

HELP CHILDREN LEARN THE NAMES OF OTHER PEOPLE IN THE ROOM, so they'll have a way of addressing, thinking about and referring to each other. Children feel more comfortable working together or joining an ongoing play situation if they know each other's names. Adults should use every opportunity throughout the day to use

children's names in conversation. Encourage children to say each other's names as they pass out food and utensils at snack time. "One cup for Joey. One for Lynette. One for Barbara. . ." Sing name-game songs at circle time.

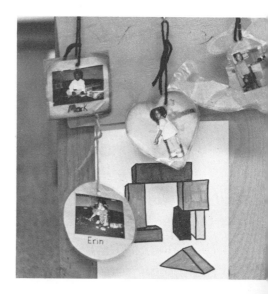

HELP CHILDREN BEGIN TO MAKE CHOICES and see alternatives throughout the day, whenever the occasion arises. Making choices is basic to all planning. "What colors do you think you'll need to mix to paint your airplane, Annette?" "Since all the blocks are already being used, what else could you use to make a road for your truck? . . . What about the carpet squares or the flat styrofoam pieces?" "That was a good idea, Mark, to fly around the circle like an airplane. Who has another idea about how we could go around the circle?"

INTRODUCE SIGNS AND PLANNING BOARDS; a sign is a tag with a child's picture and name on it that the child takes to a work area. In the work area, the child hangs the sign on a special board called a *planning board* to show himself and others that this is the area where he plans to work. This gives the child a visual reminder of his or her plan. If a child moves to a new work area, changing the sign to the new planning board will signal a change in plan. This will help children understand the relationship between plans they make and work they do. Children can also learn each other's names by identifying the child in the sign picture.

CHOOSE A TIME AND PLACE TO PLAN, suited to the needs of the children and the requirements of the schedule. In some programs the day begins with breakfast, the children plan together while they eat, or plan individually as they finish breakfast. Other programs begin the day with circle or greeting time and plan while the group is gathered, or break into small groups to plan. In some programs, the day begins with a flexible planning time where an adult plans with each child as he arrives. In choosing a place to plan, visibility is the major consideration—children need to be able to see all the work areas so their choices are visible. It's hard for many children to think of what is there if they can't see it. Children should plan at a low table or on the floor and have the adult right there with them; it's difficult to have a meaningful, relaxed conversation if the adult is towering over the child.

Planning with children

Children and adults need time to adjust to the planning process. A child may not understand for a while what a "plan" means. An adult may have problems at first knowing what to say or do, or how to get things started. Both adults and children may find themselves trapped in the same questions and responses. The following sections discuss some ways that adults can be involved in children's planning. They include

some possible strategies for adults; these are by no means the only strategies that are useful—teaching teams should try out many different ideas for themselves.

Eliciting a child's plan   What should an adult say to a child who may not understand the meaning of "plan"? The most straightforward, understandable question is, "What would you like to do today?" This question is open to many different responses and doesn't require that a child understand exactly what "making a plan" is.

Some adults fall into the trap of starting with the question, "Where are you going to work today?" This places the emphasis on where the child wants to work rather than on what the child wants to do, which is really more central to planning. It's more appropriate to discuss where a child plans to work after he's said what he'd like to do:

"What would you like to do today, Stacey?"

"Make another person."

"That's a good idea. What are you going to use to make your person?"

"The wig and shoes and dancing dress."

"I see. Where do you think would be a good place to do this work?"

"Oh, in the house area."

"You mean you're going to dress up to look like another person?"

"Um-hm."

"Good. Let me know when you've finished. I want to be sure to see what you look like."

As the adult begins to know the children better, he or she can base questions on the particular personality and interest of each child:

"I see you brought your own hammer today, Corey. Are you going to make your plan to use it?"

"You told me your plan, Joannie, when you came in the room. Tell me more about it."

"Joey, here's the Robin Hood movie you started yesterday. Let's think about how you can finish it today."

"I remember yesterday at clean-up time, Wendy, you wanted to build a house in the sand. Maybe you could make your plan to do that today."

Be sure to give each child time to respond to whatever questions are asked. Rather than hurry a child, go on to another child while the first one formulates his plan: "While you're thinking, Gary, I'll talk to Janey. Then I'll come back to you."

Recognizing a child's plan Children indicate their plans in different ways depending on

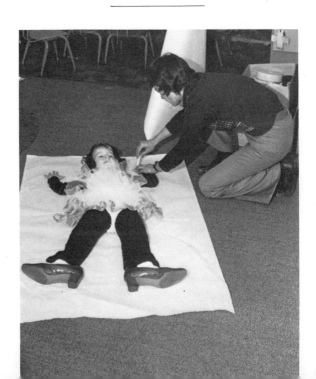

how clear a picture they have in mind and how freely they use language. Here are some ways children indicate their plans:

• Some children point to the area, object or person they wish to work with or nod their head and look in that direction. It's up to the adult to use language that supports the child's gestures. "Oh, you'd like to work in the music area today? That's a good idea."

• Some children bring the materials they'd like to work with to the adult in response to an initial question. Again, the adult should use appropriate language even though the child may never say a word. "You've got some playdough and some tinkertoy sticks. What would you like to do with them, Markie?"

• Some children describe what they want to do. "See this? My dad gave me this wood and I'm going to make a car with wheels and paint it."

• Some children recall a plan they've started and wish to continue. "I'm going to work on my dinosaur again and put the legs on."

Adults will find, too, that not only do different children indicate their plans differently, but the same children often alternate between gestures and complex statements.

Helping children who don't know what to do, or who don't indicate a plan in any way   Sometimes children say, "I don't know" or don't respond at all when asked what they'd like to do during work time. Perhaps all the choices confuse them. Perhaps they're not sure of the names of the materials, persons or places they have in mind. They may be very cautious in the still relatively new preschool setting and react to it by not appearing to respond at all. An adult plays an important role in this situation by helping the child begin to feel more comfortable and see that he *can* make a choice. Here are some ways to do this:

"How about bringing me something you'd like to work with, Toni?"

_____

"Wendy, point to the area where you'd like to work."

_____

"Let's go together and look in each area, Erica, and see if we can find something that you'd like to do."

_____

"I see Joey and Joannie working in the sand, Felix painting in the art area, Jeff and Erin building a road in the block area, Lynnette dressing up in the house area, and Stacy doing puzzles in the quiet area. Can you see something you'd like to do, Mark?"

_____

"Yesterday I remember you were stringing beads in the quiet area, Bennie. Would you like me to go to the quiet area with you and see if we can find something else to string?"

_____

"I'm going to the art area. Would you like to come with me and see if there's something you'd like to do there?"

Helping children include more detail in their plans   As adults get to know the children individually they will probably find that for some children even a very simple statement of their intent is progress. They may feel, on the other hand, that other children could be making more detailed plans. Here are examples of adults attempting to help children think through their ideas more fully:

"What are you going to do today, Lennie?"

"Play in the sand."

"That's a good idea. What do you think you'll do with the sand?"

"Play with it."

"Well, when you play with it are you going to dig, or make some piles of sand, or use the sand dishes?"

"Cups, cups. Fill all the cups up."

"Then what?"

"Turn them over. Make cakes and cakes and cakes."

"Great. Will you show me all your cakes?"

"Yep. There's gonna be lots."

———————

"How about you today, Joanie. What's your plan?"

"Cut."

"Cut. Okay, what will you need when you cut?"

"Scissors."

"Anything else?"

"Paper."

"Okay. You'll need to use scissors and paper. Where do you think you'll find scissors and paper?"

". . ."

"Look around."

"Over there in the art area."

"Yes, in the art area. Maybe you could save your pieces that you cut in this container, Joanie."

"And paste them down."

"That's a good idea. You could paste down the pieces that you've cut."

———————

"Hi, Donna. Do you know what you'd like to do today?"

"Play with Stacey."

"Can you tell me what Stacey's doing?"

"She's dressing up and being the mama."

"Well, who could you be?"

"Stacey's big sister. I'm gonna cook dinner. You can come over when it's all ready."

"Okay, call me on the phone when it's time to eat."

Helping children who make the same plan every day   As they consider a child who makes the same plan every day for an extended period of time, adults need to find out if the child actually *does* the same thing every day. For example, at planning time a child may say, "I'm going to build a road in the block area." If each day she goes to the block area, uses the same blocks to build the same road and drives the same car up and down on it, then the adults should help her think through some alternatives at planning time. If she goes to the block area, however, and makes different kinds of roads, experimenting with various materials, building techniques and vehicles, then her plan really is different each day, and the adults need to help her talk about these differences as she plans.

Here are some ways to help children who plan and do the same thing every day or who continually work in the same area:

• Encourage the child to work in another area by introducing him to materials there that are similar to the ones he always works with. "Chris, you've been working with the cars and blocks in the block area every day. I'd like to show you some different cars and blocks you might like to work with in the quiet area."

• Plan small-group activities around materials the child doesn't generally work with. Once children have had the opportunity to figure out how to use materials they may never have used or even seen before, they may be able to include them in their plans.

• Help the child plan something new for his or her first activity. "Chris, how about working in the art area first before you go to the block area today? Maybe you could trace around one of your cars, or maybe you could make a car out of milk cartons and use it in the block area."

Sometimes a child will go through a period of making the same plan his or her best friend makes. What should an adult do in that situation? Usually children separate after a while as they become more self-confident and independent, but here are some things an adult can do in the meantime:

• Let the children work together but encourage each child to state his or her own plan.

• Have the two children plan in separate planning groups.

• Support both children in the things they do on their own.

Working with children who make more than one plan at a time   Some children are able to plan and carry out a short sequence of related activities. Here are two examples:

"I'm going to the workbench and build a birdhouse and paint it in the art area."

"You're going to do two things, Lynnette. First you're going to build a birdhouse, and second you're going to paint it. That sounds like a good plan."

_____

"I'm going to work with Donna."

"But Donna isn't here yet. What could you do first before she comes?"

"First I'm going to work in the sand. Then when Donna comes we're going to dress up in the house area."

"Great. You've got two plans. First to work in the sand and second to dress up with Donna in the house area."

Some children get carried away with so many interesting things to choose from. At planning time they list more than they can possibly do in one work time. They need to focus on one of their choices first and then plan their next activity:

"I'm going to work there and there and there and there."

"Wait a minute, Erica. What did you point to first?"

"The art area."

"What would you like to do there?"

"Paint a picture of a rabbit for my mom."

"Okay, why don't you hang your sign in the art area. When you've finished your rabbit picture bring it to me and I'll write your story. Then we'll see what your next plan is."

Helping children when they make unrealistic plans   Sometimes a child makes a plan that can't be carried out, because his or her ideas are too grandiose, or the materials needed are already in use, or there isn't enough room for the child in the chosen work area. An adult's major concern in any of these situations should be to help the child retain as much of his or her original plan as possible, and then help the child alter the parts that are unfeasible. If he wants to make a tower as big as the whole room, for example, help him find a part of the room—a block area corner, a table, a large open box—that he could fill up. If she wants to make a birthday cake with the pegs and pegboard and they're already being used, help her think of some alternative materials like nails and styrofoam, toothpicks and clay, sand and popsicle sticks. If he wants to pound at the workbench and there's no room for him there, help him plan something else he can do until space is available.

As we've seen, an adult may need to intercede in children's planning in order to help them expand their usual activities, find new possibilities or deal with obstacles to their plans. If on a particular day a child has no ideas, an adult may want to suggest some activities. Occasionally an adult may want to introduce some new possibilities for work time activities to all the children. Any of these forms of adult involvement can be beneficial to children, can enhance their preschool experience and help them grow, as long as adults remember that their respect for and acceptance of children's choices is the key to making the planning process work. *If children's choices are ignored, there is little reason to ask them to choose in the first place.*

Getting a plan started

When planning is finished, children begin their work time. Some teaching teams prefer to have each child begin work as soon as he or she has finished planning. Others prefer to have the entire group begin work time at the same time. The choice depends on individual teaching styles and on the particular children involved.

It usually takes a while to learn to handle the transition between planning time and work time. Children need to finish one thing while getting another started—sometimes a difficult task. Here are two things to watch for:

(1) WHEN A CHILD PLANS TO DO ONE THING BUT DOES SOMETHING ELSE INSTEAD—When children say one thing at planning time and then begin to do something else at work time, it may be that they don't understand yet what "planning" means. A child may think that all he has to do is say the "right words" to an adult and that once he's said them he's free to do what he *really* wants to do. Perhaps he hasn't taken time before planning to look around to see what he wants to do, so he plans for the first thing that catches his attention and then on the way to getting started is drawn to something else he hadn't noticed.

Adults can help such children make the connection between planning and doing by talking with them as they are working, so that they begin to recognize that they can plan for what they really want to do. For example, an exchange like this might occur:

"Marta, you said you were going to build in the block area but you came right here to the music area instead."

"I want to plan with these."

"You mean you want your plan to be to play the tambourine and the drum?"

"Yep."

"Okay, if this is your plan, go get your sign and hang it here on the music area planning board."

Adults can also help children look around the room at planning time to be sure they have time to sort out alternatives and decide what they want to do most.

(2) WHEN A CHILD GOES TO THE ACTIVITY OR AREA HE OR SHE PLANNED FOR, BUT DOESN'T DO ANYTHING THERE—Some children can make plans and hang their signs in the appropriate areas, but have trouble actually starting their projects. They can't locate the particular materials they need, the materials are already being used by

other children, or they find what they need but can't figure out what to do next. An adult who notices a child having trouble getting started needs to find out why and then help him either find the materials or space he needs or figure out how to get started.

Changes in planning time as the year progresses

Planning time and planning abilities develop as the year progresses. As children become accustomed to planning, adults will want to evaluate the process to make sure it is a useful and positive activity for everyone involved.

Many teaching teams keep track of the plans children make throughout the year because they feel that how a child plans reflects his growth and development. One way to do this is simply to write down each child's plan as he states it, so the child actually dictates his plan.

Planning time can be video- or audio-taped at regular intervals. The team can view or listen to and discuss the tapes as well as use them to explain planning to parents, volunteers, visitors and administrators.

If writing or taping does not appeal to a team, then ways of planning should be a topic for discussion periodically at team planning sessions when the growth of individual children is being reviewed. Here are some sample descriptions of planning time at three different times during the year:

Planning at the beginning of the year

School is about to open with a room full of three- and four-year-olds who have never planned before. The signs are ready, the daily routine is set and the room is attractively and carefully arranged. The adults have decided how to proceed. Planning time for those first few days will be a leisurely time when adults greet the children

as they arrive and explore the room with them. When a child discovers something of interest, an adult will help him or her get started.

At every reasonable opportunity, adults will say the names of the areas of the room and of the materials and equipment. The children will hear "block area," "art area," "house area" and "quiet area" many times. Adults will use circle-time games and songs to repeat these names.

What clues will an adult look for before starting the first planning time? Most children will have learned to stay with an object or set of materials for a reasonable length of time, explored the room thoroughly and become comfortable in it, heard the names of the areas of the room and learned to say some of them, and learned to recognize their own sign.

Here's how a High/Scope team just learning the curriculum began the planning process:

Before school started we decided that our children's signs would be circles, triangles and squares cut from red, blue, yellow and orange construction paper. This, we felt, would be one way of helping the children become familiar with shapes and colors as well as the names of shapes and colors. Also, to identify their own and each other's signs they would have to consider two attributes at once, both shape and color.

We made two identical signs for each child, one that went permanently on the coatrack to identify his peg and his cubby, and one with a long piece of yarn on it he could wear around his neck at work time. To increase the life of the signs we sandwiched them between two pieces of clear contact paper.

On the first day of school we took polaroid pictures of each child and attached these to their signs. Seeing themselves on their signs, we felt, would make the signs more meaningful to the children. A yellow triangle could have no particular significance for Christine, but a yellow triangle with a photograph of her on it would distinguish it as hers alone.

For the first week of school our goal concerning planning was to get the children to know their own signs and to become familiar with the areas of the room and what was in them. Each morning we helped the children find their signs on the coatrack. As they worked during work time, we talked about what area they were in and what they were working on. Tee-Tee, for example, could go straight to the block area and get one of the big wooden trucks. At first, he wanted to drive it all about the room. "Tee-Tee," we'd say, "can you drive the truck back to the block area before it runs out of gas?" or "Can you back it up all the way to the block area?" To help Tee-Tee define and identify the block area, we set up a row of chairs between the block and the house areas until our toy shelf arrived.

At small-group time we used the signs to identify each child's place at the table: "Go find your signs. Your sign tells you where your seat is." We also used the children's signs at circle time for dismissal: "Whose sign is this?" an adult would ask, holding up a sign. "That's right, it's Ricky's. Take your sign, Rick, and go get your coat."

Planning by the third week   For the first few weeks similar things may happen in any classroom. There will soon be enough clues for the adults to know that most of the children feel comfortable enough in the room and with the routine to begin to plan. What next? The teaching team needs to decide how and where to plan—with individual children as they arrive? with a small group first thing in the morning? They need to decide which words to use—"work"? "play"? "plan"? All adults should use the same terms so as not to confuse the children.

Suppose, in order to start planning, a team decides to have circle time first thing in the morning. They let the children know that work time is going to be different today, everyone is going to make a plan first. The signs are in a box on an adult's lap. She brings them out one at a time. As each child identifies his own sign, he takes it and tells where he is going to work or play. If he needs help, one of the adults walks with him to the area and helps him hang his sign on the planning board. Not all children will respond; some will point, some will wait until they hear the more talkative children go along with the idea. For the reluctant ones, the adult is reassuring: "Maybe you'll tell me tomorrow." Later on, when the child is busily at work, an adult can remind him that he *did* choose a place to work: "You're in the house area, I see."

After the first few sessions with all the children in the circle, the group may become restless, so the team divides the children into as many groups as there are adults. The team may decide to ease the children into small groups by keeping the large group for several days but placing the children's signs in a circle on the floor so each child can find his own place. Once this becomes easy for the children, the team can make one smaller circle for each adult.

Here's how the same High/Scope team proceeded:

On Wednesday of the second week, just after our trip to the apple orchard, we decided to initiate planning time. As the children were sufficiently well acquainted with the areas of the room, we had all of them gather around the fireplace before heading off to their areas. Then each one of us (there were three adults) demonstrated one activity related to apples that the children could choose.

When I showed them the ingredients for the applesauce, they all wanted to sit down at the table and begin. The same happened when Martie demonstrated apple printing. They couldn't grasp the idea of sitting in one place while we showed things from three different areas. After we herded them together again we attempted to have each one tell what he was going to do at work time. Somehow they all finally planned something.

Since one of our goals was to avoid large group meetings whenever possible in favor of small groups, because we felt that three- and four-year-olds are not inclined to sit still in large groups for any length of time, we decided to have planning time with individual children. Therefore, the next day when the children came in and hung up their coats, we asked each child what he was going to do that day. After they had named or pointed to the area or material, we went with them to help them hang up their signs. As they did this we said, "You hung your signs in the block area; that means you're working here today." The children were able to take this step without any problem. If a child decided to move to another area, we reminded him to take his sign with him.

Planning went well this way, but we observed after a few weeks that while children were telling us what they would be doing, they were doing so without knowing beforehand what, if any, special things were going on. They were just happening upon some activities instead of choosing from alternatives. Therefore, we decided to review the possibilities with each child before he made his plan.

The planning process will succeed if all the adults in the room listen to what the children say, acknowledge what they do and help them carry out their ideas.

What planning can look like by the end of the year Once planning starts and the children catch on to the idea, many children will begin to carry out complex plans. It is important to keep track of what happens. Here's another example from the same High/Scope teachers' log:

We hit upon a new plan for planning time. At 9:00, as before, the children buzzed around the room checking out each area for interesting possibilities. The drumbeat at approximately 9:05 signalled planning time, only now the children went to their small-group tables. Rather than meet in one large group to plan, each adult met with the five children she meets with at small-group time. In this small-group planning time, adults and children together reviewed work areas as well as previous and upcoming trips that might have a bearing on work time. Then each child made his plan, took his sign and trotted off to his work area. Since each adult met with the same children again at small-group time, she could follow up on their plans. We could also keep track of the kinds of plans the child was making, how much help he needed in making his plans and how he recounted what he had done with his plans. We also began using planning time to review some classroom procedures that were a problem at that point.

We maintained this routine of planning with three groups and recalling with the same children at small-group time for the rest of the year. It was certainly the most satisfactory, for us and our children, of all the routines we'd tried.

Working

Work time, the heart of the preschool day and the longest single time period in the daily routine, is busy and active for both children and adults. Children carry out their planning time ideas. They use the whole room to explore materials, learn new skills, try out ideas and put together what they know in ways that make sense to them. Adults move among the children, observing and helping them carry out or extend their activities.

While most children enjoy work time and look forward to it, adults new to the curriculum often find work time confusing, because they are not sure of their work time role. Clearly adults do not *lead* work time activities—each child plans his or her own—but neither do adults sit back and watch. Work time is a time for adults to observe and learn what interests children and how they perceive and solve problems, to take cues from children and work along with them and to support, encourage and extend children's ideas.

Children need work time because they need a time to work on the things they've planned, to learn at their own pace using the materials that interest them. Work time gives children an opportunity to organize and act on part of their world, to decide which toys, tools and equipment are best for their purposes and to develop the skills necessary to use them with ease. Children begin to see themselves as people who can have ideas and act on them, who can affect their environment. They learn to think of adults as people who will assist them and support their ideas and actions. Adults, in turn, learn that even very young children have many ideas, desires and capacities, and that given the opportunity to act on their own in a supportive environment, children work creatively, effectively and eagerly.

A visitor looking in on five minutes of a typical work time might see the following: a child at the sink mixing paints—two children papier machéing a dinosaur they've been working on for the past few days—a child telling an adult about a picture she's just drawn—several children putting on a record and making up a dance—three children hammering at the workbench—two children playing a game they've worked out involving some picture lotto cards—five children, an adult and two "bears" on their way to the movies in a car they've constructed from chairs and tinkertoys—two children making a long line of cars and trucks.

Were the visitor to stay and watch the rest of work time, he or she would also see children changing their plans as they ended one activity and began another, seeking help from peers or adults as they encountered difficulties in their work and showing people what they'd done. The visitor would see adults working with children on the floor, at low tables, in the sandbox

and talking with them about what they were doing and asking questions to help them solve problems and see new possibilities.

The adult's role

Getting work time plans started   Often one of the first things an adult does at work time is look around the room to see which children (if any) seem to need help getting started on their plans. The adult may see a child hesitating at the entrance to the area he'd planned to work in, a child being ejected from an area, a child in an area doing nothing, a child getting started on something unrelated to his plan.

HELPING A HESITANT CHILD get started on his plan means first discovering the source of his hesitation. Is he timid or unsure of his reception

Work time situations

It's easy enough to talk about things adults can do at work time, but it's another thing to do them—to observe children, devise strategies and act on them on the spot. This manual outlines many different ways of observing and interacting with children throughout the day; the team planning process will help adults come up with additional strategies. The following section consists of four short work-time situations which one High/Scope teaching team encountered. Each episode describes what the team members did and how they thought about it afterwards.

EPISODE I: EXTENDING A PLAN

Mrs. Rogers. What would you like to do today, Donna?

Donna. I'm going to the workbench and make an airplane. [*Donna hangs her sign and starts working on her airplane.*]

[*Later*]

Donna. Mrs. Rogers, Mrs. Rogers, look what I made! Look what I made!

Mrs. Rogers. Why that's a beautiful airplane, Donna. How did you make it?

by other children already in the area? Is he thinking about something he'd really rather be doing instead of what he just planned? Is he watching to see what's already going on before joining others' play? Give him time to either change his plan or see for himself how he can best enter the ongoing play and carry out his plan. If he still hesitates after a reasonable period because he doesn't seem to know quite how to make his way into the area, here are some things that might assist him:

• Talk with him about what he wants to do, asking him where in the area he could work and how he could get to the materials he needs. Offer to go with him to get what he needs.

• For some children a more direct approach might be more appropriate: "Jerry, you said you were going to build with the big tinkertoys. Is that still your plan?" "Uh-huh." "Well, let's go get started."

• If a child routinely finds it difficult to begin work because he has to make his way through children who are already working, make a point to plan with him first, when possible, so he can start his work by himself. Or find out if there's a child he feels comfortable with. Perhaps they can work together occasionally.

HELPING A CHILD WHOM OTHERS REJECT requires tact, support and knowledge of the child. Sometimes a child plans to join a group of children who are already working, but when he tries to join them, they turn him away for no apparent reason. "They won't let me play with them," he reports to the nearest adult. The adult can give him some alternatives that are compatible with and supportive of the play he's trying to join. The adult might suggest that the child enter a role-play situation, for example, by knocking on the door, calling on the phone or delivering an item appropriate to the pretend situation. If, on the other hand, the adult thinks the children in the area may be rejecting the child because he is generally abusive and disruptive, he could ask the child why he thinks they may not want him and help him think of some alternative modes of behavior that might make people want to play with him. Then the adult could talk with the children in the area about the child's new plan and help him join the group, staying for a while to see that things get off to a good start.

Deciding what to do next   Once an adult has helped children get started on their plans, how does he or she decide where to go next during work time? Sometimes children make this decision for the adult by requesting or demanding his presence: "Hey, you better come over here and get your supper!" "Teacher, he's knocking down my towers." "I can't do this." "Look, this won't stay on." "Teacher, come here. I want to show you something."

At other times, however, though the adult may be needed in half a dozen situations, he has to rely on himself to spot them. Here are some typical clues:

• A child doing nothing for extended periods

• A child doing the same thing repeatedly—driving a truck up and down the same road, stirring the same buttons in the same pan

• A child almost but not quite able to do something—balance a block, reach a toy, saw all the way through a thick piece of wood

• A child flitting from area to area

• A child working for long periods without verbal contact with anyone

• A child leaving an unfinished project and starting something new

• A child getting upset with himself or another child

• A child looking around for something to do next

• A child completing a task

Once the adult has decided where a child needs to go next during work time, he then needs to decide whether to wait and observe the child, to support and encourage him, to help him extend his plan or to help him change his plan. The adult needs to ask himself questions such as these: What do I know about this child, what does he or she like and respond to? What is the child doing—exploring, building, representing? What does he think about what he's doing? What really interests him about it? Which elements of his activity can I capitalize on to help him learn?

Recognizing and supporting a child's work   A major task for all adults at work time is to recognize and support a child's work, not only when the child has completed an activity but throughout the process. Recognition, support and encouragement are conveyed both by actions and by attitude. An adult's nod and smile from across the room can be as important to a child as an intimate conversation about something he's doing. Here are some ways in which an adult can recognize and support a child's work:

• An adult can describe with genuine interest what a child seems to be doing: "Mark, you're making the propeller on your airplane go round and round. And Lynette's turning the wheels on her airplane with her hand. I'm going to try that with my airplane." This strategy is particularly but not exclusively appropriate to children who don't yet use language to describe what they're doing. By joining their play and talking about what they're doing, an adult not only supports their actions but also helps them hear the language that describes their actions, so that eventually they'll be able to talk about their accomplishments themselves.

• An adult can ask a child to talk about what

Donna. . . .
Mrs. Rogers. What did you do first?
Donna. First I put this nail in.
Mrs. Rogers. And then what did you do next?
Donna. Then I put in this nail, and then I put this part on back here.
Mrs. Rogers. Now are you finished with your airplane or is there something else you would like to do with it?
Donna. . . . No . . .
Mrs. Rogers. Well, that was a good plan you made. You planned to make an airplane and that's what you did. Can you think of some way you can use your airplane?
Donna. . . . I don't know.
Mrs. Rogers. Do you see anything in the block area you could use with your airplane, Donna?
Donna. . . . No . . .
Mrs. Rogers. Well, let's look around. Maybe you can see something in the art area you can use with your airplane. Look, maybe you could paint your airplane. Would you like to do that?
Donna. Yeah!

Mrs. Rogers. Okay, Donna, hang your sign on the planning board in the art area. Good girl. What color are you going to paint your airplane?

Donna. Blue!

Mrs. Rogers. Blue, that's a good color.

FROM MRS. ROGERS:

Donna is able to make a simple plan and carry it out but often does not seem to be able to extend it any further because, like many children, she is not aware of other alternatives available to her. I thought it was important for Donna to take her airplane-making one step further before she left it to go on to something else. Since Donna could not think of anything else to do with her airplane, I decided to offer some suggestions, but I also wanted to make her feel that whatever she chose would be agreeable to me, and that I was only trying to help her to make her own decision. I knew that imposing something on Donna or manipulating her would not help her learn to see new possibilities for herself. When she did make a decision, I tried to support it.

he or she is doing. It's important that an adult not presume to know exactly what a child is making or doing. For example, a child may be making what looks like a table to an adult but is really a birdhouse or perhaps not anything at all, just some pieces of wood nailed together. When the adult asks, "What can you tell me about what you're doing?" he recognizes and supports the child, lets the child know that a grownup is really interested in his ideas about his work and wants to hear them in the child's own words.

• An adult can find a place near a child and try out the child's ideas. "That's a different way to play the tambourine, Peter. I'm going to try playing mine just like you."

• An adult can join in and help a child who's gathering materials. "Here are some more wedges for your road, Stoney."

• An adult can have one child show another child what he or she is doing or making. "That's a big birdhouse you're making, Laurie, with a room and even a door. Can you show Jeff how you're making your birdhouse because he made a plan to make one, too."

Helping children extend their plans and ideas *John's plan was to build a gas station in the block area. He made a car out of blocks and looked around for a steering wheel. Suddenly he stopped looking and appeared ready to give up his plan. At this moment an adult arrived to help.*

"What could you use for a steering wheel?"

"It has to go like this." (John made the motions of a steering wheel.)

"It has to move. Hm."

They look around the room together. A cylinder block was not acceptable to John because it wouldn't fit into the space he had made for the steering column.

"What will fit?"

"The broom from the house area!"

"But it's got to have a wheel," said practical John.

More looking. The roundest thing they could find was a paper plate.

"How do you get it on?"

"I know. Make a hole."

With the plate pushed down over the end of the broom handle the car was ready to take lots of children for rides.

Often children stop working on their plans, not because they've finished or lost interest in them, but because they've encountered a problem and don't see any possibilities for its solution. An adult can help a child think through some alternatives and thus broaden or extend his or her way of looking at the original idea. By helping children extend their plans and activities, adults help make children more aware of their choices.

John's plan was more satisfactory to him because an adult helped him explore the possibilities of materials. She had been watching him to see if he could figure it out for himself, but before he gave up entirely, she helped. Together they went through the process of solving his problem; she helped draw out his ideas of what was and was not acceptable.

If a child's problem is with materials, like John's steering wheel, it's usually apparent to an adult when and how to step in and help. When the problem is an activity or an idea, however, when or how to help is not always so obvious:

Four children were hunting with blocks for rifles. They returned periodically to "mother" in the house area, but mother shooed them out because she didn't want guns in her kitchen. The four hunters started to chase one another and in the fun of the chase forgot their hunting. A nearby adult said, "Did you get your deer? Maybe mother will cook it for you." The play ended with venison and a nap on the block beds made by the hunters.

An adult had been keeping an eye on the progress of this plan to "play in the house area." The chase game, inspired by the mother shooing them out of the house, was an interruption of the play and didn't appear to satisfy either the mother or the hunters. The adult's question sparked a new idea that brought the plan to a comfortable conclusion. Note that the adult's question was within the same context as the children's play. Had the adult tried to suggest an entirely different activity, like painting, it probably wouldn't have worked.

An adult should be alert to the progress of children's plans. The skill with which he or she helps each child extend ideas and solve problems will develop as the year progresses. Adults will find themselves picking up ideas for activities and props in the most unlikely places and looking at all the materials in the classroom with an eye to the many ways they can be explored and used.

Here are some ways to help children extend their plans:

• Be situated so as to see the whole room during work time whenever possible. No matter where they work with children, adults should get into the habit of positioning themselves so that they can easily see all children in the room who may need immediate help carrying out or extending their plans.

• Help children find additional materials the way the adult helped John locate a room and paper plate for his car. Here's another example: *Joey built a tall tower and then wanted to build something else so his car wouldn't have to drive straight up the side to the top. He found a board for a ramp but it wasn't long enough to reach from the top of the tower all the way down to the floor. To solve this problem, Joey came up with the idea of*

EPISODE II: THE REPEATER

Mrs. Rogers. Well, good morning Mark. What would you like to do today? What's your plan?

Mark.   . . . Block area.

Mrs. Rogers. Well, what are you going to do in the block area?

Mark. Play with the truck.

Mrs. Rogers. And what are you going to do with the truck?

Mark. Build a road.

Mrs. Rogers. Okay, Mark, take your sign to the block area. [*Mark has been making the same plan every day for quite some time.*]

[*Later that day some family role-play started up in the house area.*]

Mrs. Rogers. Let's look around the room, Mark. Can you think of some other things you could do with your truck?

Mark.   . . .

Mrs. Rogers. Let's go over to the house area and see if anyone needs a ride.

Mark. Okay.

Mrs. Rogers. Mark, could your truck be a bus or a taxi? What do you think?

Mark. A bus.

Mrs. Rogers. Okay, does anyone need to go some place? There's a bus driver out here waiting for some riders!

Child. Okay, okay. Wait a minute, bus driver. Me and my baby are going to the movies.

[Later that day at a team planning meeting]

Mrs. Rogers. *[to another adult]* With a little help I think Mark was able to take part in the house area role-play for a while and be a bus driver, but it didn't last very long. Tomorrow I think I'll put materials out in the quiet area that he could use with his truck. Maybe I can extend his truck play to include some other materials.

[The next day]

Mrs. Rogers. Rum, rum, rum. Can you follow me with your truck? Rum, rum, rum . . . Oh, Mark, look at these blocks. What could you make for your truck with them?

supporting the free end of the board with a smaller tower, but his ramp still didn't reach the floor. He was ready to give up until an adult rescued him by asking, "What else could you use for another ramp?"

• Ask children questions to help them see what they could do next. Some children, for example, seem to have little trouble thinking of things to make or build, but they do need help thinking about what to do with their objects and structures once they've completed them: "You really did make lots of playdough cookies, Michael, just as you planned. Now that you've cut them all out, what else can you do with them?" If the child can't come up with any alternatives, the adult can offer some: "How about taking a trip around the room to see if there's anyone who could use your cookies?"

• Often a child experimenting with new materials needs suggestions about what to try. With a few ideas from an adult, the child is able both

to satisfy his desire to explore physical qualities and to finish the activity pleased with what he or she has done. Offer suggestions and choices to children who are exploring materials: "You've rolled these long, round blocks back and forth for a long time, Markie. Maybe you could roll them so they go under the bridge or down the ramp or all the way to the shelf."

• Help a child relate his or her work to someone else's. Sometimes children are not aware of how their work could relate or add to other activities. An adult might help a child who has finished making a book find someone to read it to—a "baby" or "sister" in the house area, or a child looking at books in the quiet area.

• Help children save or represent what they've done. Often a child is very proud of something he's done or made but can't take it home with him to show his friends and family. It may be appropriate to help such a child extend his plan by helping him take a photograph of his work, draw or trace a picture of it or dictate a story about it.

• Plan experiences and field trips that relate to children's work time interests. Perhaps some children have been playing grocery store for a number of days but include only a few details in their play. A trip to a nearby grocery store could help these children expand their idea of what people do in grocery stores and what's in them and thus help them expand their own grocery store play.

• Help each child extend his plan according to his own interests and at his own pace. There is no predetermined end toward which the extension of a child's plan is aimed. Adults should see, instead, where each child is in his work and go step-by-step with him or her from there. One child may start out making a dinosaur from

blocks and end up with a book about dinosaurs, while another child might start the same way but end up making different kinds of animals. Both represent important learning experiences.

• Take cues from children about when they're really "done" with their plans. Learn what each child means when he says, "I'm done." Does he mean, "I'm done because I don't know what to do next," or "I'm done because I can take this home now, and I want to start something else," or "I'm done and I'm done with you bothering me, too"? By taking cues from children, an adult can help them see new possibilities and also respect their desires to begin something new.

The following examples show how the above strategies could be used to evaluate work time activities and make further plans.

Troy was drawing with magic markers in the music area. At first, he seemed to be looking at the tambourines and drawing them. By the time I got to him to talk about his "tambourines" they had become clouds. An adult could say, "Let's see if we can find something in this area that looks like your picture." If the child gets a tambourine, compare it with the picture. How is it like the picture? How is it different?

Some children built a wall in the block area and then didn't know what to do with it. An adult could say, "Now that you have your wall made, what are you going to do with it?" If Wendy says, "The wall is for animals," the adult now knows that to her the wall is more like a fence. The adult might then say, "Which animals are you going to use by your wall?"

Laura smeared paste all over a sheet of paper. Maybe she thought paste was similar to fingerpaint. Since Laura didn't seem to see another alterna-

[Later]

Mrs. Rogers.   Oh, Mark, look what you made! Maybe tomorrow you can make a plan to come back here to the quiet area and see what else you can do with these blocks.

Mark.   Rum, rum, rum.

FROM MRS. ROGERS:

Mark is a very shy, quiet child who seems to find security in doing the same thing day after day. I think he probably is not aware of the possibilities of other materials, other people and other areas of the room. He seems to feel a bit afraid to venture out. I wanted to ease Mark into some other kinds of play, but I also wanted him to structure this play for himself as much as he could. Although I took an active role in Mark's play, I tried to give him as many choices as possible. I think there is a fine line between imposing one's own goals on a child and providing him with opportunities to broaden his activity. I felt Mark needed my participation because only through entering into his play could I offer suggestions or open up new possibilities.

EPISODE III: THE PLAN CHANGER

Margo. I'm goin' to the house area 'n' cook.

Mrs. Rogers. Okay, Margo, that's a good plan. Go hang up your sign on the planning board.

[*A little later Margo wanders over to watch some children painting at the art table.*]

Mrs. Hohmann. What was your plan for today, Margo?

Margo. House area . . .

Mrs. Hohmann. Okay, so now you want to change your plan to the art area?

Margo. Yes.

Mrs. Hohmann. What do you need to do if you're changing your plan?

Margo. Go get my sign.

Mrs. Hohmann. Okay, but before that, how about cleaning up what you used in the house area?

Margo. Okay.

Mrs. Hohmann. [*a few minutes later*] What would you like to do in the art area, Margo?

Margo. Paint.

Mrs. Hohmann. Well, what are some things you'll need if you're going to paint?

tive for using the paste, an adult could show her one by giving her some bits of paper and saying, "Look, you can put pieces of paper on top of paste and they stick. Let's see what else will stick!" If Laura ends up with hunks of paste on her paper, the adult might say, "Let's see what we can use this paste for," and offer her some things to paste down using the hunks of paste as a paste source.

In the music area, the children made sounds with the instruments but didn't really know what to do with them. An adult could suggest further exploration of the instruments by saying, "I've got an idea, let's play them fast and then slow." The adult could also help the children play loudly and softly, and could help them devise a signal for stopping and starting.

Lizzy made a record out of cardboard. An adult asked her if she thought it would work on the record player. After Lizzy tried it on the record player and found it didn't work, the adult asked her if she could explain why. Lizzy then began a series of comparisons of the cardboard record to a real one. She finally decided that her record didn't work because it didn't have grooves on it. The adult confirmed her observation and also said (though not expecting Lizzy to understand this) that to make a record something had to be recorded. Follow-up to this activity might be to help Lizzy make a recording on a tape recorder of some music she makes up in the music area.

Johnny planned to work with the firehose for the third straight day. The adults decided to try some of the following ideas: 1) Ask, "What things could catch on fire?" Have him make or construct the things he names. 2) Suggest that he put out a pretend fire in the house area or block area. 3) Since Johnny didn't seem to know what firemen do other than use hoses to put out fires, plan a trip to the fire station as soon as possible to see what firemen do.

Tim spent time with the take-apart truck, taking it apart and putting it back together again. The adult who was in the area felt he could be doing more than that and asked him if he'd like to make his own take-apart truck. Since his response was minimal, the adult gave him some materials to get started and offered to help him if he wanted. Tim got started on his own, using mainly tape and paste to hold his truck together. The adult asked, "How can you put your truck together so you can take it apart again?" Since Tim didn't have an idea, the adult showed him the paper fasteners. Tim wanted to put a grille on his truck but didn't know how. The adult asked him, "How do you think you could put it on?" He looked at the problem and came up with a way of solving it—he cut grooves in styrofoam and glued it on the front of his truck.

Amy started making a bus out of a milk carton but ended up taping all kinds of things to the carton. She finally papier machéd the whole thing and it fell apart. An adult could follow up on Amy's project by asking Amy if she wants to fasten things together. Depending on Amy's answer, the adult could then try to help her either make a bus or fasten things to a milk carton so they don't fall off.

Helping children change their plans   During work time, in addition to getting children started on their plans and recognizing, supporting and extending their work, adults also help children change their plans. When a child completes his initial plan before the end of work time, he begins the planning process all over again. An adult asks "What are you going to do next?" and then helps the child think through his idea in as much detail as he can. Sometimes a child's new plan is really an extension of his initial plan: "Now that my boat's all finished, I'm going to play with it with Sammy in the block area." Other times, a new plan represents an altogether new idea: "I'm all finished with the beads and I put them all away and now I'm gonna paint at the easel."

Before helping a child make a new plan, an adult can talk with him about his first plan and have him put away all the materials he used if they aren't being used by someone else. After a short, individualized recall time and clean-up time, the child can make a new plan.

Helping children deal with work time conflicts   By arranging the classroom carefully so children have space to work and can find and return materials with ease, and by having each child plan something that he really wants to do during work time, a teaching team has already gone a long way toward minimizing work time conflicts. Conflicts will occur, however, even on the best of days. Children get upset because they can't solve a problem or do something as easily as another child can. They run out of space and materials and infringe on other children's work. They get silly and in the process disturb and distract others. In these situations, adults need to help children out of their conflicts by helping them see alternative and more appropriate avenues of action.

SHARING MATERIALS often causes problems among three- and four-year-olds. Typically, a child wants something another child is using and without any verbal exchange tries to take the

Margo. A smock.

Mrs. Hohmann. Fine. Anything else?

Margo. Some paper.

Mrs. Hohmann. Good, Margo. Show me your picture when you get through so I can write down your story if you want.

FROM MRS. HOHMANN:

I don't think Margo took planning very seriously today. I think she just said something because she thought an adult wanted to hear it. She certainly didn't take the time to find out what was going on in the room. I think that if the planning process is going to be meaningful for a child, she must learn that planning means choosing something she really wants to do, really setting a goal for herself—not just choosing any old thing. My goal was to help Margo commit herself to something a little more seriously. I tried to help her think through what it was she really wanted to do and how she was going to do it. I think she really did want to paint but had to take responsibility for her first plan by cleaning up. I hoped that having her talk through the procedures of the activity she chose would help her consider more seriously what it was she really wanted to do.

EPISODE IV: THE FLITTER

Chris. I'm going to the block area to play with the truck.

Mrs. Hohmann. What are you going to do with the truck?

Chris. Build a road.

[*Chris then proceeds to: build a road, cook in the house area, play with the bunny, look at a book, string beads, play in the sand.*]

Mrs. Hohmann. Gee, I saw your road in the block area, Chris. It looked like a really good road to me. Maybe we could add some road signs or people to your road. What is this sign? Let's go. I'll follow you. Beep, beep.

Chris. Beep, beep [*passing other children in the block area*]. Hi farmers! Want to come on our road with us? Follow me!

FROM MRS. HOHMANN:

Chris is a flitter. He does not seem to know the possibilities of the block area—or any area for that matter. There were many choices available to Chris, but he chose to run off from the road

desired object away. When that fails he or she resorts to biting or hitting, to which the other child either succumbs or responds in kind. An adult intervening at this point with "Now, Lynne, Michael had the tambourine first" does not really help Lynne understand or solve her problem. Saying "Now, Michael, you and Lynne share the tambourine" fails to give them a means for doing so.

The first thing an adult can do after halting the physical dispute is to help the grabber try to identify an alternative object to use. The adult might say, "Lynne, Michael's using the tambourine right now. That's his plan, too. What else could you use that would be like a tambourine? . . . Let's take a look around and see." In the process the adult can help the child describe what about the tambourine she likes. If it's the drum part, she might like a drum. If it's the jingle

part, she might like the bells. Maybe she'd like to make her own tambourine from paper plates and buttons or from any other materials she thinks of.

Another tack an adult could take would be to have the grabbing child *talk* to the child with the tambourine. For example, "Lynne, did you try *asking* Michael if you could use the tambourine? Usually people don't like other people to hit and bite them, but they *do* like people to ask them if they could have a turn. Why don't you *ask* Michael if you could have a turn with the tambourine?" Often, but not always, this works well and the children develop their own system of turns and end up working together.

If choosing another object or activity or asking for a turn cannot solve the conflict, an adult can assist the children in using a simple, fair device—turning a sand timer or keeping an eye on the hands of a clock. An adult might say, "Michael and Lynne, since you both made plans to play with the tambourine and there's only one tambourine and two people, it looks like you'll need to take turns. The sand timer or the hands of the clock can tell you when its your turn. . ."

An additional strategy would be to purchase another tambourine. Whenever possible, equip the classroom with at least two of things that are particularly attractive. One toy firetruck, for example, can only cause problems. It's better to buy five or six small, inexpensive firetrucks than one great big beautiful one.

PROBLEMS WITH SPACE arise even in the most spacious classrooms. Perhaps too many children plan for one area or a particularly large project interferes with other work. It would be easy for an adult to move in and solve the problem immediately: "Okay, Johnny, you work somewhere else and Kerry, your house is too big so you'll have to take it down." This kind of solution, however, does not help children understand and solve their own problems.

To help children recognize and learn some ways of working things out among themselves, an adult can sit down with the children involved in the dispute and ask a question like "What's happening over here? Why is everyone mad at everyone else?" or "What do you think you could do so you're not all running into each other?" When the children come up with a possible solution, help them try it out. If it doesn't work, help them plan another. If no one has an idea, offer some possibilities from which they can choose. Here's what one adult did:

Three groups of children each planned to build large houses in the block area. When they tried to play in their houses, they all got in each other's way and tempers flared, so an adult sat down with them. "What do you think you could do instead of bother-

ing each other?" she asked. Nobody had an idea. "Well, maybe you could be different store people or next-door neighbors." The children liked the idea of being neighbors and began calling and visiting each other.

WHEN A CHILD GETS FRUSTRATED because he cannot, for example, get something to work or look right or stand up, he may take out his frustration on other children by knocking down a tower or upsetting the paints or sweeping the dishes off the table. Such a child needs an adult to help him—first, to stop disrupting other children's work, and second, to go back to his original plan to see what the real problem is.

Tracy was trying to build a tower, balancing unit blocks end on end. When the blocks wouldn't balance, he messed up Markie's road and punched in Joanie's playdough cake before an adult bailed him out. Holding Tracy firmly by the hand she briefly helped Joanie rescue her cake and Markie get his road repaired. Then she and Tracy sat down together near what remained of his tower. "Tell me what you were doing with these blocks, Tracy," she said, but he just sat there. "Well, I remember seeing you building a real hard tower with the blocks on their ends like this." Tracy nodded. "Let's see if we can figure out a way to make it work." Together they worked out a way to build the tower so that it stood up, and they used many of Tracy's original ideas. Just before she left, the adult said, "You know, Tracy, when you need help, you can come and get me or Mrs. Rogers. We'll help you. Then you won't have to make Markie and Joanie mad at you."

The adults in Tracy's room learned to anticipate when Tracy might get frustrated and tried to help him solve his problem before he got so angry he started rampaging around the room. They also tried to help him make more detailed plans so he could begin to anticipate solutions to problems before they actually occurred.

that he started. My goal in working with Chris was to help him see some of the many things he might do in the block area to continue his road building. I knew I would have to bring him back to the block area and that I would need to spend some time helping him get started again. But I also wanted his play to be as independent as possible so that he would begin to learn how to do this for himself. I tried to give him as many choices as possible. Although I initially set up a number of objects around the road, I asked him where he would place the materials and how he wanted to do things. I tried to step out as soon as I could so he and Mark and Erin would carry on on their own. I hope this helped Chris begin to see some of the many ways to play in the block area.

◇

SILLINESS AND RANDOM BEHAVIOR can also disrupt children's work. Marge, for example, had been working with the rubber farm animals by herself for a while, then had one of her cows jump over to the quiet area where Tim and Ted were building an elaborate structure with the inch cubes and cuisinaire rods. The cow jumped into the middle of it and soon all three children were jumping and rolling around in the rubble. As this activity didn't seem to abate but got wilder and wilder, an adult joined the three children, saying, "Look you guys, what's your plan here, anyway?" "We're busting up the place," they announced between giggles. There were several things the adult could do. She could remind the children of their original plans and help them return to them. She could help them make a new plan. Or she could help them figure out what the three of them could do together with the cow and the blocks besides rolling around in them. "What do you think you could do besides rolling around in the blocks?" she asked them. "We don't know." "Well, maybe you could build your house so it had a room for each of Marge's animals, or maybe you could drive these blocks to the block area and build a big animal house there where there's more room," she suggested, trying to think quickly of something that might challenge and appeal to them. "Nope," Ted said, "we're going to paint now." "Okay, I'll help you put away your blocks first. Let's do it fast." They did and then went off to paint together for the rest of the work time.

THE TWO MAIN IDEAS TO KEEP IN MIND when dealing with work time conflicts are: 1) Help children find alternative modes of behavior and plan more suitable activities for themselves rather than stress their "naughtiness." 2) Anticipate possible conflicts by helping a child before he gets himself into trouble.

Adult preparation for work time

Planning for work time   The main vehicle for team planning is the daily team evaluation and planning meeting. During this meeting the teaching team reviews and analyzes the classroom day and plans for the next one based on their observations and conclusions. Here are some questions for a team to consider as they plan for work time:

• What plans are children currently working on during work time?

• What materials could be added to the classroom to support and extend those plans?

• Which children need special help at work time because they don't know what to do next in their plan, have trouble getting started, give up very easily or repeat the same actions every day?

• Are there field trips to be planned based on children's work time interests?

• Which children might be interested in representing their plans once they're completed? Is a camera available and ready to go?

• Which materials or activities should be available to help children follow up on and recall field trip experiences?

Adult planning for work time focuses on these and similar issues rather than on specific activities each adult will be engaged in at work time. After the day's team evaluation and planning meeting, an adult's plan for work time might sound something like this: "I'm going to try to start off work time with Tracy so he gets started right away on something he feels good about. If he plans again for the workbench, I'll have him help me put a vise on the workbench so he'll have a way of holding his wood steady as he saws. I also want to keep my eye on the block and house areas to see if I can't help the store people' and the 'house people' relate to each other rather than disrupt each other as they did yesterday. If Joanie and Donna play their card game again, I want to see what they're doing—are they sorting cards, ordering them, looking at the numbers and pictures?—and how I can help them extend it so it doesn't just fall apart after five minutes." This is the kind of behind-the-scenes planning adults must do each day so that children have the freedom to say, "Today I am going to . . ." and then do it at work time.

Recording work time observations   Planning for work time depends on knowledge and understanding of what children did during the previous work time. Some teaching teams find it helpful to jot down observations during work time so they'll be able to remember everything as they evaluate and plan.

Some teaching teams put large file cards and a pencil in each area so that any adult in the area can jot down observations throughout work time. Other teams use clip boards and paper, while still others carry small file cards about in their pockets.

Any method a teaching team devises to record work time observations is fine, as long as it is speedy, unobtrusive and helpful in planning for the next day's work time.

Cleaning up

During clean-up time children put away the toys and materials they've been using during work time. They also wipe tables, wash paint brushes, jars and cooking utensils and sweep or vacuum floors. As they sort, pile, stack, empty and fit together materials at clean-up time, children learn not only where things go, but that similar things go together. They begin to understand the system for finding the things they need. As a child fills and puts a stapler away, for example, she has a chance to relate it to the other materials

on the shelf that can also be used to hold things together—string, clips, tape, glue, paste, rubber bands, wire. As she puts unused construction paper back on the shelf, she sees other kinds of paper that might be good for other projects and effects.

Sorting materials so that similar materials go together in the same bin or box helps children focus on attributes of objects—all the straight nails in one box and all the twisty screws in another, all the square blocks together on one shelf and all the rectangular blocks on another.

Sorting things out, putting materials back and cleaning up also helps children see that clean-up is part of any task they undertake. Children begin a project by thinking it through and

getting out the appropriate materials; the project ends when the materials are put away.

Suggestions for helping children clean up

Cleaning up at the end of work time helps children feel responsible for the materials they use and helps them to be aware of their effect on the classroom environment. While children clean up, adults can encourage and help them without either doing the whole job for them or leaving them to clean up completely on their own. Here are some ways to support children as they clean up:

• Encourage children to clean up throughout work time as they finish one plan and are ready to begin another. This clean-as-you-go policy will cut down substantially on the amount of clean-up everyone faces at the end of work time.

• Warn the children toward the end of work time that in a few minutes it will be clean-up time, so they won't have to end their work time pursuits abruptly.

• Decide as a team on a clear way to signal the end of work time and the beginning of clean-up, so everyone knows it's time to draw activities to a close and begin putting things away. Some teams, for example, have children take turns playing bells, a tambourine or a triangle to signal clean-up.

• Since children don't automatically know what constitutes cleaning up, help individual children define their own specific clean-up tasks. "What are you starting on today, Georgie, the cars and trucks or the big wooden blocks?" This helps a child see where to begin more than a general statement like "Come on, Georgie, it's clean-up time. You help too." Some children may need a direct suggestion in order to get started, especially on particularly messy days when even an adult might wonder where to begin. "Look,

Caddie, you start on the big beads and I'll start on the little beads and, Roddy, you pick out all the buttons."

• Work along with children as they put things away and use the opportunity to talk with them about what they are doing and observing. "That's a good way to get the furniture to the shelf, Gordy. Do you think it will all fit into your truck or will you have to make another trip?"

• Make up clean-up games based on what children are already doing and what they enjoy. Two children in the quiet area, for example, were throwing beads into the center of the room rather than cleaning up. An adult joined them saying, "Look, Gary and Jack, throwing the beads out there isn't helping at all, but if you throw them into the bead boxes you'll be cleaned up in a hurry. Let's see if you can throw all the beads into the boxes before all the sand runs down in the timer. Okay? Okay, ready, go!" Games help children do an otherwise tedious task speedily and enjoyably. One High/Scope teaching team reported the following clean-up games their children enjoyed: "Troy liked to be a robot. Markie liked to drop small pegs through holes into containers. Some children enjoyed sliding blocks across the floor, while others counted how many things they could carry without dropping them. Setting up a line and relaying objects from person to person all the way to the shelf worked well and so did racing the timer."

• Once children have completed a clean-up task, help them find another one. Each child should participate until the whole room has been restored to order.

• Once an entire area is clean, help children move to another area still in need of assistance or to a central gathering place where everyone meets as soon as they've completed their clean-up tasks. Clean-ups often consume more time than necessary because children may start playing in an area that's been cleaned and looks inviting again. Moving to a central gathering place cuts down on random play and silliness that distracts and interferes with children still putting things away. It also gives children a place from which they can survey the room and spot other jobs that still need doing.

• Alert children to the reasons for cleaning up. For example: "As soon as everything is put away we'll be ready for juice time."

• On particularly messy days, when it's hard to tell what to do first, begin clean-up time with a group meeting. Discuss briefly with the children what needs doing, help each child define his initial clean-up task and have everyone report to the meeting place for a new task upon completion of the first one. Group meetings are also helpful on days when clean-up time begins to deteriorate or drag.

• Some children will have days when they start off not only not cleaning up, but also interfering with children who are. Talk with such a child about what he or she is doing and how it's affecting other people and the task at hand, and then give him some ideas of how to proceed from there. For example, an adult might say, "Gee, Margo, you're really not helping clean-up time at all by running around hitting people. It hurts to be hit and it makes it very hard to put the blocks away when someone's hitting you. How about helping me with these blocks, or gathering up all the furniture?"

• Some children always manage to dawdle, finishing up a work time project during clean-up time so they never really get involved in cleaning up. Help such a child anticipate clean-up time before the end of work time so he can either finish his project or come to a stopping point and have a clean-up task in mind.

Recalling experiences

Recall time gives children the opportunity to remember and represent what they did during work time. Recalling work time activities completes the planning and doing process—by looking back at what they've done, children can start to see the relation, if any, between their plans and their activities, and can develop more awareness of their own actions and ideas. Children recall what they did at work time by talking about their actions, showing something they used at work time, sharing a product either completed or still in progress, drawing pictures or pantomiming their actions for others to guess.

The recall process, like the planning process, occurs throughout work time as children complete activities and talk about them with an adult before making a new plan. A child might go through the plan-do-review sequence two or three times in one work time, especially if he's new to the classroom and wants to try out many things in a hurry. By recall time, therefore, a child may already have gone through the recall process several times. An adult might then use recall time to help him remember his initial plan and the other plans he made during work time. This would help him begin to see that his work time plan is made up of all the things he chose to do.

In the process of recalling what they've done, children attach language to their actions. This makes them more conscious of their actions and more able to refer to them and draw upon them for later use. Talking about, recalling and representing their actions help children evaluate and learn from their experiences. When planning and doing are followed by recall, children can build on what they've done and learned and remember it for the next time they plan an activity.

Recalling in a small group at recall time helps children get ideas from each other about things they might like to try at work time. Recall time provides an opportunity for children to share and learn from each other's experiences (although this aspect of recall time gains significance as the children grow older) and to hear how other children describe their activities.

WHEN SHOULD RECALL TIME OCCUR? Many teaching teams schedule recall, snack and small-group time together. While the children eat, adults talk with them about what they did during work time. Then, when the children are finished eating, they are already gathered, and the transition to small-group time is easier.

Some teams schedule recall time right before clean-up time so that when small groups gather with an adult to recall, children can show things they're done that would be dismantled at clean-up time. Other teams schedule recall after clean-up in order to give children a little distance between the time they've done something and the time they talk about it. They feel many children are better able to talk about what they've done after they've had time during clean-up to let the experience "sink in."

A recall time will occasionally be included in circle time too, at the end of the day when the whole group has done something together, like seeing a puppet show, decorating a Christmas tree, picking apples in the orchard or visiting the local fire department. It's difficult to engage so many three- and four-year-olds in large-group discussion about an experience, but they do enjoy making up words and actions to an action song to describe what they've seen and done.

Regardless of when recall time occurs formally in the daily routine, the recall process occurs throughout the day—during work time as children finish one thing and begin another, after outside time when they've done something particularly pleasing or interesting. Recalling experiences whenever and wherever they occur helps children make these experiences their own. Some suggestions follow for helping children recall work time and other experiences.

Suggestions for helping children recall experiences

• Whenever possible, children should have recall time with the same adult they planned with, so the adult can help them begin to see the relation between their plans and what they actually do during work time.

• At recall time, adults and children should experiment with different ways of recalling work time experiences—talking about work done, showing materials used, sharing things finished or in progress. Not all three- and four-year-olds will be able to recall in all the suggested ways. Some children will enjoy drawing something they did, for example, but others will concentrate on experimenting with the drawing materials. Adults should accept what children do and say and not expect everyone to be able to recall the same way.

• Once an adult has a notion of how the individual children in the group are best able to recall their work time experiences, he or she should provide ways and recall materials appropriate to each child in the group.

• One key to a good recall time is a good work time. When children get involved in things that

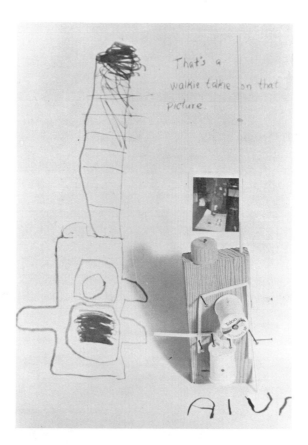

really interest and challenge them at work time, they talk excitedly at recall time about what they've done. When children are pleased with themselves and their work, they're eager to share and discuss it with others. The opposite also holds true. When children have difficult, unsatisfactory work times they often have little desire to talk about them. By helping children make good plans and carry them out, adults are also laying the groundwork for productive recall times.

• Some children may not respond at all when asked to recall their work time activities. Such children may be confused about what recall is all about; they may not yet have the language to talk about their actions, or they may have had an unsatisfactory work time. An adult can help a child by talking briefly and supportively about what the child was doing during work time. "Well, Joanie, I saw you working for a long time in the sand, filling all the containers with sand and then turning them over so all the sand came out in shapes just like the containers. And that was your plan, too, to work in the sand." If an adult doesn't know for sure what a child did at work time, some of the other children might. "Can anyone help Joanie tell about what she did at work time today?"

• Central planning boards can be used to help children recall their plans, because for everything they've done at work time they've placed a picture card on the board to represent it.

• An adult needn't worry if every single child doesn't recall his or her work activities at recall time, as long as the adult gets to these children the next day during work time and recall time.

Small-group time

During small-group time, each adult meets with five to eight children to work on the activities planned by the team to provide some of the "key experiences" discussed in the following chapters. Adults plan small-group activities around the interests and abilities of the children in their groups, allowing for individual ideas and differences. They use this time to observe their children, expose them to new materials and give them a chance to find new ways of using materials they already know.

Work time and small-group time share many characteristics. During both times, children work actively with materials, talk with other

children and adults about what they're doing and do things at their own rate and in their own way. And although children plan for work time and adults plan for small-group time, the difference is a subtle one: at small-group time, a small group of children gather in one place and find ways to use similar materials which an adult has thought about and prepared or gathered in advance, while at work time children work in various ways all over the room with a wide range of materials of their own choosing.

Because children are gathered together, it is often easier for an adult to observe and assess children during small-group time than it is during work time. Within a 15- or 20-minute small-group time an adult can see, for example, which children need more experience using scissors and which ones use them competently as tools for their own purposes.

Some adults have the mistaken notion that small-group time is their "teaching" time when they can "really teach" children things like number, color, sizes, shapes, days of the week, and so on. They view work time as "play" time and small-group time as "learning" time. In the Cognitively Oriented Curriculum, children play and learn throughout the day. Adults never really "teach" in the traditional sense of giving children knowledge by telling and showing. Rather, they teach by encouraging, supporting and extending children's choices and activities, because they know that children learn through action and the conclusions they draw from their own experiences.

WHY IS SMALL-GROUP TIME IMPORTANT? Small-group time is important for children because it opens up possibilities and choices they might not otherwise be aware of, and which they can incorporate in their work time plans. For children who generally work by themselves,

small-group time is a chance for peer contact and interchange. For children who always work in the same area, small-group time is a chance to use and find out about materials from other areas.

Because small-group time is shorter, more controlled and involves fewer children than work time, many adults find it a good time to learn about how the children in their program use language and how they sort, order, arrange and represent objects and events. Small-group time can be used by adults as a laboratory to try out new teaching strategies and to observe children in terms of curricular goals. An adult can structure a learning situation for a group of children at small-group time and observe and assess the children in terms of the focus of that activity. For example, an adult exploring apples with a group of children might learn that one child can readily describe what she sees and does with her apple while another child needs help describing his actions. What the adult learns about the children can be used throughout the day; a child who needs help connecting language with actions at small-group time probably needs similar assistance in other circumstances as well.

HOW ARE SMALL GROUPS FORMED AND HOW OFTEN DO THEY CHANGE? Each small group of children should represent a cross-section of the classroom population. If, for example, the class is made up of boys and girls, three- and four-year-olds, blacks and whites, handicapped and nonhandicapped children, each small group should reflect that composition. Such a cross-section of children provides a realistic setting in which children can support and learn from each other. One exception to this is when the age range is quite wide. Adults with children from two-and-a-half to five in the same classroom often feel that small groups work better when each group includes some but not all ages. One group might have two-and-a-half- to four-year-olds while another might have three-and-a-half- to five-year-olds.

Small-group time can also be a time to separate children who might benefit from being on their own awhile—rival siblings, next-door neighbors who are always together, two or three unusually energetic children.

Small groups should remain constant long enough for the adults and children to get to know each other. Depending on the wishes and needs of individual teaching teams, small groups could change as often as every five or six weeks or as infrequently as three times a year.

WHERE DO SMALL GROUPS MEET? Many teaching teams have the impression that small-group times have to take place around a table. Many activities do work best at a table, but small-group time should not be confined to tabletop activities. Depending on the experience an adult wishes to provide, he or she might meet with children at the workbench, around a rabbit cage, on the floor in the music or block area, in a kitchen, outside or at the sand table.

Adult planning for small-group time

Here are some questions a teaching team can consider as they plan for small-group time:

• What skill or experience should be the focus of the activity? What do the children in the group enjoy? Which materials or processes do they seem unaware of?

• Which materials can be used for the activity so that each child will have his or her own things to work on?

• How might individual children in the group respond to the activity? What can an adult look for and find out about individual children in the process of the activity? Which children might need additional ideas or materials? Which might need particular assistance?

• How can the activity be structured so that children—can use their own set of materials, have enough space to work comfortably, can make choices, can make discoveries on their own and become aware of new ideas, can have fun, can talk about what they're doing, can observe and respond to what others are doing?

Some teaching teams wonder if each small group should do the same thing at small-group time. Often each group will begin the same activity together, then branch off in different directions depending on the interests, ideas and needs of the particular children. Whether or not all small groups do the same thing is not important. What is important is that whatever adults plan, they plan for the particular children in their small groups. At the High/Scope preschool, two small groups have done such different things on the same day as make popcorn and build with boxes and wood. (The group that made the popcorn shared it with the other group, which planned to make popcorn later in the week.) On the other hand, High/Scope teams have also planned the same activity for different groups and shared materials by having one group snack while the other did the activity.

The beginning, middle and end of small-group time

A successful small-group time usually has a clearcut beginning, middle and end; small-group times can become pointless or very difficult if any one of these elements is missing or unduly prolonged.

The beginning   A brief but clear beginning to small-group time gives children an idea of the nature of the activity they're about to pursue, the materials available and what in general they might try with them. When planning the beginning of small-group time, here are some things to keep in mind:

• Have the necessary materials ready beforehand and easily accessible so the activity can begin as soon as the children gather around the table or finish their snack.

• Make a brief, simple statement about the activity. For example: "Today, as soon as we're all cleaned up from snack, we're going to the music area and see what we can find out about the tambourines, bells and triangles. When we get there, choose a bell, a triangle or a tambourine and let's see what you can do with it."

• After a few words about the activity, have children start right in on it; it's best to avoid long discussions and periods of waiting while materials are being located.

The middle   Once the children begin the activity, an adult interacts with them, supporting, encouraging and extending their efforts. Here are some things to keep in mind as the children work:

• Watch and listen to children to see how they use the materials and approach the task.

• Each child will probably be doing something different with the materials. Be ready to support and work with these differences.

• Help children think about what they are doing and discovering by asking questions: "Why do you suppose this spoon floats but this one doesn't, Ronnie?"

• Encourage children to talk with each other, to share their ideas and discoveries. One way to do this is to refer children to each other when there are problems to solve. "You know, Jack, Laurie had the same trouble getting her wood to stick together. Why don't you ask her to tell you what she did."

• Talk with children about what they're doing, seeing first if they can describe their actions. If

they can't, describe what they are doing.

• Give suggestions to children who have trouble getting started or who don't know what to do next.

• Use the materials yourself in order to try out, and thus support, children's ideas and suggestions.

The end   Often small-group time ends in the middle of an activity because the allotted time has passed. Children and adults both feel better, however, when small-group time ends at the conclusion of a process or with the drawing together of discoveries made. Here are some ways to end small-group time meaningfully so that children become aware of what they've found out:

- Have each child show, demonstrate or describe what he or she has done: "Before we clean up, let's start with Laney and go around the table and show one thing you found that would float on top of the water."

- Have the children dictate a story about what they did and found out. Write it down or tape record it, then read or play it back. A story like this might result: *"I shake the bells," said Corey. "Me, too," said Markie. "The triangle is hard. I played it loud," said Julie. "Hit the tambourine with my hand here and here, on the rounds and on the flat part," said Lynne. "Little triangle, big triangle. They hurt my ears," said Keea.*

- Take a polaroid photograph of what each child did. Each child can compare the photograph to the real thing.

- Some children might wish to draw what they did.

- If the small-group activity results in a product—playdough models, block structures, Christmas cards—put the products together and have children talk about similarities and differences.

- If the conceptual focus of the activity was on the sequence of the process, have the children recall the steps, starting with what they did first. Do this before cleaning up so they can still refer to the actual objects they used in the process.

- If the small-group activity is to continue the next day, have the children show and talk about what they've done so far and help them anticipate what they'll do the next day.

The beginning, middle and end of small-group time correlates with the plan-do-review process of work time. Although the general plan is made by the adult, the children do decide how they are going to use the materials. Small-group time ends with the children recalling what they've done and discovered and cleaning up.

Recording small-group-time observations

Since small-group time provides a natural opportunity to observe and assess children's abilities, adults should jot down their observations and findings to discuss and share during daily team evaluation and planning meetings. These observations often form the basis for subsequent small-group times as well as for work time strategies and interactions. For examples of how teaching teams have recorded their small-group time findings, see chapter 8.

Management problems at small-group time

Some small-group times may be difficult because a child does not participate fully in the activity. Perhaps he comes late or leaves the group periodically, distracting other children in his own or the other groups. There are simple solutions, but the teaching team needs to discuss the situation and generate some strategies. In the discussion the following issues could be considered:

- Does the child understand the daily routine? Can he anticipate times of the day? Does he know where his group meets each day? Does he need help getting started?

- What materials and activities might he be particularly interested in? What is he successful at and how can that be included in small-group time?

- Are small-group activities being structured too narrowly so that he can't work on his own level and be successful? Do things seem too hard or easy for him?

- Is there another child he works particularly well with who might be included in his small group?

- Can he be enlisted to help other children at

small-group time? To share ideas and solutions?

• Does he fall apart because he can't make his ideas work or because once he has tried one thing he can't come up with alternatives?

• Does he need more support throughout the day? Does he work better at small-group time after he has had a successful work time?

• What can be done to make the expectations of small-group time more clear?

Outside time

Outside time is a time when children can run, jump, skip, hop, climb, slide, push, throw, dig, race, shout, hide, roll and haul. It's also a time when they can collect and examine leaves, rocks, grasses, bugs, flowers, bottles, nuts, bark, stones and shells and can watch and feed animals and birds.

Aside from the obvious advantages to children's health and well-being, the main rationale for outside time is that it enables children to try out work time ideas and discoveries outside the classroom. Also, because outside time is less constricted and intense and perhaps more spontaneous than work time, some otherwise quiet children open up at outside time, talking and working with other children more freely than they do inside; a child who gets into trouble inside because he runs over children's work and topples shelves by climbing on them may excel outside where he can teach others to climb, swing and run really fast. Most children play outside where they live, and can carry their preschool outdoor activities into their neighborhood and backyard play.

The adult's role

Adults should play the same role at outside time as they do at work time. They should be actively involved with children in their games and activities; as they play with children, they should talk with them about what they're doing, help them solve problems and find alternatives and support, encourage and extend their activities. Adults who are used to a more traditional system, where outside time is often a time when they can take their break, may need to get used to this role of active participant.

Adults might start games with a small group of children and play as long as there are children who want to play. They may also be invited to join games the children start themselves. On rainy days, adults can take a more active role in structuring and setting up activities indoors. For example, with the help of the children, they may move some indoor furniture and equipment to make room for a large obstacle course, a game of beanbag toss or a ball game.

Circle time

At circle time the whole group of children and adults gather for an active 10 or 15 minutes of playing games, making up and singing songs, doing finger plays, learning dances, playing musical instruments, reenacting special events or briefly talking about the next day. Unlike any other part of the day, everyone is involved in the same activity at the same time.

Circle time provides an opportunity for each child to participate in a large group, sharing and demonstrating his or her ideas and trying out and imitating the ideas of others. At circle time a child can find out that there are some things that are really fun to do with other people, and that as a part of a large group he or she can sometimes be a leader and sometimes a follower.

For adults, circle time is a chance to provide "key experiences" for children in a social setting and to observe children as they participate in this setting, each with his or her own unique style. Depending on the focus of the circle time activity, adults can find out how children perceive and work with such concepts as loud and soft, same and different, fast and slow, near and far.

WHEN AND WHERE IS CIRCLE TIME? In many preschool centers or classrooms, circle time comes either at the beginning or at the end of the day, depending on the preference of the teaching team. Teams that begin the day with circle time feel that children benefit from starting the day together, because in a group they can see everyone before they get involved in small groups or individual projects, and they can find out if there is any special information about the day—if there's to be a field trip or a visitor, a new piece of equipment, a schedule change. Teams that end the day with circle time like to draw the group together to share an experience before they go home. They like to have children recall special events that might have occurred during the day.

Some teaching teams start out in the fall having circle time at the end of the day, then during the winter switch it with outside time so that the day ends outdoors and the staff and children have to wrestle with snow suits and boots only once during the day.

Circle time can be held wherever there's space for the whole group to move about and to sit down together in a circle—in an open central area of the classroom, in a large work area, on a patio, on the grass, in a hallway, in a gym. The name "circle time" makes more sense to the children when they can gather on a circle that's actually laid out on the floor; a big round rug or a masking-tape circle will make the idea of circle time more concrete.

Suggestions for adults at circle time

• Plan for circle time so that it can proceed smoothly and enjoyably. Adults need to decide what to do and how to start the activity. Make one adult responsible for initiating circle time. This responsibility can be shifted from day to day or week to week. Other adults should help children finish tasks and then join the circle as supportive participants.

• Simulate the activity planned for circle time at the team-planning session the day before it is to occur. Adults themselves must feel comfortable and sure of what they're doing so they don't use up time at circle time trying to remember a tune or a game.

• Have several alternatives in mind if the planned activity doesn't go over well, such as switching from a song to an action game or giv-

ing children a say in determining the direction of the activity.

• Keep track of the children's favorites. A list of never-fail games and songs can be very useful on difficult days when nothing seems to work.

• Start circle time with the children who are ready, allowing other children to join as they finish what they're doing. If children come to the circle eager to begin and then have to wait five or ten minutes for everyone to arrive, they may well lose their interest and enthusiasm by the time circle time finally begins. Starting right away keeps their interest and encourages others to complete their tasks so they won't miss the fun.

• Decide as a team at the beginning of the year the expectations for circle time participation. Does everyone have to come to the circle? What about children who disrupt activities? What about children who continue to be disruptive after they've been told to leave the circle? What about children who come to the circle but seem afraid to participate? Remember that active, enjoyable circle time activities go a long way towards alleviation of management problems.

• Involve the children as much as possible in planning circle time. Ask them what they would like to do, perhaps making a list on a large sheet of paper as they state their choices. Plan games

The plan was to read a story at circle time. The adults were aware of the children's response to the story and changed their plans to meet the children's needs. They recalled from previous circle times an activity that was popular with the group and that was active enough to involve even the most restless children. They didn't "punish" the children for their restlessness during the story, but rather interpreted the restlessness as a normal reaction to an activity that was not meeting the group's needs. In the future, the team might try reading stories to smaller groups of children at small-group time, or they might select shorter stories to read at circle time.

_____

III *A group of children are playing a start-stop action game with both adults. The adults started the game, one adult suggesting the actions and the other running the record player. Once the children were involved in the game, the adults asked them for suggestions. The game continued with each child suggesting something for the group to do.*

The adults had planned an activity that had a specific goal—stopping and starting. As soon as they felt that the children understood the game, they let the children take over and decide which actions to perform next. All the children were actively involved throughout the period.

_____

IV *During work time the class went to the gas station, where they saw the man filling the car with gas, putting oil in the car, washing the car's windows, raising a car on a hoist, fixing the car, etc. When they returned to the classroom, they gathered around the circle and made up a song about their trip. The song involved both singing about and enacting the events at the gas station.*

The adults used circle time to build on the children's immediate experience. By singing about and enacting the events they had seen, the children were talking about and representing their experience.

～

that give children choices about how to proceed and what to try next. For instance, in a body-part game, have the children suggest the different actions: "Timmy, what's your idea?" "Shake our hands." "Okay. Everyone, let's do Timmy's idea and shake our hands . . . Who else has an idea?"

• Once children understand an activity, let them take turns being the leader.

• Try to relate circle time activities to things the children have been doing. After a trip to the apple orchard, for example, help the children make up a song with actions about the things they saw and did.

Transitions

Between certain segments of the daily routine there are transitions a teaching team needs to think about and plan for. As children move from one activity to the next, they can easily lose control of themselves if they don't know what to expect and what's expected of them.
Here are some things adults can do to help children move easily from one time period to the next:

• The daily routine should have as few transitions as possible. In this following routine, for example, there are only three transitions:

> Planning—work time—clean-up
>   (transition)
> Outside time
>   (transition)
> Snack/recall and small-group time
>   (transition)
> Circle time/dismissal

In this routine, on the other hand, there are seven transitions to contend with:

> Circle/greeting time
>   (transition)
> Planning—work time
>   (transition)
> Recall (in planning groups)
>   (transition)
> Clean-up
>   (transition)
> Snack time
>   (transition)
> Outside time
>   (transition)
> Small-group time
>   (transition)
> Circle/dismissal time

• Plan the routine so that active times alternate with quieter times. For example, going from small-group time to outside time is an easier and more natural transition than going from small-group time to planning time, because it gives children a different type of focus and a chance to release some energy.

• Follow the routine consistently and help children learn the names of the parts of the daily routine so they can anticipate what comes next.

• Clearly signal the end of work time and the end of outside time so everyone is aware that it's time to move toward the next activity.

• Designate meeting places for transition times. For example, as they finish cleaning up and before they go to snack, have children meet in the block area. Between small-group time and outside time, meet by the door. At the end of outside time meet by an adult.

• Once children have gathered, help them make up special ways to move to the next activity—with their hands way up high, touching something blue, etc.

• Start the next activity right away even if all the children haven't got there yet. This lets them know that something fun is going to happen next so it pays to get there quickly.

Related films and publications from the High/Scope Foundation

Films—

(For a complete description of each film and instructions for ordering, see appendix 4.)

The Daily Routine: Preschool

Guidelines for Evaluating Activities series: 1. *Contrasting Teaching Styles: Small-Group Time;* 2. *Contrasting Teaching Styles: Work Time;* 3. *Contrasting Teaching Styles: Circle Time*

Exploring the Possibilities of the Room from **Helping Children Make Choices and Decisions** series

Small-Group Time: An Illustrated Checklist

Feelings in the Cognitively Oriented Curriculum

The Daily Routine (Elementary grades)

Publications—

The Cognitively Oriented Curriculum—Teacher's Guide to the Daily Routine (No. 2) (booklet, 36 pp.) by Sheila Mainwaring, 1975. (Elementary grades)

This booklet is designed to help the teacher of elementary-level children put into effect a daily process of planning, working, representing and evaluating.

The Cognitively Oriented Curriculum—The Daily Routine: Small-Group Times (booklet, 80 pp.) by Richard Lalli, 1978. (Elementary grades)

A supplement to *Teacher's Guide to the Daily Routine,* this booklet contains guidelines for planning small group instruction and 100 sample group times for teachers. The topics covered are the relationship areas of space, classification, seriation and time; language; mathematics; and the content areas of art, drama, construction, sewing, music and movement. Descriptions include the key experience and development level for which each activity is appropriate as well as suggested questions, materials and extensions.

Related reading on daily routine

Daily Program I, II, and III. HEW, Office of Child Development, Head Start Bureau, 1975, Washington, D.C., 20201.

Murphy, Lois B. and Ethel M. Leeper. *Away From Bedlam (Caring for Children* Series), DHEW Publication Number (OCD), 73-1029, Superintendent of Documents.

Murphy, Lois B. and Ethel M. Leeper. *Preparing for Change (Caring for Children* Series), DHEW Publication Number (OCD), 73-1028, Superintendent of Documents.

3/ Teaching in a team

In many classroom settings, pressures work against the formation of teams. Adults, for example, are often ranked according to title and salary. What an adult does in and out of the classroom depends on whether he or she is a "head teacher," "teacher," "assistant teacher," "helping teacher," "student teacher," "paraprofessional," "aide," "parent volunteer," "grandparent volunteer," "high school volunteer," etc. The teacher "teaches" the whole class while the helping teacher cuts out flash cards for the next lesson; the aide supervises free play while the teacher takes a break; the teacher gives lessons and the paraprofessional cleans up and takes the children to the bathroom; and so on. In such cases, although there may be two or more adults attached to the classroom, the uneven distribution of power and responsibility prevents them from working together as a team.

Interdependence characterizes a true team of adults. All members of a team are teachers regardless of their rank, educational background or salary. Each team member differs in experience, interests, strengths and weaknesses, but all members have the opportunity to grow and develop in understanding and ability within the supportive atmosphere of the team so long as they are willing to contribute to the team process.

Often one person is hired as the "official" team leader although in some cases another team member emerges as the person who generates enthusiasm and keeps the discussion moving. The team leader, who may be the head teacher or the most experienced adult, may feel ultimately responsible for the classroom and answerable to parents and supervisors, but he or she must allow the other adults to assume initiative, try things out and learn from their own mistakes. The team leader must see the classroom as "ours," not as "mine."

When one adult is more experienced in the curriculum or understands it more readily than the others, it is his responsibility to explain specific aspects of the curriculum and to relate what he does with children to the curriculum framework. In sharing his thinking with the rest of the team, he not only increases his own understanding of the curriculum but also contributes to the others' growth and effectiveness.

The team process evolves. It doesn't happen automatically because two or three people begin to work in the same classroom using the same curriculum framework. Learning to work together takes time, patience, mutual support, a willingness to persevere and a bit of humor in order to deal with the problems that will inevitably arise. One member may find another's habit of yelling across the room to children annoying. Members may have differing standards of cleanliness and safety. Some members may feel uncomfortable in an open situation and would prefer to instruct children rather than allow them to plan and make choices. Some members may use more forceful disciplinary measures than others. Some members may feel that planning for teachers and children interferes with everybody's spontaneity. Some members may spend all their energy saying why new activities can't be done or even attempted.

Whatever the problem and whatever its magnitude, a team member should discuss it with the rest of the team rather than fume about it alone. It's not particularly easy for a person to voice uneasiness, annoyance or confusion to the team, but in the long run the initial discomfort in putting it before the team is easier to bear than the potential breakdown of the group process if the problem goes unheeded.

Following are some things team members can do to help themselves work together most effectively.

Suggestions for team members

As a team, arrange the classroom and establish a daily routine

Before school starts in the fall, using the guidelines outlined in the chapters on room arrangement and daily routine, decide together how to arrange the classroom and set up a daily routine. Both the room and the order of the routine will probably change throughout the year as the need arises, but these changes should be agreed upon by the team. If each team member has a hand in establishing and organizing the environment, then everyone has a stake in what happens from the very beginning. Moving furniture and labeling materials are also good ways for the team to get to know each other and feel comfortable working together.

Plan for all members of the team to arrive in the classroom at least 15 minutes before the children

Some teams may choose to arrive earlier than this because of the amount of preparation they have to do before the children arrive. This time allows the team to review the day's plan and exchange last-minute reminders and ideas. It also permits the children to enter a relaxed and pleasant classroom rather than one in which adults are bustling around trying to get ready or resenting the fact that some team members haven't arrived yet. If it happens that a team member is habitually late, discuss the issue at a team planning meeting so that the late arriver becomes aware of the negative feelings he or she is creating.

Make a list together of specific tasks to be done before the children arrive and divide them equally among team-members

Thinking through what needs to be done and assigning tasks means that days can begin smoothly. One teaching team came up with this list of tasks:

1) Take chairs off tables.

2) Check each work area to make sure materials are where they belong.

3) Check and when necessary restock art materials—paint, paste, glue, tape, paper, staples.

4) Prepare and divide snack items.

5) Get out planning materials.

6) Gather small-group-time materials and put them near where they are to be used, if possible.

7) Set up any special work time materials.

8) Review the plan for the day—who's doing what and where, which children had plans they wished to continue.

Decide as a team who does what throughout the day

Each day unpredictable things happen. One way to enjoy and accommodate these situations is by being on top of the things that *always* happen. Having a daily routine for the team members helps ensure that the rough spots that do occur aren't ones that might have been avoided by forethought. Together decide: Who goes to the bus to meet the children? Who stays to greet the children who arrive by other means? Who makes sure that parents are greeted? Who plans with which children? Who goes to the bathroom with children (if the bathroom is too far away for them to go by themselves)? Who goes outside when the first group of children are ready and who comes out with the stragglers? Who gets circle time started? Who goes out to the bus with the children and who remains to clean up and talk to parents?

Each team will have different tasks to cover based on their particular routine. These tasks can be handled in a number of ways; for example, they could be rotated or assigned for a year, or some could be dealt with spontaneously. However they're handled they must ultimately be shared, so that one person doesn't feel he or she is the only one who cares.

Decide on common expectations for team members

If the team hasn't worked together before, members may need time to see how they work together before outlining common expectations. After a week or so discuss the following issues and any others relevant to the team's particular situation:

• What about leaving the room to answer the telephone, go to the office, smoke?

• What about talking across the room to each other or to children?

• How will team members maintain contact with each other throughout the day?

• What if a team member really gets angry with a child or another team member?

• What about talking about children while they're present?

• How will the team respond to "catastrophes" such as spilled paint or juice; to messes, accidents, and lurid tales from home?

• Will each team member's group do the same activity at small-group time?

• Should each team member stay in an area throughout work time or float from area to area as needed?

• What about the occasional times team members come to school but really don't feel like being there or being patient with children or co-workers?

• What about a child who prefers one team member or a team member who finds one child particularly difficult to get along with?

Decide on expectations and limits for children

Since the children deal with a number of adults throughout the day, consistency from adults helps them learn classroom procedures with a minimum of confusion and frustration, and spares everyone the trials of playing one adult off another. Once the team agrees on a common set of expectations, post them for visitors, parents and other adults who come to the classroom. Here are some questions the team might discuss:

• Can a child go straight to an area without indicating a plan first?

• Do children need to clean up before changing their plans?

• Can children run or tussle in the center of the room?

• Can children go outside during work time?

• What materials in particular work areas can be used in other parts of the room?

• Can children go to the bathroom by themselves?

• Do all children have to wait for everyone to be ready for the next activity before it begins, or can things begin as a small group of children are ready?

• Does everyone have to clean up just the things he or she used or work until the whole room is cleaned?

• What if a child won't clean up?

• Does a child have to go to small-group time? Does he have to remain there? If not, what specifically are his alternatives?

• What if a child doesn't want to participate in the circle time activity? What if he is disrupting it?

• How, in general, will the team deal with typical three- and four-year-old hitting, grabbing and biting?

Decide on a time each day for evaluation and planning

Forty-five minutes to an hour a day every day with the whole team present and contributing is essential to the success of the program. The next chapter discusses ways to use this time effectively.

Related films and publications from the High/Scope Foundation

Films—

(For a complete description of each film and instructions for ordering, see appendix 4.)

Team Planning in the Cognitively Oriented Curriculum

Publications—

Planning by Teachers (booklet) by Lynne Seifert, 1978. (Elementary grades)

This handbook provides guidelines for the teaching team's continued efforts in establishing a program for their specific elementary-level children. It includes descriptions of the overall and daily planning for both teams and individual teachers. Materials and organizational strategies are suggested for step-by-step implementation of a well-planned program.

4/ Planning in a team

Most adults who have worked with young children in a preschool, nursery school or day care setting have been involved in some kind of planning process. Adults might sit down once a week, for example, to generate a series of activities they feel would be interesting and beneficial to the children. At the end of each day the adults might talk about how the activity went and whether or not the children enjoyed it. Activities may be repeated either because the children enjoyed them or because the children were not successful in the activity the first time around.

Supervisors may require adults to submit lesson plans each week for approval. In these situations the adults often resent planning because it seems to be little more than a bureaucratic imposition. Turning in acceptable lesson plans means smooth sailing while turning in unacceptable plans means being made to feel incompetent. In such cases filling out the planning forms with the right words supersedes the planning process, the actual doing of the plan

and the discussion of it later with other staff.

Reporting classroom incidents presents few problems to most adults, who find the process quite natural and enjoyable. It does take time, however, to learn to observe, report and assess important details that tell something about how a child approaches and perceives materials and situations. Deciding what to do next is probably the most difficult as well as the most exciting and stimulating part of team planning. Initially many adults wish the curriculum framework gave more specific answers and directives, such as, "If a child builds a series of identical block towers then be sure to do A, B and C." Instead, the curriculum framework gives adults both a way to observe children's actions in relation to their intellectual development and a range of possible ways to interact with children in order to support and extend their interests and actions. Rather than give specific answers and directives, the framework gives *possibilities*, and makes the teaching team the curriculum developers. Knowing their unique group of three- and four-year-olds, they plan strategies and activities specifically for them.

Planning and evaluating give the teaching team an opportunity to transcend their subjective feelings about a particular day. An adult may say, "I had a terrible day today. Small-group time started out all right but then it fell apart after Jerry started rubbing playdough into Kelly's hair." With the help of the team members and the curriculum guidelines, however, this adult can look at what did go well in spite of the immediate frustration and plan ways to prevent or cope with such mishaps in the future.

In order to report, assess and plan most effectively, at the beginning of each daily planning session the team needs to set a specific focus, such as one or two key experiences, or small-group time, or how five or six children planned and carried out their plans. The rest of this chapter suggests and illustrates some ways of organizing planning sessions.

Organizing planning sessions around key experiences

A teaching team can start the planning process by selecting key experiences they feel are most appropriate for their children. The key experiences listed in the margin of this page were selected by one teaching team as a focus for planning during the first two weeks of school.

The team used the week's key experiences not only to guide their observations and assessments of children but also to generate activities and teaching strategies. They found they couldn't spend a lot of time on every key experience each day and that on some days they concentrated on just two or three key experiences. By the end of the week, however, they felt they did have a better understanding of how most children functioned in each of the week's key experiences.

Following are the team's plans and evaluations for Wednesday and Thursday of the first week of school. In reading these forms two points should be kept in mind: 1) The ideas and strategies that grew out of the team's Wednesday observations and evaluations appear on Thursday's plan under Strategies and Activities. 2) These planning forms cannot recapitulate a team's entire dialogue. They can do no more than summarize enough of the dialogue to remind the team of what they saw and what they plan to do next. The planning form only *summarizes* the rather lengthy evaluation and planning process.

FIRST-WEEK KEY EXPERIENCES
ACTION
  Exploring actively and with all senses
  Taking care of one's own needs
  Choosing materials, activities, purposes
  Acquiring skills with tools and equipment
LANGUAGE
  Describing objects, events and relations
SPACE
  Learning to locate things in the classroom
TIME
  Describing and representing past events

SECOND-WEEK KEY EXPERIENCES
ACTION
  Exploring actively and with all senses
  Taking care of one's own needs
  Choosing materials, activities, purposes
  Acquiring skills with tools and equipment
LANGUAGE
  Describing objects, events, and relations
SPACE
  Learning to locate things in the classroom
  Experiencing and representing one's own body
TIME
  Describing and representing past events
  Anticipating future events verbally and by making appropriate preparations
CLASSIFICATION
  Investigating and labeling the attributes of things

DAILY PLANS AND EVALUATIONS for **Wednesday, Sept. 8**

Daily Routine	Key Experiences	Strategies & Activities	Observations	Evaluations
PLANNING TIME	• Taking care of one's own needs • Choosing materials • Learning to locate things	Help Will and Barby find something to stand on to hang up own jackets. After children have had a few minutes to explore the room again, each adult talks to children in her small group about what each one would like to do. Help children use area names.	When asked "Can you find something to stand on so you can reach your hook?" Will didn't respond and Barby looked around but didn't say anything. "Can you see something in the block area?" Barby went to the block area and pointed to a big block. Will and Lee helped her bring it to the coat rack. It worked and both seemed pleased. Most children could say something they wanted to do, but pointed to the area rather than using name or went and got object they wished to work with.	Barby understood the problem posed although she didn't use any language to solve it. With an idea to get her started, she could solve her own problem. Children can see and name things they want to do but are still uncertain of the work area names.
WORK TIME	• Exploring actively with all senses • Acquiring skills with tools and equipment • Describing objects, events, and relations	*Art*—Help children choose from materials available so far: clay, playdough, paper, crayons, markers, paste, collage materials, etc. Talk with them about what they're doing and observing. Help Jerry find things to paste if he chooses paste again. *Block*—Talk with children about what they are doing. See what they can say. Help Will get into the area and started.	*Art*—Jerry went right to the paste again and began mounding it on the paper as he did yesterday. Charlene said, "Look, you can stick things on top of all your paste like this." Jerry watched her then put some paper on himself. Becky was the only child who spontaneously described what she was doing: "Cut, cut, cut, cut." *Block*—Ric ran the dump truck around and filled it with small blocks. Will went right to the unit blocks on his own and made stacks with them. Ric would not stay still long enough to talk to and Will left when Lee talked to him.	Jerry is beginning to move from just exploring the paste, to learning the skill of pasting. He responded positively to Charlene's alternative. He's not using much language at this point. Does Becky describe other things she does? *Block*—Both Ric and Will are exploring what they can do with blocks—filling and stacking. Ric may need help seeing what else he can do with the blocks and the truck. Will may still need time to feel comfortable with classroom adults or he may not have a lot of language yet.

Wednesday, September 8 (continued)

Daily Routine	Key Experiences	Strategies & Activities	Observations	Evaluations
WORK TIME (cont.)		*House*—Continue to see how children use house area objects.	*House*—Deann dumped all the buttons and bottlecaps into her purse, put on shoes and went to the store in the quiet area. She brought back pegs and beads which she stirred around in a pot and then spooned up onto plates. "Come over to my house for supper," she told Anne. She told Anne to eat her food and said it was "hard" and "a lot of colors."	*House*—Deann is well into role play and also describes objects. See if there are other children she can include in her play.
		Quiet—If Carrie uses a puzzle again, help her turn her pieces around rather than jamming and pounding them.	*Quiet*—Anne worked briefly with Carrie helping her turn each piece and try it. When she got the idea, she did the puzzle over and over again.	*Quiet*—Carrie is beginning to gain skill with simple puzzles.
		Add small tinkertoys. They might interest Brent.	No one worked with tinkertoys. Plan a small-group time around them.	
CLEAN-UP TIME	• Learning to locate things in the classroom.	Help children match objects to labels and find similar objects.	The square beads and square counting cubes got all mixed together.	Quiet area containers need clear labels.
			Timmy put blocks right on top of labels to make sure he got them in the right place.	Make sure there are labels in other areas that children can match objects to directly.
			Clean-up time took too long today maybe because no one cleaned up along the way. They just changed plans leaving old materials out.	Help children clean up as they go during worktime. Help them put things away before starting something new.
OUTSIDE TIME	• Taking care of own needs	Encourage children on swings to pump. Bring out bags for children who collect things.	Carrie showed Barby how to pump better than we could! Deann, Trina, and Jerry made a game of filling their bags so full they'd break. They found that stones worked best.	Deann, Trina, and Jerry are beginning to work with ideas of heavy and light. Use those terms with them.

Wednesday, September 8 (continued)

Daily Routine	Key Experiences	Strategies & Activities	Observations	Evaluations
SMALL-GROUP TIME	• Describing past events in words • Acquiring skill with tools and equipment • Choosing materials	As children eat snack have each child tell what she did at work time. After children clear table from snack, put scissors and magazine in middle of table. Have children choose magazine to cut from. Give them envelopes with signs on them so each child can save pictures to paste tomorrow.	*Lee's group* For recall, Will pointed to the quiet area but didn't say anything. Lee talked about what she was doing, Joey and Terry talked about and shared pix they made with magic markers. Barby needed help with scissors. Magazines too big for her. Ric and Joey cut out cars.	It seems easier for the children to recall when they have what they made or used in front of them to handle and show. Barby is learning how to cut. Ric and Joe cut well and are classifying by choosing just cars to cut out.
			Charlene's group Chrissy remembered where everyone worked at work time. Timmy could say "Blocks."	Chrissy is making observations about other children.
			Chrissy and Billy cut pictures with no trouble. Others had trouble just cutting, magazines too big and bulky. Chrissy and Billy took their pictures home.	Everyone but Chris and Bill are learning to use scissors.
			Anne's group For recall Deann, Trina and Jerry talked about their bags at outside time. They brought their bags to the table and everyone tried cutting things in them to see what things they could cut with scissors. This activity lasted for the entire time.	Outside time was more immediate than work time for this group so they talked about their bags. Maybe recall should occur directly after work time. Cutting objects gave opportunity to talk about hard and soft which most didn't understand.
CIRCLE TIME	• Choosing materials • Acquiring skills with equipment	Have each child pick up an instrument from the box. Charlene will conduct loud and soft.	Choosing took a long time because there were so many kinds of instruments to choose from. Children at end had to wait too long.	Circle time needs to get underway quickly.
			Playing louder easier than playing softer. Children also had to move around as they played.	Include movement in circle time activities.

DAILY PLANS AND EVALUATIONS for **Thursday, Sept. 9**

Daily Routine	Key experiences	Strategies & Activities	Observations	Evaluations
PLANNING TIME	• Taking care of one's own needs • Choosing materials, etc. • Learning to locate things	See if Will and Barby remember block. If not remind them about what they did yesterday. After child says what he'd like to do, ask: "Where do you think you could do that? In the block area (point to it), the house area (point to it) … etc."	Will kept his coat on for 1st 10 min. 'til he made his way to the block area. He saw the block he wanted but seemed afraid to get it because Joey and Terry were busy there. Anne saw his problem and said, "Want me to get your block with you, Will?" He nodded "Yes," got block with Anne and hung up coat.	Will recalled what he had done the day before.
			Every time Charlene named and pointed to an area, the children waiting to plan with her also named the areas, making it into a game for themselves.	The children are beginning to learn the work area names. Repetition and game made key experience more meaningful to children.
WORK TIME	• Exploring actively with all senses • Acquiring skills with tools and equipment • Describing objects, events and relations	*Art*—Continue to help children choose materials. Add scissors. If Lisa and Trina come, hold paper for them so they get the idea of cutting.	*Art*—Lisa finally got so she could cut while Anne held the paper. Lisa was pleased. Perhaps she could manage smaller strips by herself. Try tomorrow.	*Art*—Lisa is gaining skill with scissors.
		Block—Try talking to Ric before he starts with the truck and blocks. Also try to see when he's finishing and talk to him about another area. See if Anne can talk to Will or at least join him.	*Block*—It worked better talking to Ric before and after he used the dump truck and blocks. Charlene did most of the talking. Instead of going to the art area he went back to his truck when Charlene suggested he could use the stones in the truck too.	*Block*—Ric responded positively to suggested alternative for using truck. Continue to help him find other alternatives.
			Anne went to area with Will. He gave her blocks to make stacks, too! She talked about their stacks. He seemed to be listening but didn't say anything.	Will seemed comfortable with Anne. He understands language but doesn't use it yet in the classroom. Keep talking to him!

Thursday, September 9 (continued)

Daily Routine	Key Experiences	Strategies & Activities	Observations	Evaluations
WORK TIME (cont.)		*House*—See if Chrissy or Billy can join Deann if she goes to house again so she has child to pretend with rather than just an adult.	*House*—Deann worked in the art area making playdough snakes. Chrissy and Billy used the buttons and pine cones to fill the egg cartons and all the food boxes. They called the pine cones "prickly things." "It pinched my nose," Chrissy found when she tried to smell one.	*House*—Deann can represent by making models. Billy and Chrissy worked together though not really in a role play situation. Described objects.
		Quiet—Continue to see how children use quiet area materials. Help Carrie find another four piece puzzle.	*Quiet*—Too many puzzles out. Remove some of the more difficult ones. Carrie pulled out two hard ones before anyone could help and got very frustrated because there were too many pieces and they all got mixed up.	*Quiet*—Don't have all the puzzles out initially. Find out who needs puzzles at what level of difficulty.
CLEAN-UP TIME	• Learning to locate things in the classroom	Help children clean up before changing their plans as well as at clean-up time. When children begin putting away cubes and beads in quiet area, explore differences with them and tape a cube to the cube box and a square bead to the bead box.	Better today. Not everyone could clean up before they changed plans because materials were still being used. Becky and Brent did a good job sorting the cubes and the beads. Lisa and Billy didn't want to clean up their block house. We explained about the afternoon class and took a picture of it.	Clear labels help the clean-up and sorting process. Photo helped Lisa and Billy "save" their house. Also gave them a chance to interpret the photo for others at recall.
OUTSIDE TIME	• Taking care of own needs • Actively exploring • Choosing	Talk with children about what they're doing and seeing and finding. To make coming in more fun have someone choose a way to come in like running, hopping, etc.	Chrissy named a lot of things she saw from on top of the climber, and Becky joined in with a game "Can you see a telephone pole?" and so on. Lisa said everyone should go in like airplanes. That was a hit.	Once one child begins naming things outside, others pick it up and it becomes a game with the challenge of "how many" (things can you see). Lisa had no trouble thinking of a way to move.

Thursday, September 9 (continued)

Daily Routine	Key Experiences	Strategies & Activities	Observations	Evaluations
SMALL-GROUP TIME	• Describing past events in words • Acquiring skill with tools and equipment • Choosing materials	Recall during snack. Have children find an object they worked with or something they made to talk about. *Lee's group* Continue with scissors and magazines. Add car magazines for Ric and Joey. Add construction paper strips for Barby.	*Lee's group* Barby did much better with the strips of paper. She cut out pieces and fringes. Ric and Joey cut more cars and Terry and Will just cut pieces of paper. All are ready to paste tomorrow. Ric and Joey may be able to sort their cars as they paste because they began sorting them today.	*Lee's group* Barby is still mastering the skill of cutting. Terry and Will can cut but are not yet sorting out specific things to cut. More interesting cutting per se. Ric and Joey able to cut *and* sort.
		Charlene's group See if Chris and Bill can choose one kind of picture they want to cut out. Have construction paper for others for fringing and cutting into small pieces.	*Charlene's group* Bill just cut pictures at random but Chris cut out only people. We talked about making a people book tomorrow with them at work time. Timmy cut fringes. Carrie and Lisa began cutting pieces and also on short lines Charlene drew.	*Charlene's group* Bill cuts well and cuts around outlines. Chris sorted—just people pix. Tommy, Carrie, Lisa, still experimenting with cutting itself.
		Anne's group Have scissors, paper, and magazines since this group didn't get to this yesterday.	*Anne's group* Brent needs more help and practice cutting. Becky cut out pictures. Deann and Trina cut out whole pages. Jerry cut fringes and also tore pieces when cutting got too frustrating. Strips might be easier for him.	*Anne's group* Brent and Jerry learning the skill of cutting. Deann and Trina cutting large pieces. Becky able to choose and cut specific pix although they weren't all the same in any way.
CIRCLE TIME	• Choosing materials	Just have tambourines, bells, and triangles, so choosing goes faster. Have children take turns conducting loud and soft. Before putting instruments away march around room.	Went faster. Also had a chance to compare different sounds. Played each kind of instrument by itself loud and soft. Children thought of different ways of conducting. Try a march record played not too loud to give a simple beat to follow when marching.	Starting out with fewer instruments made differences easier to compare. Children could generate own ways of being leader. Music needs a steady, easily identifiable beat. Otherwise it just becomes background noise.

Organizing planning sessions around the daily routine

Some teaching teams may find it useful to evaluate and plan for specific times in the daily routine, especially in the beginning of the school year. What happened during planning time? What did it mean? What does the team want to happen during planning time? Once the team has lived with the daily routine and dealt with some of the issues it raises, they may then choose to change their daily planning focus to appropriate key experiences. Some teams may do both at once.

The following questions may help to guide the team that chooses to focus on the issues raised by the daily routine:

Planning time

- How do children indicate their plans?
- How can adults respond to support each kind of planning?
- How do children use their signs?
- How can planning be made more graphic for children?
- What are the advantages/disadvantages of small-group planning?
- What are the advantages/disadvantages of individual planning?
- What works best for a particular child?

Work time

- How often does a child change his or her plan?
- How and when should an adult intervene to extend a child's plan?
- When is it appropriate for children to change their plans?

- How can an adult help children solve problems?
- What are some strategies for the child who does the same thing day after day?
- When is doing the same thing day after day appropriate?

Recall and small-group time

- How can adults help children recall things they've done during the day?
- Should recall follow directly upon work time?
- Under which circumstances do the children spontaneously recall things they've done?
- Which key experiences does a child's recall relate to?
- Should every child recall something he's done every day?
- How can recall be interesting to all children?
- What is the purpose of a particular small-group time?
- How are small-group times planned?
- What can be done if a child does not want to participate?
- What could nonparticipation indicate?
- How can small-group activities be made developmentally appropriate for individual children?
- What kinds of materials can be used?
- What if there are not enough materials for each child?

Circle time

- How can the whole group participate actively without chaos?
- What is the purpose of a particular circle time?
- What is the role of each adult?

- What about children who distract the group?

Outside time

- How do children use this time?
- How can it be a learning time?
- What kinds of equipment and activities are appropriate?
- How should adults interact with children outside?
- What limits should be enforced for safety's sake?

Organizing planning sessions around individual children

All daily planning, no matter what its focal point, deals with individual children. Occasions will arise, however, when the team will wish to focus their planning explicitly on one or more children. Perhaps, for example, a child continually disrupts small-group time or the work of other children at work time. Or perhaps the team members realize they haven't even mentioned some children during recent planning sessions. Certain children may create problems the team feels it must deal with: the child who doesn't talk, the child who's been working with the trucks in the block area for the past month, the two girls who thoroughly depend on each other and who monopolize the house area, the boy who seems to be asking for new and exciting ideas to work on, the girl who starts a project but doesn't finish it and then gets upset because she doesn't have anything to show at recall time.

The team needs to spend some time pooling what they know about these children—what they like or dislike, what they're good at, where in the daily routine they have difficulty and where they respond well. Then they can use the curriculum framework to plan strategies specifically for these children. They may decide to focus on one particular time in the daily routine with which a child has difficulty, or they may decide that a child has difficulty making choices and plan strategies to help him do that throughout the day.

Recently a High/Scope teaching team spent time planning for a four-year-old child who was developmentally delayed and causing problems for both staff and other children. Here's a transcription of part of their planning session:

1st Adult. I've noticed recently that Amy and Troy are more accepting of Leon than some of the other children are. Joanie, for example, asked me if he was crazy, I think because his language and behavior must appear so strange to her. I didn't know what to say to her.

Curriculum Assistant (CA). Maybe you could ask Joanie what makes her think he's crazy and then respond with a simple statement like "He hasn't learned to talk yet" or "He hasn't learned to do that yet." This strategy satisfied Tommy when he asked about Mike. I think it's important to try to make the child who's asking the question feel he can help the "different" child.

2nd Adult. Some things I've noticed are that Leon is learning Joanie's name, and he does respond to simple directions like "Come with me" and "Find the truck." He's also delighted when other people imitate the sounds he makes.

1st. I've also seen brief moments of parallel play with Joanie and Amy. When Leon does something Amy doesn't like, she tells him "No" which from her he responds to.

2nd. Corey, Jeff, Wendy and Erin don't want anybody to interfere with what they're doing, especially Leon, so they don't even give him a chance. They shout "No" at him before he even comes near them, and that doesn't seem fair to him.

1st. Let's talk to those children and at least get them to stop shouting "No!"

2nd. Okay. Maybe they can learn from Troy, who often seems to enjoy Leon. Today, for example, Troy built towers, Leon knocked them down, and Troy built them up again.

1st. Yes, I saw that, so I tried to build some towers for Leon after Troy left to see if he would knock them down, but Leon was off to something else.

2nd. I wonder if Leon does some negative things deliberately just for attention. Today, for example, I saw him smack the rabbit, run off, come back, do it again, and look at me specifically for my reaction. I told him, "No, that hurts the rabbit" and led him away.

CA. I think that was a good way to respond because you gave him a reason for not hitting the rabbit but you reacted matter-of-factly instead of very emotionally. Where do you think we should go with Leon from here?

1st. We've seen tremendous progress in him in the past three days, but we're afraid he won't continue to improve unless one adult works with him every minute, and that's not fair to the other children.

2nd. What if we try zone defense. If he's in your area, follow up on him.

1st. I tried that but if I'm involved with other children, I have to stop mid-sentence to take care of Leon.

2nd. Maybe we should add some toys younger children like, such as pull toys to the quiet area.

CA. That's a good idea. You could also try to extend the time he does things, and plan specific activities for him like dumping and pouring rather than expect him to plan. I think for the next few days, you should try the things we've thought of so far—giving other children ways of helping him, giving him simple directions, imitating his sounds, picking up on things he likes to do like knocking down towers, giving a reason when you tell him "No," "zone defense," adding toys he might have more success with like pull toys, and planning specific activities for him rather than asking him to come up with something which is too hard for him. Another thing we haven't mentioned that we should be sure to do is to encourage and support him when he does do something appropriate. Let's evaluate these strategies after we've given them a try for a couple of days.

After a series of discussions evaluating Leon's actions and planning strategies to try, the team came to these conclusions:

LEON'S ADJUSTMENT TO PRESCHOOL.   *In September, Leon spent work time moving rapidly from one thing to another, looking out the window and interacting very little with other people. He seemed to be constructing a sense of the room as a whole, moving around the room but always returning to particular materials (books, trucks, small blocks, stuffed bears, shape sorters). Later on, Leon stopped working with materials altogether and spent several weeks trying to establish social relationships with other people, often by hitting, pushing, screaming and trampling structures or projects. Although this was a difficult time, we were heartened by his energetic social efforts and his attempts to meet his new needs. For the past two or three weeks, Leon has integrated his actions with materials and people in a more realistic manner. He is once again working with materials and is content to play with them near other children with occasional interactions rather than continue his former strategy of forcing con-*

frontations. Leon does seem to have a general understanding of the daily routine and often spontaneously predicts what comes next. He responds to verbal directions without physical cues and understands some rules. For example, although he still goes outdoors at work time, he usually comes right back in without adult direction. There is an increase in Leon's appropriate language usage and considerably less babbling. He spontaneously uses short sentences and repeats the key words.

LEON'S SOCIAL-EMOTIONAL PROGRESS.   *He controls his impulses to hit or push children by stopping his hands midair. He does touch gently and his hitting is becoming rarer. He continues to dislike any attempts at isolation. He maintains eye contact now, which helps him initiate peer interactions. He is also turning to the adults as reliable people to do things with and is less attracted to our numerous visitors, preferring people who are consistently present.*

LEON'S MOTORIC PROGRESS.   *Leon is more adept at manipulating objects and is particularly good at dumping and filling. He enters groups and work areas more slowly, is more aware of what is by his feet and now often steps over rather than on top of things.*

OTHER CHILDREN'S RESPONSES TO LEON.   *The children often tell us what Leon says and occasionally show him how to do things, build small towers for him to knock down, and attempt to include him in their play. They have learned to say "No" to Leon, but usually without any further explanation.*

This is something to work on. The children sometimes notice his progress—"He's not using a double cup today"—and interpret his actions—"I guess we gave him too much juice."

STRATEGIES THAT WORK WITH LEON

1) *Reinforcing Leon's positive and appropriate actions.*
2) *Spending some time with him every work time.*
3) *Taking Leon with us occasionally to see what children are doing and to involve him in their activities. He especially likes going to the house area.*
4) *After Leon hits a child, telling him "No" very sternly, making him sit down, telling him why he can't hit people and requiring that he sit for 5-10 seconds.*
5) *During work time, acknowledging what he is doing, directing him to an activity or offering him a choice between two activities.*

IMMEDIATE GOALS FOR LEON

1) *Extending the time he plays cooperatively near other children.*
2) *Helping him see new ways to use materials.*
3) *Increasing his number of spontaneous verbal requests and verbal exchanges.*
4) *Increasing his ability to remain at the table for snack time.*

As part of their daily planning sessions, some teaching teams talk about five or six children, or each child when they have the time, and record specific observations and strategies to try. Having a list with a place to make notes about each child helps the team think about all the children and reminds them to pay more attention to children they may have nothing to say about on a particular day. Following are examples of how two teaching teams used such a system:

Example 1: **ASSESSMENT OF CHILDREN'S ACTION AND LANGUAGE**

	Corey	Erin	Wendy	Mark	Joanie	Karl
Representation	10/30: Made machine out of wood with a button (bottle cap) to turn it on.	11/4: Made bed cover for bed; used material for cover. Pillow was wood rectangle nailed onto bed.	10/30: Progressed with box barn. Attached barn to yard with connecting doors. Cut windows and planned for front door and back door.	10/30: Mark & Corey made a barn out of hollow blocks for the house.	10/25: Role played as baby. Didn't talk, couldn't get out of bed.	10/25: Made an E with flat beads. "This is an E for Elizabeth" (his sister). Also made a tall building out of hollow blocks. "I want to build a building like this" (referred to picture).
Classification	11/4: Said that his car started itself. Wheels have batteries inside that make wheels go round. Had a sense that car was different from ordinary.	11/4: After discussion of hard & soft, glued a piece of aluminum foil next to a cotton ball; felt the textures.	10/30: Described all the parts of the barn and yard.		10/28: Washed apples. One container for dirty apples, tub to wash, tray to dry, container for clean ones. No problem keeping 4 separate.	10/25: Made a distinction between bath water & water with boats in it. Said he liked bath water. Suggested that Joanie wear a bib. "Babies wear bibs."
Seriation or Number Concepts	11/4: Painted a picture of his car. Counted wheels in picture, then painted the numeral "4" below car.	11/4: Wanted to pantomime 6, 7, 8 hammers to song, her action was to move whole body. Did not associate number with actual body parts.		11/4: Said he picked up 2 blocks at same time to put away.	10/25: Looking at my necklace, pointed to different beads, saying, "Little, little..., big."	10/31: After Troy counted 5 cookies, Karl added quickly 6, 7, 8, 9, 10, 11, 12 with no one-to-one correspondence. Did this many times, beginning to be joke. Did use 1-to-1 correspondence with 3, 2, 1 cookie(s) on plate.
Spatial or Temporal Relations	10/24: When asked if today would be same as yesterday, immediately said, "No, we went to the apple orchard yesterday."	10/25: Added a new complexity to barn by starting to attach 2 boxes together as continuation of the barn.	10/30: Figured out how to place 2 boxes with doors so they could connect. Talked about placement of doors.	10/15: After looking at bus & cars & talking about front & back wheels with me, I asked what would happen to car or bus if no back wheels. Said, "It would fall down." Made 2 axles and put seats between them.	11/4: Wanted to ride horse and play in sand at same time; moved horse accordingly.	10/25: Continues to be interested in measurement. Made a long "chain" out of tinkertoys—measured it by comparing it to me.

Assessment of Children's Action & Language (continued)

	Laura	Jeff	Amy	Troy	Erica	Peter
Representation	10/25: Pretended to be Joanie's Mommy (Troy was Dad). Dressed in dress, bracelets, high heels, purse. Role-appropriate behavior and language.	10/31: House made out of big blocks is not being spontaneously elaborated. It remains a simple rectangle with sometimes a bed inside.	10/25: Joined in outside dramatization of pony song with others; did not try to be separate from them.	10/25: Troy was the Dad in the house. He got so involved with arranging caps in muffin tin that role was secondary (called bottle caps cookies).	10/30: Glued small wood A's on wood block upright and later identified as castle. Said would paint it pink.	10/31: Recognizes bunnies, ducks, truck, men from picture in book.
Classification	10/30: Started to make 2 piles of signs for the Goodby Song. Also held her sign up before the end.	11/1: Felt the oil, said it was smooth.	10/30: Identified 2 shades of red as dark and light.	11/1: Felt oil in top layer of oil/water; labeled it shiny.	10/30: Asked if dark red & light red in color tray were same, she said "No, it's the same as this one," pointing to another dark red.	10/25: Peter spontaneously said "Put away" while putting away the bus even though it was not clean-up time. Put it on top shelf where he always puts it. Progressed with identifying where truck belongs.
Seriation or Number Concepts		10/29: Counted 12 hanging monkeys.	10/30: Counting cards at group time; if 1 added or taken away, how many? Amy counted each time, not relying on mental operations.	10/31: Counted 8 cookies in row easily, 5 in stack. When placed around plate, counted 1 twice. Very confident of his results.		
Spatial or Temporal Relations	11/4: Painted: very intent on painting all of a box. At other times works very hard to paint all of her hands.	10/29: I asked to have a separate bedroom in his house, but he only made my room. To make walls taller so no one could see me sleep, used lots of unit blocks piled up; did not see easier solution of using larger cardboard blocks.	10/30: Planned ahead. Thinking she wanted wheels to roll, wanted to put nail in right place. Did one easily, next by trial & error. Did not compare 1st to 2nd spot.	10/28: Spent all outside time with cider press turning wheel, putting apples in. At circle time, asked why not going outside. Change in routine confusing.	10/31: Wrote story about castle she made yesterday, labeling parts as beds, pillows, & other parts. These were not apparent to observer; perhaps she is labeling & defining more for the adult.	10/25: Peter, faced with a very extended work time, anticipated that it was time to go "outside." He opened the door without words several times, but was able to control impulse sometimes without our help.

Example 2: PRESCHOOL DAILY OBSERVATIONS AND PLANS FOR NOVEMBER 12

Joey	Seriated spontaneously today: "I'm going to build a big house for Frank, a one not so big, and a little one." He did. See if he seriates with other materials. See if he can represent seriated things he makes.
Rebecca	Noted similarities of actions at circle time: "They both did the same because they both used their hands like this." Can she begin to describe things more fully?
Tim	Worked on car again. Needs to go out and look at real car to get placement of wheels.
Lynette	Sang a long song in music area about her room and new baby. Try to take dictation from her. She might illustrate.
Tracey	Really talked at outside time much more than he's ever said at work time. Watch for outside language tomorrow.
Tonio	Worked with Tim on car and really helped him at recall time. Might enjoy dictating his recall.
Lisa	Played baby again in house area with Margo. Since she plays baby so much could she represent baby in any other media?
Margo	For the first time really did a good job at clean-up time. Had a game with Lisa. She might also like a beat-the-sand-timer game. Try it.
Ryan	Hard time at circle time. Left because he didn't understand "different from." Use terms with him at work time when appropriate and use "same as" in circle game tomorrow.
Michelle	At recall talked about her picture spatially. "There's two towers *next to* the house and two people *on top of* the house." Ask her about spatial relations in things she works on at work time.
Jon	At planning time, recalled plan from yesterday and used term "yesterday." See if he would like to dictate his plans and keep a "plan" book.
Kerry	Was going to paint yet another house picture today but Carole asked her if she could think of another way to make a house. Worked on block house. Continue helping her think of alternatives.
Stacey	Absent. Remind her of birdhouse she started when she comes back.
Melissa	Made a plan on the way to school to make a birthday card for her grandmother, which she did! Got involved in counting number of people on card and seeing how many would fit.
Felix	Had to sit next to Lisa at small-group time. Okay. He works well with her and is much more willing to try things when she's around. He also helped her staple. Help him see himself as a helper.

Later on this teaching team used their daily observations of children to write a short paragraph about each child for visitors and parent volunteers, a few of which are reproduced here:

TRACEY—*Tracey started school just before Thanksgiving. At first he spent a lot of time filling containers with anything available. He rarely spoke, smiled or played with other children. Now he plays ball with other children and pushes them in the car.*

At work time he often becomes very intensely in-
volved in activities such as tower building, painting,
finger painting and pasting. At clean-up time he
enjoys sorting buttons and chestnuts in the house
area or washing the paint brushes. Although he
doesn't say much, he's very responsive to language.
Sometimes he'll forget himself and say, "These two
are the same!" Often he communicates by whining
or tugging. You usually can tell what he wants, but
if you say, "Tracey tell me what you want," he'll
say "paint," or whatever. Tracey is the only three-
year-old who has shown signs of sorting objects into
groups of identical objects rather than into graphic
or serial collections. He is initially very cautious in
responding to new adults.

MARGO—*Margo generally comes in with a*
plan to work in the house area and be a baby. In
order to carry out this role, however, she depends on
Lisa to be her mommy. As a baby, she responds
happily to the mom's directives, but when the mom
is busy elsewhere, she gets busy cooking or tele-
phoning or dressing up. Often after a while she'll
announce, "I'm changing my plan," get her sign and
then look around for an interesting activity to join.
She sometimes needs a little encouragement from an
adult at these transition times. At clean-up time she
needs her own specific task.

LYNNETTE—*Lynnette works in all the areas.*
She generally comes in with a plan but needs help
matching what she wants with what she says. In the
house area she enjoys working with Lisa and Margo.
In the art area she likes to have you ask her about
what she's making and is especially pleased to have
you write down what she says about her picture and
have you read it back. She's very eager to commu-
nicate using language and picks up and uses new
words readily. Once after we had talked with her
about a complex patterned structure she had built in
the block area, she brought Margo over and ex-
plained, "It goes up and down and up and down."

REBECCA—*Rebecca often plans to work in the*
art area and changes her plan frequently as she sees
and wants to sample other activities about the room.
Like Margo she enjoys being the baby. When things
get dull she demands something from the mom like a
book or a doll or a toy. More than anyone else in the
room, she likes to look at books, be read to and tell
her own fanciful stories. She also enjoys imitating
the things people or animals in the story are doing.
At circle time she often comes up with "I've got a
game" or "I've got a different way" and proceeds to
direct a new game or action.

JOEY—*Joey is very enthusiastic and verbal*
about practically everything he does. Since he comes
on the second bus everyone is usually busy working
by the time he comes striding in announcing "I'm
here." He usually makes his plan to join Timmy or
some activity that looks interesting to him. In the
house area he often becomes the dad and goes to
work and generally assigns any available adult to a
supportive role like mom or big brother. He also
builds block houses for Frank, the guinea pig, and
transports him about in the big wooden truck. In the
art area he's begun painting and finger painting.
"These things are the same," he often comments
during the course of working or cleaning up.

Relating seasonal themes and holiday activities to the curriculum framework

Teaching teams will probably wish to plan
around holiday and seasonal themes at appropriate times throughout the year. At such times,
team planning sessions often begin with activity
ideas which the team then attempts to modify so
that certain key experiences can occur. After
doing the activity with the children, the team
evaluates it in terms of these key experiences.

One teaching team, for example, selected the following activities to do at Christmas time and then discussed the relevant key experiences:

SELECTING AND BRINGING BACK A CHRISTMAS TREE (FIELD TRIP). *Key experiences to focus on:* time sequence of the trip; describing and comparing sizes, shapes, parts of different trees.

MAKING AND HANGING DECORATIONS FOR THE TREE OUT OF A VARIETY OF MATERIALS (A WORK TIME CHOICE). *Key experiences to focus on:* helping children make choices and see alternative uses of materials; rearranging materials in space; fitting things together; manipulating, transforming, combining materials; noticing and describing similarities and differences; comparing sizes, lengths, amounts; counting objects made; describing position of decorations on the tree in relation to tree and other objects.

MAKING BOOKS ABOUT CHRISTMAS BY DRAWING OR CUTTING OUT PICTURES AND DICTATING STORIES (A WORK TIME CHOICE). *Key experiences to focus on:* relating pictures to real places and things; recognizing that words can be written down; describing something in several different ways; interpreting representations of spatial relations in drawings and pictures.

REPRESENTING CHRISTMAS TREES WITH A VARIETY OF MATERIALS (A WORK TIME CHOICE). *Key experiences to focus on:* choosing materials and procedures; constructing models; making drawings and paintings.

MAKING CHRISTMAS CARDS AND ENVELOPES WITH PHOTOS AND DRAWINGS OF CHILDREN, HANDPRINTS AND DICTATED STORIES (A SERIES OF SMALL-GROUP PROJECTS). *Key experiences to focus on:* experiencing and representing one's own body; relating pictures and photos to real people; relating index of hand to hand on body; fitting things together; rearranging materials; having one's language written down and read back by an adult; anticipating and recalling a sequence of events.

SINGING CHRISTMAS SONGS USING INSTRUMENTS AND MOVEMENT (CIRCLE TIME). *Key experiences to focus on:* discovering relations through direct experiences; starting and stopping on signal; soft and loud; comparing similarities and differences.

[The adults didn't plan all the activities, however. After the children and adults set up the tree, the children generated these additional activities, with the team supplying the appropriate key experiences:]

MAKING SANTA CLAUS OUTFITS AND SLEIGHS. *Key experiences to focus on:* fitting things together; comparing sizes and amounts; shaping objects by folding and tying; comparing similarities and differences.

PLAYING "NIGHT BEFORE CHRISTMAS" (EVERYONE GOING TO SLEEP, SANTA LEAVING PRESENTS UNDER THE TREE, WAKING UP AND OPENING PRESENTS). *Key experiences to focus on:* role play, pretending; imitating actions; anticipating and sequencing events; describing events; expressing feelings.

Planning from a series of activities makes more sense to some teaching teams than starting with key experiences and generating activities that would provide them. In starting with activities, however, a team must not stop after describing the activity. "Let's make cupcakes at small-group time tomorrow" is a good beginning as long as the team then decides how they will use the experience, what they will emphasize, what they will try to find out about the children as they make cupcakes. Evaluation of the activity then has the possibility of going beyond "the cupcake-making went well" to a discussion of why it did and what children and adults learned along the way.

Planning for field trips and follow-up activities

Every team will probably spend time periodically planning and evaluating field trips and follow-up classroom activities. Some teams schedule trips regularly, while others try to plan them around the children's interests and projects of the moment. In either case, the team must agree on goals for the trip, how they can realize the goals and how they can build on the children's experiences back in the classroom. An example follows in which a High/Scope teaching team plans a trip to the gas station in order to extend children's representations of gas stations:

[Planning the trip]

1st Adult. The children have been doing a lot of gas station play lately.

2nd Adult. Yes, both in the block area with the small cars and blocks and in the house area with the sit-on car and pots and pans.

1st. What if we took a trip to the gas station so that they'd have a better, clearer idea of the things they're trying to represent in their play.

2nd. There's the gas station right around the block where I take my car. The people are very friendly, and I don't think they would mind having children visit them.

1st. Why don't we go tomorrow during outside time and have our snack when we come back. We could walk and look at cars on the way.

2nd. Since we want to help the children in their gas station role play, I guess we should focus on the equipment in the gas station and on what the people do there—the men putting cars on the hoists and fixing them, putting air in tires, putting gas in cars and washing the windows.

1st. Why don't I stop by the station on my way home and talk to the mechanic I know. I'll ask him what kinds of things he would allow the children to do while they're there. Maybe they could hold the hose while he's filling a car up with gas and help wash windows, especially if I left my car there for them to operate on! Maybe there are things inside he would let them touch and feel like tires and the lifts.

2nd. I'd like to take the camera with us so we can get some photographs of the children doing some of these things to bring back to the classroom. Photos might help remind them of things they saw and could add to their own play.

1st. And at circle time tomorrow while the experience is still fresh in their minds we could make up a song with the children about the things they saw and did. Once they talk about or sing about what they've seen I think they can recall it better later. I don't play the guitar very well but I could probably strum a couple of chords, enough to get a tune going.

2nd. Okay, great. Now about planning time tomorrow. Don't you think we should tell the children at planning time about the change in schedule so they'll know what's going to happen next and won't be confused?

1st. Yes, and we could also take the opportunity to talk with them about what's the same and what's different about tomorrow's schedule and the regular daily routine.

2nd. Probably not everyone will be able to see those differences, but we should point them out ourselves for those children.

1st. I think the trip for tomorrow is settled, but there's something that happened today at small-group time...

[The next day: evaluating the trip and planning follow-up activities]

2nd. I think the trip went really well today. It took us longer than I anticipated to get organized for the walk there, perhaps because the children were excited and we hadn't really thought much about the walk itself.

1st. Next time maybe we should have the children walk with the adult they have small-group time with.

2nd. Anyway, once we got there first there was the oil man in the red-spotted hat who very kindly showed the children how he pumped the oil from his big tank truck.

1st. Yes, and Joey got all excited counting all the tires on his truck. You got a picture of the truck, didn't you, so in case Joey wants to build a truck at the workbench he can refer to it and get all the tires on?

2nd. Yes, I did. The c going up and down on the hoist was good to see because it happened so close to the children and they got to see the bottom of the car. The mechanic also turned the wheels so they could see the wheels turning above them.

1st. Yeah, the hoists were really good for seeing the car from a number of different perspectives and also seeing that that's one way a mechanic can fix a car.

2nd. They also got to see the men working under the hood of the car. And Tim and Margo talked about all the different sizes of fan belts on the wall which were seriated by size.

1st. Now that we've gone to the gas station I think it's important for us to think about some follow-up activities to build on the gas station experience.

2nd. I think there are a lot of things that we can put out in each work area for the children to use if they choose to. We can put the sand table out with some cars and pipe cleaners to use for hoses. We can put the tinkertoys and the photographs that we took today in the quiet area.

2nd. In the art area we could put out some car pictures in case anybody wants to make a book. We could even have some little toy cars available if they want to trace cars.

1st. Right. And of course there's always the easel for painting as well as clay and playdough.

2nd. I think in the block area they could use the big car and maybe use some of the boxes to make a gas pump. There's also the gas hose, and I could bring in an oil can. What I'd like to do is to stimulate some play acting in the block area. Maybe some children can build a gas station and act out some of the things they saw the gas station men doing. What we need to do is put out some gas station props.

2nd. I think one of us will probably need to be in the block area to support the role play, adding some language to what the children are doing and helping them extend the things that they may start there…

[The third day: evaluating one of the follow-up activities]

1st. I was in the quiet area while the children were looking at the photographs we took of the gas station. At first, they were just looking at each other in the picture and saying, "Oh there's Michael. There's Timmy." They were talking to each other about themselves and what they were doing in the pictures so I asked some questions to determine if they could interpret some more abstract things from the photographs. They were able to tell me where things were in relation to each other like whether the car was up or down, and if they were standing under the car or beside the car, and where the gas station man was in relation to the car or to them.

2nd. So you used the opportunity to help children talk about the spatial relations of the things in the photos. Who were the children?

1st. Tim and Lisa.

2nd. That's great. We should try the same thing with some of the other children…

Summary of suggestions for planning and evaluating

• Set aside a regular time each day for evaluating and planning by the team.

• Set a specific focus for planning.

• Make up planning and evaluation forms and try out different ones. Keep the forms that work best for the team.

• Share the recording tasks—have one member record the evaluation, for example, while another records plans and another keeps notes about individual children.

• Make specific statements about what individual children and adults did in relation to the focus of the planning session.

• Don't stop after stating a problem. Go ahead and generate strategies for dealing with it.

• Get help when necessary from the curriculum assistant, an adult more experienced in the curriculum, another teaching team, a parent.

• Make sure every team member has a chance to contribute observations and ideas.

• Periodically, look at how effectively the team works together.

Related films and publications from the High/Scope Foundation

Films—

(For a complete description of each film and instructions for ordering, see appendix 4.)

Team Planning in the Cognitively Oriented Curriculum

Supporting Children's Intellectual and Physical Development

Guidelines for Evaluating Activities series: 1. *Contrasting Teaching Styles: Small-Group Time;* 2. *Contrasting Teaching Styles: Work Time, the Art Area;* 3. *Contrasting Teaching Styles: Circle Time*

From Direct Experience to Representation from **Experiencing and Representing** series

Observing a Child in the Block Area from **The Block Area** series

Publications—

Planning by Teachers (booklet) by Lynne Seifert, 1978. (Elementary grades)

This handbook provides guidelines for the teaching team's continued efforts in establishing a program for their specific elementary-level children. It includes descriptions of the overall and daily planning for both teams and individual teachers. Materials and organizational strategies are suggested for step-by-step implementation of a well-planned program.

Active
Learning

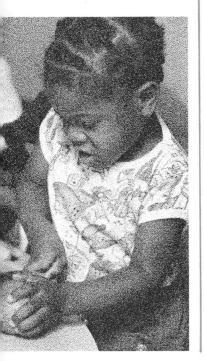

Language

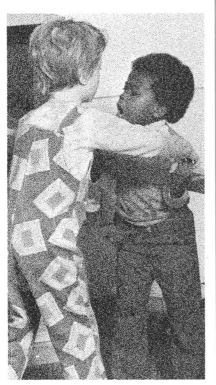

Experiencing
and
Representing

Classification

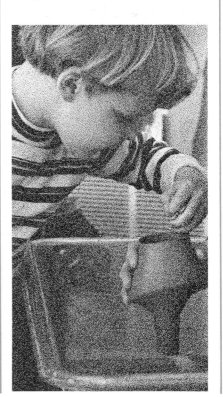

Part Two

Seriation

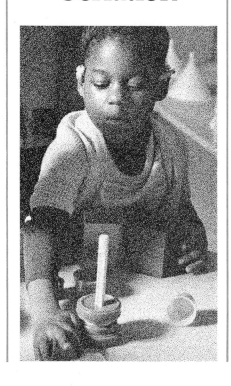

Number

Spatial Relations

Time

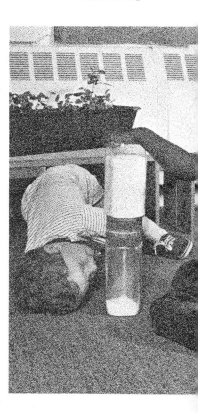

Key Experiences for Cognitive Development

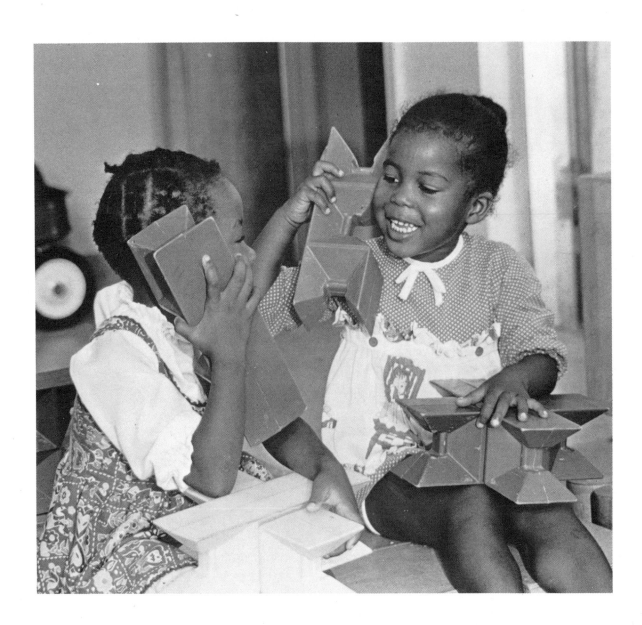

5/ Active learning

...in order to know objects, the subject must act upon them, and therefore transform them: he must displace, connect, combine, take apart, and reassemble them...

From the most elementary sensorimotor actions (such as pushing and pulling) to the most sophisticated intellectual operations, which are interiorized actions, carried out mentally (e.g., joining together, putting in order, putting into one-to-one correspondence), knowledge is constantly linked with actions or operations, that is, with *transformations*.

...Knowledge...at its origin, neither arises from objects nor from the subject, but from interactions—at first inextricable—between the subject and those objects.

—JEAN PIAGET

Piaget's concept of action includes both overt motor behavior and internal mental processes. The use of the term "action" to refer both to mental activity and physical activity is not a semantic accident; Piaget believes that the two are inextricably related, with systems of mental actions, or operations, deriving ultimately from sensorimotor actions, which are self-initiated and self-directed.

"Active learning," as we propose to use the term, connotes learning that is initiated by the learner, in the sense that it is *carried out* by the learner rather than simply "handed" or "transmitted" to him. With preschool-age children it usually has a sensorimotor component—moving, listening, searching, feeling, manipulating.

Active learning also connotes creativity on the part of the learner, who is trying to construct a better "theory" of reality and to invent new combinations of means and ends. This is also

what we mean when we say that the child "initiates" his own learning.

For Piaget, internalized actions lead both to the unconscious mental operations that distinguish the logic of one developmental period from that of another, and to representational symbols such as mental images, drawings and language. Internalization occurs through progressive "miniaturization" of sensorimotor actions and through a process of abstracting general systems of logical transformations from numerous particular actions. As sensorimotor "schemes" become internalized at about age two, the child is increasingly able to perform actions "in his head," anticipating consequences before actually doing something.

In the preoperational subperiod, in which most preschoolers are located developmentally, actions are being internalized to become representational thought, but the logical operations are not yet fully developed; the fluid mental transformations that make logical thought function will not appear until the child is in the first or second grade and enters the period of "concrete" operations. The preschool child still has difficulty representing transformations, keeping in mind several dimensions at once and understanding other viewpoints and perspectives.

Experiences in which the child produces some effect upon the world (in contrast with, say, watching television) are crucial to the development of thought processes because the child's logic develops from the effort to interpret the information gained through such experiences; interpretation of new data modifies the interpretive structures themselves as the child strives for a more logical internal model of reality.

Stepping for a moment outside of the Piagetian psychological perspective, we can see from simple observation of young children how "taking the initiative" and "producing effects upon the world" are virtually synonymous with learning— the child has an *interest* in what he's doing and is therefore fully involved in anticipating and solving problems. If we desire that children become intelligent problem solvers, it seems clear that the best way to do so in school programs is to give students plenty of opportunity to work on problems of interest to them— that is, problems that arise from their own attempts to comprehend the world. Piaget consistently underwrites this view when he speaks of classroom teaching. Thus—

> ...what is taught...is effectively assimilated only when it gives rise to an active reconstruction or even reinvention by the child...

and

> ...each time one prematurely teaches a child something he could have discovered for himself, that child is kept from inventing.it and consequently from understanding it completely. This obviously does not mean that teachers should not devise experimental situations to facilitate the pupil's invention.*

The progressions from *concrete to abstract, simple to complex, things to relations,* and *here and now to more remote in time and space* (see *A curriculum framework* in the Introduction) apply to active learning in the following ways:

*The quotations from Piaget in this section are taken from *Carmichael's Manual of Child Psychology* (third edition, volume 1), edited by Paul H. Mussen, chapter 9: Piaget's Theory; published by John Wiley & Sons, 1970.

- Concrete ⟶ abstract

Action on real, "concrete" objects is the developmental starting point for language, representation and logical operations. Active learning begins concretely, with manipulation and whole-body movement. As children become more familiar with a particular concept or object, they may work with it on a "symbolic" level— they may draw it or talk about it or listen to stories about it without requiring "it" to be actually present.

- Simple ⟶ complex

Active learning is a process of increasing complexity in that simple actions evolve into complex coordinations of actions. This is manifest in the child's attainment of the ability to use tools (e.g., scissors, hammer), to build with blocks and to use art media.

- Here/now ⟶ there/then

One of the reasons to stress the here and now at the preschool level is that a young child can more readily act on things that are spatially and temporally *present.* As the focus moves to distant places and to future and past events, there is a tendency on the part of the teacher to become more verbal and more abstract and therefore for the children to become less active. It's a challenge to the teacher to keep learning active as the child's ability to go beyond the here and now increases. One device we use is the plan-do-review cycle, in which a child makes a plan, carries it out and represents it in a variety of ways. In this cycle, active learning remains central as it's integrated with the child's growing ability to deal with remote events symbolically.

Sometimes the activities adults plan and the things they do with children don't involve active learning. Consider the following example:

At small-group time in a nursery school, eight children were seated on chairs in a semicircle. An adult had brought a fresh pineapple, paper plates, one very sharp knife and napkins. The adult settled herself comfortably on the floor and began by holding up the pineapple for the children to see and asking "Who knows what this is?" Then she held the pineapple for the first child to feel and smell. While the other children were waiting for their turn to touch the pineapple, the adult pointed out that the pineapple has a very prickly stem and that unless they sit very still on their chairs someone might get hurt. She passed it after her warning. Meanwhile, the children at the end of the semicircle were squirming and fidgeting in their chairs. They couldn't see the pineapple now, because the adult was kneeling in front of it as she held it for another child.

After all the children had a chance to touch and smell the pineapple, the adult took the knife, warned the children about the danger of sharp knives and cut the pineapple. As she lifted off the top she breathed in the aroma of the freshly cut fruit. Still the children were sitting, watching. She cut a slice, held it up and asked the children questions. "Who knows what the hard part in the middle is called?" "Can we eat it now or does something else have to be done?" "Is this piece shaped like a square?"

Only a few children responded; many were staring off into space and squirming on their chairs. The adult began slicing and peeling pieces and passing them out for the children to eat.

Touching and smelling a fresh pineapple, preparing it and eating it for snack is an appropriate, exciting activity for a group of preschoolers. The adult in this example had obviously planned the activity and provided materials and time for it. The children were watching and listening, touching and tasting. Why, then, were the children "staring off into space?" The answer is that they were not actively involved: The chil-

dren watched while the adult held, cut, smelled and sliced the pineapple herself; they listened while the adult talked and asked questions, but they didn't talk and ask questions themselves. In fact, they spent much of the time waiting for a turn. *The children were watching, listening and waiting, not acting.*

Now consider this example:

For a small-group time the adult brought a fresh pineapple. "I don't want to touch that. It's got stickers," said Teresa. "Let me feel it, let me feel it," said Sam.

"Let's pass it around so everyone has a chance to feel the pineapple," the adult said. "Teresa said it has stickers. What can you say about it, Pepe?" "It's prickery to me," Pepe said.

"Look at me! I'm holding it by the leaves and it's really heavy!" exclaimed Jennifer. "I can make it roll," said Kadith, "see?"

After each child had a chance to feel and talk about the pineapple, the adult asked, "What do you think it's like inside?" "Wet!" "It will have seeds!" "It will be soft like a banana!"

"How could we find out?" asked the adult. "Cut it, cut it!" The adult cut the pineapple into slices and gave one to each child. "Now what can you say about the pineapple?" Joanie immediately started licking her slice. "Oh, it tastes yukky to me." "I like it," said Jeff. "It's sweet." Teresa ran to the house area and brought back some blunt knives. "I'm gonna cut the stickers off mine." "Me, too," said Felix.

"How does it smell?" asked the adult. Antoine, who was still very much involved in feeling and tasting the pineapple, said, "Squishy, mine's squishy." "Yes, Antoine," said the adult, smiling, "the pineapple does feel squishy. How about trying to smell it. How does it smell?"

"Mine smells like a, like a, like a...pineapple!" exclaimed Sarah.

The key experiences described in this chapter are the heart of the curriculum framework. Every learning experience should be an active one in at least some of the senses discussed here. The discussions, and the accompanying suggestions for adults, will help adults provide active experiences for young children—the kinds of experiences that are the foundation for cognitive and social development.

Key Experience:
Exploring actively with all the senses

A young child learns what an object is like by experimenting with it—holding, grabbing, climbing on, crawling under, dropping, touching, seeing from many angles, smelling, tasting, hearing. Appearances alone can be misleading. For example, a small, red rubber ball and an apple might appear similar to a young child who has had little previous experience with apples or rubber balls. Facts that would be obvious to adults, such as *one bounces and one doesn't* or *one is good to eat and one isn't* wouldn't be obvious to the child until he explored the objects.

When children have explored an object and discovered its attributes, they begin to understand how the different parts function and fit together, how the object "works" and what the object is really like rather than how it appears. When children discover that the outside part of a pineapple is hard and sticky while the inside part is sweet and juicy, they're beginning to understand that an object may *look* forbidding but may in fact be pleasing to the taste. They learn this by finding it out for themselves, not by being told.

It is important not to confuse passively "experiencing" an object with actively exploring it. A child's experience with an object can indeed be passive—merely watching and listening. We can infer from the following that this is the kind of experience young Charles had at a farm:

Charles' father, knowing that his four-year-old son had visited a farm that day, asked Charles if he knew where milk comes from. Charles said, "Sure. It comes from the store."

Adults often assume that what seems obvious and simple to them will be obvious and simple to young children. We may have forgotten that much of our knowledge of objects was gained through discovery. It's easy to confuse the verbal "knowledge" a four-year-old has with his actual understanding of objects and experiences. The knowledge of objects that comes from direct experience is more likely to remain with the child than knowledge founded on the ability to name or point to an object.

Preschoolers are by nature active explorers of objects. For example, a four-year-old exploring an empty oatmeal box might take the lid off, put some small blocks in it, put the lid back on, shake it, empty it and attempt to put it on his head as a hat. In a group situation, this natural bent of young children may prove challenging to adults. It may be difficult to maintain order and safety at times. It may also be difficult to provide the materials, the time and the space needed for each child to explore actively. Often it may be tempting to have children wait in line, take turns or watch and listen as the *adult* explores an object and talks about it. But if an adult respects the children's desire to explore and understands that this is *one of the most important ways young children learn,* then he or she will see to it that there are ample opportunities for action. Here are some ways to provide these opportunities.

Suggestions for adults

Provide materials that encourage active exploration

Each area of the room should be amply stocked with materials that can be used in a variety of ways—materials that children can manipulate and explore. For example:

HOUSE AREA: egg beater, sifter, coffee pot with insides, food mill, telephone, containers with lids, egg timer, briefcases, small stepladder, boots, gloves, radio, clock, vacuum cleaner.

ART AREA: clay, stapler, pipe cleaners, fabric and carpet scraps, glue, tape, scissors, paint equipment, hole punch, cotton, sponges, small cardboard boxes, styrofoam, egg cartons, paper bags, string, yarn.

BLOCK AREA: take-apart cars and trucks, small rubber people, blocks of all sorts, boxes, boards, sheets, plastic tubing, large styrofoam pieces, carpet samples, small push-cars.

QUIET AREA: beads of different sizes, shapes and colors, small building materials, sound bottles, sandpaper shapes, smelling bottles, puzzles, nesting shape sorters.

Here are some other materials to include in the various areas: real tools, nuts, bolts, nails, wood, screws; musical instruments; sand and water; animals; plants; collections of stones, pinecones, nuts, leaves and other things children find on field trips.

Encourage exploration

As a child is working with materials, ask questions about how things sound, smell, feel, taste or what can be done with them. Such questions can help to extend the child's initial explorations. For instance, as a child is working with playdough, an adult might ask: "How does the playdough feel?" or "What can you do with it?" or "How does it smell?" An adult might also combine observations with questions: "The playdough feels gooey to me, how does it feel to you?" Another technique is to elicit an action from the child rather than a verbal response: "Show me how you could make a noise with the straws." "I can make a house with the blocks; let's see what else we could do with them."

Plan active small-group times

At small-group time, provide materials for each child. When possible, involve children in gathering these materials. Encourage children to do things for themselves and to help each other. They can, for example, open glue bottles, cut their own fruit, use the stapler and mix paint. When the activity is finished, involve children in putting away materials, wiping tables, sweeping the floor and storing finished products.

When planning activities for small groups, consider these questions:

• Can all the children in the group actively participate, not just sit and listen, or look and answer questions?

• Will there be materials for each child to work with?

• Will children be given time to explore materials in their own way?

Explore actively outside the classroom

Take field trips around the neighborhood on which children collect, bring back and explore the things they find: stones, leaves, cans, gum wrappers, twigs, grass, etc. Plan ahead with the place or person being visited to see what active experiences the children can be involved in. For example, plan with the grocery clerk to have the children help fill their grocery bags, or with the gas station attendant to have the children wash the windows of one of the adults' cars. Repeat walks and visits whenever possible. Exploring takes time.

Provide outdoor equipment that allows children to move and use their bodies in different ways. Encourage children to participate in and make up games that involve running, jumping, hopping, rolling, skipping, sliding, crawling, bending, stretching, climbing, pulling, pushing.

Enthusiasm and involvement can be sparked by the addition of new things to explore outside. Here are some examples: animals (rabbits, kittens, a puppy, raccoons, possums, worms, chickens), materials for an obstacle course (barrels, boards, short ladders), large cardboard boxes, telephone-wire spools, rope, chain, digging equipment (and a place to dig), water play, bales of hay or straw.

Key Experience:
Discovering relations through direct experience

As young children become familiar with the objects around them and continue to experiment with them, they become interested in putting them together and using them together. They love to put smaller things inside larger things; they love to stack a set of pots and pans or measuring cups. These activities offer information to children about what objects are like in relation to each other and how they work together. Figuring out how objects in the environment are related is the child's way of structuring his or her world.

Relations between objects that seem obvious to adults (big/little, over/under, heavy/light, inside/outside) aren't obvious to young children. Young children are in the process of discovering these relations and learning to express them. For example, a two-year-old may not be able just to look at two cardboard boxes and say which is bigger, wider, deeper, or taller. The child's knowledge of such relations is acquired through direct experience—bringing the objects together, trying to fit one inside the other, stacking them, and so on. Through direct experience a child learns that one box fits inside another, that juice cans overflow a cup, that one block is on top of another, that the truck is inside the hollow block, that one tower is taller than another, that one truck went faster than the other—

discoveries that are the foundation for an understanding of math and logic, space and time.

The child who is trying to find a block to span the gap between two other blocks is involved in a discovery process. We adults may have forgotten that we learned relations by discovery. Often we're too eager to help a child finish a product—to make something "right" or to do something "right" the first time—and we want to feed children the solutions to their problems. In so doing, we deprive the children of the chance to find out for themselves, which is to say that we deprive them of the chance to learn. Whether the child finds the right block isn't nearly so important as the fact that he or she is discovering relations through direct experience.

Suggestions for adults

Help children discover relations

Encourage children to talk about what they're doing. For example:

"Joanie, you've been working hard all morning. Tell me about your building."

"I see that you painted two pictures, Harry. How is this one different from the other?"

Make observations about children's work, pointing out relations. For example:

"You *did* make a tall tower, Lynnette! And you know what else you did, you made it taller than the block shelf."

"You made such a long necklace with the beads, Angelette. And you used all different colored beads."

"John made a neat tunnel. Now he's driving his car through it."

"The rock Liz dropped in the water went straight to the bottom of the tub."

Avoid doing things for children that they can do on their own. Sometimes adults don't stop to think that a task, while trivial from a grownup point of view, is significant for a child; for the adult it is more important to have it done "correctly" or quickly. Some common examples are putting on boots and coats, mixing paint, washing brushes, pouring juice. Children discover relations through such small, "routine" tasks, just as they do by turning on lights, arranging chairs around a table, cleaning the table after a snack.

When a child needs help in solving a problem, help him think of alternatives instead of solving the problem for him. These children need help in solving problems:

• *Wendy has built a "toybox" for all the animals in the block area by stacking three small hollow blocks on top of each other. Now she's frustrated because not all of the rubber animals will fit inside.*

• *Karl is trying to put a roof on the school he built in the block area. None of the blocks will span the area between the walls.*

• *Corey is having trouble attaching a flattened can to a collage he's making in the art area.*

Here are some ways an adult could help:

Wendy—Help her to think of some ways she could change her box so that all the animals would fit inside. If she can't come up with any ideas, offer her some choices. For example, she might use one big hollow block instead of three little ones, or she might use a fourth little one.

Karl—Help Karl to think of other things besides blocks to make a roof. If he can't see any possibilities on his own, offer some alternatives. For example, he could use a piece of carpet, or pieces of paper taped together.

Corey—Suggest to Corey that there are other ways to make the can stick. Encourage him to look around the room for other materials. If he has trouble, offer some suggestions. For example, he could try glue, or tape, or string.

Key Experience:
Manipulating, transforming and combining materials

As children become familiar with the materials around them, they begin to explore the ways in which these materials can be combined, changed and used. Consider a four-year-old playing in a sandbox. The sand, which was loose while being poured from spoon to pan, becomes hard as the child packs it to make a level panful. The child adds water to the sand, and now the loose, dry solid has become soupy, almost a liquid. As the child molds the wet sand, the smooth, flat surface becomes a series of mounds and craters.

Sand play is just one of countless activities in which young children manipulate, transform and combine materials. Other examples can be found in art activities such as painting, cutting and pasting, drawing and making collages; in building with blocks or tinkertoys; in bead stringing; in blowing bubbles with soap and water. As children manipulate, transform and combine materials they discover relations between objects and between actions and events. For example, while actively involved in a seemingly simple activity such as stringing beads, a child is learning the relation of cause and effect: tying the knot at the end of the string (cause) keeps the beads on the string (effect).

The child's actions upon materials give adults clues about what types of discoveries he's made. Some young children may be more interested in the active *process* of manipulating, combining and transforming materials than in the *products* of such activities. For example, a child who is painting may be more interested in mixing the paints and dipping and stroking with the brush than making a "picture" of something.

For the young child, *access* to materials, *freedom* to manipulate, transform and combine them in his or her own way and *time* to do so are the essentials of the process of discovery. Adults can provide these essentials. Here are some suggestions.

Suggestions for adults

Provide materials that children can manipulate, transform and combine

Here are some suggested materials:

BLOCK AREA—a variplay, large tinkertoys that can be reassembled in a variety of ways

HOUSE AREA—blankets, scarves, large pieces of fabric for dress-up; wigs and dress-up clothes; buttons, pokerchips, bottlecaps, stones and nuts for "cooking;" real foods that can be made by children—popcorn, hot cereal, chocolate milk, frozen orange juice

ART AREA—playdough, clay and materials that can be added to them like toothpicks, styrofoam bits, popsicle sticks; material scraps, needles, thread, buttons; paints the children can mix; liquid starch for combining with paint to make fingerpaint; food coloring; bendable things like wire, rubber bands, elastic, pipe cleaners, aluminum foil, plastic straws; sawdust, glue

QUIET AREA—magnets and magnifying glasses; stringable objects other than beads such as washers, buttons and straws; "connecto" straws

OUTSIDE AREA—sand, water, containers, spoons and shovels; forms for making dirt and snow "bricks" (a wooden box without a top or bottom into which snow or dirt can be packed

Each child makes his own fingerpaint by combining liquid starch and powder tempera paint. The adult asks questions and talks with each child about the changes that occur as he mixes the starch and paint and makes designs or pictures and "erases" them by smoothing them over with his hands.

Each child has his own musical instrument. Pairs of children play their instruments together. The adult asks questions and talks with them about the sounds they have combined. The sounds can be recorded and played back to see if the children can identify the instruments.

Support children's use of materials

Adults must be attuned not only to the products of a child's manipulation of materials but also to the process of discovery the child is experiencing. It's often easier to praise a product than to support and encourage a process. In the following example a child was involved in using materials and an adult was supporting this process:

Jeff was at the construction table. He'd been trying for several minutes to make a hole in a small board. He'd tried a screwdriver and a pair of scissors and finally succeeded with a hammer and nail. An adult said, "Good, Jeff. You tried several things to make a hole in that board and now you made one with a nail and a hammer."

Extend children's use of materials

Adults can sometimes extend a child's involvement with materials by offering the child choices when he or she seems to be stumped. Adults can also redirect a child who is frustrated or whose activity is inappropriate. For example:

Marky was playing with the large tinkertoys. He'd put several together end to end to form a pole and was now standing on tiptoes, hands stretched over his head, trying to touch the ceiling with the

and easily removed); gyms that come in several pieces and can be combined by children in many ways; logs, boards, sturdy boxes

Plan small-group activities in which children manipulate, transform and combine materials

At the beginning of the school year it's usually a good idea to introduce each child to the areas and the materials in each area. A good small-group activity for the first week of school is to use some of the materials from each area. This will help the children to become familiar with the materials and the adults to become aware of how each child in the group uses materials. Here are two examples:

pole. An adult said, "What do you need to do to your pole to make it touch the ceiling?" Marky thought, then shrugged his shoulders. "Would a round disc like this work or do you need a stick?"

Todd was banging two pots together in the house area, creating a great noise. Several children in that area were holding their ears. An adult said to Todd, "Wow, they really make a loud noise. But I think it's hurting Leslie's ears. You could use the pans to make a soft noise or you could fill them with bottle caps."

Now think of choices to offer the children in these examples, choices that will extend or redirect their use of materials:

Troy is in the quiet area. He has three containers filled with wooden beads of different shapes in front of him. He grabs a handful of beads from one container and tosses them. They scatter and roll across the floor.

Erin and Betsy have built an elaborate train using hollow blocks and flat boards. Peter begins to use the top of the train as a road for his toy car.

Talk to children about what they're doing

If a child is using pipe cleaners to make jewelry for his mother, for example, an adult might say, "I bet your mother is really going to like this necklace, Johnny. It's got big loops and little loops all joined together."

The adult can ask an open question about how the child is changing or transforming his materials. If the child is unable to respond, the adult can make the question more specific: "How did you change the straight pipe cleaners so they turned into circles?"

The adult must give the child time to respond. If he can't articulate what he did, she can ask him to show her. Then she can say some-

thing like, "Oh, I see. You're taking a straight pipe cleaner and bending it into a circle and then twisting the ends together. That's a good idea."

Key Experience:
Choosing materials, activities, purposes

Our discussion of active learning so far has been concerned with children's experience of their environment—their explorations and discoveries. Another important aspect of active learning is children's freedom to initiate—to decide where they will work, what they will work with, what they will do and how they will do it.

The process of choosing materials, activities and purposes helps young children see themselves as people who can generate ideas and structure their own time. It gives them a view of themselves as "doers" and problem solvers.

But three-, four- and five-year-olds in a new group situation can be amazingly timid and acquiescent. They don't calmly master the routine and the room arrangement the first day and then proceed to make choices about what they're going to do and how they're going to do it. So it's not enough merely to say that young children should make choices and structure their own time. They need the help of adults. Here are some suggestions.

Suggestions for adults

Provide a consistent daily routine

A consistent routine helps children structure their own time and be responsible for their own actions. It gives them a way of understanding time and of knowing what is happening next and preparing for it. Chapter 3 presents a detailed view of the daily routine for cognitively oriented programs.

Suggestions for helping children learn the routine:
- Post a daily schedule using objects, photographs, pictures and/or names of the times of the day.
- Follow all of the parts of the routine each day.
- During planning time review the parts of the day.
- If a field trip is to be taken, discuss how the routine will be different that day.

Help the children learn the arrangement of the room

These questions will help teaching teams evaluate their room arrangement:
- Does the room have several well defined work areas for the children (block area, house area, art area, quiet area)?
- Can the children see and reach all the materials they can use themselves?
- Is space provided for each child to store his personal belongings?
- Are there materials that can be used in a variety of ways?
- Are there various materials that can all be used to do the same thing (glue, tape, stapler, hammer and nails, thumbtacks)?

Chapter 1 discusses these and other aspects of arranging and equipping a classroom.

Help the children learn where materials belong

Have the children themselves put away the materials they have played with. When new materials are brought to the room, have the children decide where to put them and how they should

be marked. They could look through magazines for pictures of the new materials or trace them, draw pictures or even take photographs.

At small-group time, use materials from each work area. Let the children explore the materials and then put them back.

Help the children work imaginatively with materials

Bette has been playing alone in the block area with the dump truck for two weeks. What are some things an adult could do?

If Bette is still exploring the truck, learning all the things it can do (that it can roll, that things can be put in it, that part of it lifts up, that it can be pushed), an adult might want to add to her experience by talking with her about it. However, if she seems to be at a loss for things to do with the truck or does the same thing each day, the adult might offer her alternatives. For example, the adult could suggest that she use or make a similar object in another area. Perhaps she could make a dump truck at the workbench, paint a picture or make a model of a dump truck in the art area, or build roads in the sandbox for the smaller trucks.

The adult might also try to involve Bette with other children. Perhaps she could drive the truck to Joanie's house or haul animals to Billie's farm.

Sometimes a child stays in one area because he is unaware of the other things he can do. Having an adult explore possibilities with him before he begins to plan might help him make a different choice. He and an adult could tour the work areas or play with some materials before he makes a plan for work time.

Some children seem to have little trouble thinking of things to make and build, but they do need an adult's help in thinking about what to do with their object or structure once they've completed it. Adults should be able to identify and assist children who need help in extending their plans. (See chapter 2, the section on work time, for ways to help children extend plans.)

Help children recognize that they've made choices

Sometimes children don't describe or say aloud every choice they make, but adults can still help them recognize that they have made choices. Here is an example of an adult acknowledging a young child's choices:

Angelette has taken a small balloon and pasted bits of paper and some glitter on it.

Adult: "Oh, Angelette, look what you made. What can you tell me about it?"

Angelette: "It's a fish."

Adult: "You made a fish out of your balloon. What a good idea. And you pasted some paper on— all different colors of paper—and some glitter. What are these parts here?"

Angelette: "Those are the eyes and this is the mouth and these are the scary parts."

Adult: "So you used round pieces of paper to make eyes and the glitter to make it scary. Boy, it sure looks scary to me. Those were good ideas. Is there anything else you've planned to do with your fish?"

Provide opportunities for choosing even in "structured" small-group activities

By planning small-group activities to which each child can respond in his or her own way, adults can offer children choices. Consider these three questions when planning any small-group activity:

• If the activity focuses on a product, is there attention to the process, the "how-you-do-it" aspect?

• Are the steps to be followed in the activity flexible or are all children expected to be doing the same thing at the same time?

• Are divergent products and processes encouraged or are children expected to follow the adult's example?

Key Experience: Acquiring skills with tools and equipment

As children grow, they acquire more complex and sophisticated means of interacting with their environment. Babies act on objects in such simple ways as pushing, pulling, grasping, shaking, dropping and banging. By age three, children are capable of putting two or more of these actions together and coordinating them to use tools and equipment. Consider the actions involved in making a "pushcar" go. The child must grasp the wheel, turn it to steer and push with his feet, all at the same time. When a child hammers he must grasp the hammer, steady the grasp, aim and pound.

Experiences with simple tools and equipment (by "equipment" we mean such things as wheel toys, climbers, swings, egg beaters, cameras, cider presses, food grinders, staplers, etc.) are important for developing the skills necessary to perform more controlled, complex actions. As young children use tools and equipment, they're developing skills which lead to competence—the ability to do things on their own and to solve ever more complex problems.

Opportunities for problem-solving are plentiful when children work with tools: a child tries to find a nail that's long enough to make two pieces of wood stay together; another tries to find a piece of wood the right size for one side of his birdhouse. Children also experience cause-and-effect relations when working with tools: sawing fast makes lots of sawdust; turning the handle of the egg beater faster makes more bubbles. Experience with tools and equipment also helps children develop coordination of their small-motor and large-motor actions.

Suggestions for adults

Set up a construction area

A sturdy table, a large piece of wood or an old tree stump will do for the core of a construction area if a workbench isn't available. Include tools such as hammers, saws, clamps, vises, a hand drill, a screwdriver and pliers. Some materials to include might be wood (soft pine), styrofoam, cardboard, wire, carpet scraps, spools, plastic containers, aluminum containers, lids, bottlecaps. An ample supply of nails, woodscrews, nuts and bolts, wire, paste, rubber bands, thumbtacks and glue gives children many ways to bind materials. (See chapter 1, the section on arranging and equipping a construction area, for further ideas.)

Support children's use of tools and equipment

Activities that require complex tools and equipment (such as cooking, making popcorn, playing the phonograph, using the electric vacuum cleaner) are often appropriate for young children but require constant and careful supervision by adults. These activities are good for small-group time because then the adult has a fixed number of children to work with and an opportunity to structure the time.

Make a list of tools and equipment and keep track of each child's progress

List the skills with tools and equipment you wish the children to acquire and plan ways for each child to become proficient. One teaching team came up with this list: painting, mixing paints, gluing, stapling, taping, cutting, stringing, pouring, hammering, sawing, dressing and undressing. They worked with each child throughout the year as situations arose and sometimes during small-group times specifically planned around one or more of those skills.

Key Experience:
Using the large muscles

Active learning for a preschooler means learning with the whole body. It means climbing on top of a large block tower to see how things look from up there, moving the chairs and table in the art area to mop up the paint that spilled there, crawling fast on all fours pretending to be the baby, pushing five people all over the playground on the taxi. This whole-body learning need not be synonymous with chaos but rather should be expected, planned for and delighted in.

Suggestions for adults

Include physical therapy for children with special needs

In many programs, children with physical-therapy needs are taken from the classroom to a special therapy room for individual treatment. This can be very disruptive to the child's social development and nascent feeling of belonging. When physical therapists and regular classroom adults work together, however, very often they can come up with ways of integrating the child's special physical needs into the daily routine so that the child's deficits aren't singled out but are worked on naturally throughout the normal day. Perhaps a child needs exercises to strengthen his legs; these might be built into a game that all the children could participate in and enjoy. A physical therapist can also work with a child during outside time when everyone else is engaged in similar activities.

Provide equipment on which children can exercise their large muscles

Be sure to include some of the following: climbers, slide, swings, balls of different sizes, large packing barrels and boxes, railroad ties for balancing, wagons, tricycles, wheelbarrows, sandbox, ropes and pulleys, ladders, large sewer pipes, large wooden spools.

Provide space and a time in the daily routine for children to be involved in vigorous indoor or outdoor activities

Include both "structured" activities (relay races, obstacle courses, dances) and activities in which children use play equipment as they wish. Encourage all children to take part. Some children may need adults to swing or climb or bounce balls with them to get started.

Support each child at his or her own level of coordination and muscular development

Some children, for example, may be able to swing and pump by themselves, while others may be unable to get on the swing unassisted. Each child is entitled to an adult's support and encouragement.

Key Experience: Taking care of one's own needs

Children enjoy doing things for themselves and grow in ability and self-confidence as they do so. Even infants, once they've figured out how, want to hold their own bottles and then feed themselves with their fingers with no help from anyone. The just-turned-toddler doesn't want a

hand to hold any more. He climbs up and gets down by himself and proudly carries his own book just like his big sister, who at 2½ undresses herself, carries her own books back to the library, puts her blocks away with no help from mom or dad, fills up the dogs' dishes with dog food and washes her hands all by herself. Respecting a young child's insistence that "I do it" often requires time and patience, but the child's pride in accomplishment is well worth any inconvenience it may cause an adult at home or in school.

By the time children reach preschool age, their repertoire of self-help skills has greatly expanded, unless they've never had the opportunity to help themselves. They're quick to respond to an environment which supports their desires for more independence. Adults who expect, encourage and provide time for children to do things for themselves are actively nurturing the child's concept of himself as one who can do, who has the capacity to help himself as well as others. This applies to all preschoolers—preschoolers with "special needs," "gifted" preschoolers and "normal" preschoolers. Helping children learn to help themselves is one of the most important ways adults can be of service to young children.

Suggestions for adults

Provide time for children to do things for themselves

When cold weather sets in, remember to provide extra time in the daily routine for children to get into and out of boots, hats, mittens and jackets. Although it may be faster and more convenient for adults to tend to the buckles and zippers, given a chance to master these skills, preschoolers become quite adept and efficient themselves.

The same is true at snack and meal times. Allow and encourage children to pass, pour, mix, stir, cut, spread and wipe up spills, even though the adult in charge could execute these tasks speedily and without any mess. Remember that the importance of snack and meal times isn't just in the eating but also in the social and physical learning that takes place.

It's never too early for children to learn that cleaning up is part of any activity they undertake. For young children, cleaning up can be a source of pride and satisfaction if adults show that they're confident in the children's ability to do a good job, and if they have the patience to see it through—young children often don't clean

up rapidly because this "task" is still a form of play for them.

Make self-help a part of every activity

Art activities in particular are often ones in which adults prefer to overlook opportunities for children to do things for themselves. But with a little initial guidance children are perfectly able to select and mix their own paints, cut their own strips of paper and glue, paste and tape their own collages.

Plan for children in terms of doing things for themselves

Children differ in their ability to do things for themselves. A child from a large family may already be quite self-sufficient, while a child confined to a wheelchair, for example, may never have helped himself in any way. Adults could capitalize on the first child's knowledge by encouraging him to help others, particularly the handicapped child. Helping a handicapped child do things for himself takes some ingenuity on the part of the teaching staff as well as the understanding and cooperation of the parents. One teaching team, for example, devised a tray that attached to the arms of a child's wheelchair so that he could carry whatever he needed to any area—by himself.

Related films and publications from the High/Scope Foundation

Films—

(For a complete description of each film and instructions for ordering, see appendix 4.)

Helping Children Make Choices and Decisions series: 1. *A Good Classroom is a Classroom Full of Choices;* 2. *Questions That Help Children Develop Their Ideas;* 3. *Exploring the Possibilities of the Room;* 4. *Acknowledging Children's Choices and Decisions;* 5. *Planning Activities that Include Choices*

Guidelines for Evaluating Activities series: 1. *Contrasting Teaching Styles: Small-Group Time;* 2. *Contrasting Teaching Styles: Work Time, the Art Area;* 3. *Contrasting Teaching Styles: Circle Time*

Starting with Direct Experience from **Experiencing and Representing** series

A Way Children Learn from **Experiencing and Representing** series

Supporting Children's Intellectual & Physical Development

A Place to Build All Kinds of Structures from **The Block Area** series

A Place to Explore New Materials from **The Block Area** series

Parental Support of Early Learning series: 1. *Opportunities for Learning;* 2. *Babies Like Attention;* 3. *A Special Kind of Mother;* 4. *Learning Through Problems: A Baby's Point of View;* 5. *Cans: Toys for Learning;* 6. *Responding to Baby's Actions* (Parent-infant education)

Publications—

The Cognitively Oriented Curriculum—Learning Through Music (No. 5) (booklet) by Lynne Seifert, 1979. (Elementary grades)

Children of all ages can be music makers—from exploring sounds to playing instruments. This guide encompasses both the practical aspects of organizing, introducing and helping elementary-age children make their own music and the theoretical rationale upon which this approach is based. Sections on key music experiences, practical considerations, and group activities provide teachers with activities and strategies for establishing music in the classroom.

The Cognitively Oriented Curriculum—Learning Through Play and Drama (boklet) by Richard Lalli, 1979. (Elementary grades)

This guide looks at drama from its informal roots as role play and casual interaction to the more advanced forms of scripted performances. It discusses in detail the various elements of drama for elementary-level children, (i.e., role play and language opportunities) and offers teachers practical suggestions for 1) introducing drama into the classroom, 2) extending children's spontaneous role play into more planned drama experiences, and 3) helping children make their own dramatic events. The booklet details ways of extending play to include writing experiences in the forms of scripts, stories and scenarios.

The Cognitively Oriented Curriculum–Learning Through Sewing & Pattern Design (No. 4) (booklet) by Sheila Mainwaring, 1978. (Elementary grades)

How to set up a sewing area in the elementary classroom and how to make it a vital center for learning and cognitive development.

Home Teaching with Mothers and Infants: The Ypsilanti-Carnegie Infant Education Project (book, 129 pp.) by D.Z. Lambie, J.T. Bond, D.P. Weikart, 1975.

An account of an experiment in home-based parent-infant education. Chapters on the project's philosophy, the implementation of the program, the experimental design, and the results of the research are included.

Related reading on active learning

Almy, M. "Spontaneous Play: An Avenue for Intellectual Development," in *Early Childhood Education Rediscovered,* J.L. Frost, ed. New York: Holt, Rinehart, and Winston, 1968.

Chittenden, Edward A. "What is Learned and What is Taught?" *Young Children,* October, 1969. pp. 12-19.

DeVries, Rheta and Constance Kamii. *Why Group Games? A Piagetian Perspective.* Urbana, Illinois: ERIC Publications Office, 1975.

Dewey, John. "My Pedagogic Creed" in *John Dewey on Education, Selected Writings,* Reginald D. Archambault, ed. Chicago: The University of Chicago Press, 1964. pp. 427-439.

Duckworth, Eleanor. "The Having of Wonderful Ideas," *Harvard Educational Review,* Vol. 42, No. 2, May, 1972. pp. 217-231.

Flavell, John H. *The Developmental Psychology of Jean Piaget.* Princeton, New Jersey: Van Nostrand, 1963. Chapter 2.

Ginsburg, Herbert and Sylvia Opper. "Implications for Education," in *Piaget's Theory of Intellectual Development, An Introduction.* Englewood Cliffs, New Jersey: Prentice-Hall, 1969. pp. 218-232.

Hawkins, F.P. *The Logic of Action–Young Children at Work.* New York: Pantheon Books, 1974.

Johnson, Harriet. "The Art of Block Building," in *The Block Book,* Elisabeth S. Hirsch, ed. Washington, D.C.: NAEYC, 1974.

6/ Language

The precise role played by language in intellectual development is still a matter of great controversy among developmental theorists. Historically, we have moved away from the notion that language *is* thought, or that language *precedes* thought. Piaget stresses the primacy of mental transformations over language; the development of a child's language abilities *follows* more profound changes in the child's thought processes, rather than being the cause of these changes. A position taken by many American developmental psycholinguists is that cognitive and linguistic development proceed hand-in-hand, in a mutually constraining relationship.

Other controversies in the area of linguistic research and theory bear more directly on classroom practice. Much research has been devoted to the issue of the alleged incompatibility between subcultural dialects and the "standard" language of the school, this being a possible cause of school failure. There have been debates over "deficit" versus "difference" interpretations of ethnic, regional and social-class dialects and over the question of bilingualism in education. By and large, the attitudes of educators and parents towards the specific language goals of educational programs are more strongly influenced by ethnic, social-class and national group values than by linguistic theories.

It seems clear, regardless of one's predilections in these matters, that language is both a tool for thinking and a means of communication, and that it should be supported as such by educators. Language should not bear the burden of the teaching/learning process in young children

but should be embedded in what we call "active learning." Language is not to be separated out from the key experiences of the curriculum but integrated with them. Some of the strategies that apply in general to the key experiences apply specifically to language in the following ways:

• Concrete ⎯⎯⎯⎯→ abstract

Language is an arbitrary symbolic system in the sense that words typically bear no similarity to the things and concepts they stand for. Since it is such an "abstract" symbol system to begin with, yet one that even very young children are already struggling to master, *language should be tied in wherever possible to direct experience;* new vocabulary, concepts and linguistic forms should be introduced by the adult in connection with a concrete activity undertaken by the child.

• Simple ⎯⎯⎯⎯→ complex

A child's language becomes more complex in a predictable, sequential way. Researchers have charted this progress for preschool-age children. The complexity evolves, not in response to adults' patient modification of teaching objectives, but rather as a result of the conversational give-and-take between child and adult, in which the invitations to talk presented by the adult are more important than explicit reward contingencies or learning sequences. Adults naturally model language that's more complex than the child's. This seems to be effective if it doesn't give the child the message that his or her language is inadequate. Complexity in the child's language will evolve—at a different rate for each child.

• Here/now ⎯⎯⎯⎯→ there/then

Language permits us to convey to others information about unseen or remote events.

Sometimes this capacity of language fools us into thinking that we've taught a preschooler something that he or she hasn't experienced directly. Frequently we've only taught the child to parrot our words. For one thing, the relational concepts which convey information about remote events (the where/when/why kinds of information) have not been securely mastered by the preschooler. Our recommendation is to extend language gradually into the future and past, via the *planning process,* talking about what the child has done and what the child will do, with whom, how, and so on. As children develop in the years between three and five it certainly is reasonable that adults should be expanding the temporal and spatial perspective of conversations. We add a caution that this be done gradually and always in relation to a core of shared experience; this will help the child to master abstract concepts and become a better communicator and problem-solver.

～

The growing mastery of language is one of the signal differences between the preschool-age child and the infant. Preschoolers are learning both the syntactic rules of their dominant language (and perhaps others) and the meanings of specific words. By the time they enter school many children have mastered most of the grammar of their dominant language.

Children evolve language rule systems in predictable stages, stages which show great consistency of sequence across children, just as do the stages of cognitive development. Psycholinguists have not, however, found the specific mechanisms by which adults can accelerate or inhibit language development. Like cognitive development, language development proceeds as a matter of course in the normal child. However, we regard it as axiomatic that the *richness* and *scope,* rather than the pace, of development in any sphere—be it that of logic or "affect" or language—is strongly influenced by the quality of the child's transactions with the environment; this, indeed, is the *raison d'être* of the developmental approach to education.

Key Experience: Talking with other children and adults about personally meaningful experiences

Ms. Flores begins small-group time by saying, "Let's all cut open our pumpkins." The children start right in. Liz asks, "Can I mark a line, and then cut?" "Hey, that's a good idea, Liz," Ms. Flores replies. As they get their pumpkins open Ms. Flores asks them how they might get the seeds out. "I'm gonna get a spoon to get mine out." "Look, Lisa's dumping hers over." She asks them about the insides of their pumpkins. "Icky." "Yuk, it tastes awful." "Timmy's has little hairs inside." Juan passes on some family knowledge: "My mom said we can eat these seeds. They taste like peanuts." Ms. Flores replies, "That's a good idea. What could we use to put them in?" "We could put them in a cake pan," Victor suggests. "I'm gonna keep mine in my juice cup," Erin decides.

Notice that Ms. Flores doesn't insist on "teaching" the names for things and doesn't impose her own ideas and preconceptions. Instead, she allows the children to discover things for themselves, encourages them to talk about their discoveries and responds to what they have to say, because she realizes that when children are free to converse about personally meaningful experiences, they use language to deal with ideas and problems that are real and important to them. As the children communicate their thoughts through language and listen to each other's ideas and comments, they learn that their personal way of speaking is effective and respected.

Listening to and talking with children is full of rewards for children and adults: children enjoy the respect and attention of a responsive adult, and adults are continually rejuvenated by the children's freshness of thought and perception. Even the most routine question—"What is your plan today?"—can evoke an unexpected response—"I want to rock and play and stare at the sky."

Key experiences: Language
- Talking with others about personally meaningful experiences
- Describing objects, events and relations
- Expressing feelings in words
- Having one's own spoken language written down and read back
- Having fun with language

When children are free to talk about subjects of their own choosing, and free to respond in their own way to topics to which they've been directed, they reveal unique perceptions, interests and concerns. Consequently, the more opportunities children have to talk with other children and adults about personally meaningful experiences, the more opportunities adults have to come to know each child. One extremely important role of classroom staff, therefore, is to create and maintain an environment in which children enjoy conversing, feel free to express their thoughts and feelings and know they will be listened to and acknowledged by a sympathetic respondent. Here are some ways adults can provide such an environment.

Suggestions for adults

Take advantage of opportunities for communication in the plan-do-review sequence

One reason for the plan-do-review sequence is the numerous occasions it presents for children to talk with one another. By having a time for planning, followed by work time and recall time, adults are giving children the opportunity to talk with each other about their plans, ideas, problems and experiences.

Whenever possible, encourage children to talk about their plans together. Such opportunities occur when two or three children want to work with each other at work time but haven't settled on the object of their united energies. Or two or three children might want to use the same blocks or musical instruments or tools; their planning together will entail ways of coordinating or modifying their original ideas.

At work time when a child is having difficulty completing or extending a project, encourage the child to solicit help from other children; help the child see and approach other children as possible resources.

At recall time, adults can encourage children to discuss what they saw each other doing, ask each other questions and offer each other suggestions and ideas. Such exchanges help children begin to realize that communicating is more than just talking. It's listening, thinking and sharing ideas, too.

Encourage interaction and cooperation among children

Young children are able to interact positively and cooperate with one another when they are given incentives and reasons to do so. In the context of their self-chosen activities, children can be en-

couraged to talk to each other instead of pushing, grabbing or shoving, and to help each other if they have skills others can use. By allowing children to help each other in their activities, adults are putting children in contact with each other and thus promoting natural conversation.

Adults can initiate large-group tasks like scrubbing down the art area or planting or weeding an outdoor garden in which each child must coordinate his or her efforts with someone else's. Adults can also provide indoor and outdoor equipment which can be used by several children at a time, for example, tents, sheets, wagons, rocking boats, two- or three-seater riding toys, large take-apart toys, a standard-size wheelbarrow. One teaching team was amazed at the amount of conversation and cooperation that occurred between two usually quiet children

who were successfully operating a large tank-type vacuum cleaner together at clean-up time:

"Okay, Markie. You push this metal thing."

"Can't go. Stuck."

"Wait. I got it now. I got this hose thing. Now go."

"There it goes. There it goes. Ohhh, eee!"

"The dirt goes up under. Here's some more."

"Stop! Cut it off . . ."

Another important way adults can provide opportunities for verbal interplay and cooperation among children is to support and encourage role play. When children assume roles, they often speak more volubly and with more animation to their fellow role-players than they do when they're not pretending. Specific suggestions for role play can be found in chapter 7.

Refer one child's questions or problems to another

Rick was having trouble getting his block tower to stand without wobbling. An adult suggested that Dorie, who was building nearby, might have some ideas.

_____

Arlene was concerned about the bandage over Peter's eye. When she asked an adult about it, she suggested to Arlene that maybe Peter would tell her.

_____

"Ivan, Bill is trying to make these two cans stay together with glue, but they keep falling apart. Do you have an idea how he can make them stay together?"

Adults can promote conversations between children by redirecting one child's question to another child, by asking a child to see what another child has done to solve a similar problem and by asking one child to help another.

Interpret and deliver messages

Mr. Yanez observed M.G., an English speaker, roaming around the block area, and went over to see if he needed help getting started. Aquiles, a Spanish-dominant child, was just placing his sign on the block area planning board.

Mr. Yanez: *"M.G., I thought your plan was to build a house in* el rincon de los bloques.*"*

M.G.: *"I was gonna, but Totor and Jimbo have 'em all."*

Mr. Yanez: *"They did get all the blocks because they made their plan and got started before you did. Is there anything else you could use to build your house?"*

M.G.: *(shakes his head)*

Mr. Yanez: *"Let's look around and see if there's something else you could use. Hey,* maybe Aquiles would like to help you. Aquiles, podrias ayudarle a M.G.? Quiere construir una casa pero los bloques ya estan ocupados. Que mas podriamos usar para hacer una house?*"*

Aquiles: *"Los tinker toys."*

Mr. Yanez: *"Aquiles said we could use the tinker toys. What do you think, M.G., would that work?"*

M.G.: *"And we could cover it with that thing and hide inside!"*

Mr. Yanez: *"Oh, the sheet! That sounds like a good idea!* Aquiles, M.G. dice que podrian cubrir la tinker toy house con esta sabana y esconderse adentro! *Would you two like to work together building your* casa? Les gustaria trabajar juntos a construir la casa?*" Mr. Yanez helps them get some giant tinker toys, and the boys start working together.)*

In every preschool classroom there are likely to be children who do not speak or whose speech is difficult for other children to understand for any one of a variety of reasons: developmental delay, a speech impediment, deafness or another language or dialect. For these children it's vital that classroom adults serve as interpreters and message-givers. This means that at least one adult must "speak the child's language," know sign language or, through close observation and trial and error, be able to learn a child's personal language of gestures and sounds. Thus, interpretation and message-giving could include anything from translation, as Mr. Yanez did for M.G. and Aquiles, to interpreting a child's non-verbal cues. For example, an adult might say, "Rayette, when Bobbie points to your road and smiles and says 'Ga ga ga' it means he'd like to run his car on your road. Ask him if he'd like to join you."

Some children will eventually begin to take over the role of interpreter themselves, which is good both for the child doing the interpreting and the child being interpreted. The latter feels good because he can talk directly to his friend who can understand him, while his friend has the morally valuable experience of stepping outside of himself to meet another's need.

Fill in the context for children's out-of-context statements

Grisha leaves his friends in the block area to watch a fire truck rush by on the street outside. When it has passed he returns to his friends who are still building the elaborate tower he had been helping them with, saying, "Went there yesterday. Come on, let's get the poles and the beds." His friends look at him uncomprehendingly, then return to their building. He tries to add two broom handles to the tower. "Look, we need the poles to go down fast." An adult helps him out by explaining to the others, "Grisha saw the fire truck go by and remembered our trip to the fire station last month. Now he wants to pretend the tower is a fire station and the poles are the poles the firemen slide down to get to their fire truck." "Okay," one of the builders responds. "Let's make a station right here next to the tower. Poles go here . . ."

Children frequently make statements that seem to be "out of the blue" because they've been following their own thought processes without informing their playmates of the links between one topic of conversation and the next. Adults who know the children in their classroom and are aware of some of their immediate and past experiences can often help fill in the context for out-of-context statements and so make it possible for conversations to occur or continue.

Encourage active listening

Part of helping children have conversations with other children and adults is helping them learn to listen to the other half of the conversation. Here are some ways adults can encourage active listening:

Ask a child to look at what another child is trying to show him. It's easier for a child to listen if he can focus his attention on the object under discussion.

_____

Call a child's attention to what another child has just said to him. Some children become so absorbed in what they're doing that they don't respond to conversational openers or requests addressed to them. If they do this all the time, other children may no longer attempt to speak with them.

_____

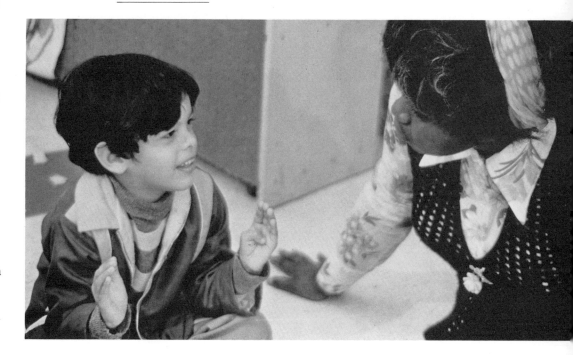

Help a domineering child find ways to control his desire to have the first and last word and to understand that other people also want to express their thoughts and feelings.

Be available for conversation

If children are to have meaningful conversations with classroom adults, they must feel that adults desire and enjoy such exchanges. Adults can display their willingness to converse by:

Using a conversational tone of voice rather than a "teachery" or "sugary" tone. Children are unusually adept at detecting a facade.

Listening to what a child is saying. Look at the child and at the object he or she may be showing you. There's nothing more discouraging than trying to talk with someone who doesn't appear to be paying attention to you.

Making physical contact with the child. It can be brief; it shouldn't be excessive but it shouldn't be withheld, as long as the child is willing to be touched. Holding a child's hand, putting an arm around a child's shoulder, holding a child on your lap are ways of letting children know that what they say and do are really important.

Learning and remembering each child's particular interests. Ms. Adams, for example, knew that Tommy was particularly interested in and knowledgeable about farm equipment, so she brought in an advertisement for tractors she had received in the mail and asked him to explain the different tractors pictured on it. "I'll help you," he said, very pleased at her request.

Acknowledge and respect the child's role in conversations with adults

Years ago, children were supposed to be seen but not heard and speak only when spoken to. When adults did address children it was more often for instructive purposes than for an informal chat. Unimaginable as this approach to children seems today, many classroom adults, once they do engage children in conversation, tend toward didacticism by dominating the conversation, correcting "mistakes" and telling children how to do what they're trying to do or say what they're trying to say.

Adults who acknowledge and respect children's role in conversation usually listen as much as they talk and recognize the children's ideas by including them in their own speech:

Child: *Hey! Look at here! Look at my way-high-up boy.*

Adult: *My goodness. You do have a way-high-up boy. What's he doing way up there?*

Child: *He's a lookin' and a lookin'. "There he is," he says and his dad gets his truck and gets it in his truck and takes it home for the little boy. It's a little dog for the little boy.*

Adult: *Oh, I see. The little boy got way high up so he could find a little dog?*

Child: *Yep. And his dad helps him, too, 'cause he wanted a little dog so much but he couldn't see on the ground so he went way high up to see. Hey, Ronnie, come here and see this way-high-up boy . . .*

This way of dealing with children requires focusing on *what* children say rather than on how they say it. Worries about grammar, dialect or pronunciation are misplaced with preschool children, who are learning to use language as a tool; success in using language to communicate, to represent and to solve problems is more im-

portant for them than "correct" language usage or syntax. Respecting and accepting each child's way of speaking is critical to his or her language development.

Stick to the subject, as set by the child, and let the child take the lead in conversation. If a child wants to talk about trains or about a building he's making, talk about trains or the building. Don't entice children into conversation or respond to their desire to converse and then use the opportunity to "quiz," "instruct" or introduce an unrelated topic.

Maintain a balance between child and adult talk throughout the day

Adults should be ready both to initiate conversations with children and to respond to conversations children begin. An adult who was learning to implement the Cognitively Oriented Curriculum in her day care center was aston-ished to hear herself in the background of a videotape made of one of her co-workers. Although the intent of the videotape was to examine the role play that was developing during work time in the house area, all she heard was herself talking nonstop in the block area. She was so shocked to hear so much of herself and so little of the children that for the next couple of days she didn't say much at all during work time but concentrated instead on listening to what the children were saying as they worked and talked with one another. Gradually she began to say more, but she tape-recorded herself periodically to make sure she wasn't returning to her former habits of excess. She found that she learned more about the children from listening to them, and she came to understand that *they* learned more about their world when they tried to put ideas, discoveries, problems and observations into their own words.

Converse with children who do not talk

In any classroom it's easier to talk with the children who are already quite verbal and enjoy sharing and exchanging ideas; it's most difficult to talk with those children who offer very little, if any, response. Yet parents of infants and toddlers still too young to talk realize the necessity for talking to them and do so throughout the day as they bathe, dress, feed and play with them; three- and four-year-olds who won't talk must be talked to with the same persistence, interest and concern. They must begin to feel that people wish to communicate with them.

Once a teaching team gets to know a nonverbal child, it's often appropriate to expect the child to begin replacing grunts and gestures with words. "*Tell* me what you want and I'll help you," an adult might say to a child who has developed such an effective nonverbal system of communication that he sees no reason to use words.

Establish verbal contact with children whose language you don't speak

In classrooms where there are children who don't speak English, it's important to establish some kind of verbal rapport: talk in a natural, conversational tone, listen to what the child is saying and learn and remember the child's particular interests. Gestures can be used whenever possible as well as the few words in the child's language the adult has been able to pick up or has asked a bilingual adult or child to supply. The point is that each teaching team member must establish contact with all the children in the class, not just with those children whose language they speak, because children must feel that adults value them regardless of their linguistic heritage or abilities.

Key Experience: Describing objects, events and relations

The *content* of conversations is the focus of this key experience. After creating an environment in which children feel free to converse easily and naturally among themselves and with adults, adults must turn to the task of tuning themselves into *what* children are saying so that they can both support and extend children's thoughts, ideas and observations, and enrich the content of their own conversations with children. Many adults are very warm and receptive as they talk with children, as they should be, but often much of what they say consists of comments like "Oh, that's a beautiful picture." While it's very impor-

tant to praise children, it's equally important to provide verbal stimulation and support for their emerging ability to connect language with actions and experiences. Three- and four-year-olds have the developing capacity for generating increasingly precise descriptions of objects, events and relations. With the support and encouragement of adults who recognize and appreciate this ability, they can learn to express their thoughts and observations as clearly as they are able. Without support and encouragement they are more likely to lapse into less articulate speech patterns resulting in imprecise statements like "Take that one over there," instead of more elaborated statements like "Take the biggest chair and put it next to the table with the globe on it." Following are some ways adults can provide opportunities for children to describe objects, events and relations.

Suggestions for adults

Direct children's attention to objects, events and relations worth describing

Two preschoolers are examining a large, wooden, three-dimensional Aztec calendar in the quiet area. "Look at this man with the big round eyes and the long points on his head." "Here's a bird and another bird with a long beak and long, long legs." "And here's a monster made out of lots of squares and lines . . ."

Providing children with interesting things to explore and use is essential to the development of descriptive language. Children aren't going to describe things if there isn't anything in the environment to excite and delight them. But they are going to explore, manipulate, use, experiment with and, consequently, talk about things, places and events that intrigue them, that challenge them, that they've never seen before, that they have some kind of control over, that can be used and experienced in an endless variety of ways, and that involve them closely with peers.

Many specific classroom materials, places to visit and events to participate in are suggested throughout this volume. If a teaching team follows these suggestions and comes up with their own additions, they will certainly be setting the stage for descriptive language production by providing children with things worth describing.

Encourage children to describe things by having them try to answer their own questions

Germond: *What's that you've got, Mrs. Mahama?*
Mrs. Mahama: *What do you think it is, Germond?*

Germond: *Well, I don't know. It looks like a*
tube with a handle here and a hose
here . . .

Children ask lots of questions, many of
which they can answer for themselves if they're
encouraged to do so. Answering them means
that they must make, put together and describe
the observations they originally requested from
someone else. The more often adults turn children's questions back to them with "What do
you think?" or "I don't know, how could we find
out?" the more opportunities they are giving
children to think out and describe possibilities
and observations.

Provide opportunities for children to describe what they're going to do, what they've done and what's going to happen next

Once adults become accustomed to the dynamics
of planning, working and recalling experience,
they can begin to extend the plan-do-review process and the resultant descriptive language to
other parts of the day. Here are some examples:

Outside time—"What are you and Niva going to
do with all those balls?"
"See how many we can throw into the big
barrel. We're gonna get 'em all in."
"Hey, Leah. How's the taxi business
going?"
"Fine. Wally's going to his Gran's house
over by the bushes and Paula's got to get to
the hospital under the slide real fast because
she got hurt in the leg by a big dog. Look at
her bleedin'."
Small-group time—"Jose, tell us what just happened to your blocks. We missed it down at
this end of the table."

"They were way up high, then boom!
These top ones fell into my chair."
Circle time—"What would happen if we all went
around in a circle with our eyes closed?"
closed?"
"We would bump."
"Go slow."
"Someone might step on me."
"We could hold hands."
"It would be very dark."
"We would have to open our eyes to see
. . ."

Play descriptive games with children

Any teaching team can adapt games they know
to include opportunities for describing things.
With a little ingenuity they can also create their
own. Here are some examples:
"Simon Says"—Instead of having Simon say,
"Do this," have Simon describe the action:
"Put your legs far, far apart." The same
change can be made in "Everybody Do
This."
"Little Foxes"—The leader tells the little foxes to
"run to the stone steps" or "hop to the biggest log." As soon as the foxes get to one
place, the leader describes another place for
them to go to.
"Let's Be"—Each child takes a turn describing
someone or something for everyone else to
pretend to be. "Let's be people carrying lots
of balloons." "Let's be a man paintin'."
"Let's be a dog licking his feet."

Be precise when describing objects, events and relations in talks with children

As adults converse with children thoughout the
day, they need to be precise in their own language so that what they say has some content
and children can hear and imitate language being

used descriptively. Instead of saying, "This goes over there," for example, an adult could say, "This tambourine hangs on the pegboard on the wall with the other instruments you shake."

Read stories to children

Among the many reasons for reading to children is that it gives them the opportunity to hear descriptive language used imaginatively.

Key Experience:
Expressing feelings in words

An adult was struggling to untangle a mess of wheel toys for a group of preschoolers. They were all crowding around her screaming in chorus, "I want the bus!" "I want the tractor!" "I want the big trike!" "I want . . ." "I want!" She stopped and said, "Wait! I'm getting angry because everyone keeps yelling 'I want' at me. Please wait 'til all the wheel toys are out, and then we can begin sharing." There was quiet and bewilderment until one boy came up and whispered in her ear, "Teacher, teacher." "What, John Paul?" she acknowledged. "I WANT THE TRACTOR!"

Throughout the day in a cognitively oriented classroom, children are encouraged to speak freely about what they're doing, observing and feeling. Communicating thoughts and feelings is essential if children are to learn how to relate to others and get along in the world.

Language gives children a socially appropriate means of communicating their feelings of sadness, anger, fear, frustration, excitement, happiness, friendliness and delight. Language provides a basis for a cooperative, problem-solving approach to conflict as an alternative to aggression by giving children a way to delineate problems, think them through and come up with solutions. Expressing feelings in words also helps children begin to understand that other people's points of view are often different from their own. This new understanding of language as a key to social interaction is essential to children's social and cognitive development.

Here are some ways adults can help children express their feelings in words and use language to deal with conflicts.

Suggestions for adults

Establish and maintain a secure environment

Since children are more likely to express and talk about their feelings in an environment that is caring and secure, adults need to do all they can to provide a sense of security in their classroom. One major way they can do this is to set clear limits and maintain them consistently. Adults need to formulate a simple, reasonable set of rules and discuss with the children the reasons for the rules and the possible consequences of breaking them. Then these rules must be followed consistently and discussed as often as needed, with individuals and with small groups.

Another way to lend security and reasonableness to the environment is to make a habit of accompanying "No" with an explanation. Children who are continually assaulted with "No, don't do that!" often feel bewildered, frustrated and angry because they get a negative response without knowing what they're doing wrong or what behavior would be acceptable. Instead of saying, "No, Laurie, don't knock Bretta's tower down," an adult could say, "Laurie, be careful with Bretta's tower. It took her a long time to get it to balance and she'll be very upset if you knock it down. Would you like me to help you start a tower like Bretta's? Maybe Bretta could show us how to start."

Speak matter-of-factly with children when they bring up questions and concerns

In establishing an environment in which children feel free to express and discuss their feelings and observations, adults must be ready to deal with children's concerns sympathetically yet matter-of-factly. This includes discussing rather than avoiding questions children raise about frightening or embarrassing subjects like, "My Daddy's head got all bloody. Is he going to die?" or "How's your baby going to get out of your tummy to get born?" There is no set way for adults to answer questions like these, but they must do their best to discuss them in a straightforward manner to the satisfaction of the questioner. Some questions can be turned back to the child ("How do you think the baby will get out?"), giving the adult a chance to find out how much understanding the child already has; sometimes all a child really wants is affirmation or reassurance rather than a lengthy explanation.

Children may also have concerns about other children and adults in the classroom that will demand the same kind of matter-of-fact discussion. When children make statements like, "I don't like him 'cause he don't talk right," "Why does she look so sad?" "What's that big bump on Joey's back? I don't like it," adults can help them by providing the information they need in a way they can understand it. For example, in the first situation, concerning a child whose speech is developmentally delayed, an adult could say: "Well, you know something, Barry? Ikie is just learning to talk and he's doing the very best he can. When I was learning to talk, no one could understand me very well, and when you were learning to talk, no one could understand you very well either. Some people learn to talk before they come to school, and other people wait till they come to school to learn."

Adults can also help children think of ways they can assist the people they're concerned about: "Since Ikie's just learning how to talk, what do you think you could do to help him, Barry?" By helping children plan ways to help, adults are giving them a means of changing negative feelings into positive interactions. In the case of Ikie and Barry, the adult could also help Barry think of all the things Ikie enjoys and can do well so that Barry can begin to recognize Ikie's strengths rather than dwell on his shortcomings. In the process, the adult can also help Barry see what he and Ikie have in common.

Recognize and acknowledge children's feelings

Crysta, usually a very cheerful, active child, just wants to sit on Ms. Bersuder's lap. Danny's tearing up his paintings. Timmy's crying outside the fire station and refuses to come in. Carole and Paul have left small-group time and won't come back. Through their behavior, each of these children is wordlessly expressing a feeling and a desire for assistance. What can adults do to assist?

Go to the child and verbally acknowledge his or her concerns.

_____

Assume that the child has a legitimate concern and is not just trying to be annoying.

_____

Ask the child what's the matter so that he has an opportunity to shape and control his feelings by putting them into words.

_____

Listen to the child and help him plan a more appropriate action.

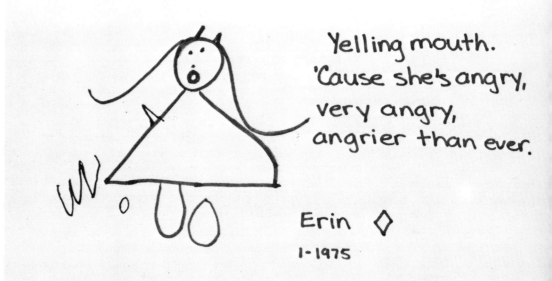

Yelling mouth. 'Cause she's angry, very angry, angrier than ever.

Erin

1-1975

If the child can't say what's the matter, make a guess, but if your explanation proves wrong, refrain from further questioning. Let the child know you're willing to listen whenever he or she wishes to talk, and in the meantime, take the lead in planning more appropriate actions. If the situation persists, talk with the parents to find out all you can do to help.

Express your own feelings in words

Joe had planned to make peanut butter with the children at small-group time. Before school he had collected everything needed, but at small-group time the peanuts were gone. He said, "I'm disappointed and a little angry because someone took the peanuts we were going to use to make peanut butter. Now we can't make peanut butter for snack. We'll have to do something else."

Adults need to express their own emotions honestly. The "stonefaced" teaching team member, parent or caretaker may succeed in covering up emotions, but rarely can he or she hide the tension and strain that results. In the example above, Joe spoke about his disappointment and anger to "clear the air," and he pointed out the consequence of the loss of the peanuts, but then he moved on to an alternative activity instead of deliverying a homily about peanut thieves. And negative feelings aren't the only ones that need verbal airing; adults also need to express positive feelings and encourage children to do the same.

Help children find alternatives when conflicts arise

Conflict is a common occurrence among preschoolers, arising from frustration and impatience. When things don't work out just right—the tower won't balance, there's no room at the easel, someone is already using the xylophone, the house area "family" doesn't want any more members—children often resort to hitting, kicking, biting, grabbing, pushing and shouting. These direct, physical actions, usually aimed at another person, do little to alleviate the problem and generally leave the child feeling worse than he did to begin with. The role of adults in these situations is to redirect the children in conflict back to the original problem so they can find a workable solution. This is done chiefly through language.

By dealing with conflicts in a matter-of-fact manner as they arise, adults can help children replace physical abuse with (nonabusive) speech and locate or generate alternative materials or procedures. The first thing an adult can do is stop the disrupting child and ask him or her what the trouble is. "Tell me why you're hitting Bernie, Tracy." If Tracy can answer (" 'Cause I want that truck!"), talk briefly with him about

how hitting hurts but *talking* and *asking* are much more likely to produce the desired result. If Bernie still needs the truck, help Tracy find something else he could use until Bernie is finished. "Let's look around and see if there are any more trucks, Tracy, or if we can find anything else you could haul your blocks in. Maybe we could make a truck. What do you think?"

Help children anticipate and avoid conflicts

Adults can help children learn to avoid some potential conflicts or upsetting situations by helping them verbally anticipate what's going to happen next. Just before a trip to the fire station, for example, an adult might ask, "What are some things we might see and hear at the fire station?" in an effort to alert children to the fact that the sirens will be loud but the fireman will say when he's going to blow them and he'll only blow them for a short time.

Adults can also talk as needed with individuals or groups of children about "What might happen if . . .?" and "What could we do instead?" in order to help children put potential difficulties into words and plan ahead to avoid them.

Encourage children to think about other people's needs

Preschoolers are often more capable of altruism than many adults will give them credit for. If adults regard small children only as "egocentric," they won't expect or encourage them to see things from another person's point of view. A look around any preschool classroom, however,

will usually reveal a child comforting another, a child sharing a toy from home, a child showing another child how to do something.

Adults should verbally acknowledge the helpful, thoughtful things children do. "That was very kind of you, Susanna. You saw that Tommy needed the stool so you got it for him."

Adults can support children's inclination to respond to one another's needs by asking them to describe how they think other people feel in a specific situation: "How do you think the little bear felt when he came home and found his porridge all gone and his chair all broken to pieces?" "How do you think Matt feels when you won't let him sit next to you?"

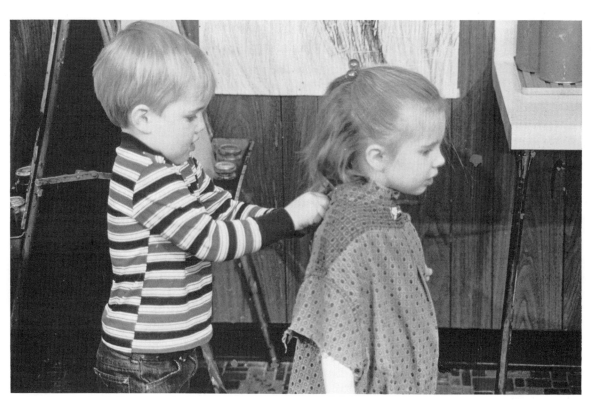

Key Experience:
Having one's own
spoken language
written down and read
back

As children use spoken language and encounter written language, they begin to understand that written language is another means of representing their thoughts and feelings. When children talk about something they've done or seen or made, and someone writes down exactly what they say and reads it back, they are witnessing the writing and reading of their own ideas. They learn that they can talk about what they think

and feel, that what they talk about can be written down, that what they dictate can be read aloud and that eventually they will be able to write and read.

Not only does the dictation process demonstrate to a child that written words are representations of spoken language, it also generates enthusiasm for speaking, reading and writing. The child becomes confident that his language works and that his or her ideas are important. The child also becomes interested in acquiring writing and reading skills.

Here are some ways adults can provide opportunities for children to have their own words written down and read back.

Suggestions for adults

Ask children to describe their drawings

This is a good starting point for dictation. An adult can introduce the process by saying, "Tell me about your picture, Max, and I'll write down what you say. I'll write down your story."

Write down the child's exact words

It's important to write down the child's words exactly as the child says them. Don't edit or "correct." This helps the child understand more clearly the connection between spoken and written language. If the child dictates in a language you don't understand, try to write it phonetically or get the help of a bilingual child or staff member.

Say each word as you write it

Again, this emphasizes the connection between spoken and written language. An adult should say each word or phrase after writing it and encourage the child to repeat the words that have been written.

Take dictation whenever possible throughout the day

After children understand the process of dictation, it can be used in many activities; for example:

• Labeling and describing a structure built in the block area.

• Writing down what happened while visiting the "dentist" in the house area.

• Writing down the steps for making applesauce.

• Making signs and labels for the toy village set up in the quiet area.

• Making labels for new materials in the classroom.

• Making cards, letters or thank-you notes for friends and relatives.

• Writing the words to a song about a field trip.

• Writing a group story about a pet animal in the classroom.

• Writing a plan to build a model plane during work time.

• Recalling things accomplished during work time.

Collect dictations

As children dictate regularly, their ability to include details and more elaborate descriptions increases. Some children might want to collect their dictations for a book. Adults might also want to keep their own collections of children's dictations in order to watch their development throughout the year.

Respond to children's interest in letters, sounds and words

During the process of dictation, many children begin to pay attention to letters, sounds and words. If a child's name begins with S, for example, she may enjoy finding all the S's in her story as well as the other letters she can name and identify. Other children may begin to pick out entire words. The important thing for adults to do is to follow up on children's interests in these pre-reading and pre-writing processes.

Key Experience:
Having fun with language

Many children have been enjoying language long before starting preschool. In their beds while supposedly napping, they've been making up stories and songs. Children enjoy the sounds of words, they enjoy repeating words and trying out new words and expressions, like the little girl who delighted herself by saying over and over again, "Silence goes by, silence goes by." They enjoy hearing and saying other people's words even if they don't understand them—words like "opined" and "carburetor."

Even the most active, rambunctious two-year-old will pause with respect when a short picture book is being read aloud to a small group. A few preschoolers who during work time may have threatened the very structure of the building will easily be captivated by a story. Some young children memorize, word for word, each page of a beloved book and will "read" their favorite stories to themselves or other children.

When children listen to stories, they are experiencing part of the complex relationship of writing and reading. When they make up a story or poem, they are learning that they can express their own ideas, and that these ideas can be recorded and read back. Listening to and making up stories, poems and songs also prepares children to become effective writers and communicators. Young children who understand the relation between spoken and written language and who have connected speaking, listening and writing to the reading process will begin to read naturally and to write for pleasure as well as communication.

Suggestions for adults

Provide books for children to look at and "read"

Designate an area of the room for children's books that's accessible to children at all times and affords privacy and quiet. Stock it with all kinds of books: picture books, story books, books relating to field trips taken, books relating to individual children's particular interests, books of poems, song books, books of photographs, books the children have made, nursery-rhyme books, books in all the languages spoken by the children, books in braille if there are blind children.

Read books, stories and poems to children

Read to children whenever the opportunity arises—during work time at a child's request, after school when the last few children are waiting to be picked up, before school to the early arrivals, after lunch just before nap time, before lunch after hands are washed and everyone is waiting for the food. Plan to read once a week or at least occasionally at small-group time or as children are eating their snacks, and at circle time to the whole group. Let children have a chance to choose what to read. Acknowledge and respond to children's questions and comments about the story.

Tell stories and recite poems, nursery rhymes and verses

Sometimes instead of reading, tell stories you know by heart. These can be traditional stories, folk tales, myths, legends, tall tales, stories about historical figures, stories you were told as a child, stories about things you did as a child, stories you invent about the children in the class. Tell any story you enjoy telling that you think the children would understand and enjoy. Some adults use props and puppets, while others feel more comfortable without them.

Recite verses you know by heart whenever there's occasion. One adult always recited "Up in the air we go so high, up in the air so blue. Oh I don't know of a pleasanter thing, ever a child could do" whenever she pushed a child on the swing, while another chanted "Thumbs in the thumb hole, fingers all together, this is the song we sing in mitten weather" as she helped children with their mittens.

Make up chants, rhymes and limericks with children

Many children make up their own spontaneous chants and rhymes to the rhythm of something they're doing: "Round and round. Round and round. Round and round." "Beady, bead. Beady, bead. Beady, bead." "Up and down to get the

crown. Up and down to get the crown." "Golly, jolly, golly, dollie. Golly, jolly, golly, dollie." Listen for children's chants and rhymes, and if it's possible to do so without disrupting, join in to let the children know you appreciate and enjoy their word play. Sometimes other children will join in, too, and add to the rhyme or even start a new one.

Adults can start rhymes, too. At snack time, as the children were making sandwiches, one adult started to say, "Spread the bread." To which the children added, "Go to bed. Hands on your head. Nobody said. I like lead." The adult wrote it down and it became the beginning of a book of rhymes the children created over the year. One favorite rhyme started on the bus on a field trip when a child saw a man crossing the street and said, "There goes Popper Noodle." From this developed the limerick,

There goes Popper Noodle.
He likes apple strudel.
When he eats with a spoon
He goes to the moon.
Mister Popper Noodle.

Make up stories and songs with children

Encourage children to tell stories or sing songs about things they've done and imagined, and record these stories and songs through dictation or tape recording. When children dictate stories, encourage them to illustrate them too; the stories and illustrations can be covered with clear contact paper and added to the book area.

In one classroom, a favorite song book originated from a set of pictures Corey drew for his friend Susanna. Susanna, who had just got a new song book for her birthday, decided to make Corey's pictures into another song book, so she sang a little song for each picture, and one of the adults wrote down the notes and words.

Related films and publications from the High/Scope Foundation

Films—

(For a complete description of each film and instructions for ordering, see appendix 4.)

Supporting Communication Among Preschoolers series: *Part I—An Important Opportunity; Part II—Opportunities in the Classroom; Part III—Encouraging Interaction and Cooperation; Part IV—Referring One Child's Questions or Problems to Another; Part V—Interpreting or "Delivering" Messages; Part VI—Encouraging Active Listening; Part VII—Examples for Discussion*

Questions That Help Children Develop Their Ideas from **Helping Children Make Choices and Decisions** series

Acknowledging Children's Choices and Decisions from **Helping Children Make Choices and Decisions** series

Experiencing and Representing series: *Part I—A Way Children Learn; Part II—Starting with Direct Experience; Part III—From Direct Experience to Representation; Part IV—Strategies for Supporting Representational Activity*

Publications—

The Cognitively Oriented Curriculum—Writing and Reading (No. 6) (booklet, 40 pp.) by Oon Bee Hsu, 1977. (Elementary grades)

A plan for developing writing and reading abilities in elementary-age children based on the following premises: 1) that writing and reading are best learned together; 2) that the child's initiation into literacy is a matter of his discovering the connection between spoken and written language; and 3) that the child discovers this connection when his own experiences are the content for his first attempts at writing and reading.

Related reading on language and language acquisition

Anastasiow, Nicholas J. and Hanes, Michael L. *Language Patterns of Poverty Children.* Springfield, Illinois: Charles C. Thomas Publishers, 1976.

Bates, Elizabeth. *Language and Context: The Acquisition of Pragmatics.* New York: Academic Press, 1976.

Beilin, Harry. *Studies in the Cognitive Basis of Language Development.* New York: Academic Press, 1975.

Blank, M. "Language, the Child and the Teacher: A Proposed Assessment Model," in *Psychological Processes in Early Education,* H. Hom and P. Robinson, eds. New York: Academic Press, 1977.

Bloom, Lois. *Language Development: Form and Function in Emerging Grammars.* Cambridge, Massachusetts: The M.I.T. Press, 1970.

Bloom, Lois. "Language Development Review," in *Review of Child Development Research,* Vol. 4, Frances Degen Horowitz, ed. Chicago: University of Chicago Press, 1975. Chapter 5, pp. 245-303.

Bloom, Lois and M. Lahey. *Language Development and Language Disorders.* New York: John Wiley and Sons, 1978.

Cazden, Courtney B. *Child Language and Education.* New York: Holt, Rinehart, Winston, 1972.

Cazden, Courtney B. "Children's Questions: Their Forms, Functions, and Roles in Education," *Young Children,* March, 1970. pp. 202-219.

Cazden, Courtney; Cancino, M.; Robansky, F. and J. Schumann. "Second Language Acquisition Sequences in Children, Adolescents and Adults." Final Report Project No. 730744, Grant No. NE-6-00-3-0014, U.S. Department of Health, Education and Welfare, National Institute of Education Office of Research Grants, August, 1975.

Cazden, Courtney B.; John, Vera P. and Dell Hymes, eds. *Functions of Language in the Classroom.* New York: Teachers College Press, 1972.

Ervin-Tripp, Susan. *Language Acquisition and Communicative Choice.* Stanford, California: Stanford University Press, 1973.

Dato, D.P. "American Children's Acquisition of Spanish Syntax in the Madrid Environment." ERIC ED 053-631, 1970.

Lambert, W.E.; Just, M. and N. Segalowitz. "Some Cognitive Consequences of Following the Curricula of the Early School Grades in a Foreign Language." Report of the twenty-first roundtable meeting. Monograph No. 23, Washington, D.C.: Georgetown University Press, 1970.

Moore, Timothy E. *Cognitive Development and the Acquisition of Language*. New York: Academic Press, 1973.

Piaget, Jean. *The Language and Thought of the Child*. New York: Harcourt, Brace, 1926.

Ravem, Roar. "The Development of Wh-Questions in First and Second Language Learners," in *Occasional Papers*, University of Essex, Language Center, Colchester, December, 1970.

Ravem, Roar. "Language Acquisition in a Second Language Environment," *International Review of Applied Linguistics*, Vol. 6, No. 2, 1968. pp. 165-185.

Sinclair-De-Zwart, Hermina. "Developmental Psycholinguistics," in *Studies in Cognitive Development, Essays in Honor of Jean Piaget*, David Elkind and John H. Flavell, eds. New York: Oxford University Press, 1969. pp. 315-336.

Slobin, D.I. "Cognitive Prerequisites for the Development of Grammar," in *Studies of Child Language Development*, C.A. Ferguson and D.I. Slobin, eds. New York: Holt, Rinehart, and Winston, 1973. pp. 175-208.

Swain, Merril. "Working with French-English Bilingual Children." Modern Language Center: Ontario Institute for Studies in Education. Toronto, Canada, 1971.

7/ Experiencing & representing

One of the most important kinds of developmental progress that preschool children are making is in their ability to represent their knowledge of the world in many different modalities and media. Many of these are not dependent on language at all, or are only partly infused with language: drawing, making three-dimensional models such as clay or block structures, imitative actions and "pretending," as well as singing, dancing and other musical pleasures.*

*For those who wish to place nonverbal representation in a theoretical perspective, perhaps it will help to note that Piaget talks about nonverbal representations, whether physical products such as drawings or mental processes such as images, as being "figurative" or "symbolic" representations, because, unlike language, they resemble that which they represent. Piaget is using "symbolic" here in a way that distinguishes "symbols" from "signs" such as words. Signs are arbitrarily related to what they stand for. Piaget believes that the ability to imitate something seen previously but no longer present (deferred imitation) is the beginning of the ability to use mental representations to stand for objects or events. He sees deferred imitation as evolving from the imitation of things while they are present, and further believes that mental images and other picture-like representations evolve from the action-oriented imitation processes. The predecessor of imitation, in Piaget's description of development, is seen as the infant's response to "signals" or "indexes." These are representations that are not yet differentiated from what they represent in the infant's mind. Indexes are parts of other phenomena or are caused by other objects. Mother's voice, the dog's barking, footprints in the snow "indicate" (or are indexes of) the presence of mother, dog or someone walking in the snow, but they do not "stand for" mother, dog, etc. in the way that a picture does for a preschool child; the preschooler has learned that the picture and the dog are not the same thing but rather that one "stands for" the other.

For Piaget, the essence of the preoperational subperiod is the growing ability of the child to use "symbolic" representations. Piaget calls the preoperational years the "period of representative intelligence."

Nonverbal representations, mental images, dominate the thinking of the preschooler. These representations are a tremendous advance over the infant's total dependence on the here and now, but they do have limitations because, in Piaget's description, they are not used in conjunction with the mental operations, which have not yet been attained. Preschoolers can't yet reverse a process mentally, they have difficulty considering more than one dimension at a time, and they find it difficult to "see things" from another person's perspective. Their thought processes cannot adequately represent transitions and transformations because imagistic thinking is static and nonreversible.

Although it does not constitute the principal means for attaining logical thinking (nor, by the way, does language in Piaget's theory), nonverbal representation continues to be an important element in any creative thought process. The ability to "picture" relationships and to encode with the muscles as well as with words how some action or process occurs may be vitally important to the competent adult. Recent research on the functioning of the brain suggests that nonverbal, nonlogical systems are located separately in the brain from other thinking modes. The preschool years seem an opportune if not critical time in which to strengthen the nonverbal thought processes, before they are submerged by verbal and logical thought.

～

The key experiences described in this chapter are ways to organize efforts to extend and support the child's emerging abilities to represent the world through a variety of symbolic processes. The basic strategies of moving from concrete to abstract, simple to complex, things to relations and here/now to there/then apply very clearly to these key experiences.

- Concrete ————→ abstract

The basic principle is to start out with an active experience with real things, and then to represent the experience in a variety of ways. This applies to introducing new objects or living things, new places, new concepts.

- Simple ————→ complex

The progression from simple to complex will be made in every area of symbolic representation. Children's drawings, block structures, imitative gestures, role play, clay models, etc. all become increasingly differentiated, integrated and complicated during the preschool years. Teachers and parents should facilitate this process rather than force premature complexity on the one hand or limit the available media on the other. It's the *process* of representation that children are trying to master, not an adult conception of what constitutes an adequate symbol. Providing models for children-to copy (as, for example, when the teacher displays his or her own drawing) or providing coloring books and the like may inhibit the process of representation and encourage only completion of a product that *seems* to be a representation. It is important, though, to remember that representation of the real world is a very basic skill that preschoolers are highly motivated to master. It does not make sense to see this as somehow opposed to "creativity." Some early childhood teachers are so determined not to stifle creativity that they're embarrassed when children are clearly trying to represent something real with "art" media. This embarrassment may be the result of good intentions but it is inappropriate if the initiative is coming from the child in regard to (1) the child's interest in using the media for representation, and (2) the child's choice of the actual structure of the representation, its complexity and degree of "realism." Adults can help children form more complete, detailed representations by helping them to observe real things closely, rather than by criticizing the representations that they produce.

• Here/now ————————→there/then

As children develop, they're increasingly able to remember and "imagine" things that aren't present, and to imagine things that don't exist. The development of fantasy, dreams and creative imagination is very much a part of the development of nonverbal representation in early childhood. It makes sense to support imagination by helping children expand their representations to include past, future and distant

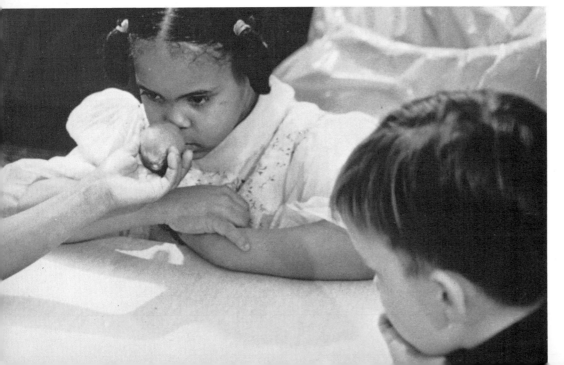

events, but only after they are comfortable with the process of representation and have a thorough grounding in active experience.

Key Experience:
Recognizing objects by sound, touch, taste and smell

Preschool children are beginning to represent their experiences—what they think and feel about people, objects, events and social roles—in many different ways. One way very young children begin to represent is by recognizing that the sound, smell, taste, or feel of an object can "stand for" the object when it is not present or visible or when it is only partially visible. By looking at a bootprint in the snow, for example, they conclude that somebody has been out walking. Or they can sniff the air and tell that an angry skunk has been by. A siren brings them rushing to the window to see if they can see a fire engine or an ambulance. A brown corduroy coat hanging beneath Tommy's sign tells them that Tommy has come to school that day. These cues—a bootprint, a skunk smell, a siren, a brown corduroy coat—call to their minds a picture of the whole object—the person, the skunk, the fire engine or ambulance, their friend Tommy.

To interpret a sensory cue a child must have had experience with the object to which it refers; a child who hears a tambourine, for example, but has never seen, heard or used a tambourine can't tell what's making the jingling sound. A child who has had a wide variety of active experiences can identify many objects from their sensory cues. He can picture the whole object from the part he sees, hears, smells, tastes or touches. The sensory cue serves as a reminder from which the child can complete his own mental representation of the object.

Recognizing objects by sensory cues is the intermediate step between an infant's sensorimotor perceptions and an older child's understanding of symbols. An infant, for example, hears the sound of popcorn popping and becomes attentive to the sound itself, with no notion of what it's connected to. A preschooler, on the other hand, hears popcorn popping and puts the noise together with everything he knows about making and eating popcorn.

Here are some ways adults can provide opportunities for children to recognize objects by their sensory cues.

Suggestions for adults

Play sensory-cue games

After children have had an opportunity to explore some materials, have them use a sense other than sight to identify them:

Put familiar objects in a paper bag, or under a cloth, and have children try to identify them by touch alone.

———————

Place a small amount of familiar material with a distinctive odor in a container. Have the children try to guess what the material is by smell alone. Some things to try are coffee, peanut butter, chocolate, cinnamon, banana, perfume, paste.

———————

See if children can identify foods by taste alone. At snack or small-group time, ask each child to close his eyes and identify what he or she is tasting.

Ask children to identify familiar sounds as they occur throughout the day: a plane flying overhead, the sirens of a firetruck or police car, a dog barking, a familiar person talking in another room, people clapping, running, bouncing balls outside.

———————

Cover all but one part of a familiar object and ask children to identify it. Take advantage of natural situations as they arise throughout the day. For example, children enjoy burying or partially covering things in the sandbox and then having someone guess what they've "hidden." Talk with the children about what they see when a toy truck is half covered by blocks, a paint brush is partly hidden by paint, the pet rabbit is hiding under the shelf and only his nose is visible.

During small-group time, play games in which one child covers his eyes or turns his head while another talks or makes a noise by turning water on, knocking on wood, clapping, coughing. Ask the child who is not looking to identify the person or sound.

Provide tape recorders and tapes

Children can record and identify their voices, sounds in the room, things heard on field trips. Don't be upset, however, if the children are more interested in the recorder itself and what it's saying than in identifying who is speaking. Many three- and four-year-olds do not make the connection between speaking into the microphone and what comes out on the tape. Even if they've just recorded something, they often don't understand that the recorder plays back their voice; they feel the recorder itself is speaking.

Help children notice imprints and make their own

Provide opportunities for children to identify objects from their imprints by *talking with them about the imprints they make* at the sand table using cars and trucks, cups, silverware, their hands; *encouraging plaster, paint and playdough printing* using hands, feet, fingers, sponges, vegetables, rocks, clay flowerpots, sticks, spools, a potato masher, forks, corks, string and whatever else the children suggest; *talking with them about the imprints they see,* such as tire tracks, animal footprints, human footprints, imprints of their bodies in snow, sand or leaves.

Help children notice and make shadows

Outside, talk with children about the shadows they see, what they think is making the shadow, how its parts correspond to the parts of the shadow.

Key Experience:
Imitating actions and sounds

- *Lanny grips the handle of an old iron and guides it slowly across a pair of pants.*
- *Timmy stands in front of the mirror in the house area, his face covered with shaving cream, using a small spatula to shave.*
- *Kara stops her work in the block area, picks up the telephone and calls Jeff.*
- *Joey walks on hands and feet. "Look! I can walk like a spider!"*
- *Tracy whizzes by Maurine, then turns his steering wheel sharply to avoid the corner of the shed. He makes a screeching sound as he slams on the brakes and brings the wheel-toy bus to a stop.*

These three- and four-year-olds are imitating the actions of people and animals they've seen. They began the process of imitation as infants as they copied such adult actions as drinking from cups, waving and making sounds. As they grew into toddlers and preschoolers, they continued to learn through imitation, and they began to imitate increasingly complex actions—driving a car, riding a horse, "doing" their hair, setting the table. Through imitation preschoolers learn to represent with their own bodies and voices what they know about the world. Imitation is the beginning of pretending, or role play, in which children integrate a series of imitations into a recognizable role like "mommy" or "store person."

Here are some ways adults can provide opportunities for children to imitate actions and sounds.

Suggestions for adults

Encourage children to imitate at work time

Children can add sounds to their play at work time such as car and truck sounds when pushing cars and trucks, the sound of a bell ringing when pretending to push a doorbell, the sound of a phone ringing after dialing the phone.

As children work, adults can imitate their actions and sounds and thus model imitation for them. For example, a child may be using an eggbeater in a mixing bowl while making a cake. An adult might say, "That looks like a good idea. I think I'll make a cake, too," and then proceed to use a pretend eggbeater, imitating the child's actions and sounds.

Encourage children to imitate at recall and small-group time

Have children recall what they did at work time by having them imitate their own and each other's work time actions—making pudding, building with blocks, stringing beads, painting, playing the drums, hammering.

At small-group time read stories and see if the children can imitate the actions they see in the pictures.

Encourage children to imitate at circle time

Sing songs like "This Is the Way We Wash Our Clothes" in which children can imitate a familiar sequence of actions such as going to bed, getting up in the morning, dressing, eating, going to school. Modify these songs so they reflect the actions the children participated in at work time or on a field trip. Ask the children to suggest actions to add to the song.

Play games like "Everybody Do This" in which children imitate each other's actions and sounds.

After a field trip make up stories or songs in which children can imitate the actions and sounds of things they saw on the trip. After a field trip to a farm, for example, they might come up with these ideas: a cow mooing, a farmer milking the cow or driving a tractor or putting bales of straw on the wagon. After a trip to a fire station, the children might imitate the sequence of steps a fireman goes through when he receives a call—jumping out of bed, putting on his boots, coat and hat, sliding down the pole, climbing onto the firetruck, driving to the fire, putting out the fire, driving back to the station.

Key Experience:
Relating models, photographs and pictures to real places and things

Infants use toys, photographs and pictures as they use any other objects—to chew, push, bend, carry around—but they do not interpret them; a real orange, a plastic orange and a picture of an orange in a book, for example, are three different things to play with and carry around and have no particular relation to each other. By the time children reach preschool age, however, they're beginning to relate toys, photographs and pictures to the objects they represent.

"This is my grandma's house," says Antoine as he walks a little rubber doll through the door of the doll house.

While playing dentist, nurse Michelle decides to read her patient a story. She gets a picture book about firemen and begins to "read." "Once upon a time, there was a fireman . . . with cavities. He ate all that stuff."

"This truck's like my dad's truck, but his truck is great big and it's blue and I can honk it and I can really turn it on. This one, you have to push it like this."

"Ouch. Can't bite this," says Latrice trying to bite into a plastic banana. "I had me a soft 'nana at my house . . . Here, baby, you eat this 'nana, and don't you miss that bus!"

Three children are gathered around a photograph album in the quiet area. "Look, here's William! Here's Jenny! Here's Ventrice. He's bald-headed!" Gales of laughter. "Uh oh. Here's Jarline. She's bad." "Here's Biddy and Tony. Them two's the same 'cause they got boots. Their daddy got 'em."

Adults should provide many opportunities for preschoolers to relate toys, photographs and pictures to the objects they represent, because this experience helps children make sense of the many representations that occur in their everyday world—billboard pictures, television and film images, toy models, photo albums, picture books and magazines. Experience in interpreting such representations also gives children the background for the more abstract representations they'll be interpreting later on—letters and numbers.

Suggestions for adults

Provide toy models of real objects
In each work area provide models of objects, events and people children encounter in the classroom, on field trips and at home—wooden or rubber people and animals, a dollhouse and dollhouse furniture, a child-size stove, sink and refrigerator, small vehicles of all kinds, dolls, animal- and object-shaped cookie cutters, puppets, a Playskool village set, plastic nut-and-bolt sets.

Compare models to the objects they represent
Throughout the day as children use models in their play, encourage them to compare the models they're using to the objects they represent whenever this can be done in a natural and enjoyable way. Here's an example:

"Hey, Ms. Stewart, look at my bunny. Here he goes hopping, hopping, hopping into his little house."

"Your bunny is quite a hopper, Charlotte. When he comes out of his house, maybe he'll hop over to visit our real bunny."

"That's what he's doing now. Hop, hop, hop . . . look, they're sniffing each other!"

"So they are. What do you think, is your bunny the same as the real bunny?"

"Yep. They got noses and ears and lots of white but my bunny's very, very tiny so I have to hold him in my hand so he won't get hurt. He's going back to his house now. Hop, hop, hop . . ."

Display photographs of the children and classroom

Photographs of the children working and playing and of classroom and outdoor materials and equipment can be placed in the quiet area so that children can look at them whenever they wish. Talk with the children about what they see and help them compare the photographs to the real people and objects.

Provide picture books

Have a variety of illustrated books in the quiet area for children to look at whenever they choose. Picture books about what the children saw and did on field trips can be included. Give the children the opportunity to "read" or interpret the pictures to you as you look at the books and read with them.

Be sure to select books with large, clear illustrations or photographs of people, places, animals, objects and actions with which the children have had some experience so that they have some basis for interpretation. Also be sure to accept a child's interpretation of what he sees even if it isn't the conventional one. A child might look at a picture of a crane, for example, and call it "a tractor with a long neck."

Place catalogs and picture magazines in the art area

As children cut and paste pictures, talk with them about what they see. When possible see if they can locate corresponding objects or people doing similar things in the classroom.

Key Experience:
Role playing

Timmy and Ricky, outfitted in fire hats, boots and coats, are busy loading their "firetruck" with a ladder and hose when the phone rings. Ricky answers. "Fire at Becky's!" he shouts. "Fire at Becky's!" echoes Timmy as they hop aboard the truck and rush off to the block area where they battle with Becky's burning house.

Lisa is busy washing dishes inside a cardboard "house" when Billy walks up wearing a bus driver's cap and shouts through the window, "I'm home, honey!" "O.K., baby," Lisa replies. "I need some clothes," Billy says as he grabs some pants and a dress. He sizes up the pants for himself and throws the dress to Lisa. "Here's yours, honey," he says.

Role playing, making believe—pretending to be someone else by doing and saying what that person does and says—is another way young children represent experiences they've had and what they know about people and situations. Through role play children sort out and use what they understand about events they've witnessed or taken part in—making breakfast, going to work, going to a party, visiting friends, taking care of a baby, going to the dentist, attending a wedding or a funeral, putting out a fire. The logic, meaning and context of many situations and events in the adult world often confuse or escape young children, but role play helps them make their own sense of these situations and events.

It's important for adults to recognize that three- and four-year-old children represent experiences through role play and to encourage and support such play. In providing materials and opportunities for role play, adults are providing opportunities for children to represent and thus consolidate and strengthen what they know about their world. Here are some ways adults can encourage and support children's role play.

Suggestions for adults

Provide a place in the room specifically for role play

In many classrooms the house area is set aside for role play, although the children often need more room and so extend their play to the block area and to other parts of the room. Children may "go off to school" under the sandbox or near the coat rack, for example, or "go to the store" in the quiet area.

Equip the role play area with a variety of materials for props

For a list of role play equipment and materials for prop boxes, see the section on arranging and equipping a house area in chapter 1.

Children will also use materials from other areas of the room in their role play. For example, a child who needs some "money" to put in her purse might decide to make some money in the art area, or to hunt in the quiet area for some things to use (e.g., beads, shape-sorter chips, puzzle pieces).

Provide equipment outside for role play

Because there's usually more space outside and fewer boundaries, outdoor role play is generally noisier, freer and more mobile than indoor role play. Children include whatever they can find— wagons, tricycles and other wheel toys for cars, buses, trains, boats; large packing boxes, boards, ropes and tires for houses, stores, forts and caves; sand and sand utensils for cooking, eating and "going to work."

Encourage children who are just beginning to role play

Some children who have had little role play experience may want to assume a role but may need help from an adult in carrying it through. Here are some things to try:

Provide opportunities for the children to see different people in different roles by inviting adults to come to the classroom and demonstrate what they do. A mother and her baby might come to visit, for example, and the children without younger siblings could see some of the things "being a mother" entails. Taking field trips is another way children can see people working. Bringing back objects children can use as props in their play and taking photographs of people in their roles help children recall what they saw different people doing.

Model the use of role play props with children during work time. An adult might call a child on the telephone and ask to come over to see what he's doing. An adult could also use puppets or dollhouse people to talk with children about what they're doing.

If a child shows some interest in a particular role play situation but doesn't know how to take part, an adult can assume a role appropriate to the ongoing play and invite the child to join in. Ask the child who he'd like to be, and if he can't think of a role himself, suggest several roles from which he could choose. Stay with him until he's in his role with other children and then gradually withdraw. Here's how one adult did this:

Billy and Becky had set up a hospital and were looking around for a patient. They tried to enlist Faye, who was watching from the sidelines. "You pretend to have a broken leg, okay, Faye?" they said, trying to guide her to their hospital bed improvised from cloth blankets and towels. Although Faye resisted their suggestion, she didn't leave the area. Perhaps she really wants to join the play, one of the adults, Ms. Ransom, thought, but doesn't quite know what to do. "Let's both pretend to be patients with broken legs," Ms. Ransom said to Faye, who nodded in agreement. "Maybe you could knock on the hospital door so Billy and Becky will let us in." Faye and Ms. Ransom entered the hospital as patients. When Ms. Ransom saw that Faye was comfortable in her new role, she said, "I'm going home now, but I'll be back soon to visit you. Doctor, when are visiting hours?" Ms. Ransom left, returning about 10 minutes later with some visitors from the block area and some flowers they'd made for Faye from tinkertoys.

When children indicate they'd like to assume a role but don't seem to be carrying it out, try talking with them about some of the things the person they have chosen does. For example, if a child says he's going to be a "store man" but then stands around not doing anything, an adult might say, "Dennis, you said you were going to be a store man today. What are some things store men do?" If Dennis can't come up with anything, the adult could give him some suggestions and arrange a field trip to a store in the near future.

Role play at small-group time

Plan small-group activities in which children assume roles. Here are some ideas:

Give the children puppets or dollhouse people and see if any role play situations occur. An adult can help the children get started by having her puppet or doll go for a visit or call someone on the phone, or the adult could set the stage by saying, "I hope somebody comes to my grocery store today. I sure have lots of food here to sell."

Using large pictures, photographs or a picture book, tell a simple story and ask the children if they'd like to enact it by taking roles themselves. Be sure to ask them who or what they would like to be and what things they might need in order to be that person or thing.

Have children who have role played during work time tell the rest of the group what they did, or take photographs of role play situations during work time and ask the children who were photographed to talk about what they were doing. This may give children who aren't yet role playing an idea of what they could do.

Role play at circle time

Here are some ideas for circle time activities in which children carry out a sequence of actions related to a particular role:

Make up and sing action songs with the children about people they've seen in various roles. Here's a song, for example, about a fireman, to be sung to the tune of "This Is the Way We Wash Our Clothes":

I.   What does a fireman do?
                a fireman do?
                a fireman do?
      What does a fireman do
      At the fire station?
II.   The fireman slides down the pole . . .
III. The fireman puts on his boots . . .
IV.   The fireman puts on his hat . . . etc.

Play group story games in which the children act out the actions of the main character. One such game is "Going on a Bear Hunt," in which the leader chants one line and the group repeats it with appropriate actions:

Going on a bear hunt
(Going on a bear hunt)
Put on my boots
(Put on my boots) . . . etc.

The children especially enjoy being the leader.

Help children sustain their role play

Sometimes children are able to take roles, define a setting and situation for their role play and get started, but then they don't know what to do next, so the role play begins to disintegrate. Here are some things an adult might try when this happens:

Assume a role appropriate to the situation and introduce a new problem or possibility for the group to deal with. Here's how one adult did this:

Mike, John and Amy had made fishing rods and fish and gone fishing with them. They'd pulled their fish in and out of their paper pond a number of times and were beginning to race around and act silly. An adult joined them as a fellow fisherman, saying, "I've caught a lot of fish, too, and now I want to cook them but I don't know what to do. Can you help me?"

Try offering new props the children haven't thought of: "Mike, here's a frying pan. Maybe you could cook your fish in it and maybe this sheet could be your tent in case it rains."

Encourage children to interact in role play situations

Sometimes children carry out a role all by themselves even though there are other children pres-

ent to share it with. If one child is playing mechanic alone, for example, an adult could suggest that another child playing with a truck in the block area take his truck to the mechanic's garage for a tune-up. Be sure there are props available that stimulate cooperative play, like telephones and dress-up clothes that require zipping and tying.

Use the Role-Play Observation Guide

The Role-Play Observation Guide can help adults identify the elements of role play occurring in their classroom and determine which elements each child uses as he plays.

Role-Play Observation Guide

Child _____

Observing a child, do you see him doing the following:

Activity _____

Observing a role play episode, do you see the children doing the following:

	NOTES
• pretending to be someone else	
• sharing the pretend role with others	
• using one object (or "prop") to stand for another	
• using actions and sounds as substitutes for the real actions or sounds	
• using words to represent a make-believe situation or setting	
• talking with others within the context of the role play situation	
• remaining in a role play episode for a significant amount of time	

Key Experience:
Making models out of clay, blocks, etc.

Donna hammers three pieces of wood together to make an airplane in the construction area.

———————

David and Don make a house using blocks and carpet samples. They divide it into rooms and put appropriate furniture in each room.

———————

Corey molds some playdough into a bumpy, oblong shape, puts a small round wooden bead on top of it and two small tinkertoy sticks on either side of the bead. Then he uses his deepest voice to make the sound of an engine as he moves it over the table.

———————

Alisa pretends to be a photographer. Margo decides she'd like to take pictures, too. Because Alisa has the only camera, an adult suggests that Margo make her own. They find an empty Jello box in the art area, punch a hole in it for the viewer and paste a button on to snap the pictures. Then Margo joins Alisa in the house area.

Children enjoy making models of people and objects from three-dimensional media— wood, blocks, carpet pieces, playdough, clay beads, tinkertoys, boxes. But not all three- and four-year-olds use three-dimensional media to make models. Some use blocks for stacking and hauling, wood for sawing and pounding nails, playdough for squeezing, rolling and flattening, boxes for filling and emptying. When these children have had ample opportunity to explore materials, they'll then begin to use them as tools for representation.

Children's representations vary in the amount and arrangement of details and in the similarity of the representation to the thing represented. These differences depend on the degree of the child's familiarity with the object he's representing and his skill with the materials he's using. A child may have a very clear mental picture of a dog, for example, because he plays with his own dog every day, but he may construct a very primitive sort of dog at the workbench because he hasn't acquired the skill to saw out the detailed pieces he needs; his clay dog, on the other hand, may have many more details because it's easier for him to shape the clay to fit his internal picture.

Here are some ways adults can provide children with opportunities to make models.

Suggestions for adults

Provide materials for making models

Include materials for making three-dimensional models in appropriate work areas. For lists of such materials, see the section on arranging and equipping an art area in chapter 1.

Help children acquire skill with tools and equipment

In order to make three-dimensional models, children need to develop motor skills and coordination for such activities as cutting, pasting, stringing, hole-punching, sawing and hammering.

Talk with children at planning time about the models they plan to make

Ask questions to help children think through the model-making process: "What will you need to make your birdhouse?" "What will you do next after you've gotten your wood, hammer and nails?" Always give the child time to answer before asking another question or offering some suggestions.

Some children enjoy dictating a "recipe" and having an adult draw accompanying pictures so they can "read" it themselves. Here's Angie's recipe for a birdhouse:

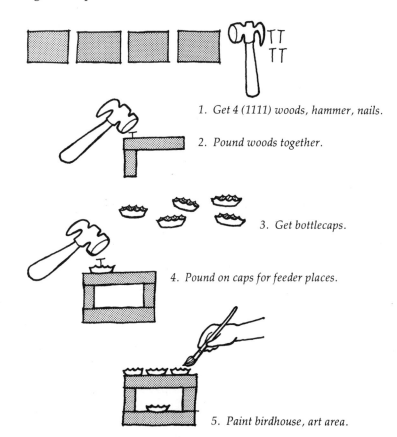

1. *Get 4 (1111) woods, hammer, nails.*

2. *Pound woods together.*

3. *Get bottlecaps.*

4. *Pound on caps for feeder places.*

5. *Paint birdhouse, art area.*

Sometimes a child needs help envisioning a model that's possible to make. The child may plan, for example, to make a giraffe "as big as the one we saw at the zoo." This isn't realistic, of course, but it *is* possible to gather some large cardboard boxes, empty ice-cream tubs and papier mâché supplies and make a "really big" model of a giraffe.

Provide time for making models

Work time (or small-group time) should be long enough to give children time to complete the models they've planned. If a child doesn't finish, however, plan with him to continue the activity the next day at small-group time or suggest that he plan to finish his model at the next work time.

Encourage children to complete or elaborate models

Sometimes children stop working on their models because they don't know what to do next, or they can't get a part to stay on where they want it, or the model doesn't "look right" to them. To help them, an adult can ask questions: "What else does a car have?" "What can you put on your car for when it's dark or rainy?" The adult can help the child nail on the wheel that keeps falling off, or if the model car doesn't "look right" they can take it outside and compare it to a real car.

Some children work on a model for an entire work time but still have things they wish to add before they feel it's complete. At the end of work time, therefore, talk with the children about what they've done so far and what they still need to do the next day at work time.

Encourage children to use a variety of media

Sometimes children get into the habit of making the same kind of model out of the same materials over and over again. Kerry, for example, built houses out of blocks day after day until the adults in her classroom helped her think of some other materials she could use to build houses. After that she began building houses out of wood pieces, clay, large and small tinkertoys, empty food containers and a combination of beads, counting rods and cubes.

Ask children to talk about their models

An adult should not assume he knows what a child's model represents or even that the child is making a model and not just gluing boxes together or pounding nails into wood. A child is likely to feel uncomfortable when an adult says, "Oh, Jimmy, that's a nice boat you're making," when, in fact, Jimmy is making a school bus that just happens to look more like a boat than a bus to the uninformed adult eye. Jimmy is then left with the choice of either feeling bad because his bus looks like a boat or agreeing with the adult that it's a boat even though it started out in his mind to be a bus. Rather than name the object himself, the adult needs to find out from the child what *he* thinks he's making, either by listening to him if he's talking about it as he works or by asking him questions.

Key Experience:
Drawing and painting

Another way preschool-age children represent things they've seen and done is by making their own drawings and paintings. Using paint or implements for drawing, they put down on paper what they can hold in mind about a person, place, object or situation.

The more children use what they know about an object to make a picture or model of it, the more they strengthen their knowledge of that object, and thus the easier it is for them to act on that knowledge in problem-solving situations.

Suggestions for adults

Provide materials for drawing and painting
Stock the art area with a wide variety of materials for painting and drawing. Be sure these materials are accessible and available for children to use during work time whenever they wish to paint or draw.

Help children learn to prepare and use painting materials on their own
Early in the year help children learn the processes of mixing their own paint, getting ready to paint, unrolling paper from the paper roll, tearing off sheets of computer paper. Many teaching teams plan small-group times around learning these procedures.

Some adults feel uncomfortable about allowing children to mix their own paints because they feel that children will waste limited supplies and make a mess. Once children understand what the procedure involves, however, and how they can accomplish each step, they're

"A GIRL ON A BICYCLE. SHE'S GONNA HIT A ROCK."

quite able to mix their own paints with a minimum of waste and mess. Here's a "recipe" one teaching team devised and used successfully with their children:

1 scoop of paint . . .

. . . into jar.

1 scoop of water . . .

. . . into jar.

Stir to form paste.

Add water up to the line.

Assist children who want to draw or paint but don't know how to begin

Sometimes when children are drawing or painting a picture of something, they have difficulty remembering what it looks like. A child may be drawing a person but may be unable to think of any attributes of a person besides a head, arms and legs. An adult can help by suggesting, for example, that the child look in a mirror.

Often children want to make a picture of something they've used or made in the classroom but have no idea how to go about drawing or painting it. An adult might suggest tracing the object. To do this, the child may need help fitting the object onto a piece of paper and keeping the object steady as he or she traces. When the drawing is finished, the adult can help the child compare the tracing to the object.

When children are attempting to draw something that's not available in the classroom, like a firetruck, an adult can suggest they go to one of the work areas and bring back a realistic toy model to draw or trace.

Sometimes children want to draw something but are overwhelmed by its size or complexity. An adult can help them get started. Jeff, for example, had built a very tall, complex building in the block area. He wanted to make a picture of it to show his mother, but it was too large to trace, and he didn't know how to begin drawing it. An adult offered to help him. "What part should we draw first?" she asked. Jeff pointed to a block on the bottom of the structure, which the adult then drew. "Okay, Jeff, your turn. Which part are you going to draw?"

Ask children to talk about their paintings and drawings

The amount and arrangement of detail in children's drawings and paintings varies from child

bouncing
the
ball
Ryan

Key Experience:
Observing that spoken words can be written down and read back

My mama makes breakfast. Then the school bus comes. She waves. She goes back inside and watches her programs. She makes lunch. I watch "Spider Man." Then she watches her program. Then she takes me to the store and she buys me toys. She buys me all the toys. She makes dinner.

to child depending on each child's familiarity with what he's representing and his skill with the media. One child, for example, may draw what looks to an adult like a mass of squiggles and say, "This is me on the swings." Another child may draw herself on the swings in a much more detailed and recognizable fashion. It's important that adults acknowledge and accept all children's drawings and paintings, whether they're squiggles or recognizable images. One way to do this is to say to a child, "Tell me about your picture"—this gives the child a chance to give his or her own interpretation and so avoid the awkward situation in which an adult imposes an interpretation on the child's work.

This is Timmy's story about his mama. As he said the words, an adult wrote them down. Timmy watched the adult say the words as she wrote, and he watched her pencil making the words. When he was finished dictating, he listened to her read back his story just as he had said it. "That's what I said," he said with a great big smile. "I'm 'na show it to Miss Linn so she can read it," and off he went with his story proudly in hand.

Like Timmy, many preschool-age children are fascinated and pleased by the dictation process, another way in which they can represent their experiences. They dictate stories about familiar people and situations as well as stories about pictures they've made, structures they've built, situations they've enacted in role play. Their stories may be a series of coherent sentences, like Timmy's, or a series of words or phrases.

Through dictation children begin to understand how written language can be used to represent their thoughts. As they hear their own words read back, children begin to get a sense of the power of their words to communicate their experiences and ideas. They begin to realize, too, that they can be *makers* of stories as well as listeners.

Here are some ways adults can encourage and support children who are observing that spoken words can be written down and read back.

Suggestions for adults

Take dictation from children throughout the day

Make the process of writing down a child's words and reading them back a regular classroom procedure. At appropriate moments throughout the day—e.g., at planning time, work time as children are finishing projects and talking about them, or at recall time—ask children if they'd like to have their stories written down. On a fresh sheet of paper, or on the child's picture if he so desires, write down exactly what he says without editing or correcting his grammar. Read back the child's words, pointing to each word as you read.

Sometimes a group of children may wish to dictate a group story about a project they've worked on together or a role play situation in which they were all involved. Follow the above procedure, giving each child a turn to speak and inserting the child's name in the form "_____ said" before his or her contribution.

Read books to children

Read both picture books and storybooks to children. With picture books, point out that there are no words to read, and encourage the children to tell their own stories from the pictures. Take the opportunity to write down the stories the children tell and read them back. With storybooks, point to the words as you read them.

Encourage children to make their own books

Many children enjoy putting together their own books with illustrations and dictated stories. In order to support and encourage this process, be sure to equip the art area with a variety of bookmaking materials: paper of various sizes, colors and textures; writing and drawing implements; tape, glue, a stapler, a hole punch, scissors, yarn, string, magazines and catalogues. Some children will have no difficulty constructing a cover, gathering the number of pages they want and figuring out a way to hold the whole thing together.

Other children will need help identifying the parts of a book and finding a way to keep the parts together.

When a child has finished making a book, read his words back to him, pointing to each word as it's read. Some children will want to make up a title for their book and number the pages; other children won't be concerned with these details.

When a child has made a book during work time, be sure to have him talk about how he made it at recall time and read it to the group so they can enjoy the story and perhaps get the idea that they, too, can make their own books.

Help children recognize their own names in written form

Often the first word a child recognizes and learns to write is his or her own name. An adult can help a child learn to recognize his own name in its written form by clearly printing it on his sign, on the box he uses to store his personal belongings, under his coathook and on the pictures, books and constructions he's made.

Some children will enjoy arranging large wooden or plastic letter blocks to form their names, and some will be able to trace or even copy their names from a model the adult provides.

Related films and publications from the High/Scope Foundation

Films—

(For a complete description of each film and instructions for ordering, see appendix 4.)

Experiencing and Representing series: *Part I—A Way Children Learn; Part II—Starting with Direct Experience; Part III—From Direct Experience to Representation; Part IV—Strategies for Supporting Repesentational Activity*

A Place to Represent Things from **The Block Area** series

Observing Role Play

Contrasting Teaching Styles: Work Time, the Art Area from **Guidelines for Evaluating Activities** series

Representation series: *Part I—An Important Opportunity; Part II—Opportunities in the Classroom; Part III—Encouraging Interaction and Cooperation* (Elementary grades)

Publications—

The Cognitively Oriented Curriculum—Learning Through Play and Drama (booklet) by Richard Lalli, 1979. (Elementary grades)

This guide looks at drama from its informal roots as role play and casual interaction to the more advanced forms of scripted performances. It discusses in detail the various elements of drama for elementary-level children (i.e., role play and language opportunities) and offers teachers practical suggestions for 1) introducing drama into the classroom, 2) extending children's spontaneous role play into more planned drama experiences, and 3) helping children make their own dramatic events. The booklet details ways of extending play to include writing experiences in the forms of scripts, stories and scenarios.

The Cognitively Oriented Curriculum—Writing and Reading (No. 6) (booklet, 40 pp.) by Oon Bee Hsu, 1977. (Elementary grades)

A plan for developing writing and reading abilities in elementary-age children based on the following premises: 1) that writing and reading are best learned together; 2) that the child's initiation into literacy is a matter of his discovering the connection between spoken and written language; and 3) that the child discovers this connection when his own experiences are the content for his first attempts at writing and reading.

Related reading on representation

Almy, M. "Spontaneous Play: An Avenue for Intellectual Development," in *Early Childhood Education Rediscovered*, J.L. Frost, ed. New York: Holt, Rinehart, and Winston, 1968.

Athey, Irene. "Piaget, Play and Problem Solving," in *Play as a Learning Medium*. Washington, D.C.: NAEYC, 1974. pp. 33-51.

Curry, Nancy E. "Dramatic Play as a Curriculum Tool," in *Play as a Learning Medium*. Washington D.C.: NAEYC, 1974. pp. 59-73.

Franklin, Margery B. "Non-Verbal Representation in Young Children: A Cognitive Perspective," *Young Children*, November, 1973. pp. 33-53.

Furth, H. *Piaget and Knowledge*. Englewood Cliffs, New Jersey: Prentice-Hall, 1969.

Ginsburg, Herbert and Sylvia Opper. *Piaget's Theory of Intellectual Development, An Introduction*. Englewood Cliffs, New Jersey: Prentice-Hall, 1969. pp. 72-85 and 152-161 (mental imagery) and pp. 168-179 (development and learning).

McFarland, Margaret B. *et al. Play: The Child Strives Toward Self-Realization*. Washington, D.C.: NAEYC conference proceedings, 1971. pp. 8-12.

Piaget, Jean. *Play, Dreams, and Imitation in Childhood*. New York: Norton, 1951.

Piaget, Jean and Barbel Inhelder. *The Psychology of the Child*. New York: Basic Books, 1969. Chapter 3, "The Semiotic or Symbolic Function," and "Conclusion: Factors in Mental Development."

Sigel, I. and B. McBane. "Cognitive Competence and Level of Symbolization among Five-year-old Children," in *Disadvantaged Child*, Vol. 1, J. Hellmuth, ed. Seattle: Special Child Publications, 1967. pp. 435-453.

Singer, J. *The Child's World of Make Believe*. New York: Academic Press, 1973.

Smilansky, Sara. *The Effects of Sociodramatic Play on Disadvantaged Preschool Children*. New York: John Wiley and Sons, Inc., 1968. Chapter 2, pp. 5-18.

Smilansky, Sara. "Can Adults Facilitate Play in Children? Theoretical and Practical Considerations," in *Play: The Child Strives Toward Self-Realization*. Washington, D.C.: NAEYC, 1971. pp. 39-50.

Sponseller, Doris. "Schema for Play and Learning," in *Play as a Learning Medium*. Washington, D.C.: NAEYC, 1974. pp. 115-123.

8/ Classification

Jeff and Jesse are pulling on their boots, getting ready to go outside in the snow. "Hey, Jesse," says Jeff, "our boots are the same. Mine are red here and yours are red and mine have these snapper things like yours. Look, teacher, me and Jesse wore the same boots!"

———————

"Those two bunnies is the same," announces Joannie as she looks into the rabbit cage. "He's the same and he's the same. And they wiggle their noses like this!"

———————

Rebecca and Lynnette are building a tower in the block area. "I found something outside we could put right here," says Rebecca, taking a small stone out of her pocket. "It's very tiny and soft and it's got some white things on it. We can't let anyone see it, okay?"

These children are exercising their capacity to observe attributes of objects, to note similarities, to put similar objects together, to distinguish the meaning of "same" and "different." In short, they are beginning to classify, to use the logical thinking skills they command to distinguish characteristics of things and to sort and arrange them according to these characteristics.

* * *

How the capacity to classify develops in children

In what Piaget calls the *sensorimotor* stage of development, babies as young as one to four months learn to make different responses to different objects. For example, they suck on some things and not on others, they regard some things more intently than others and smile at some people and objects more readily than at others. Babies are intensely involved in perceptual learning—tasting, touching, hearing, seeing—using what they discover with their senses to distinguish one thing from another. Later on they learn that different objects call for different actions—a rattle is to shake, a ball to roll, a squeaker toy to squeeze, a bell to ring. Differentiation and perceptual learning are not classification, but they are essential to its development because they help infants learn that not all things are the same and that different attributes call for different actions.

In the next stage of cognitive development, the *preoperational* period (ages 2-7), children are still actively involved in the exploration of objects and their attributes, but they are also beginning to use class names for objects, although they may not yet understand the logic of the classes. A preschool-age child may use the class name "fruit," for example, to refer to particular fruits he doesn't know the names for. He calls an apple by its name but refers to limes as fruit. If someone else refers to an apple as fruit he disparagingly corrects him: "Oh brother, that's not fruit. That's an apple!" He doesn't realize that apples and limes both belong to the same class, fruits.

When very young children begin to sort objects they start by making what Piaget calls "graphic collections," carefully arranging things in a way that appears to have nothing to do with their similarities and differences. In the block area, for example, a child may sort out a heap of blocks, very carefully arranging them in a group the logic of which escapes anyone but himself. When asked what's the same about all the things in his collection, the child, if he is able to respond, is likely to point to one block after another and say something different about each one. "This one's red. This one's got a hole. This one's long. This one's a funny shape."

As young children develop, they move from making graphic collections to sorting objects according to consistent criteria. These first non-graphic collections tend to be groups of objects that are exactly the same along every dimension.

are not identical, and they choose a criterion for grouping objects and use it consistently until all objects are accounted for.

In the next stage of development, the period of *concrete operations*, seven- to eleven-year-old children deal with the logic of classification as they begin to understand and work with multiple class membership and class inclusion.

Here's an example of some elementary-age children working with multiple class relationships—the idea that a set of objects, ideas or events can be sorted several different ways and that an object, idea or event can thus be a member of more than one class:

Some children are making caramel apples for a Halloween party. Before they start they separate all the materials they've gathered for the process into two groups—the things they bought at the store (caramel and sticks) and the things they gathered at school (pot, spoon, cinnamon and waxed paper). When the adult brings over a bag of apples she had brought from home, they point out that the apples don't belong in either group because they hadn't bought them or found them at school. The adult suggests they think of two different groups into which they can re-sort their items so that the apples will also be included. This time the children come up with "things you can eat" (apples, cinnamon and caramels) and "things you can't eat" (pot, spoon and waxed paper).

Unlike preoperational children, these children have the capacity to realize that objects have multiple attributes and therefore don't belong exclusively to one class. They had no trouble making two large classes to account for all the items they were using, and they also saw that each object could belong to more than one class— that the caramels, for example, were at the same time both "bought at the store" and "things to eat."

Children begin by sorting things into many small groups, but later they are able to sort into fewer groups with a wider variety of objects in each group. For example, they might sort the same buttons into the same muffin tin using fewer groupings, perhaps putting all the red buttons together, all the blue buttons together and all the white buttons together. At seven or eight years of age they'll probably be able to sort all the buttons into just two categories—all the four-holed buttons and all the not-four-holed buttons. One thing they wouldn't understand, however, is the idea of class inclusion, the idea that the four-holed buttons and the not-four-holed buttons all belong to the larger class of buttons regardless of their differences. When asked, "Are there more four-holed buttons or more buttons?" they wouldn't be able to figure out the problem.

Towards the end of the preoperational stage, children exercise these classification-related capacities: they see similarities among objects that

Class inclusion is the process of combining small groups—cats, dogs, rabbits—to make large groups—animals—and reversing the process by separating the parts from the whole. As they look at their gerbil family, these elementary-age children are tangling with the logic of class inclusion:

An adult and several children are looking at their family of two adult gerbils and five new babies born the night before.

Adult: *What do you think, Willa? Are there more babies or more gerbils?*
Willa: *More babies.*
Adult: *More babies than what?*
Willa: *Than gerbils.*
Adult: *What do you think, Joanne?*
Joanne: *I think there are more babies than there are mothers and fathers.*
Adult: *Are there more babies or more gerbils?*
Joanne: *There are more babies.*

Willa and Joanne don't yet understand that the subset babies is contained within the whole set gerbils. Jessica, who is older, has mastered the logic of the problem:

Jessica: *They're all gerbils.*
Adult: *Well, what do you think, Jessica?*
Jessica: *Well, then, there's more gerbils.*
Adult: *More gerbils than what?*
Jessica: *Than babies because these five babies plus those other two are seven.*

Children like Jessica who understand class inclusion can accurately compare the number of members in a class and can understand the relations "some" and "all," that is, the relation of the part to the whole.

When children reach *formal operations,* at around twelve years of age, not only can they deal with multiple relations among classes and with class inclusion but they can control variables and work with hypothetical classes.

The importance of classification experiences for preschool children

Three- and four-year-old children use many objects with skill and imagination. They've had experience with heavy and light things, hard and soft things, round things and prickly things, but they aren't necessarily conscious enough of these attributes to be able to call upon them when they need them in a specific situation. Three-year-olds, for example, often want things other children are using. Three-year-old Corey grabs the truck Susanna is filling with stones and yells, "I want that, I want that. Gimme. Gimme." If Susanna doesn't give in and an adult doesn't intervene soon enough, he hits Susanna and she

Summary: How Classification Capacities Develop

The child	Sensorimotor Stage (0-2½ yrs.)	Preoperational Stage (2½-7 yrs.)	Concrete Operational Stage (7-11 yrs.)	Formal Operational Stage (12+ yrs.)
Makes different responses to different objects	X	X	X	X
Explores attributes	X	X	X	X
Uses class names		X	X	X
Makes graphic collections		X	X	X
Sorts by identity		X	X	X
Sorts by similarity		X	X	X
Sorts into two groups		X	X	X
Uses multiple class relationships			X	X
Uses class inclusion			X	X
Controls variables				X
Generates hypothetical classes				X

bites him back and they're both out of hand. An adult can aid Corey in this situation by helping him distinguish the things about the truck that appeal to him so that he can find something else that meets the same requirements. Corey already has the capacity to distinguish attributes and to find similar objects, but he needs opportunities to learn how to use these capacities so he can begin to solve problems on his own. There's no point in trying to drill a three- or four-year-old in class inclusion or to explain to him how to sort all items in a set into two groups, because pre-operational children do not yet possess these logical capacities. They can be good at what they *can* do, however, and the more opportunities they have to do this, the broader and richer the base from which they will continue to develop.

Key Experience:
Investigating and describing the attributes of things

Three- and four-year-olds actively explore and investigate objects. With their command of language they can name and organize what they find out from their investigations. They are able to ask and answer for themselves such questions as, What can I do with this? Where can I find another one? How does this look, feel, taste, sound, smell? What parts does this have? What can I use with it?

Darla, a four-year-old, was working in the quiet area with a set of interlocking building squares. As she fit them together in a number of ways she reported the following observations to her friend stringing beads next to her: "These have slots . . .

You just punch the slots together like this . . . These are the same color . . . You look green when I look through these . . ." A few days later, when Darla was building a window in the block area, she included the building squares from the quiet area because she remembered that she could see through them.

The ability to describe the attributes of things they explore and observe allows children like Darla to use this information when they need it to solve a problem or to communicate their ideas and discoveries.

Suggestions for adults

Provide materials worth investigating

Children will wish to investigate and talk about materials they find intriguing—things with moving parts, things they haven't been able to get close to before like tools, kitchen utensils, cloth and carpet scraps, real foods, musical in-

Key experiences: Classification
- Investigating and describing the attributes of things
- Noticing and describing how things are the same and how they are different; sorting and matching
- Using and describing objects in different ways
- Talking about the characteristics something does *not* possess or the class it does *not* belong to
- Holding more than one attribute in mind at a time
- Distinguishing between "some" and "all"

struments, objects they find on field trips, a record player, a tape recorder, a simple camera, animals and plants.

One adult made this comment about materials that were particularly interesting to an active child: "Ric's intrigued with objects over which he has control, which he can operate and change so that he can see the results immediately—things like a sponge, flashlight, metronome, squeeze bottle, clock and screw toys."

Children are eager to use and investigate real tools at clean-up time—a broom and dust pan, sponges and water, a vacuum cleaner. With help they can learn to use and operate these tools on their own. An adult who felt a little wary of letting children use the vacuum cleaner was rewarded when she heard this description: "Look Markie, you push on this metal thing here. I hold onto this bumpy part. This here cuts it on. It moves easy. Okay, go . . . See the dirt go up under that black thing?"

At the beginning of the year and throughout the year when new materials are added to the classroom, use small-group times to investigate and describe new classroom materials. Provide an object or set of materials for each child in the group. Ask each child to talk about an object. When possible, take dictation from children about objects and read it back.

Use outdoor time to collect, investigate and describe natural objects with children: leaves, grass, stones, pinecones, trees, bushes, animals, sidewalks, walls, cans, sand, puddles, dirt.

Plan field trips on which children can collect objects to bring back to the classroom: trips around the block, to a chestnut tree, to a park, to an orchard or garden, to a grocery store.

Use meal and snack times to help children investigate and describe the attributes of the foods they're eating.

Ask questions of children about the objects they're investigating

"What can you tell me about the things you're building with?" "What are you doing with the things you're holding in your hand?" "What else do you think you could do with all those beads?"

If a child can't respond to such questions, ask questions that give a little more direction: "What can you tell me about the parts of your truck?" "What can you tell me about the way your blocks feel (sound, look)?"

If a child can't respond to any questions about the objects he or she is working with, talk with the child in a pleasant, conversational way: "Mark, you're rolling all the round blocks. I bet I can roll these round blocks back to you." "Laura, it looks as though you're filling up the big cup with water and then pouring it into the metal pot with all the holes in the bottom. Look, the water's coming out the holes."

Accept the names for things children generate themselves

Support children's investigations by using the descriptive labels they generate as well as the conventional labels: "That's right, Mark. You're using the noisy beater thing, or the egg beater, to make your pancakes."

Ask children what *they* would call objects rather than supplying them with all the "correct" labels. This gives the adult a chance to see what attributes the children are focusing on: "What do you think you could call those things you are gluing onto your paper, Henry? . . . White squishies? That's a good name. Why do you call them that?"

Take dictation from children about things they're investigating

For some children, describing the attributes of something they're using or something they've made is more meaningful if an adult writes down their "story." Be sure to take down their words verbatim even though the sentences may be incomplete and the grammar incorrect. The important thing is to see how the child is thinking. Be sure also to read the whole story back to the child. Stories about objects taken down during work time can also be read back to a wider audience at recall or small-group time.

Take opportunities outdoors, at circle time and on field trips to help children investigate and describe the attributes of things

For example:

Sing "Mary Wore a Red Dress" and have each child make up a verse by naming something another child is wearing. Go around the circle so each child has a turn.

Outside, try a game in which all the children playing run to something wooden, for example, as an adult counts to five. After the children get the idea, have them take turns being "it"—naming the kind of thing to run (or hop or skip) to and counting to five. For children who end up at something that's not wooden (if that is the attribute), be sure to acknowledge positively what they've located. For example, "Casey ran to the wooden ladder. Marie's at the wooden bench. Kelly and Stacey are on the wooden rim of the sandbox. Chris ran to something metal, the legs of the swing set, and Annie found a part of the swings that's wooden, the seats."

Field trips to places where children can touch and handle things give them a chance to investigate and describe objects usually not available in the classroom. This means talking in advance to the people at the field trip site to arrange possible "up close" opportunities for the children. One adult, for example, had neighbors who raised sheep. In the spring, when the lambs were corralled in small pens with their mothers, the neighbor let the children pet and feed them from a bottle. As they did, they talked about the lamb's "hard stubby hair," the mother's "long brown hair," the lamb's "sharp black feet," "ears with pink insides" and "tongue all wet and slimy."

Help children investigate and describe objects at small-group time

In planning a small-group time in which children investigate and describe attributes of objects, ask and answer the following kinds of questions with teaching team members: *Which objects would interest the children—objects from the classroom they don't seem to be aware of? objects from a field trip? things the children have collected themselves? things relevant to their geographic area or cultural heritage? Will there be enough objects for each child to have something to work with on his or her own? Should some additional objects be available for children to use? How will the activity begin? How can I give the children some idea of what to do with the materials without being too directive? How will the activity end? How can I help the children describe their discoveries? How can I help make them conscious of the attributes they've been exploring?*

It's important that small-group time have a brief but clear beginning in which children find out which materials they will be using and what, in general, they're to try with these materials:

"The people who worked in the house area today made some dough that's something like playdough. I'm going to give some to each of you. Let's play around with it and see what it feels like."

"Remember where we went yesterday? . . . That's right, to the apple orchard. Here are some of the apples we picked. I want everyone to take one and see what you can do with your apple."

"Here are some new Lego blocks we just got for the quiet area. After you each get some, see if you can make them go together somehow. See what you can do with them."

Children will explore and use objects in a variety of ways. Some will be intrigued with one or two aspects of the object, and others will try out a number of different things. In either case the adults should support and acknowledge what each child is doing. Try to follow this acknowledgment with a comment that will either help

children become aware of what they're doing or help them see something new to try. Here are some examples of what an adult might say as a small group of children are exploring playdough:

"Yes, Tracy, you've rolled your playdough into lots of balls. And look, they're all pretty much the same size. Maybe you could try making some that are a different size."

———————————

"Liz, you have a good way of spreading your playdough out using the spoon. I'm going to try your idea and spread mine out that way. I think I'll use the handle of my spoon, too."

———————————

"That's a good idea, what you're doing with your playdough, Jerry. You put your hand in it and made a print. Can you see something else on the table you could use to make a print in it?"

———————————

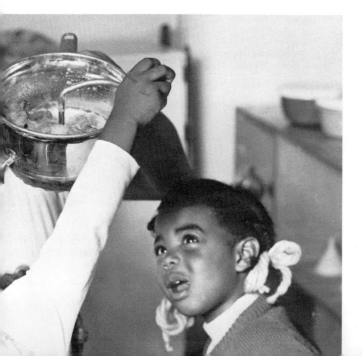

"Felix, you're mashing the playdough through your hands so it will squish through your fingers. What does it look like on the other side of your hand?"

Bring small-group time to a meaningful end for children by helping them become aware of all the things they've discovered about their materials. Here are some ways to do this:

Write a group story with the children about the objects they've been exploring. For example, if the children have been exploring apples, ask each child to say something about his or her apple and write down what each child says. A "story" like this might result: *"This apple rolls,"* said Margo. *"Mine does, too, and I can roll it between my hands,"* said Tommy. *"Red,"* said Joannie. *"It tastes good,"* Felix said. *"Mine has lots of seeds,"* said Andy. *"Skin on the outside,"* said Lavonne.

———————————

Have each child say something into a tape recorder about what he or she did or found out. Play it back.

———————————

As children are cleaning up, talk to them about what they found out about their materials.

———————————

Build some of the children's discoveries into a clean-up game. For example: "Some of you found out that some of your blocks roll. Let's see who can roll their blocks across the table into the can . . . Felix, you were spinning some of your blocks. Do you think we can spin some blocks into the can? . . . Laurie stood her blocks up into a line and when she pushed the end block, it knocked the others down. Do we have enough blocks left to do that so that the end ones go into the can? . . ."

Key Experience:
Noticing and describing how things are the same and how they are different; sorting and matching

Kendra is showing an adult a picture she made by cutting out squares of wrapping paper and gluing them onto a piece of construction paper. "This goes with this. This goes with this," Kendra says, pointing to pairs of squares. "Why do they go together?" the adult asks. "Because this one has a snowman and this one does, too. And this one has a bird and this one has another bird." "Oh, you mean these two are the same because they both have snowmen and these two are the same because they both have birds?" "Yeah, and this and this have red circles with yellow around them." "That's right. They're the same, too."

———————————

Tracy has filled a pegboard with red pegs on one half of the board and yellow ones on the other. He thrusts it proudly at an adult, saying, "Birthday cake." "What a great cake, Tracy," the adult says, putting her arm around him and squatting down to get a better look. "Can you tell me something about it?" "Candles," he says, running his hand across the pegs. "Yes, it has lots of candles, Tracy, and they look pretty special to me because you've put all the yellow candles together on this side and all the red candles together on this side. The red ones are all the same and the yellow ones are all the same." "Blow," says Tracy, indicating the red candles. "Okay, I'll blow out all the red candles and then you blow out the yellow ones, okay?" Tracy laughs and nods.

———————————

As Jimmy and Wendy march their animals along a road they've built of stones and blocks, they chant as the animals move first along the stones, then along the blocks, "Bumpy, noisy, bumpy road. Bumpy, noisy, bumpy road. Soft, soft, soft road. Soft, soft, soft, road."

Kendra, Tracy, Jimmy and Wendy are all dealing with similarities and differences. Wendy, Jimmy and Kendra can describe the groups they've created, and Tracy can do the actual sorting of his pegs but needs help describing what he has done.

Sorting intrigues three- and four-year-olds. They usually don't sort, however, just for the sake of sorting, as older children are apt to do. Rather their sorting occurs within the context of something else they're doing, like pasting, making a birthday cake or building a road for the animals.

Generally, three- and four-year-olds begin sorting by making groups of things that are exactly alike. Kendra, for example, put two identical snowman squares together and two identical bird squares together. Another, older child who was working next to her described his groups, however, on the basis of similarities rather than identities. He said all the squares with blue edges went together even though the pictures on them were different.

Although young children are able to generate groups of identical and sometimes similar objects, the word "same" is often confusing to them because of its ambiguity: it can mean either identical (exactly the same) or similar (the same in some way). Children like Tracy, for example, need to hear the word used many times in appropriate contexts before they're able to attach the word to their actions.

Responding to and using the words "same" and "different" often but not always precedes the ability to describe *how* things are the same or different, and initially similarities are usually easier for children to describe than differences, although there are always exceptions. An adult asked one little boy, for example, if there were any things that were the same in a picture he had just painted. "Well," he answered, "these two birds are different because this one has a tail and this one has no tail."

An adult who looks carefully at what children do with objects will find that three- and four-year-olds put similar objects together. It's important for the adult to help them find ways to describe what they're doing so that the process becomes conscious for them, and they can call upon it deliberately when it's needed. Here are some ways adults can help children describe how the objects they're working with are the same and how they are different.

Suggestions for adults

Provide sets of identical and similar materials

Provide pairs or sets of identical materials in each area of the room. For example: pairs and groups of trucks, cars, rubber people, animals, blocks, dollhouse furniture, dishes, utensils, hats, scissors, tools, musical instruments.

In each area of the room, provide pairs or sets of materials that are similar but vary along one dimension. For example: dump trucks that are the same make, shape and color but are different sizes; blocks that are the same shape, color and size but are different weights; silverware that is the same size, shape, weight and color but has different patterns on the handles; sandpaper pieces at the workbench that are the same size and shape but have different textures.

Also provide groups of materials that are similar but vary along more than one dimension. For example: blocks that are the same size and shape but are different colors and textures; buttons that are the same shape and have the same number of holes but are different colors and sizes.

When adding new materials to the classroom, ask children where they think the new materials should go. A conversation might go like this:

Adult: Where in our classroom do you think we should put these chestnuts we found on our walk yesterday?
Child: House area.
Adult: The house area is a good place. What do you think you could do with them there?
Child: Cook.
Adult: Cook with them? Can you find some other things in the house area you cook with?
Child: Buttons.
Adult: Is there a place near the buttons for the chestnuts?

At clean-up time help children define their clean-up tasks by referring to specific attributes of objects they're responsible for. For example, an adult in the music area might say, "Lois, can you put away all the instruments that you shake to make a noise?"

When arranging the room, group similar objects together.

In each area of the room, group materials that are the same and similar. For example, put all the paper in one section of the art area, then within the paper section, put all the manila paper together, all the newsprint together, all the red construction paper together, and so on. Children will use paper in other areas of the room, but if it's all stored in one area they will always know where to find it, and they will also learn that different kinds of paper have different uses.

Label places in the classroom where materials are stored—use pictures, photographs or outlines so that children can match the objects to the labels, but don't go overboard in labeling materials so that all the children do is match objects to labels. To avoid this, provide divided containers into which children can sort as they clean up. For example, provide a silverware tray but don't label the divisions within it. This allows the children to make up their own silverware categories. On a shelf containing dollhouse furniture, attach a few labels to the shelf or shelf back so children can see that that's where the furniture goes. Then let them arrange the rest of the furniture in their own groups. Some children may put all the chairs together and all the tables together. Others might group the furniture by rooms—all the bedroom furniture together, all the kitchen furniture together.

Talk with children about materials they're using that have clear similarities and differences

Observe how children are using objects during work time and throughout the day. If they're working with materials that are the same or similar or are sorting things in some way, talk to them about what they are doing: "You've built four tunnels for your truck to drive under, Lisa. What's the same about all four tunnels?"

For the child who can't respond to questioning, describe similarities and differences in what he or she is doing: "Lynnette, you've put all the carpet pieces together and all the red blocks together in your building. You're putting things that are the same together."

Before questioning children about the similarities and differences in materials they're using, watch and listen to find out how they view their projects. Here are two examples:

An adult is watching Erica cut out and glue wrapping-paper squares on a piece of paper. "This is a wipe-mat for my Mom and I'm going to give it to her." The adult picks up on Erica's interest and talks about similarities at the same time: "When you give this to your Mommy are you going to show her anything that's the same?" Erica proceeds to point out and talk about all the parts of her picture that are the same.

———————

One day following a trip to the hardware store, Chris cut out and pasted doorbells onto a sheet of yellow paper after leafing through a pile of pictures and brochures about things at the hardware store. An adult asked which doorbell she'd like to have on her door. She pointed to one: "This one, because it's on my daddy's (Air Force) uniform." Chris found two series of small doorbell pictures, many of which were identical. After she pasted them down the adult asked her if she could find any that were the same. She responded by connecting identical ones with lines. They then talked about similarly shaped doorbells—round, square, long, thin and ones that looked like medals on uniforms.

Sometimes an adult asks a question and the child answers a different question instead: "You're using all kinds of cartons as you work, Troy. How are they all the same?" "This is different and this is different," Troy replies. Then it's necessary for the adult to change the focus to fit the child's concerns: "How are they different, Troy?" "This one's yellow and this one's white."

Be sure to acknowledge and support the work of children who have made their own things that are the same or similar: "Kerry, you've painted two pictures of houses and they're both the same. They both have houses with red roofs. They both have trees next to the house. What else can you see that's just the same? . . . That's right. They both have a person under the tree. I'll come back and see your next picture to see if it's the same as these two or if it's different."

Another special way to acknowledge a child's work is to take a polaroid photograph of things the child has made that are the same or similar. Children enjoy comparing the photograph to the original object.

Take dictation as children describe similarities and differences

In talking with children and asking questions about similarities and differences, ask if they'd like to have what they say written down. This is usually more appropriate when children are in the final stages of their projects. Remember to write down the child's exact language and to read the "story" back to the child.

Take field trips to investigate similarities and differences

Take the children to places where they'll see groups of things that are the same or similar. For example, at a grocery store they would see all the breads together, all the fruits together, and so on. Other possibilities: an open market, a farm, a hardware store, a lumber yard, a greenhouse, a high-school orchestra or marching band. Whenever possible bring back materials that the children will be able to describe and compare in the classroom.

Build similarities and differences into the games children play

With a little brainstorming a teaching team can come up with variations of games and activities that will help children notice and describe similarities and differences. Here are a few starters:

- "Red rover, red rover, let everyone wearing pants the same color as Harvey's come over."
- "Who can think of a way to play the tambourine? Good, Cara has a way. Let's see if we can play our tambourines like Cara."
- "Boy, Tommy, you've found lots of different stones out here on the playground. I'm going to close my eyes and see if I can feel any that feel the same. Then you try it, okay?"
- "That looks like a pretty hard obstacle course you've set up with the boxes and the jump ropes. Let me see if I can go through it the same way you do . . . Let's see if we can go through the same way Elana's doing it."

Help children notice and describe similarities and differences at small-group time

Children *notice* and *describe* similarities and differences in the objects they are using. They *use* similar objects to make things that are similar or different. And they use a wide variety of materials to *generate* their own groups of objects that are all the same or similar.

If an adult doesn't yet have a clear idea of how each child in the group deals with similarities and differences, it might be useful to plan a small-group time in which children can use and describe objects that are the same or similar. Later on, when the adult knows more about the children, he or she can plan an activity in which each child has the opportunity to make a group of similar objects.

In planning a small-group time in which children notice and describe how things are the same and how they're different, consider the following questions: *Which materials would children be interested in describing and sorting? Which particular materials would appeal to the particular children in the small group? How can the activity be done in such a way that it's fun and interesting for the children, so that they're not just being asked questions about similarities and differences? Can any game-like elements be built into the activity? Which children in the group might be apt to describe similarities and differences spontaneously? How will the activity begin so that the children have an idea of what to do and choices about how to do it? How will the activity end so that the children are aware of the similarities and differences the group has described?*

Materials whose similarities and differences children are inclined to *describe* are those whose similarities and differences are fairly obvious: pairs or groups of fruits and vegetables purchased or gathered with the children; collections of fabric samples, some with similar and others with varying textures, thicknesses, colors and designs; a collection of bottlecaps, buttons and washers; a collection of rocks and polished stones; a collection of shells; collections of leaves, pinecones, grasses, flowers, weeds; collections of things gathered on field trips; collections of photographs or pictures of things and situations the children are familiar with.

Materials children *use* on the basis of their similarities and differences are usually collections of similar materials they can do something with—build with, take apart and put together, pretend with. Here are some examples:

Collections of things to build with: table-sized blocks, inch cubes, cuisinaire rods, picture dominoes, shape blocks from shape sorters, small boxes

Collections of things to take apart and put together: small tinkertoys, large Lego blocks, play plax (interlocking plastic squares), beads, bottlecaps with holes, straw pieces, macaroni and string, sets of containers and lids, pegs and

pegboard, nuts, bolts, screws, thin wooden boards with holes

Collections of things to pretend with: small metal and wooden cars, wooden and rubber people and furniture, wooden and rubber animals

Materials children use to *generate* their own groups of objects with obvious similarities or differences could be art or construction materials the children already know how to use: play-dough, magic markers and paper, fingerpaint, wood bits, nails and hammers, styrofoam bits and glue, wire and pipe cleaners, popsicle sticks and glue.

Some children enjoy the idea of a game or a challenge. In making an activity more game-like, try to keep the "rules" simple and minimal and try to have the children challenge themselves rather than work against each other. Here are some ways to make a small-group activity dealing with similarities and differences game-like.

Be sure to add other strategies that work to the list.

After the children have had a chance to work with their own collections of materials, try playing "I'm looking for something that is the same _____ as _____." For example, an adult might say, "I'm looking for all the things on the table that are the same color as my button. Who has something that's the same color?" After the adult has been "it" for a couple of turns, give a child a chance to be "it."

Try the "how many" game: "How many things can you say about your (grapefruit)?" "How many things can you build that are the same from your (blocks)?" "How many things can you make that are the same from your (wire and pipe cleaners)?"

Try giving each child his or her own board on which to assemble a bag of materials. Each child assembles the materials on the board, then passes the board and bag to the next person.

Three- and five-minute sand timers add the element of "how fast" to the activity. An adult might say, "See how many things you make out of playdough that are the same before all the sand runs out. When Gary turns the sand timer over, that means go. And when all the sand is in the bottom, that means stop." A timer might also be used with the "board and bag" game. When the sand runs out, it's time to pass your board and bag to the next person.

A "spinner" can add the element of chance to a game. It might be made from the children's signs or from photographs of the children. One game with the spinner might be to give each child an identical set of objects. The child to whom the spinner points builds something from the materials, and the other children try to make something that's exactly the same or different in some way.

Key Experience:
Using and describing objects in different ways

"Brrrum, brrum, round and round, brrum, brrum, round and round," said Corey as he drove a small dump truck along a block road he'd built. "What goes round and round, Corey?" an adult asked. "The wheels," he said, turning the truck

upside down and showing how they spin. A few days later Corey used the same truck to haul blocks from one block pile to another and back again. "Down dumper," he'd say as he pushed the "dumper" down and all the blocks spilled out. "Up dumper," he'd say as he reversed the process. "Boy, you can really make the dumper part of your truck go up and down, Corey," the same adult said. "Does your truck do anything else?" Corey looked at his truck for a moment and then continued filling it up. The adult said: "The other day you showed me how the wheels go round and round, and today you're making the dumper go up and down. Your truck sure can do lots of things."

Describing more than one characteristic of an object at a time is difficult for most preschoolers. Many, like Corey, may note one characteristic one day and another the next, depending on what aspect of the object they're focusing on at the moment, but they have difficulty switching their attention to other possibilities. Most three- and four-year-olds need help linking their observations so that things can be used and described in several different ways.

Many preschoolers have the same difficulty re-sorting groups they've made. One day at clean-up time, for example, a child may arrange all the dollhouse furniture on the shelf so that all the wooden furniture is on one side and all the plastic on the other. Another day the same child may sort the same furniture so that all the bedroom furniture is together, all the kitchen furniture is together, and so on room by room. Operationally this child is defining some furniture as "wooden" and some as "belonging in the kitchen," but the child needs help in verbalizing and linking these two observations. The more ways a child can describe an object, the more conscious the child becomes of the possible ways to use it.

Here are some ways adults can help three- and four-year-olds link their actions and observations to describe things in different ways.

Suggestions for adults

Provide materials that can be described and sorted in different ways

Most materials already mentioned in this chapter can be described and sorted in different ways.

For example, if the house area has been provided with a variety of buttons that can be used for pretend cooking—buttons of different sizes, shapes, colors and with different numbers of holes—containers can be added that children would enjoy filling with buttons. As a child makes "muffins" or "cupcakes," talk about the kind he is making and ask him if he can think of another kind he could also make. "George, you've made some big-button cupcakes, and some little-button cupcakes. What other kinds of button cupcakes can you make?"

At clean-up time, be aware of how children are sorting and arranging materials on their own. For example, if a child has arranged the furniture on the furniture shelf over a period of several days, see if he does it the same way all the time. If he does it the same way, ask if there's a different way he can put the furniture back. If he does it differently, point out and support these differences: "Garth, yesterday you put all the furniture with legs on one end of the shelf and all the furniture without legs on the other end of the shelf. How did you do it differently today?"

In talking with children about what they're doing, describe the attributes of objects

"Markie, you've really got to pull hard to get your red rubber boots on. The tops of your boots are smooth but the bottoms are rough and full of ridges. And your boots have zippers, too. You zipped them all the way up to the top. Now you're ready to go outside in your red, rubber, zipper boots."

———————

"You sure do a lot with your legs when you swing, Renee. You push them way out in front of you, you pull them back, and you drag them on the ground to make you stop."

———————

"You're going to give me a ride in your wagon, Rhonda. Gee, that's great. Let's see. Take me to the place with the wooden roof (the rabbit hutch) . . . that's right. The rabbit cage has a wooden roof . . ." Later: "Take me to the place with the wire sides (also the rabbit hutch) . . . that's right, the rabbit cage again. It has a wooden roof and wire sides. Can you see anything else it has?"

Ask questions about the attributes of materials children are using

After talking with children about the attributes, similarities and differences of the things they're working with, ask a question: "How does the guinea pig feel?" "How does the guinea pig look?" Always give children ample time to respond to questions. After a child has said a few things in answer to a question, sum up what the child has said: "You've said a lot of different things about the guinea pig, Frank. You've said he's got feet and eyes, he feels soft, and he's brown and white. You can say lots of different things about the guinea pig."

Plan small-group activities that help children describe objects in different ways

One way to think about such small-group activities is to refer to the small-group strategies for the key experience, Investigating and Describing the Attributes of Things (page 195). Plan small-group times in which each child has materials to explore and describe. As children work with materials, attempt to get each child to say several things about the same object. Here are some ways to do this:

When talking to children about what they're doing with their materials, listen to what they say, then ask: "What else can you say about your (pinecone)?" An exchange like this might occur:

Child: *My pinecone's got prickly things on it.*
Adult: *That's right. These things do feel prickly.*
           What do you think you could call these
           prickly things?
Child: *Prickly hard leaves.*
Adult: *That's a good name for them because they*
           are hard and prickly and they do look like
           leaves. What else can you tell me about the
           leaves on your pinecone?
Child: *They're brown, and you can break them off*
           into pieces, but watch out you don't hurt
           your hand.

Whenever possible, link one child's observations to another's:

First child: *My pinecone rolls.*
Second child: *Mine stands up.*
       Adult: *Look at that. Pinecones roll, and*
                they stand up. See if you can try
                rolling yours and then standing it
                up.

Toward the end of the small-group time, play some "how many" games with a spinner or a sand timer. With a spinner, have the child the spinner points to choose an object and say as many things as he or she can about it; spin again and repeat until each child has had a turn. Turn a sand timer over and go around the table having the group say as many things as they can about the object before the sand "runs out."

At the end of the small-group time, write a group story with the children about the objects they've been using. After reading the story back and commenting on all the different statements the children have made about the same object, try underlining and counting all the different attributes mentioned.

Another way to plan small-group times in which children describe something in several ways is to encourage children first to sort objects and then re-sort the same objects into different groups. An adult might give each child a lunch bag full of bottlecaps, buttons and washers, and suggest that everyone sort his or her objects so that the things that are "the same" are together. Some children will make groups of things that are exactly the same—all the big red buttons together, all the little red buttons together, all the clear buttons together, all the Pepsi bottlecaps together, all the orange soda bottlecaps together, and so on until every item has been accounted for even if some have to be in groups all by themselves. Other children will use the materials to build with or arrange into various configurations which may or may not incorporate series of objects that are the same. Some children may sort into more general groups of things that are similar as well as things that are identical. And still other children may need an idea to get started—an adult may need to pick out an object and ask the children if they can find anything like it.

Some children are more likely to sort materials if they have containers into which they can put the groups of objects—a red box for red things, a yellow box for yellow things, for example. Other children may be able to make their own groups on their own "board" (a large sheet of paper), then draw a circle around each group to separate one group from another.

Don't be surprised if many children, especially the younger ones, do more building with materials than sorting. Work with the builders and arrangers on similarities and differences, and work with the sorters on describing their groups and re-sorting if they are able.

Key Experience: Talking about the characteristics something does *not* possess or the class it does *not* belong to

"I don't want that truck. It doesn't have any wheels."

In this very personal way, many three- and four-year-olds begin describing things in terms of attributes they do not possess. Some children are able to make more complex "not" statements:

"Look, teacher!" Jeff holds up the two halves of the apple he has just cut apart. "This part has seeds and this part has no seeds."

Spontaneous comparative statements like Jeff's are not frequent among three- and four-year-olds, but such children are often able to grasp them when others use them. Generally three- and four-year-olds don't group objects into "not" groups such as the "red dress-up shoes" and the "not red dress-up shoes." They're more likely to refer to the red dress-up shoes, the green ones, the brown ones, and so on. It's important, however, for adults in the classroom to use "not" statements in appropriate contexts in their own conversations with children so that children will begin to distinguish classes (roses, for example) from their complements (other flowers that are not roses).

Here are some ways adults can provide opportunities for children to learn that something can be described in terms of characteristics it does not possess.

Suggestions for adults

Try labeling some classroom materials using "not" labels

Some children might be able to decode "not" labels. For example, a shelf for cars and trucks might be labeled with two outlines, one on either end of the shelf:

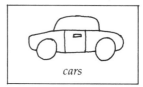 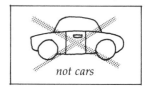

cars   not cars

Some children might be able to put all the cars together and all the vehicles that are not cars together. This kind of labeling may be too abstract, however, even after some explanation. If so, discontinue it.

Use "not" statements in conversations with children

Here are examples of what an adult might say to children at different times of the day:

WORK TIME:

• "Joanie, could you bring me my baby, too? She's the one who's not wearing shoes."

• "Look, Tommy, your picture has lots of red in it, but Lennie's picture does not have any red in it at all."

• "In your tower, Jarvis, you used all the brown blocks on the bottom and all the blocks that are not brown on top."

• "Lois, you're stringing the beads that are in the box, and Tillie is stringing the beads that are not in the box."

• "I'm playing the tambourine, Joanie's playing the tambourine and Eddie's playing the tambourine, but Sylvia's not playing the tambourine. She's playing the drum."

CLEAN-UP TIME:

• "Linda, can you hand me all the animals that are not horses, and I'll put them on the shelf?"

SMALL-GROUP TIME:

• "Kristen and Leo, bring us some things from the quiet area that do not have holes. And Brady, you bring us some things from the art area to draw with that are not crayons. Jenny, we need some paper, too, that is not white."

• "Look, Clarice, you're using all the red blocks to make a road. And Mabel is making a road, too, but she's using blocks that are not red. She's using yellow, and green and blue blocks."

OUTSIDE TIME AND CIRCLE TIME:

• "Red Rover, red rover, whoever is not wearing a hat come over."

• "Jill and Clarence, you've been running lots of races today. What's a different way to race each other, a race that is not a running race? How could you race but not run?" *If the children can't come up with an idea, give them some alternatives like,* "One way you could race but not run is by having a jumping race. Or you could have a rolling race."

• "If you're not wearing red touch your head . . ."

• "If you're not wearing blue touch your shoe . . ."

Ask children "not" questions as they work with materials

Try out some "not" questions to see how children respond. Continue to use them in appropriate situations.

• "How can you tell that's not a banana you feel inside the grocery bag?"

• "You've made applesauce for your babies out of all the red buttons. What else could you make for supper with the buttons that are not red?"

• "Hello, Mr. Grocery Store Man. I'd like to buy some milk. Can you find me two cartons in your store that are not the same? . . . That's great, Mr. Grocery Store Man. You brought two cartons of milk that are not the same. When you were looking for them on the shelf, how could you tell they were not the same? . . . You're not sure? Well, one way I bet you could tell they were not the same, Mr. Grocery Store Man, is that this carton has a cow on it and this one doesn't."

Key Experience:
Holding more than one attribute in mind at a time

Holding two things in mind at the same time and describing something in different ways require similar thinking processes that are difficult for many three- and four-year-olds. When asked to find something that's both red and made of wood, for example, many preschoolers bring back something that's either red but not made of wood or made of wood but not red. They can remember one attribute and search it out but have trouble holding more than one attribute in mind at a time. Instead of "both . . . and" they're more likely to think in terms of "either . . . or."

Repetition of two attributes doesn't in itself represent comprehension, either. After hearing a story about a brown, furry, honey-loving bear, preschoolers can repeat that he was brown and furry and liked honey, but if asked to find something in the room that's also brown and furry (besides the Teddy bear), they have great difficulty. Children can't be drilled or taught to think about two things simultaneously, but they can profit from hearing adults describe objects, situations and events that are both one thing and another.

While it's important for adults to support and encourage children in the things they can do, such as describe attributes, similarities and differences, it's also important to offer challenges to children who may be ready for them. An opportunity to think about two things simultaneously challenges those children who are just beginning to develop that capacity. Here are some suggestions for providing such opportunities.

Suggestions for adults

Try labeling some storage places in terms of two attributes

If the house area is stocked with a variety of black dress-up shoes, for example, try labeling one storage box like this:

(black, buckle)

and another like this:

(black, tie)

Many children may concentrate on one attribute at a time, putting all tie shoes in the "tie" box regardless of color or all black shoes in the "buckle" box whether or not they have buckles. The important thing is to see if there are children who can interpret the labels properly. If there aren't, remove the labels and try again later in the year.

Throughout the day, make comments and observations about objects in terms of two attributes

As appropriate situations arise, talk to children about what they're doing using the idea of "both . . . and." For example, as a child comes in talking about his new hat, an adult might say: "That really is a neat hat, Rocky. It's red and you can snap it. And you know what? You have on something else that's red and snaps, your boots. See, here's the snap on your boots and here's the snap on your hat and they 're both the same color, too."

Ask questions that refer to more than one attribute of an object

As children are working with collections of similar objects, find out if they can hold two attributes in mind by asking questions about the objects:

"Peter, you've made one long necklace with different colors and shapes of beads. Now you're starting another necklace and you have three yellow square beads on it. Do you think you can make this necklace with beads that are just yellow and square?"

_____

"Your building is made out of all red plastic pieces, Cindy. What else can you find to add to it that's also red and plastic?"

_____

"What a beautiful bunch of leaves you've found, Harry. They're all green and long. What can you add to your bouquet that's also green and long?"

If a child can't hold two things in mind at once, if he concentrates on one attribute and not on the other, don't press him. Many three- and four-year-olds are able to look at one attribute at a time, but not two.

For children who can hold two attributes in mind, set up situations throughout the day for them to do so:

"Mike, you planned to make your dinosaur with round, metal legs. Is there anything else you want to add to it that could be round and metal, too?"

_____

"Willa, to shake up the chocolate milk, we need some things that will hold water and have tops. Will you and Eddy go to the house area and see what you can find for us that will hold water and have tops?"

_____

"Boy, Donna, the rabbits sure like eating grass. What else is there that's green and grows in the ground they might like to eat? . . . Good, you've found some clover that's green and grows in the ground, and this looks like dandelion leaves, and they're green and grow in the ground. See if the rabbits like clover and dandelion leaves."

_____

"Laura, jump and clap your hands,
   jump and clap,
   jump and clap,
Laura, jump and clap your hands.
Jump and clap your hands."

_____

"Paul, what two things could you do at the same time? . . . Hop and hold your ear? That's a good idea." "Paul, hop and hold your ear . . ."

Key Experience:
Distinguishing between "some" and "all"

Preschoolers are just learning to use the terms "some" and "all" and to see that "some" is less than "all." They're beginning to understand that there's a difference, for example, between cleaning up all the blocks and cleaning up some of the blocks, between using all of the pipe cleaners and some of the pipe cleaners, between hearing the whole story and just part of it. It's important for adults to support and encourage children as they begin to make these distinctions, because by grappling with the concepts of "some" and "all," children are strengthening their understanding of the difference between a part of something and the whole of it.

Adults can help children make the distinction between "some" and "all" in a number of ways. Here are some suggestions.

Suggestions for adults

Store similar materials together

In each work area, store similar materials next to each other so that as children get and return materials they see the relation between "some" and "all." For example, as children get and return scissors, they see that *all* the scissors are together and that *some* are sharp and *some* are blunt. At clean-up time an adult could say: "Bonnie, you're putting all the scissors away. Some are sharp, and you're putting those together; and some are not sharp, and you're putting those together."

Use "some" and "all" in conversation with children

Since most three- and four-year-old children haven't yet developed the logical capacity to think of a group of objects in terms of "all" and "some," probably the most important thing an adult can do is to use these words in talking with children throughout the day:

"You've used all the blocks in the block area in your structure, Barry and Candice. Some of the blocks you built into towers, and some you built into long lines, but you built with all of them."

_____

"All the children in our class came to school today, but some came on the first bus and some came on the second bus."

_____

"You know, all of us are drinking juice out of cups, but some of us have plastic cups and some of us have paper cups."

———————

"Julie, you ran all the way to the swings, and I only ran some of the way, and then I walked!"

Ask questions using "some" and "all"

"Renee, what can you tell me about all these things you've made out of clay?"

———————

"What can you show your baby that's the same about all the toys you have for her, Joey?"

———————

"Beth, what do you think? Will all your animals fit into Georgie's barn or just some of them? . . . How can you find out?"

Record observations about how children classify

As adults begin to identify classificatory behavior in children, and as they begin to broaden children's capacities by providing for other classification experiences, it's helpful for them to record their observations in order to plan further experiences. The adult who wrote the following report was particularly excited about seeing how the children were classifying.

WORK TIME, QUIET AREA, THURSDAY 11 MAY 1972—

Becky began a guessing game using the lotto cards. She'd hold one against her so I couldn't see the picture and say, "Guess what this is." Lisa and Trina joined her once they got the idea.

When I asked "categories" questions like, "Is it an animal? . . . plant? . . . something you wear?

. . . ride on?" Becky answered yes or no, usually appropriately. She could also give me clues: "It flies" (accompanied by hand motion), "It goes in the water," "Something you can roll on" (roller skates), "Something you are and something else" (a person and a dog). Some objects she couldn't yet generalize into categories. For example, a shark was a shark to her. When I asked, "Is it a fish?" she answered, "No," because she knew its specific name.

At one point I had a picture. Becky could ask me some questions like, "Is it an animal?" but soon exhausted her supply of categories, so I said, "It's something you ride on." She guessed, "Car, truck, bus." So I said, "It doesn't have wheels." She still couldn't guess so I showed her the picture, a sailboat, which elicited this response: "Boats have wheels 'cause they're on the bottom of the sea."

Lisa and Trina couldn't give clues. In fact, when I asked Lisa to tell me something about a picture she generally told me what it was and showed me the picture. Once I asked her, "Is it an animal?" "No," she replied, "it has stripes. It's a zebra."

Trina had a picture of what looked like a bandsman's hat and coat with big gold buttons. When I asked her if it was something to wear she said no. She finally showed me the picture but wasn't quite able to figure out what it was. Becky described it as "a drummer's coat." Apparently Trina can't yet deal with the concept of "coatness" upon seeing a picture of a particular kind of coat she probably hasn't had any experience with. On the other hand when she had a picture of a watermelon and I asked if it was something you could eat, she said, "Yes, it is."

Becky was able to deal with some categories and could give clues. Trina could deal with categories when both the objects and the categories were very familiar to her, but she couldn't give clues. Lisa couldn't deal with categories or give clues except by showing the picture. Many of the pictures she herself couldn't name.

Now that I think about it, these children could deal better with a category when I described it in the manner of, "Is it something that . . . (you wear, eat, ride on)?" When I asked, "Is it a fish, flower, plant?" they seemed to treat this as the name of the object rather than as the category to which it belonged. Perhaps children begin first of all to describe and categorize things in terms of what you do with them or how they're used.

Becky had a picture of an ear of corn. When I asked if it was a plant she said no, but she answered yes when I asked if it was something you could eat. When I saw the picture I made the remark that you could eat plants. Becky thought I was completely crazy. "Plants are green things in the ground," she informed me!

Related films from the High/Scope Foundation

(For a complete description of each film and instructions for ordering, see appendix 4.)

Contrasting Teaching Styles: Circle Time from **Guidelines for Evaluating Activities** series

Contrasting Teaching Styles: Small-Group Time from **Guidelines for Evaluating Activities** series

Classification—A Sequence of Exercises from **Cognitive Development** series (Elementary grades)

Related reading on classification

Flavell, John H. *The Developmental Psychology of Jean Piaget.* Princeton: Van Nostrand, 1963. pp. 303-309.

Ginsburg, Herbert and Sylvia Opper. *Piaget's Theory of Intellectual Development.* Englewood Cliffs, New Jersey: Prentice-Hall, 1969. pp. 119-134.

Inhelder, Barbel and Jean Piaget. *The Early Growth of Logic in the Child.* New York: Norton, 1969.

Kofsky, E. "A Scalogram Study of Classificatory Development," in *Logical Thinking in Children,* I. Siegel and F.H. Hooper, eds. New York: Holt, 1968.

Olver, Rose R. and Joan Rigney Hornsby. "On Equivalence," in *Studies in Cognitive Growth,* Jerome S. Bruner, Rose R. Olver, Patricia M. Greenfield, *et al.* New York: John Wiley and Sons, Inc., 1966. pp. 68-85.

Piaget, Jean and Barbel Inhelder. *The Psychology of the Child.* New York: Basic Books, 1969. pp. 102-103.

Sigel, Irving E. "The Development of Classificatory Skills in Young Children: A Training Program," *Young Children,* January, 1971. pp. 170-184.

9/Seriation

One of the important logical abilities developing in the preschool years is the ability to seriate, or arrange things in a series according to some property, as when children arrange dolls from shortest to tallest. Seriation is a general cognitive skill that involves the coordination of relations as objects are ranked or ordered along some dimension such as weight, cost, age, temperature or sweetness. As with classification, children's ability to fully master the logic of seriation is far from complete during the preschool years.

How the capacity to seriate develops in children

By the time children are "concrete operational," at about seven or eight years of age, the ability to seriate has fully emerged. These children seriate when they rank their ten favorite songs in order of preference, or when they mix up five batches of lemonade made from five different recipes and then rate each recipe according to the sweetness (or sourness) of the lemonade it produced. Seriation begins in the years before this, however, with an awareness of difference. In the sensorimotor stage, infants between the ages of one and eighteen months learn to distinguish and initiate actions of graded intensity. An infant responds to and can make very soft and very loud sounds. He can say "da-da" or "da-da-da" or "da-da-da-da-da-da," making his utterances short or long at will.

One- and two-year-olds show their awareness of difference when they build pyramid towers with the largest blocks on the bottom and the smallest blocks on the top, and when they fit smaller nesting boxes inside larger ones.

"Preoperational" three- and four-year-olds can build more complex pyramid towers and can fit together more nesting boxes than their younger peers. They can also make comparisons: "I am very big now but my baby's very little." "I want all the heavy blocks." "I want a longer turn than Timmy." "This house is higher than this one." Through trial and error, some three- and four-year-olds can begin to fit one ordered set of objects to another. Given three pans of different sizes and three outlines to hang them on at clean-up time, with some experimentation they can fit each pan over its outline.

Older preoperational children, between four and five years of age, can construct a series of objects of different lengths but often pay attention to only one end of each object. A child arranging all the pencils in the pencil box might end up with a series that looks like this:

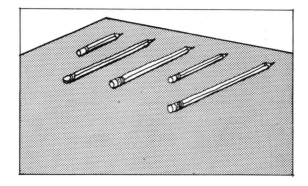

Six- and seven-year-old preoperational children, on the other hand, can construct a "stairway" of sticks, paying attention to both ends, and they can even insert additional sticks in their appropriate places in the series.

In concrete operational children, the ability to seriate includes the ability to comprehend "transitivity" and "reversibility." For example, a concrete operational child who systematically constructs a "stairway" series of sticks,

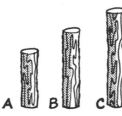

knows that

If stick A is shorter than stick B, then stick B is longer than stick A. (reversibility)

He also does not have to test physically to know that stick A is shorter than stick C, once he finds out that

Stick A is shorter than stick B and stick B is shorter than stick C. (transitivity)

He understands where each stick fits in relation to the other two.

A concrete operational child can construct a series based on two different attributes. The child might arrange some leaves according to both size and intensity of hue:

small • medium • large • very large • giant

very light red • light red • red • dark red • very dark red

Concrete operational children can also make correspondences between series. They might select five sheets of paper of different sizes and mount the smallest leaf on the smallest sheet, the medium leaf on the medium sheet, and so on.

Children in the formal operational stage can represent a series of relations abstractly and hypothetically. They can solve verbally stated problems such as, "If Linda is taller than Sally and Sally is taller than Betty, who is taller, Linda or Betty?"

The importance of seriation experiences for preschool children

Although preschool children are not yet able to seriate a set of objects, they're very much involved in making and describing comparisons, from which the ability to seriate evolves.

Juanita and Paula were building a structure in the block area; it had got so tall they could no longer reach the top. Paula tried standing on a block but it wasn't high enough. They enlisted the help of a

Summary: How Seriation Capacities Develop

The child	Sensorimotor Stage (0-2½ yrs.)	Preoperational Stage (2½-7 yrs.)	Concrete Operational Stage (7-11 yrs.)	Formal Operational Stage (12+ yrs.)
Distinguishes and initiates actions of graded intensity	X	X	X	X
Builds pyramid towers and fits nesting blocks together	X	X	X	X
Compares differences		X	X	X
Fits together simple ordered sets through trial and error		X	X	X
Constructs series of objects of different lengths but only attends to one end		X	X	X
Seriates systematically			X	X
Constructs two-dimensional arrays			X	X
Corresponds one serial array to another			X	X
Seriates abstract and hypothetical arrays				X

nearby adult who asked, "Why didn't the block work?" Paula looked carefully at the block and decided, "It wasn't high enough." "We need something higher," said Juanita, who went off to find a chair. Standing on the chair, the girls were able to finish their structure themselves.

By providing opportunities for preschool children to make comparisons among a wide variety of objects and materials, adults help them become aware of their ability to discern differences. Preschoolers like Juanita and Paula, who are encouraged and supported as they make comparisons, respond thoughtfully to a problem and use their skills to solve it.

The best way to help preschool children develop the ability to seriate is to provide an environment full of interesting materials that invite comparison, and to support and encourage children as they make comparisons throughout the day. The more aware children are of differences and the more opportunities they have to make comparisons, the more they're able to solve problems and develop a rich repertoire of experiences to draw upon when they begin to seriate.

Key Experience:
Making comparisons

At small-group time children are scooping out and decorating pumpkins they've gathered on a field trip to a local pumpkin patch. As they work they make many comparisons.

"Mine's the scariest. Watch out."

"Mine is more scarier 'cause he's got long teeth."

"This part's heavy (lid) and this part's more heavy (rest of pumpkin), but I can still lift it with one hand. It's not too heavy for me 'cause I am very strong."

"These (fresh pumpkin) seeds are wetter than these (baked) seeds. And these (baked seeds) taste more saltier. Mmmm . . . Yuck! These (fresh seeds) taste yuckier."

"Mine's very bumpy here (on the outside) but it's more bumpier and ouchier here (on the stem). Sometimes it hurts me. Mr. Philips, Mr. Philips, touch this ouchy part."

Preschool-age children make comparisons as they explore and use objects. Scooping out and carving pumpkins provided this group of children with a context in which to see, feel and taste as well as use comparative terms like "scarier," "heavier," "wetter," "bigger," "bumpier" and "ouchier."

Since children learn to make comparisons through actual contact with the objects they're comparing, it would have done them little good if Mr. Philips had provided only one pumpkin which he himself cut open, scooped out and

talked about while the children watched and listened. Children need the opportunity to experience objects directly with all their senses and to make their own comparisons if they're to develop a real understanding of the attributes of objects.

Preoperational children have not yet developed the ability to make the subtle comparisons concrete operational children are able to make. They focus on obvious differences rather than on subtle ones. Given three pumpkins, for example, a very light one, a quite heavy one and one just a little bit heavier, preoperational children won't distinguish between the two heavier pumpkins. They'll call the first one "light" and the second two "heavier." Given just the two heavy pumpkins to compare, they'll call both of them heavy.

Suggestions for adults

Provide materials children can easily compare

Make sure the classroom is stocked with materials that invite comparison. One way to do this is to make a list of comparative terms, such as the following, and then think of materials that can be compared in these ways: *heavier/lighter, sharper/blunter, rougher/smoother, wetter/drier, harder/softer, bigger/smaller, thicker/thinner (fatter/skinnier), louder/softer.*

Ask questions throughout the day that help children make comparisons

As children work with materials that lend themselves to comparison, ask them questions that call for comparisons and relate to what the children are doing.

It's planning time and Brian is planning to build two buildings in the block area.

"They're not going to be the same," he tells the adult he's planning with. "One's going to be this high, and one's going to be this high."

"You mean one building's going to be bigger than the other?" the adult asks.

"Yep," says Brian, "and it's going to have bigger blocks, too."

"Teacher, teacher, do this for me," Danny says, thrusting a piece of hard clay toward his teacher.

"Do what, Danny?" she asks.

"Make it flat like this one," he says, holding up a flat piece of clay.

"Well, how did you make that piece flat?" she asks.

"I pushed it down like this," he answers, demonstrating his technique.

"Well, why don't you push this piece down?"

"See, it won't go."

"Why not?"

"It's too hard."

"What about a softer piece of clay? Would that work?"

Danny finds another hunk of clay. "Here's a piece. It's softer 'cause I can push it down."

"I am very strong," Bernadette says, "'cause I can pick up this heavy hammer with one hand."

"Okay, strong lady," an adult responds, "will you pick up all the heavier hammers and put them away while I put away all the lighter hammers?"

"Okay." Bernadette picks up two hammers. "These are both heavier so these are for me." She picks up another. "This is too light for me. I need a heavier one."

It's Bonnie's turn to show and tell about two pictures she made at work time. "Made lines," Bonnie says proudly.

"Did you use the same brush for each picture?" the adult asks.

"Nope," says Bonnie.

"Show us the brushes you used." Bonnie brings back a thick brush and a thin one. "Which brush did

you use to make the thin lines?" the adult asks. Bonnie matches the brushes to the lines. "That's right. You used the thin brush to make the thinner lines, and the fat brush to make the fatter lines."

Play games that call for comparisons

Many standard children's games can be modified to include opportunities for making comparisons. Here are three examples:

Red Rover—Red rover, red rover,
> Let anyone *shorter than Mrs.* _____
> *taller than the rocking boat*
> *bigger than the rabbit*
> *smaller than the climber*
> come over.

Simon Says—Simon says,
> Run to something that is *rougher than the blacktop*
> *smoother than the gravel*
> *harder than the grass*
> *softer than the sidewalk*
> *drier than the garden*
> *smaller than the rabbit cage*
> *bigger than the rabbit cage*
> *fatter than the telephone pole*
> *thinner than the pine tree*

Giant Steps—Everybody can take a step that's
> *shorter than the sandbox*
> *longer than the wagon*
> *higher than the tree stump*
> *lower than the swing set*

Take dictation about comparisons

When children are comparing objects, write down what they say and read it back to them. The small-group time described above in which the children scooped out and decorated their pumpkins would have been a good opportunity for an adult to take down a group story that included many comparisons.

Key Experience: Arranging several things in order and describing their relations

Preschoolers often arrange three or four things in order by size, and many preschoolers are able to say that in a pyramid tower, for example, the big block is on the bottom, the middle-sized block is next and the little block is on the top. Block pyramids are probably the most frequent way preschoolers arrange objects according to size, because this arrangement has a very practical appeal. Young builders quickly learn that the bigger the base, the sturdier the tower, so they use all the big blocks first, then add the medium-sized blocks and last of all add the small blocks on top. They often do the same thing at the workbench, starting with a big board and adding smaller and smaller boards and pieces till their creation is finished. They also find that carrying a stack of plates, puzzles, books or records is easier if they put the largest ones on the bottom and the smallest ones on top.

Preschoolers often line up dolls and toy animals from biggest to smallest (dad to baby). Their paintings and drawings of people often depict this same kind of ordering, although many preschoolers take the liberty of depicting themselves as the biggest or, at least, bigger than, an older brother or sister.

As they work with clay and playdough, preschoolers often make objects of varying sizes. "Snowmen" are made with three balls of decreasing size, and "snakes" vary in length and width.

Children should have opportunities to use words like "big," "bigger," "biggest" in relation to things they themselves are doing and making. Adults should be aware of how and when preschoolers arrange things in order, so they can encourage and support children's efforts as well as talk with them as they work.

Suggestions for adults

Provide materials in three or four sizes

Many classroom materials can be purchased, gathered or made in three or four sizes. Here is a beginning list organized by work areas; be sure to add other items.

Block area—three or four sizes of blocks, boards, boxes, tinkertoys, vehicles, rubber/wooden people and animals (particularly families of people and animals)

House area—three or four sizes of pots, spatulas, coffee pots, ice-cube trays, mixing bowls, cake tins, muffin tins, measuring spoons and cups, cannisters, dishes, buttons, stones, empty food containers (gallon, half-gallon, quart and pint milk cartons, for example), dolls, stuffed animals, dress-up clothes, jewelry

Art area—three or four sizes of paper, paper plates, paint jars, brushes, paper clips, rubber bands, cookie cutters, macaroni, pencils, crayons

Quiet area—sets of nesting cups and boxes, graduated stacking rings, cuisinaire or counting rods, three or four sizes of beads, pegs and peg boards, puppets, magnifying glasses, books

Construction area—three or four sizes of hammers, nails, screw drivers, screws, drill bits, jar lids, wood pieces

Music and movement area—three or four sizes of triangles, bells, maracas, tambourines, drums

Outside area—three or four sizes of balls, boards, boxes, tunnels, ramps, wagons, tree stumps, buckets

Talk with children and ask them questions about size relations

As children use and construct things of various sizes, talk with them and ask them about the relative sizes involved. Try to relate questions and comments directly to what a child is doing. Give the child a chance to respond to each question, and refrain from this approach when questions and comments appear to disrupt rather than complement the child's activity.

"Hey, come on over t'my house," Joey calls, "an' ring the doorbell, right here."

"Ding, dong, ding, dong."

"Come in. Come in."

"Oh, Joey, what a big house you've made."

"I'm not Joey. I'm your daddy."

"Okay, Daddy, you have all kinds of chairs in your house. Can I sit down in the biggest one? I'm so tired."

"No, you can't sit in the biggest one. That's mine 'cause I'm the daddy."

"Can I sit in the smallest one, then?"

"No, you're too big. That's for the baby. You're the little girl. You sit in this one."

"You mean this medium-sized chair?"

"Yeah. That medium one's for you. And the big one's for the mom. An the biggest one's for me 'cause I'm the dad. I'm 'na go out now. You stay right here till I get back and you watch TV . . ."

Use materials in three or four sizes at small-group time

When planning small-group times include materials in three or four sizes, and provide an opportunity for children to order and describe the relations among the materials.

Most preschoolers probably wouldn't be interested in spending a whole small-group time just ordering a set of three or four materials by size, but they might be interested if they were using the materials for another purpose. Here are some examples:

During a small-group time in which the focus is drawing something done at work time, each child might choose a large, medium or small piece of paper.

———————

After exploring materials at small-group time—apples, pumpkins, stones, blocks, things collected on a walk, things from the quiet area—children might enjoy cleaning up by first locating and putting away the largest stone or the

biggest thing from the quiet area, then the next biggest thing, and so on down to the smallest.

———————

A child cutting an apple or pumpkin into lots of pieces might enjoy ordering the pieces from largest to smallest.

———————

Perhaps children are learning how to cut in their small group, or they're making texture collages. As they finish, see if they can order the

pieces they've cut or the objects they've glued to their collage.

Encourage children to order things by size at clean-up time

When children need help getting started at clean-up time, suggest they find a set of things they can order, starting with the biggest or the smallest. An adult might say, "Grady, you were working with the animals today. You be the animal-putter-away. How about if you make a parade on the shelf with the biggest animal leading the parade and the smallest animals at the end." Be sure to check back to see how many objects the child has been able to arrange in order.

Encourage children to represent stories that deal with size relations

Two traditional children's stories in which size relationships play a prominent role are *The Three Billy Goats Gruff* (featuring a big, a medium and a small billy goat) and *Goldilocks and the Three Bears* (the bears, their bowls, their chairs and their beds all come in three sizes).

After the children have heard one of the stories a number of times, plan some small-group times in which they can represent the story. Here are some ways they might represent *Goldilocks and the Three Bears* at small-group time:

Have the children take turns telling parts of the story from the pictures. Then provide materials so the children can make their own pictures and dictate their own version of the story. See if any of the children order the bears, bowls, chairs, beds or anything else by size in their pictures.

———————

Provide a variety of materials—playdough, buttons, blocks, pipe cleaners, etc.—and encourage the children to make their own bears, beds, chairs and bowls. See which children are able to make things in three sizes. Probably not all of them will be able to do this.

———————

Help the children reenact the story, making themselves big for the papa bear, medium-sized for the mama bear and small for the baby bear. See what they can find around the room or make to use as bowls, chairs and beds of different sizes.

Key Experience:
Fitting one ordered set of objects to another through trial and error

Another seriation-related activity preschoolers engage in is fitting one ordered set of objects to another through trial and error. At clean-up time a preschool child works for a while, trying each pan over each outline to see where it fits before hanging the big pan over the big pan outline, the medium pan over the medium pan outline and the small pan over the small pan outline. Or a child tries to put the small doll shirt on the medium doll and then puts it on the small doll; he tries the medium doll shirt on the large doll and then finds that it fits the medium doll; finally, because only the large doll and the large shirt are left, he dresses the large doll in the large shirt. This child may go through a similar process with the same dolls and the three doll beds, trying each doll in each bed before he finally fits the large doll into the large bed, etc. Or perhaps a child is making mixtures in three different-sized coffee cans and then, because she wants to

save her mixtures, tries out a series of lids until she finds the right size lid for each can.

Preschoolers are most apt to fit one ordered set of things to another when there are no more than three or four items in each set and when they have a practical reason for fitting the sets together. Because they fit and match by trial and error (instead of saying to themselves, "I've got the biggest jar—now, of all the lids, which one is biggest?"), more than four items in a set can cause frustration and abandonment of the task. Preschoolers usually do not fit sets together merely for the sake of matching, but because the match serves a practical purpose. They want to dress the different-size dolls so they can take them out for a walk, or they want to cover their three mixtures so they won't dry out. The activity of fitting one set onto, into or around the other also intrigues and challenges them. Preschoolers, therefore, are more likely to get absorbed in fitting lids on cannisters as they pretend to cook than in matching precut cardboard circles with precut cardboard squares.

Here are some ways adults can provide appropriate opportunities for preschoolers to fit one set of objects to another.

Suggestions for adults

Provide ordered sets of materials that fit together

Ordered sets of materials that go together should include *three or four items*, they should be materials the children will *use* in their everyday work and play, and they should involve *fitting* rather than just matching one set to the other. Here are some examples:

three or four sizes of —flower pots and saucers
  purses and wallets
  wallets and play money
  broom handles and broom heads
  mixing bowls and lids
  coffee cans and lids
  buttons and muffin tins
  cups and saucers
  boxes and covers
  nuts and bolts
  drill bits and screws
  dolls and doll clothes
  dolls and doll beds
  doll beds and mattresses
  animals and cages

  bird cages and bird-cage covers
  toasters and toaster covers

Encourage children to fit ordered sets together at clean-up time

If a child is having trouble figuring out where to begin at clean-up time, suggest a specific task that involves fitting one ordered set of things to another. An adult might say, "Jimmy, you were doing a lot of cooking today. You find all the cannisters and all their lids and fit them back together. Show me when you're finished, O.K.?" Outlines may be used to label places where ordered sets belong; in cleaning up, children can match the sets of ordered objects to their corresponding outlines.

Talk with children about what they're doing as they fit ordered sets together

As children search for the right nut to go with the big bolt, or struggle to put the medium-size shoes on the large doll, talk with them about what they're doing to help them understand the size relations:

"That nut doesn't seem to fit onto that bolt you've screwed into your car, does it, Cindy? Since it's a really big bolt, why don't you try a really big nut, the biggest you can find . . . That's good. You fit the big nut onto the big bolt. Is your car all finished now?"

Include ordered sets in small-group activities

Each child in the small group can start a project in a different-sized container and then find the cover that fits his container when it's time to store the materials. In an activity such as making playdough, for example, children can hunt for the lids that fit each bowl when the playdough is finished and ready to be stored for use.

Related films and publications from the High/Scope Foundation

Films—

(For a complete description of each film and instructions for ordering, see appendix 4.)

Seriation—A Sequence of Exercises from **Cognitive Development** series (Elementary grades)

Understanding and Using the Concept of Number (K-3) (Elementary grades)

Publications—

The Cognitively Oriented Curriculum—Mathematics: Number (booklet, 68pp.) by Sheila Mainwaring, Sam Hannibal, Jan Diamondstone, 1979. (Elementary grades)

Mathematical information and ability are a useful part of daily child-initiated activities. This guide describes materials and questions which strategically provoke mathematical thinking in the elementary classroom. It also illustrates the developmental progression from gross comparison ability to one-to-one correspondence and conservation ability for the six concepts of number, length, area, weight, volume and time. Many ways that children represent mathematical information are shown as they lead to the learning of standard computational systems.

Related reading on seriation and number

Brainerd, C.H. "The Origins of Number Concepts," *Scientific American,* March, 1973. pp. 101-109.

Brearly, M. and E. Hitchfield. *A Guide to Reading Piaget.* New York: Schocken, 1966. Chapters 1 and 2.

Flavell, John H. *The Developmental Psychology of Jean Piaget.* Princeton, New Jersey: Van Nostrand, 1963. Chapter 9, pp. 298-322.

Ginsburg, H. and Sylvia Opper. *Piaget's Theory of Intellectual Development: An Introduction.* Englewood Cliffs, New Jersey: Prentice-Hall, Inc. 1969. pp. 119-152.

Hunt, J. McV. *Intelligence and Experience.* New York: The Ronald Press Company, 1961. pp. 195, 212-215.

Lovell, K. *The Growth of Understanding in Mathematics: Kindergarten through Grade Three.* New York: Holt, Rinehart and Winston, Inc., 1971.

Nuffield Mathematics Series: *Beginnings; I Do and I Understand; Pictorial Representation.* New York: John Wiley & Sons, 1968.

Piaget, Jean. *The Child's Conception of Number.* New York: Norton, 1965.

Piaget, Jean. *The Early Growth of Logic in the Child.* New York: Norton, 1969. pp. 247-279.

Piaget, Jean. "How Children Form Mathematical Concepts," reprint 420 from *Scientific American,* November, 1953. San Francisco: W.H. Freeman & Co.

Piaget, Jean and Barbel Inhelder. *The Psychology of the Child.* New York: Basic Books, 1969. pp. 101-102, 104-105.

10/ Number

Through experiences with counting, matching, grouping and comparing, preschool-age children begin to form an understanding of number; this understanding is of course the basis for understanding mathematical operations that transform and combine number, as in elementary-school arithmetic. In Jean Piaget's theory of development, *two landmarks of children's advance in their understanding of number are one-to-one correspondence and conservation.*

In *one-to-one correspondence,* two or more groups of objects are paired, one for one. If a person has a bunch of apples and a bunch of oranges, and if he puts one apple with each orange, he is placing the apples and oranges in one-to-one correspondence. If he finishes pairing the two groups and there is no apple or orange left over, then the one-to-one arrangement has concretely demonstrated that there is the same number of apples and oranges. This

pairing can be done by physically placing the two sets together, or it can be done by counting, in which case the physical actions aren't necessary.

Whether you arrange the apples and oranges into groups on the table, set them in a large circle, or pile them in a basket, there is still the same number of apples and oranges. That is the idea of *conservation:* the number of objects in a set remains constant no matter how the objects are positioned or arranged.

Both these ideas—conservation of number independent of spatial arrangement and one-to-one correspondence—are elementary to an adult, and adults use them every day in various ways. But Piaget found that very young children must go through a period of development before they achieve an understanding of these two ideas, which are basic to comprehension of number.

How the concept of number develops in children

During the sensorimotor stage of development, the stage of infancy, the human being discovers that objects exist, that they can be moved, that often two objects can be fitted together or one put inside another. These discoveries help the infant build an understanding of objects, which later develops into the understanding of classification, seriation, one-to-one correspondence and conservation of number.

At around three or four years of age, in the preoperational stage, the child begins to see that two kinds of objects can be matched one-to-one (one big block with one little block), but he doesn't see that the two sets are equal in number when there are the same number of big and little blocks unless they are arranged the same way—for example, in two lines of equal length.

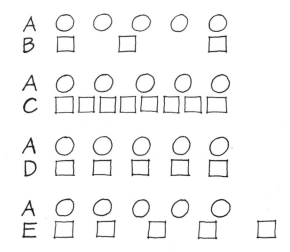

To a preoperational child, set A and set B have the same number, sets A and C have the same number, and sets A and D have the same number because they "look" the same—they are the same length. The same child, on the other hand, would say sets A and E are "different" or don't have the same number because set E is longer than set A.

Piaget conducted the following type of experiment that gave further proof of preoperational children's inability to conserve number. He would set out a row of vases, and a child would be asked to place one flower in each vase. The child would usually say that there were as many flowers as there were vases. However, when Piaget took the flowers out of the vases and bunched them together, the child would declare that there were now more vases—because the vases were in a longer row.

Piaget also found that counting didn't help four- and five-year-olds conserve number. When he asked a five-year-old to count a row of six glasses and a row of six bottles, the five-year-old could say there were six glasses and six bottles. But in spite of that, the child maintained that there were more bottles than glasses, because the six bottles were arranged in a longer row than the six glasses:

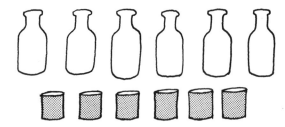

Concrete operational children (7-11 years old) understand the concept of number. That is, they both conserve number and use one-to-one correspondence. They also grasp the use of a standard unit (inches, pen lengths, paces) in measurement, and they can divide a group into two smaller groups of equal number as well as equalize unequal piles of objects.

Children in the formal operational stage (12 and up) are able to deal with more complex ideas, such as infinite sets and hypothetical unknowns (like the x in algebra), and they can reason both deductively and inductively.

Since preschool-age (preoperational) children have not yet fully developed the concept of number, adults must be careful to provide the kinds of experiences that are appropriate to their pre-number logic and judgment. Preschoolers compare and make judgments about amounts of things. They perform actions that involve one-to-one correspondence, like passing out one cracker to each child at snack time. They also count objects they're using, although the numbers they say aloud may not always be in numerical order. In this chapter, we'll discuss these key experiences and the ways adults can provide them.

Key Experience:
Comparing amounts

• *"I want that big box of beads 'cause it has more."*

• *"Jimmy's got less blocks than me 'cause he's littler. When he gets big he can have more like me."*

• *"Joanie and me are taking home the same (amount) because we both got big bags to carry our stuff in on the bus."*

• *"I got more than you, Jeanie."*
"No, you don't."
"Yes, I do."

Preschoolers often compare amounts of things using the terms "more," "less" and "the same," but because their perceptions are colored by their desire to have the most for themselves, and by their inability to conserve, their judg-

ments about amounts are often incorrect. Although a smaller box may actually have more buttons in it, they think the bigger box must have more buttons because it's bigger. They think that ten cookies spread out in a line are more than ten cookies bunched together. They also believe that pouring sand (or any other substance) from a smaller container into a larger one increases the amount of sand.

Because preschoolers are making the best judgments they can about amounts of things, it's important for adults to accept their judgments, even when those judgments are incorrect by adult standards. It's pointless and frustrating to preoperational children to have their logic "corrected" to conform to adult logic—they simply haven't developed a firm enough base of understanding. In order for children to learn to make more mature judgments about amounts, they need opportunities to exercise their emerging numerical capacities, opportunities that are suited to those capacities. Here are some ways adults can encourage and support preschool children as they compare amounts of things.

Suggestions for adults

Provide both "continuous" and "discontinuous" materials

Continuous materials are materials that can be measured and poured from one container to another but cannot be broken down into countable parts. Water, sand, flour and salt are continuous materials children can pour, mold and compare according to amount. *Discontinuous* materials are materials that can be lined up and counted, like beads, blocks, cars, dolls, buttons, cans, and so on. Make sure the children have access to both kinds of materials for comparing.

Ask questions about number and amount as children work with materials throughout the day

As children work with materials, ask them questions about number and amount and then ask them to explain their answers. Eddie, in the following example, explains how it is that one collage has more things on it than another:

"You've made two big collages, Eddie, one on red paper and one on yellow paper. Which collage has more things on it, do you think?"

"This one."

"The one on the yellow paper?"

"Yep."

"How can you tell it has more things?"

"Well, it has all the things from here (one side) to here (the other side) and this red one just has these things here."

"You mean the yellow one has things all the way across the paper, and the red one has things just in the center, so the yellow one has more?"

"Yes. This one's got more things and the red one's got just a little bit."

At snack time, Michelle chooses the taller pitcher of milk for her table even though the amount of milk in each pitcher is the same:

"Michelle, do you think both these pitchers have the same amount of milk in them?"

"Nope. This one has more."

"You mean the tallest pitcher has more milk in it?"

"Yeah. We want the biggest one for our table."

"Why do you think it has more milk in it?"

"Cause it's the biggest."

"But look, the milk comes up to the same line on both pitchers."

"Yeah. But this one's got more 'cause it's the biggest."

Encourage children to rearrange materials they're comparing

Because preschool children do not yet conserve number, the arrangement of the materials they're comparing influences their opinion about amounts. As they compare numbers of items, encourage them to rearrange the materials and compare them again:

"Look, Mr. Antonesse, this board has more pegs than this one."

"Why does this board have more, Shantel?"

"Because these pegs are longer."

Shantel gets a "bright idea" and arranges the pegs on the second board in a line that's longer than the line of pegs on the board she thought had the most pegs. "Look, this one has more now!"

"How can you tell?"

"Because they're the longest."

Encourage children to compare the number or amount of things they see in pictures

As children look at books, magazines, photographs and pictures, ask them about the number of things they see and why, for example, they think one basket has more eggs in it than another. This may be difficult for some children, because they'll have to make judgments about things they can't manipulate.

Key Experience:
Arranging two sets of objects in one-to-one correspondence

Young children are often confused about one-to-one correspondence, because they believe that the physical arrangement of two sets of objects determines whether the number of objects in the sets is the same. A preschool child building two parallel roads, for example,

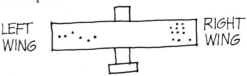

believes the first road has more blocks in it because it's longer than the second road. Likewise he believes there are more tacks in the left wing of his airplane

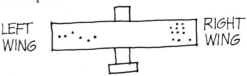

than in the right wing because the tacks in the

left wing are spread out and the tacks in the right wing are all bunched together.

There are situations, however, in which preschoolers can and do arrange two sets of things in one-to-one correspondence. When they're passing things out at snack time, for example, they make sure that each child has one cup, one napkin and one cookie, although they still remain confused about whether there are more cookies or more children at the table. In make-believe play in the block area, they may line up the animals, giving each one a "block of hay," and make one garage for each car. In the art area, they put one brush in each jar of paint, or paste or draw one picture on each page of a book they're making.

As children arrange sets of objects in one-to-one correspondence in the course of their work and play, adults can support and encourage them. Here are some suggestions:

Suggestions for adults

Provide materials that fit together in one-to-one correspondence

Young children are more apt to arrange things in one-to-one correspondence when they fit together some way—for example, pegs and pegboards, muffin tins/egg cartons and ping-pong balls or stones, jars/containers and lids, nuts and bolts, felt-tip pens and tops, dolls and hats, toothpicks and styrofoam bits, empty spools and pegs, Chinese checker board and marbles.

Talk with children in terms of one-to-one correspondence

As children are putting things together in one-to-one correspondence, talk with them in a pleasant, conversational way about what they're doing:

"That looks interesting, Maxie. You're putting one marble in each hole. Will you show me how you play your game?"

———————

Alexis is putting one peg in each spool hole, saying, "Down the hole, down the hole. Another man down the hole."

"What are the men doing down in the holes, Alexis?"

"Fixing the water. Down the hole. Down the hole."

"You mean for each hole you put one man down to fix the water?"

"Yep, so it won't get out on the streets and all the people."

Encourage children to generate their own sets of materials in one-to-one correspondence

There are some situations in which children can be encouraged to use one-to-one correspondence in a way that complements and extends rather than interferes with what they're already doing. A child making a book, for example, might enjoy pasting or drawing just one picture on each page. A child making balls and snakes from clay or playdough might enjoy making one ball for each snake or wrapping one snake around each ball. A child making a collage might respond positively to the suggestion that she make lots of circles on her paper and then paste one thing inside each circle. Children can make a garage for each toy car and a house, bed or chair for each make-believe person or animal.

Encourage children to pass things out at snack and meal times

At snack and meal times, give children turns passing out cups, napkins, silverware, plates, cookies, etc.—the same number of things for each child.

Play games that include one-to-one correspondence

Card games in which children pass out one card at a time to each child can be played with regular playing cards, the children's signs, cards the children make themselves or whatever else they choose to use in place of cards.

Musical chairs is a good one-to-one correspondence game. It's best with young children to keep the number of chairs (or carpet squares, boxes, tree stumps) constant and equal to the number of children playing the game, so that when the music stops, each child can find a place. Eliminating chairs creates hurt feelings and confusion for this age group. Before putting the music on, the adult can tell the children there's one chair for each child.

Key Experience:
Counting objects

Preschoolers are intrigued by counting and impressed with numbers. Their own ages and the ages of their classmates are very important to them, and they know that four is older than three and that after they're four, on their next birthday, they'll be five. In guessing an adult's age, they choose a really big number like twelve or fifteen.

Many preschoolers count the number of blocks they've used in a building, or the number of people in a painting they've made, or the number of crackers on the plate in front of them at snack time. They also rote count, chanting or singing a series of numbers that may or may not be in numerical order—more for the sake of saying the numbers than to count a set of objects.

Counting doesn't mean the same thing to three- and four-year-olds as it does to adults. For example, in the situation Piaget set up with the six bottles and the six glasses, although the child counted six bottles and six glasses, he still maintained there were more bottles than glasses, because the bottles were in a longer row than the glasses. Although he could count each row correctly, the length of the row carried far more significance for him than the actual number "six" that he counted in both cases. That is to say, children may count objects, but the result of their counting has no meaning for them until they develop their capacity to conserve.

In order for adults to support and encourage preoperational children as they begin to count, they need to understand that three- and four-year-olds count objects as well as rote count; that the numbers they use as they count aren't always in numerical order; that the meaning of the numbers themselves is outweighed by the physical arrangement of the objects being counted; and that written numerals are generally too abstract for them. Knowing these limitations, adults can encourage children to use numbers in one-to-one correspondence with objects they are using. This will help children to develop the concept that each object being counted is counted once and only once.

Here are some ways adults can support and encourage children as they count objects.

Suggestions for adults

Provide sets of countable objects

A preschool classroom should be filled with sets of interesting, usable, countable objects. Together as a teaching team, go from work area to work area and note all the sets of things children can count.

Make counting a part of child-initiated activities

Counting should be directly related to the work and interests of the children. Encourage children to count things as they use them. (Planning "special" counting activities, in which children are to count various numbers of circles, blocks, buttons, etc. removes counting from a meaningful context and turns it into mere drill.)

Try to make counting a natural part of the children's work:

Joey has built a very tall garage for his car and is telling an adult about it. "See, my car has to drive way up to the tippy top."

"It looks pretty steep to me, Joey."

"He has to drive right up the side for a long, long ways till he gets to the garage part."

"How many blocks does he have to drive on till he gets to the top?"

"I'll show you. One . . . two . . . three . . ."

Accept children's numerical ordering

Many preschoolers are able to assign one number to each object as they count, but the number order they use is their own creation. It's not unusual for a preschool child counting the cookies in the snack basket, for example, to say, "One, two, three, six, seven, five, six, eight." An adult, realizing that giving each cookie one and only one number is more important at this stage than assigning the "right" order, will accept the child's tally. When the adult counts the objects and models correct numerical order, the child will imitate and eventually use the correct order.

Help children represent numbers in a way they can understand

Occasionally, preschool children will wish to write down or keep track of how many blocks they've hauled in their trucks, how many pages they've made in their books, how many times they've put the ball through the hoop. An adult might help them keep track of the numbers involved by showing them how to tally. For each item or turn, a child makes a mark or a line. When the child is finished, he can count all the marks or lines the same way he counted all the objects or turns.

Related films and publications from the High/Scope Foundation

Films—

(For a complete description of each film and instructions for ordering, see appendix 4.)

Seriation—A Sequence of Exercises from **Cognitive Development** series (Elementary grades)

Understanding and Using the Concept of Number (K-3) (Elementary grades)

Publications—

The Cognitively Oriented Curriculum—Mathematics: Number (booklet, 68pp.) by Sheila Mainwaring, Sam Hannibal, Jan Diamondstone, 1979. (Elementary grades)

Mathematical information and ability are a useful part of daily child-initiated activities. This guide describes materials and questions which strategically provoke mathematical thinking in the elementary classroom. It also illustrates the developmental progression from gross comparison ability to one-to-one correspondence and conservation ability for the six concepts of number, length, area, weight, volume and time. Many ways that children represent mathematical information are shown as they lead to the learning of standard computational systems.

Related reading on number

(For related reading on Seriation and Number, see Bibliography on page 227.)

11/ Spatial relations

When a baby leaves the womb, it enters what Webster defines as "the boundless expanse within which all things are contained; a three-dimensional entity that extends without bounds in all directions and is the field of physical objects, events, and their order and relations." This is space. There are simple spatial relations, such as perceiving that one object is to the left of another, folding a piece of paper into a paper hat, figuring out how big a bowl to use for the green beans, tying a knot, tilting a large piece of furniture to fit it through a small door, making a simple map, hanging a picture straight; and there are more complex spatial relations, such as reading or making blueprints, changing a flat tire, fitting the pieces of a dress pattern, threading a film projector, laying a floor covering. These are spatial understandings that most adults possess, but which didn't just come naturally—they were acquired over the years through experience and intellectual maturation.

Just as adults need practice in solving spatial problems in order to master them, young children need to experience and represent spatial relations and solve spatial problems in order to master the simpler spatial skills grownups take for granted.

How spatial concepts develop in children

Spatial awareness and mastery are a long time unfolding. In the sensorimotor stage, infants

gradually learn to track or follow objects visually, as well as reach for them and grasp them. In the first eight months of life, an infant is aware only of objects he can see; if a ball he's been playing with rolls out of sight, it no longer exists as far as he's concerned. He doesn't search for it but turns to something else within his visual space.

Between 8 and 12 months, infants learn to move their bodies so they can search for things outside their immediate field of vision, and they learn to manipulate objects in space in order to see them from different angles. Between 12 and 18 months, a toddler learns that *he* is located in space, not just his arms and legs. He also studies the way objects change positions in relation to each other; for example, when he drops his stuffed rabbit out of his crib, he watches it fall to the floor. He also enjoys opening mommy or daddy's hand and "finding" something there that he's seen his parent hide.

Near the end of the sensorimotor stage, toddlers between 18 and 24 months have developed the ability to represent space mentally. For example, a toddler can find a toy car that has rolled under the sofa and out the other side.

The relations of proximity—how close things are in space—and of separation—how far apart they are—are fundamental to a child's understanding of space. Preoperational three- and four-year-olds are actively exploring these relations as they take things apart and fit them together and arrange and rearrange things in space. They are also learning to describe where things are, the distances between things and the directions in which things are moving, although their judgments are not always accurate by adult standards. Piaget found, for example, that preoperational children's judgments of proximity and separation are influenced by the presence or absence of barriers. A child may say that the

sand table is close to the door until someone builds a large tinkertoy house between the two; then he believes the sand table and the door are farther apart, even though the actual distance between them hasn't changed. Preschoolers also confuse distance with effort—they believe, for example, that climbing up a slide involves going farther than sliding down.

Three- and four-year-olds are beginning to work with the notion of spatial enclosure. Piaget found that they can discriminate between objects with holes and objects without holes as well as between a closed loop of string with something inside it and a closed loop of string with something outside of it. They also construct their own enclosures and use words like "inside" and "outside" to talk about them.

While three- and four-year-olds have difficulty producing a straight line in space, either by drawing with a pencil or lining objects up, older preoperational children (5-7 years) are able to do so by following the edge of a table or by trial and error. They also attempt to actually measure distances, using a primitive method such as spreading their hands apart. Spatial order is also just beginning to make sense to them. Given a few objects arranged in a line or a circle, they may reproduce the same order through trial and error with another set of objects. (Three- and four-year-olds may be able to arrange things in an order they create, but they generally can't reproduce the same order following the pattern of the first arrangement.)

By the time they are concrete operational (8-11 years), children are able to deal successfully with many spatial relations. Younger concrete operational children are able to interpret and represent the projective and geometrical aspects of space. They can conserve length and distance; that is, they realize that an object's length is independent of its position in space, and that the distance between two objects is not affected by barriers placed between them. They can line objects up in straight lines by end-on sighting, and they can use a standard unit to measure length.

Older concrete operational children can apply measurement to a two- or three-dimensional coordinate system, can conserve volume and area, and can, with a fair degree of accuracy, represent alternative spatial perspectives as well as angularity, parallelism and distance.

Children in the formal operational stage can do all of the above plus grasp and deal with geometrical abstractions such as the idea of the infinite extension and divisibility of a line or figure in space.

Key Experience:
Fitting things together and taking them apart

Infants learn that their fingers can fit into their mouths, and that other objects can fit into their mouths as well. Later, when they are able to distinguish objects from actions in space and have some control over their limbs, they begin to manipulate objects, turning them every which way, feeling and tasting them. Between 8 and 12 months, they begin another "fitting" process—dropping things into pots, cups, cans and cartons, and taking them out again, and wedging themselves into and out of spaces. With their increased dexterity, toddlers are able to fit lids on boxes and pots and fit two snap beads together by pushing the bump on the end of one into the hole on the end of the other.

During the preschool years, children become increasingly aware of the spatial relations of objects and increasingly able to fit things together and take them apart. A three- or four-year-old fits checkers into an olive jar, puts shapes into a shape sorter, puts puzzles together, fills and empties containers of sand, puts three big blocks into a wagon, carefully fits the tools into the toolbox, and in the process makes some functional discoveries—some things screw together, others snap or slide together, some things have to be lined up carefully in order to fit inside the container, each puzzle piece fits into its own place.

Usually preschool children make gross comparisons of objects and the spaces they fit into, and they often approach the problem of fit by trial and error. It's common to see a preschooler shoving a puzzle piece around until, by acci-

dent, it falls into place. Concrete operational children, on the other hand, will observe the contour of a puzzle piece and then match it with other pieces. Preschoolers have trouble estimating fit unless the difference in size and shape is obvious.

Fitting a toothbrush into a slot, scissors into a holder, magic markers into their box; snapping pants, buttoning a coat, zipping boots, putting feet into shoes; fitting metal climbers together to make a long ladder, making a house out of giant tinkertoys—these are important active experiences for preschool children, through which they come to understand the spatial concepts involved in fitting things together and taking them apart. Adults working with preschoolers can find many opportunities to support and encourage them in this process. Here are some suggestions.

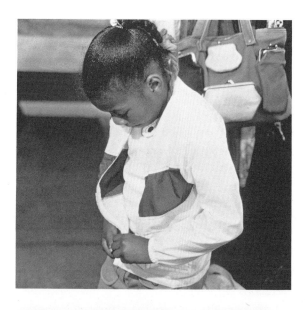

Suggestions for adults

Provide materials that can be put together and taken apart

Block area—hollow and unit blocks, plastic "take-apart" trucks and cars, wooden "screw-apart" vehicles, large tinkertoys, interlocking blocks, clip-on wheels and blocks, snap-together train tracks

Quiet area—large and small pegs and pegboards, stacking round-about rings, small tinkertoys, large Lego blocks, interlocking plastic squares, nuts-bolts-screws-and-board set, puzzles, parquetry blocks, connecto-straws, geoboards

House area—jars and lids, mixing bowls and lids, pans and lids, wind-up clock, old jewelry that fastens or snaps, keys and key ring, empty make-up articles (compact, lipstick, after-shave bottles) dress-up clothes that snap, button and zip

Art area—magic markers and tops, paint jars and lids, paste jars/glue bottles and lids, staples and stapler

Construction area—wood, hammer, nails, saw, drill and drill bits, screws and screwdriver

Provide materials from which children can make their own fit-together-take-apart toys

puzzles—magazine pictures, glue, wood or cardboard

necklaces—string, paper clips, thread spools or other "recycled" materials

take-apart trucks—boxes, paper, glue, cardboard, metal fasteners, string

interlocking squares—scissors, cardboard

Provide time for children to work with materials on their own

Children need time to try to fit things together and take them apart on their own. The time for an adult to step in with suggestions is when a child is clearly frustrated by his or her own unsuccessful attempts. (See the key experience, *Discovering Relations through Direct Experience*, in chapter 5.)

Encourage children to demonstrate and talk about how materials they used fit together and came apart

• "Arthur, you put the truck together all by yourself. Show me how you did it."

• "Hey, Joanie, you discovered how to keep the lids on the mixing bowls. What did you do?"

• "Mark, your wall is fixed. What did you do to keep that blanket from falling down?"

• "Gregg, how did you get that wheel to stay on your car?"

Some children will re-enact the process they went through, some will only point to what they did, and others will both demonstrate and talk about the process. The important thing is for each child to communicate his or her discoveries in some way to an appreciative adult.

Make observations about how things fit together and come apart, and point out things a child may not have noticed

• "Margo, you put all the small pegs into the holes in the pegboard. What a good idea you had for making a birthday cake!"

• "So that's where that green tinkertoy stick fits, Eddie. Right through the middle of the round piece. And you can make the round part spin around."

• "You had to turn that screwdriver around and around to make that screw go into the wood."

• "First, you put the stick part through the hole and then you twisted the end part, and that kept the wheel on. That was a good idea, Traci."

When a child is baffled trying to fit something together or take it apart, make suggestions

Sometimes children get frustrated because they can't get something to fit together or come apart. Unaided, they become angry, or they leave the problem for something more satisfying. Sometimes a suggestion or a little help from an adult can turn a frustrating situation into a successful one:

• "Here Pancho, let's try that puzzle piece right next to the one you just put in."

• "Tinkertoys really stick sometimes, Nancy. Let me help you get that one out so you can put it where you want it."

Provide simpler materials for some children

Evan got very frustrated trying to put the small Lego blocks together. An adult suggested he work with the unit blocks instead, but Evan didn't want them because they didn't "snap."

The small Legos were too hard, and the unit blocks were not challenging enough. After some looking, the adult discovered that Lego blocks came in three sizes—small, large and giant. He borrowed a set of giant Lego blocks with which Evan worked happily on his own.

———————

A teaching team found that twelve nesting cups was too many for any of their children to fit together at one time, so they reduced the number to five, and the children enjoyed greater success with them. They found the same principle was true for puzzles. Puzzles with more than eight or nine pieces were too frustrating, so they removed them in favor of puzzles with fewer pieces.

———————

Donna couldn't fit together a puzzle made from a magazine picture of a person. Realizing that Donna was having difficulty because the material was so abstract, an adult decided to provide experiences with more realistic materials. Donna might need more experiences using her own body to focus on the relationships of body parts. She could work with dolls and puppets, take apart and try to fit together the parts of a figure made from playdough or try a wooden puzzle of a person with fewer details and pieces.

Plan small-group activities around materials that can be put together and taken apart

Review the general suggestions for small-group times in chapter 2. Included here is a sample plan for one small-group time focusing on fitting together and taking apart, with notes on how the adult extended the children's actions.

Objectives	Materials	Observations
Fitting together, taking apart. Encourage children to notice the attributes of the materials and how the objects are used together. Opening statement: "Let's see how many different ways you can fit these tinkertoys together"	Set of tinkertoy sticks, wheels and paper shapes with holes in bags for each child. Put child's sign on bag.	*Tania* fingered, stacked wheels, put all wheels on one stick and spun them around. Labeled objects.
		Mike stuck sticks in every hole in wheel, called it a "flower." Aware of parts of wheel. Described how to fit together.
		John watched and imitated Mike, showed rather than told how to fit together.
Things the adult did		*Debbie* made a long "pole" using sticks and wheels, measured with it.
• Watched each child.		
• Asked what each child found in his bag.		*Stevie* dropped short sticks through holes in paper—tried to interest him in holes of round tinkertoy.
• Labeled objects for Stevie, imitated him.		
• Asked if he could find other holes to drop the sticks through.		*Kadith* planned to make a person—used sticks and wheels to make body, taped paper on for clothes, described attributes of materials and person.
• Asked what John and Mike did to get the flower to stay together.		
• Asked "how else" they could fit their materials together. Children began to notice more possibilities.		*Gregg* sorted objects—at first didn't notice how sticks fit in wheels—made identical units of wheel and stick—not yet aware of possibilities.
• Ended the small-group time by asking each child to show the group what he or she had done.		
• Cleaned up by putting identical objects together.		

Key Experience:
Rearranging and reshaping objects

Guided by their immediate perceptions, young children believe that because the changes objects undergo cause them to look different or to take up more or less space, the objects themselves are no longer the same objects they were before the changes. A preschooler may not believe, for example, that the group of blocks scattered on the floor, then stacked into a high tower, are the same group of blocks and not more. Nor does the child believe that a round ball of playdough remains the same when it's rolled into a footlong hotdog. At this age, children can't keep in mind the process that changes objects. They focus on what objects look like before and after they're changed or rearranged, not on what happens in the interval.

When they've reached the concrete operational stage of development, young children are able to understand change, or transformation, because they can keep the *process* of transformation in mind, conserve mass or amount (realize that nothing has been added or taken away) and mentally reverse the transformation process to remember the object in its original state. Preoperational children, however, are still dominated by their perceptions of objects before and after they're transformed. Although they don't understand the process of transformation, they do transform objects by folding, twisting, stretching, stacking and tying them, and in so doing they gain first-hand experience in how objects can be rearranged in space and still retain their essential characteristics.

Regardless of how they perceive the transformation process, and regardless of their belief that physical manipulation of objects changes their characteristics, preschoolers need many opportunities to rearrange and reshape objects. The more opportunities they have to exercise their preoperational understanding of transformation, the broader the base they will have on which to build later concrete operational understandings of transformation and the conservation of mass and volume.

Suggestions for adults

Provide materials that can be rearranged and reshaped

House area—silverware, dishes, shoes, dolls, teddy bears, pinecones, poker chips and other pretend food, pillows, doll blankets, scarves, shoes with laces, doll clothes, washcloths, towels

Block area—blocks, boards, pieces of carpet, cars, trucks, rubber people, wooden furniture, cardboard boxes, rubber animals, cardboard pieces, sheets, blankets, rope, large tinkertoys

Art area—scraps of material, paper of all kinds, paper tubes, magazines, leaves, branches, styrofoam, rubber bands, yarn, string, elastic, paper clips, toothpicks, pipe cleaners, playdough clay, papier maché, straws, wire

Construction area—wood, cardboard, nails, plastic lids, wire, string, rubber bands, pipe cleaners, material pieces, styrofoam

Quiet area—footprints, cubes, small blocks, playschool village, puzzles, shape-sorter shapes, small tinkertoys, Lego blocks, geoboards, interlocking plastic squares, connecto-straws

Provide different surfaces for rearranging and reshaping materials

flat surfaces—table and floor space, boards, heavy cardboard, carpet squares, linoleum pieces

round surfaces—paper tubes, carpet tubes, plastic piping, wooden doweling, balloons, ping pong balls

enclosures—boxes, cartons, plastic containers

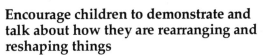

Encourage children to demonstrate and talk about how they are rearranging and reshaping things

Showing and talking about what they're doing helps children put words to actions and thus become more aware of what they've done. Here are some examples of how adults might encourage children to point out or tell how they've rearranged or reshaped things:

• "Jeremy, I saw you squish your playdough out into a long skinny shape. Now what are you doing with it?"

• "You changed your furniture all around, Clark. The last time I was here it was all along the walls. What did you do to make it different?"

• "A few minutes ago your necklace was straight, Bobbie, but now you changed it so it has all kinds of circles in it. How did you do that?"

• "Your napkin sure looks different from mine, Nasca. What did you do to it?"

• "First I saw you stacking all the blocks in a big, high tower, Susanna. Now what are you doing to make them look so different?"

• "What's happening to your rubber band as you're pulling it, Marva?"

Describe changes in objects for children who can't do so themselves

Many children can effect changes in objects but don't have the language to describe what they've done. Adults can assist them by talking with them about changes they've made:

• "First you lined all the shells up in one long line, Patrice, and now you've changed them so they are in lots of short lines."

• "You made the wire look different, Evan, by twisting it around your finger. See all the circles it has in it now?"

• "First you had the blanket draped over you like a tent, Celeste, and now you've folded it all up so you can lie on it."

Encourage children to try different ways of rearranging and reshaping

• "You know, we've been folding our napkins the same way for a long time. Let's see if we can come up with a different way of folding them."

• "Look what Lance is doing with his clay, Mimi. Do you think you and I could try rolling ours out real long the way he is?"

• "What do you think would happen if you tried stacking your blocks another way, Ida?"

• "Look, Kirt. Maybe you could try putting the tinkertoys together another way like this so the sticks all go around . . . or like this so they all go together in a long line."

Assist children who are attempting complex transformations

Making even the most elementary paper airplane requires a number of folds that are difficult for young children to remember or to duplicate from looking at a properly folded airplane. One way to assist children in carrying out such relatively complex transformations is to work alongside them, demonstrating or explaining each step. Another way is to make a "picture recipe" chart showing each step in order.

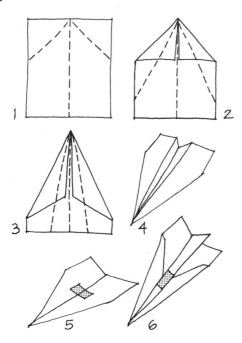

Plan small-group times in which children rearrange and reshape objects

Review the general suggestions for small-group time in chapter 2. Included here is a sample plan for one small-group time in which children rearranged and reshaped leaves they had gathered on a walk.

Objectives	Materials	Observations
Rearranging and reshaping leaves gathered on walk	Provide large piece of colored paper and box lid full of leaves of different shapes and sizes for each child.	*Laura* put leaves in rows, then a circle (observed Tara)
Opening statement "Here are some of the leaves we found on our walk yesterday. Put some of them on your paper and see how many different ways you can arrange them. See what designs you can make. Maybe you can fold or bend them, too."	Have masking tape, glue, paste, rubber cement available for when they want to stick leaves on.	*Traci* made piles of leaves, larger leaf on bottom, smaller on top, all stems faced same way.
		Rico first made circle. All stems in middle. Forgot his arrangement and began adding leaves to empty spaces.
		Tara made circle with leaves then began to cover every space. Folded some larger leaves.
		Eddie made collage. Intended to cover the whole space.
Things the adult did • Observed children's actions. • Asked children to think of another way to arrange leaves. • Imitated Tara's circular pattern. • Labeled certain shapes: "row," "circle," "tube." • Called attention to how Tim bent his leaf into a tube to help children become aware of other possibilities. • Ended with guessing game—"The person whose leaves are put in piles can put his (her) picture in her cubby and go to the circle . . ." • Asked children to describe their arrangements. • Described arrangement for those who couldn't themselves.		*Tim* first classified leaves putting maple leaves on top row, birch leaves on bottom. Then rearranged them all around the edge of the paper. In the middle put leaves bent into tubes he formed around his finger and taped together.

Key Experience:
Observing and describing things from different spatial viewpoints

A person's capacity to see and imagine things from various viewpoints changes as he or she matures. A baby's spatial viewpoint is very limited until he learns to move and grasp things and achieves some mobility; then it expands as he or she learns to crawl and walk and manipulate objects with greater freedom and dexterity. Preschoolers are mobile and dextrous compared to their younger counterparts and can get them-

selves into all kinds of positions to see how things look from there. They hang upside down from climbers and tree limbs; they climb to the top of hills, trees, jungle gyms and block towers to see things from way up high; they get on their stomachs to scoot through a tunnel; they crawl around and inside of big things they've made from wood or packing crates to make sure they've painted every spot. As they move up, down, around, through and inside they see things from a variety of spatial viewpoints.

When children reach the concrete operational stage of development, they can begin to imagine and represent how things look from other spatial points of view. They can imagine, for example, what a friend can see from across the street without actually being there themselves.

While preschoolers cannot yet imagine spatial points of view different from the ones they perceive at the moment, they do place themselves in many unusual positions to view their world. Adults can assist children in viewing and describing things from many spatial viewpoints by supporting and encouraging their mobility, curiosity and desire to experiment with physical positions.

Suggestions for adults

Provide materials and equipment for looking at things from different spatial viewpoints

Outside—swings, climbers, tree stumps, merry-go-rounds, ladders, hills, bridges, slides, tree houses, tunnels, seesaws, wheeltoys, a sand pit, a small trampoline or large inner-tubes

Inside—large sturdy blocks, heavy-duty boxes, stools, chairs, tables, small stepladder

Encourage children to look at things from various spatial viewpoints

This can be done quite naturally and enjoyably outdoors as children play. Encourage them to try as many positions as they can safely assume on each piece of equipment. Adults can even demonstrate some new positions themselves.

Indoors, encourage children to inspect their creations from all sides and positions: "You've made a very big, long building, Clyde. Come over here and see how it looks from this side."

Encourage children to describe how things look from their spatial point of view

As children look at things from different spatial viewpoints, encourage them to describe what they see and how things look:

- "You've climbed way up to the top of the climber, Enid. What can you see from way up there?"
- "Hey, teacher, look at me. I'm a snake crawling."

"Well, Mr. Snake, tell me what you see crawling way down there in the grass."

Some children may not be able to describe what they see or how things look. Then an adult can join them on the climber, the swings, under the table or wherever they are and talk about what can be seen from this position:

"You really have to make yourself little to fit under this table, Dawn! But now that I'm here I can see people's legs and shoes. I see Glenn lying on the floor looking at the ant farm. I see the bottom of the block shelf . . ."

TRIP TO THE PARK

Objectives	Materials/Equipment	Observations
(1) Walking, running, climbing, using large muscles, finding out and describing what your body can do. (2) Observing and describing things from different spatial points of view.	hill, climbers, swings, tunnel, trees, seesaw, slide, tall grass to crawl through and hide in	*Tal and Rino*—rolling down the hill—described everything as "turning around." *Jeb*—hanging upside down, said it looked like I was walking on the sky. Also tried to hide behind a tree. Had no idea that I could see him—since he could not see me. *Cathy and Tara*—on top of slide telling others they looked little. *John*—had idea of running to the top of the hill to be better able to see the train across the river. *Mark and Traci*—on swings. Learning to pump, wanting to go higher and higher. *Eve and Bethany*—stayed together whole time trying different places to hang by their knees. Hung upside down from climber, low tree limb, and lay with heads facing down hill. Eve: "The grass is by my head." "The leaves are standing on the sky." *Brenda and Kelly*—spied on people through the grass. "We see Tal's knees (giggle, giggle)." *Bruce*—shinnied up the swing leg to the crossbar and slid down like a fireman. "High." "There goes Tal. There goes Rino." *Derek and Leo*—crept through tunnel then climbed on top of it and jumped off. Derek in tunnel told Leo what he saw from there while Leo told Derek what he saw from on top.

Statement at meeting before trip and again just before arriving at park: "Let's see how many things you can do at the park and what you can see when you move to new places."

Things the adults did
- Focused on parts of bodies children were using to climb, swing, run, etc. Labeled parts of bodies used. "Mark, you really are moving your legs to pump." "Cathy, did you ever try holding on tight with your hands to the sides of the slide as you go down? Do you know what happens?"
- Asked children to describe what they could see when they were at the bottom and on top of the slide, on top of and underneath the climber, in the middle of the tunnel vs. out of the tunnel . . .
- Encouraged children to guess what John could see from the top of the hill.

Take photographs of familiar things and places from different spatial viewpoints

Take photographs from the spatial viewpoints often assumed by the children—from the top of the climber, from the swings, from the tunnel, from under the table, from a block tower. Take photographs of classroom objects and of things the children have made—photographs of the resident rabbit from the top, front, back and sides, photographs of a block structure from various angles and positions. Add the photographs to the quiet area so that children may look at them and describe them whenever they wish.

Encourage interested children to represent things from different spatial viewpoints

Many preschool children are interested in drawing pictures of things they've made—a block house or tower, a wooden airplane, a long paper chain, a cardboard doll bed. As a child draws a block house, for example, encourage him to make a series of pictures of it from several spatial viewpoints. He can sit in front of it to draw it, then sit in back of it and make a second picture. Remember that preschool children cannot yet *imagine* spatial points of view. The preschooler drawing his block house would have to *see* the back of his house in order to draw it.

Take walks and trips in which children can experience a number of spatial viewpoints

Something as simple as a walk around the block can provide many opportunities for looking at things from different spatial viewpoints. How does the school look when you're standing right next to it? How does it look from the corner? What part of the school can you see from the hill? What else can you see from the hill? Included here is an example of one teaching team's plan for and observations of such a trip.

Key Experience:
Experiencing and describing the relative positions, directions and distances of things

As preschoolers fit things together, rearrange and reshape them and observe them from different spatial viewpoints, they are not only developing an understanding of how things relate to each other in space, but they are learning to use the words that describe these spatial relations. Many spatial words, however, are quite confusing to preschoolers.

Although preschoolers have spent a lot of time and energy all their lives arranging objects in different positions as well as assuming all kinds of positions themselves, they are just beginning to try out words to describe them, words like *on, off, on top of, over, above, under, below, beneath, underneath, bottom, top, in front of, behind, in the middle of, between, beside, next to, on the side of.* One problem is figuring out which word to use when a particular position can be described in several different ways. A doll lying under a blanket, for example, could be described as being under, beneath, underneath, below, covered by or wrapped in the blanket. The easiest way out of this dilemma for many preschoolers and even many hasty adults is to point to the little bundle saying, "The doll's right there!"

Moving in all directions is another thing preschoolers have been doing vigorously ever since they learned to scoot around or crawl. Now, however, they're beginning to be aware that their movement has direction, and they're trying to use words like *to, from, into, out of, toward* and *away from* to describe the direction something or someone is moving in.

Preschoolers are also beginning to describe relative distances. The words *close, near, far, next to, together* and *apart,* however, can be confusing because the same word can cover a wide range of distances depending upon the context in which it is used. Take *close to,* for example: Sitting close to someone may mean there is a distance of a foot or two between people, or it may refer to no distance at all, while living close to someone may mean that two people live next door or that they are separated by a distance ranging from a few blocks to a few miles. This confusion is compounded by the fact that more than one word or phrase may be used to describe the same spatial distance—for example, an adult might ask a child to place the cups *close to, next to, together with* or *near* the juice container—as well as by the fact that preschoolers' judgment of distance is influenced by the presence or absence of barriers. A preschooler may view a chair a few yards away from him, for example, as being close to him, but if someone builds a house between him and the chair, though the distance actually remains unchanged, he sees the chair as no longer being close. The barrier formed by the house has made it farther away from him according to his perception of distance.

Spatial terms describing relative positions, directions and distances are just emerging in preschoolers' vocabularies. Although they've probably heard these terms used for a good part of their lives, they're just beginning to connect them with their own actions. Here are some suggestions to help adults support and encourage children's attempts to describe positions, directions and distances in space that they've experienced.

Suggestions for adults

Provide materials that encourage children to explore positions, directions and distances

Positions—most materials and equipment (indoor and outdoor) already mentioned in this book can be placed in various positions by children

Directions and distances—The following kinds of materials lend themselves particularly well to the exploration of direction and distance:

  Toys with wheels—toy vehicles, ride-on toys
  Toys with legs—dolls, stuffed animals, wooden/rubber animals, dollhouse people

Living things—classroom pets, hardy plants
Things that drip—water, paints, finger paints, plaster of Paris, wheat paste, glue, rubber cement
Things that roll—balls, spools, beads, tubes, cans, jars, dowels, marbles, bearings, washers, plastic piping, pegs, stacking rings
Moving outdoor equipment—swings, merry-go-round, seesaw, wagons, scooters, riding toys, ropes

Provide opportunities for children to experience various positions, directions and distances

Obstacle courses imaginatively set up allow children to assume a variety of spatial positions in sequence. Obstacle courses can also be arranged in zig-zag fashion to emphasize directional changes, and they can be shortened and lengthened to cover various distances.

"*Follow the Leader*," like obstacle courses, can be played so that the leader (and followers) assume a variety of bodily positions, move in a number of directions and cover various relative distances (for example, going from one tree to a tree that's close to it, then going from that tree to the top of the hill which is further away).

Circle games provide various spatial experiences. In "A Tisket, a Tasket" and "Duck, Duck, Goose" children go *around,* stop *behind* someone and sit *between* people. In "In and Out the Window" children go *around, into* the circle, *out of* the circle, *between* people and *under* their arms. In "London Bridge" children go *under, through, between, behind, in front of* and are captured *inside* the gates of the bridge.

"*Simon Says*" can be modified to emphasize positions; "Simon says sit *next to* somebody . . . stand *on top of* a block"; directions: "Simon says hop *toward* Mr. Norton . . . jump *away from* the school" or distances: "Simon says roll to a tree that's *close to* you . . . walk to another tree that's *far away.*"

Encourage children to describe the spatial positions, directions and distances they're experiencing

One way adults can encourage children to describe spatial relations is to ask them questions:

• "I can't see the animals on your farm, Anita. Where did you put them?"

• "Yes, Mr. taxi driver, I do need a ride. What direction are you going?"

• "That's a long road you've built, Roxanne. How far can your truck go on it?"

Adults can also ask children to give directions about where to put things and where and how far to go:

• "Denny, I'll help you put away all these trucks and cars if you tell me exactly where on

the shelf they should go. Don't *show* me where they go, just *tell* me, and I'll put them right where you say."

• "Sure, I'll pull you in the wagon, Izzie. Just tell me where you want to go."

"Over there."

"Where's over there?"

"To the bunny cage."

"Okay, here we go to the bunny cage."

Use specific spatial terms when talking with children

As adults talk with children throughout the day they should be as specific as possible when referring to positions, directions and distances. For example, instead of saying, "I saw you putting the paste away over there," an adult could say, "I saw you putting the paste away in the art area on the top shelf next to the scissors." Or instead of saying, "Look, Jenny, the rabbit is hopping over there," an adult might say, "Look, Jenny, the rabbit is hopping toward Shelly and Celia."

As opportunities arise naturally in conversation with children, comment on where they are or where they're going:

• "You're building your garage between Peter's road and Nikita's tinkertoy house."

• "You're hopping on one foot toward the swings."

Accept children's judgments of positions, directions and distances

It's important to accept and acknowledge children's efforts to use spatial terms even if their spatial descriptions are sometimes erroneous from an adult's point of view. One child, for example, when asked which block she was going to put on the top of her tower, responded by pointing to a number of blocks already part of

Objectives	Materials	Observations
(1) Arranging objects in space (2) Gaining skill with glue (3) Exploring and describing things in relation to each other—especially inside, top, bottom, sides, next to	Provide each child with a large milk carton, glue, scissors, and a personal tray filled with sandpaper and wrapping paper scraps, fabric pieces.	*Tammy* knew which side to put the glue on wrapping paper. Covered side of carton nearest her. After we turned carton around looking for difference between sides, she realized she had covered only one side.
		Ron very carefully covered the inside. Cut pieces into rectangles or squares and lined up edges. Said that he put things "next to" each other and "inside the box."
		Jackie put identical paper scraps on each side of carton, said 2 pieces were "near the top," 2 "near the bottom."
		Terrance kept gluing on paper on top of another on one side. Mostly interested in the gluing, less in covering space. Could not describe "on top" so I did for him.
Opening statement "I'd like you to see where on your milk carton you can glue these pieces of paper and material. When we're finished, I'd like you to tell where you decided to glue your pieces."		*Martha* explored with glue, dripping it onto her carton making drip patterns. After observing, I asked her what she thought she could stick on top of her drips. She covered each drip with a piece of sandpaper. I talked with her about "on top of" and "next to."

(left margin: SMALL GROUP TIME I)

Objectives	Materials	Observations
(1) Exploring relative distances (2) Using large muscles	Outside— snow	*Karl and Tim* walked "to the rabbit cage." Other children noticed that Tim got there first. I asked why. Some confusion between speed and distance. We compared footsteps—how close they were to each other.
		Laura went "to that big tree" and tried taking tiny footsteps and counting them.
		Joanie and Rino tried to take long jumps so their footprints would be farther apart. They went "to the swings which are far away."
Opening statement "Today everyone's going to have a chance to make footprints. Pick out a place you want to walk to, then when it's your turn, tell us where you're going and we'll watch to see if you make your footprints close together or far apart."		*Traci* began to walk in circles, lines, more interested in spatial arrangement. We ended with adaptation of "Mother May I." For example, Karl said, "Mother, I'm'na take close together steps over there to the slide."

(left margin: SMALL GROUP TIME II)

the tower saying, "This one's on top. This one's on top. This one's on top . . ." Rather than "correct" her, the adult, looking at things from the child's point of view said, "That's right, Benita, this block is on top of this one, this block is on top of this one, and this block is on top of this one. And here's the very top of your tower. Which block should go here on the very top?"

Take photographs of the children as they experience different positions and directions and encourage them to talk about what they see

Take photographs of the children on top of the slide, going down the slide, running toward the school, sitting next to each other, and so on. Probably the first thing the children will notice in a photograph is who's in the picture. "There's me. There's Greta and Freddy." After they've done this ask them to describe where each child is or where he or she is going.

Encourage children to describe the spatial relations of things they see in picture books, magazines and in pictures they make themselves

As children are looking at pictures, ask them to describe positions, directions and distances. Also ask them if they'd like their descriptions written down and read back.

Plan small-group times in which children can experience and describe relative positions, directions and distances

Review the general suggestions for small-group time in chapter 2. Included here are examples of plans and observations from two small-group times in which children experienced and described spatial positions, directions and distances.

Key Experience:
Experiencing and representing one's own body

When all other perceptual channels are blocked—sight, sound, taste and smell—people can still experience space with their bodies. The more aware they are of what their bodies can do, the more aware they are of the space around them and the relations among objects in space.

Newborn infants begin life with very little idea of their bodies. One of the first things infants learn is to move their heads at will and focus their eyes on objects within their range of vision. Then they learn to wave their arms and legs, batting and kicking at things. They become fascinated with their hands and find they can grasp and hold things with them. They learn to roll their bodies over, sit up, stand, crawl, walk and climb. Through trial and error, they learn where their bodies will fit and where they won't, and they begin to master some finer skills such as untying shoes, pumping the handle on a top to make it spin and turning the pages of a book.

Compared to infants and toddlers, preschoolers are quite adept with their bodies. As they work with materials and equipment, they increase their knowledge of what their bodies can do—cut, pound, fit together, stack, twist and fold things; climb, swing, pull, push and balance. At the same time, however, they are adding a new dimension to their understanding of bodies. They are learning to name various body parts, describe what they can do and represent this knowledge in models and pictures.

As preschoolers make pictures and models of themselves, their families and friends, they are using everything they know about how a body fits together and how all its parts relate to one another. Young children's earliest representations of people reflect a very rudimentary understanding of body parts and their relations. As their awareness of their own bodies increases, however, their "people pictures" show greater detail and more realistic interrelations among body parts.

As preschoolers continue to explore new ranges and qualities of movement and how the different parts of their bodies move in relation to each other, they also begin to label and describe these parts and actions as well as represent what they know about bodies in pictures and models. Here are some ways adults can encourage and support children in these endeavors.

Suggestions for adults

Provide opportunities for children to use their bodies in a variety of ways

During outside time, encourage children to use equipment in many ways so they can use their bodies in different ways. Be sure to join them in their play and talk with them about what they're doing.

Play circle games which focus on specific body parts and positions:
- "This time think of some way we can make just our fingers move."
- "Can you think of another way to move while we're sitting down?"
- "What's an exercise we can do lying on our backs?"
- "Who can think of a way to move our bodies but not move our hands and feet?"

At work time and small-group time, talk with children about all the different things they're doing with their bodies—lifting, balancing, carrying, stringing, sorting; using crayons, pencils, paint brushes, scissors; stirring, pouring, shaking, hammering, pounding, sawing; buttoning, zipping, putting on and taking off coats and boots.

Provide materials and equipment that help children learn how their bodies are put together

Full-length mirrors enable a child to see what his or her whole body looks like from many angles. Very simple *cameras* allow children to take pictures of each other and to have "people photographs" to refer to when they're drawing people. *Rolls of wrapping or butcher paper* enable children to make life-size body tracings to which they can add body parts and clothing. *People puzzles, people pictures, rubber and wooden people* and *dolls*

encourage children to label and describe body parts. *Shadows and silhouettes* help children focus on major body parts and movements by blocking out extraneous details.

Help children learn body-part names

Talk with individual children about the body parts they see as they look at themselves in mirrors, as they look at body prints or tracings, as they make models or pictures of people. Use body-part names when describing children's actions:
- "You sure have strong arms, Chris. You're carrying four blocks at one time!"
- "Maria has new shoes. I can see all her toes."
- "That was a good idea, Monique. Your hands are full so you pushed the door open with your hip."

Use precise terms when talking with children about body parts to avoid confusion and to help them learn the names for the less easily distinguished ones:
- "Amy, you have some red paint on your cheek." (instead of "face")
- "Julie has a pretty bracelet on her wrist." (instead of "arm")
- "When Bobby fell he bumped his ankle." (instead of "foot")

Also encourage children to identify the body parts of classroom pets and to compare them with their own.

Help children begin to notice how their bodies are similar to other people's and how they're different

Preschoolers are often curious about differences they notice in physical appearance and are pleased by physical similarities. Help them describe their observations and feelings: "Yes, Troy, David's skin is a different color from yours.

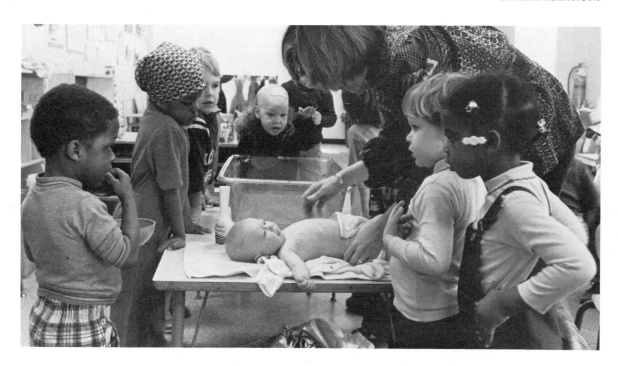

Yours is dark brown and his is light brown. In that way you're different. What's one thing you're doing with your bodies right now that's just the same?"

Plan small-group times in which children can make models or pictures of bodies

Review the suggestions for small-group time in chapter 2. Some activities for focusing on body parts: making life-size body tracings on wrapping or butcher paper; cutting out magazine pictures of people, describing and pantomiming their actions, pasting them into a book about people; making puppets; drawing people using crayon, magic markers, paints. Included here is a sample plan for such a small-group time and the observations one of the adults shared about the children in her small group.

Objectives	Materials	Observations
(1) Represent a body (2) Label body parts	playdough and different sizes of tinkertoy sticks for each child and adult	*Corey* had problems starting. Needed me to simplify and go step by step. Knew head and legs. Representation's name changed several times.
		Carolyn was not interested in representing self. Made bird with wings, beak.
		Joey made head plus limbs, no body.
		Laura asked "What's a body?" and made a person like Joey's. Hands very important.
Opening statement "I'd like you to make a person today. You can make a boy, girl, a woman or a man. It can be you or someone else. That's up to you."		*Tom* made head, body, legs, arms, hands. Started to put clothes on. Labeled parts.
		Sam is not representing in this medium yet. Explored playdough, squeezed, pulled, stuck sticks in and hid them in mass of dough.

Key Experience:
Learning to locate things in the classroom, school and neighborhood

"Look, dad, over here in the workbench area. I made a big house out of wood here and used that hammer that's hanging up there and lots of these big nails. And see that gas station over there? We went there and that man put the car way up in the air and brought it down real slow."

This preschooler knows where things are in the classroom and where in the neighborhood she and her classmates went for a walk that day and is excitedly sharing this knowledge with her father as he picks her up after school.

Once very young children gain mobility and are given the freedom to use it, they quickly learn to locate things in their immediate, everyday environment—their toys, the kitchen waste basket, the stairs, the stool they like to climb on, the cupboard full of paper bags.

By the time they are of preschool age, children can locate things within much larger, more complex environments. Given a consistent classroom arrangement, they learn to locate particular materials they need and to determine which work areas are most appropriate for particular activities. With this information they also learn to carry out plans and ideas on their own without constantly waiting for or seeking out an adult to help them get started.

Preschoolers also know where things are on the playground or in a park they often visit. They can also point out landmarks and turns to make on a familiar route. Given the opportunity, they can also learn to locate places in their immediate home and school neighborhood—the way to a friend's house or to the fire station around the block from the school.

This immediate knowledge of where things are in their environment provides preschoolers with a sense of security and control. It also forms an experiential basis from which their ability to understand and make their own maps of places will later emerge.

Preschoolers are developing a sense of location and are beginning to think of themselves in relation to things in their immediate environment. A thoughtful adult can provide experiences which guide and foster this development.

Suggestions for adults

Divide the classroom into several distinct work areas

In a well organized classroom, children quickly learn to locate things. A room divided into a block area, house area, art area, quiet area, music area, construction area and sand-and-water area provides consistent location for materials and activities. Start the year with three or four of these work areas; when the children feel comfortable with the initial areas, gradually add others. Use the names of the work areas and the materials in them whenever possible; preschool children usually feel more comfortable and in control of the environment when they can name and thus talk about the things and places in it.

Begin the year with a limited amount of material in each work area

A classroom initially too full of materials may frustrate and overwhelm children. Limit materials at the beginning of the year. Then gradually

add new materials, involving children in deciding where new materials should go and in making labels for the materials.

Have planning boards in each work area

Hanging their signs on the planning board helps
children become aware of the various work areas
and reminds them of the particular areas they've
chosen to work in.

Play circle games about where things belong

One such circle game centers around a collection
of materials from all the different work areas. Let
each child choose one thing from the collection,
tell where he or she would put it at clean-up time
and then put it away. Make up a song to clap and
sing as the child does this. For example, to the
tune of "Did You Ever See A Lassie?" sing,

> Emily put the block back
> the block back
> the block back,
> Emily put the block back,
> She knows where it belongs.

In another game, each child gets something
from a work area and brings it back to the circle.
Then, going around the circle, everyone claps
and sings about each thing to the tune of "Old
MacDonald Had a Farm."

> Mary went to the art area
> E-I-E-I-O
> In the art area she found a brush,
> E-I-E-I-O

Take new children on a tour of the classroom

A classroom tour can help new children learn
where each area is, what materials are available,
where the bathroom is, where to hang their
coats, and so on. After such a tour, involve children who are familiar with the room in helping
new children learn to locate things.

Help children learn about the area surrounding the school

Take walks around the block where the school is
located. Look at the school from different angles
and vantage points and help children notice
places and permanent objects which can be used
to mark the way: "First we walk down the sidewalk to the stoplight . . . Now we turn and go
toward the big tree at the corner . . . Here at the
corner we turn again and go toward the fire station . . . Now we're passing the pizza place and
the gas station."

Take photographs of landmarks on these
walks, then cover them with clear contact paper
and put them in the quiet area or have the children talk about them during a small-group time.
Also encourage children to make their own pictures of things they've seen on such walks.

Take walking or riding field trips to different places in the community

Field trips acquaint children with people and
places in the neighborhood and community. In
deciding where to go, consider places that relate
to the children's everyday lives and cultural heritage as well as places they would find interesting. Banks and real estate agencies, for example,
are not particularly meaningful to preschoolers;
preschoolers are interested in places where they
can watch and even join people in action—the
local fire station, gas station, office, hardware
store, homes of classmates and teaching staff. Be
sure to arrange trips beforehand with the people
the children are going to visit, explaining to
them what preschool-age children are interested

in and planning together some simple ways the children might participate in the activities—for example, getting into the fire trucks, bagging the groceries they buy, feeding the calves, weighing nails.

Take photographs of the things the children see and do on each field trip and also bring back any props which will help children recall or reenact the trip.

Key Experience:
Interpreting representations of spatial relations in drawings, pictures and photographs

Children learn spatial concepts and gain an understanding of spatial relations through active experiences with things, people and places. On the basis of these direct experiences, preschoolers begin to interpret representations of spatial relations in pictures.

Often, however, preschoolers' interpretations differ from those adults would make, because preschoolers are just learning about what happens when three-dimensional objects are portrayed on a two-dimensional plane. They are learning, for example, that things meant to be far away in pictures are smaller than things meant to be closer. Looking at a picture of a man in the foreground and a car far away in the background, a preschooler might say, "There's a big man and a little tiny car." One preschooler looking at a fairly realistic drawing in a book of some

children playing in a nursery school laughingly pointed to a little girl near the top of the page and said, "That girl's painting up in the air!" She perceived the top of the page as up and the bottom of the page as down, which is true, of course, in some pictures (when the sky is on the top and the grass on the bottom), but not all pictures. The more experience preschoolers have comparing reality with pictorial representations, the more they will understand the conventions of depicting spatial relations on flat surfaces.

By providing a variety of pictures, drawings and photographs of people, places, events and objects with which children have had experience, adults can encourage and support children as they begin to interpret spatial relations in two-dimensional representations.

Suggestions for adults

Provide a wide variety of pictorial materials

Include in the classroom a wide variety of pictorial materials related to children's experiences: picture books (including books with photographs, realistic drawings and more abstract drawings); magazines and catalogs; photo albums (of classroom experiences, field trips, the children in their homes); drawings, paintings, books the children make themselves.

When possible, show children slides and videotapes of themselves, and encourage them to identify who they see and their relative position in the picture.

Children always enjoy looking at and talking about each other's pictures, so it's a good idea to provide a display space in each work area for children's pictures.

Encourage children to compare people, objects or scenes with pictures or photographs of them

When possible, call a child's attention to the actual person, object or scene he or she is looking at in a picture or photograph. Encourage the child to compare the actual object with its two-dimensional representation:

"How's our pet bunny different from the bunny in the book, Linus?"

"Well, this bunny's brown and ours is white and our bunny's ears are down and this bunny's ears are up."

Encourage children to describe the spatial relations in their own and others' pictures

The first thing children usually say about pictures they've made is what's in it—a man, a car, a scary house, etc. In order to describe positions, directions and distances, they'll probably need some questions from an adult to help them look at the picture in terms of space:

• "Yes, Rhody, you did draw Frank the guinea pig and his cage. Where is Frank in your picture?"

• "That's right, Eddie. There's you and Laurie and Kim and Barry and the gas station man at the gas station. Where are you all standing?"

"Right there."

"Right there. Where is right there?"

"Underneath the car."

"That's right, but how can you stand underneath the car?"

"The car's up. The man made it go up on the lifters."

Encourage children to recreate the spatial relations they see in pictures and photographs

Children often enjoy imitating spatial relationships as they listen in a group to a story:

"Who can tell me what Andy's doing in this picture?"

"He's standing on his toes with his hands way up in the air."

"Let's see if we can stand the same way as Andy."

A child may be intrigued with a photograph or with a picture someone has done and decide to make "a big building just like the one in the picture." Often the child needs help in figuring out where to start. An adult can help him sort out and describe where things are in the picture:

"Well, what's on the very bottom of the tower in the picture, Angie?"

"A big red block."

"Okay, what's on top of the big red block?"

Play "I'm looking at a picture which. . ."

One game some children enjoy as they're looking at pictures and photographs is *finding the picture being described.* An adult looking at pictures with a few children in the quiet area, for example, might say, "I'm looking at a picture in which two people are standing next to a tree," or "I'm looking at a picture of two ducks under a bridge." Be sure to acknowledge and talk about the pictures the children do pick out, whether or not they're the correct ones. Children looking for a picture of two ducks under a bridge may pick out a picture with only ducks in it or only a bridge in it because they may be concentrating on only one thing at a time. An adult might then say, "There are two ducks in that picture, Terry. What are they doing? . . . Can you find another picture with the ducks under the bridge?" Chil-

dren in the group can also be "it" and describe a picture they want people to find.

Key Experience:
Distinguishing and describing shapes

Learning about the shapes of things is part of children's increasing awareness of space. Before they reach preschool age, young children begin to discover the properties of different shapes through active exploration and manipulation of objects. They discover, for example, that a ball dropped on the floor rolls, while a block dropped on the floor does not, and that blocks but not balls can be piled on top of each other.

Preschoolers learn to sort things out by shape, putting all the round beads together on a necklace followed by all the square beads, for example. Most often children use and sort things out according to shape before they use shape names. This is a logical sequence of development because a child first needs many experiences using square things in many different ways before the word "square" makes sense to him. In other words, children distinguish shapes through their actions before they can describe them with terms like "circle," "square" and "triangle." That's why drilling children in shape names, as many adults working with preschoolers do, is a pointless undertaking. Adults who really want to help children learn to distinguish and describe shapes should provide many objects with different shapes for children to use and talk about.

It's important for adults to realize that preschoolers attend primarily to surfaces rather than

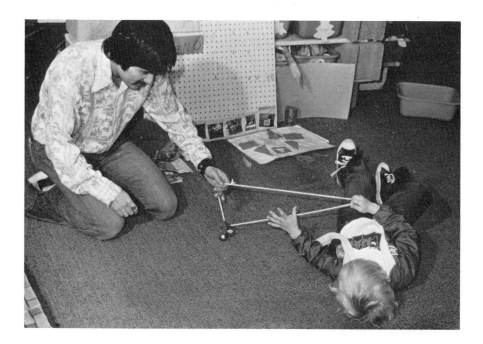

dimensions. This means that, in describing the shapes of things, preschoolers don't distinguish between a two-dimensional circle and a three-dimensional sphere. Shapes adults distinguish as circles and spheres are all circles to preschoolers.

Many preschool-age children are also beginning to make their own regular shapes as they paint and draw and model things from clay, playdough, wood, sand and papier maché. Circles are the first shapes they master; squares and triangles take much longer to learn to make because it's difficult for young children to change directions abruptly to make angles. At the same time, preschoolers continue to explore and experiment with irregular contours, lines and forms, and many of their paintings and drawings which they call "designs" combine both regular and irregular shapes and lines.

Suggestions for adults

Provide a variety of materials with distinguishable shapes

Not all classroom materials are equally easy to describe in terms of their shape. What shape is a pair of scissors? Here are some classroom materials whose shapes are more regular and are therefore most easily described: blocks, boxes, carpet pieces, plates, lids, food containers, cookie cutters, blankets, scarves, towels, rings, bracelets, necklaces, buttons, beads, bottlecaps, cards, books, dominoes, Lego blocks, tinkertoys, shape sorter shapes, attribute blocks, cuisinaire rods, pieces of wood, triangles, tambourines, wood blocks.

Many teaching teams keep a collection of collage materials in the art area—bits of paper, cloth, sandpaper, cardboard, ribbon, netting, carpet pieces, styrofoam, balsa wood, foam rubber—cut into circles, triangles, rectangles and squares.

Encourage children to make their own shapes

As children make their own pictures and models, they often wish to include regular shapes in them but aren't always sure how they can make ones that "look right." One solution is to ask an adult to make the shape they need. An adult can respond by asking children how big they want their shape to be and helping them find an object of the same shape to trace. The important thing is to demonstrate to children that they can make their own shapes by tracing.

Talk with children throughout the day about shapes they're using and making

• "What a tall tower you've made, Amanda. And look, first you put all the rectangle blocks on top of each other, and then you put all the square blocks on top of each other."

• "What a good idea, Lee. You pounded all your nails in so they make a big circle on your piece of wood."

• "Thanks for the cereal, Jesse. I like cereal made from round buttons and served on a round plate."

Encourage children to observe the properties of shapes

"That's a long ramp you've made, Paula. Which blocks do you think would roll down your ramp? . . . How come this one rolled down but this one stayed at the top? . . . "

Encourage children to notice shapes in a variety of settings

Throughout the day talk with children and help them see different shapes on the clothing they wear, on buildings, in windows, doors, signs, playground equipment, vehicles, furniture, flowers, leaves.

Be careful about asking children the question, "What shape is this?"

Many adults tend to overuse this question, a question that puts the child in the awkward position of having to come up with the right answer or to be corrected. Adults can best help children learn to distinguish and describe shapes by using the suggestions already mentioned and using the direct question, "What shape is this?" only when they are relatively sure that a child is able to label shapes correctly.

Related films from the High/Scope Foundation

(For a complete description of each film and instructions for ordering, see appendix 4.)

Spatial Learning in the Preschool Years

A Place to Build All Kinds of Structures from **The Block Area** series

Spatial Relations—A Sequence of Exercises (Elementary grades)

Related reading on spatial relations

Flavell, John H. *Developmental Psychology of Jean Piaget.* Princeton, New Jersey: Van Nostrand, 1963. pp. 322-341, 388-392.

Laurendeau, Monique and Adrien Pinard. *The Development of the Concept of Space in the Child.* New York: International Universities Press, 1970.

Piaget, Jean and Barbel Inhelder. *The Psychology of the Child.* New York: Basic Books, 1969. pp. 15-17, 106-107.

Piaget, Jean; Inhelder, Barbel and Alina Szeminska. *The Child's Conception of Geometry.* New York: Basic Books, 1960.

Piaget, Jean. *The Child's Conception of Space.* London: Routledge and Kegan Paul, 1956.

Piaget, Jean. "How Children Form Mathematical Concepts," reprint 420 from *Scientific American,* November, 1953. San Francisco: W.H. Freeman & Co.

12/ Time

Ed, a four-year-old, was absent from preschool yesterday. Today, just before planning time, an adult says, "Ed, you weren't at preschool yesterday. Were you ill, or were you somewhere else?" Ed replies, "My grandma and me went to Greenfield Village. But I was here, too."

Was Ed trying to say he was in two places at one time? If not, what was he thinking and trying to say? A brief look at how young children think about time will help to answer these questions.

At about the age of three, children are just beginning to view time as a continuum, to understand that things existed *before now* and things will exist *after now*. This is a marked change from an infant's one-dimensional conception of time—that things exist *only now*. When a young child realizes that time is a continuum, he can reach into the past and reconstruct—mentally represent—events and experiences. But many preschool-age children cannot yet *sequence* past events; for them there is no chronology. Ed, for example, recalled having gone to Greenfield Village, but he also recalled having gone to preschool recently. What he couldn't do was separate the two events chronologically.

As he recalled both going to Greenfield Village and going to preschool, Ed was bringing into play some important new knowledge—that time is a continuum, and that past events can be reconstructed. The adult helped him understand some words adults use to describe the sequence of events: "That's right, Ed. Yesterday you went to Greenfield Village with your grandma, but the day before yesterday you were here at school."

As young children describe past events in words, they strengthen their ability to understand and deal with the continuity of time. They begin to think about a sequential order for past events and learn the words adults use to represent time. They still have a long way to go, however, before their understanding of time begins to resemble that of an adult. Any adult who has tried to explain to a four-year-old how long it will be until his birthday, or how long it will be until his mother comes home, is probably aware that young children do not understand time in the same way adults do. The passage of time is a kind of mystery to young children, and the idea of measuring the passage of time may be even more mysterious. The conventional time units adults use to measure time and talk about past and future events—minutes, hours, days, "weekend," "tomorrow," etc.—have little meaning for most preschoolers. That's why the following questions are relatively common among young children:

"Is it time yet?"

"When will it be tomorrow?"

"Is it my birthday yet?"

"Is it yesterday now?"

Preschool children do not yet have an "objective" view of time. They understand the passage of time subjectively—in terms of their own feelings—rather than in terms of an external event like the movement of clock hands. Adults, too, sometimes view time subjectively; for instance, two hours of waiting in a doctor's office may seem like an eternity. However, adults do compare their subjective feelings to objective measures. Young children do not. Because they lack understanding of the objective dimension of time, time really does "fly" and "crawl" for young children, depending on what they're doing.

Each key experience in this chapter is concerned with a particular aspect of the young child's conception of time. They key experiences will help adults understand how a child conceives of time, and how adults can help children consolidate the gains they're making in building a more objective understanding of time. The key experiences are organized around two major themes: understanding time units or intervals and sequencing events in time.

I UNDERSTANDING TIME UNITS OR INTERVALS

Key Experience:
Stopping and starting an action on signal

Preschool children confuse the time taken up by an event or action—when it begins and when it ends—either with the space taken up by the event or with the speed at which it occurs. For example, if two preschool children leave the classroom at the same time and one reaches the slide, which is closer to the school, at the same time as the other reaches the swings, which are farther away, they both believe that even though they started and stopped at the same time, the child who got to the swings ran for a longer time because he ran farther than the child who ran to the slide. Likewise, if one child walked to the slide while the other ran to the swings, even though they both stopped and started at the same time, they believe that the child who ran, ran for a longer time than the child who walked for the same time.

Adults can't change a preschooler's notion that each event occurs in its own time or their reasoning that simultaneous events of the same duration can take up different amounts of time. But adults can provide a wide variety of experiences in which children observe the beginning and ending of actions, events and time periods. By helping children note when they start an action and when they stop it, adults are helping them realize that time units do have a beginning and an end regardless of what happens in the interim.

Suggestions for adults

Provide materials children can use to signal the beginning and end of time periods

Materials children can use to mark the beginning and end of time periods include timers—three-minute egg timers, sand timers, mechanical kitchen timers that tick and ring, clocks with alarms, metronomes—as well as things children can use to produce noise—musical instruments, voices, hands, records, tape recorders, rattles and shakers. Be sure to give children plenty of time to explore and use these devices on their own before using them as timers.

Signal the beginning and end of time periods within the daily routine

One way adults can help children become more aware of when time periods start and stop is by signaling the beginning and end of each time period within the daily routine. Some signals may be verbal; others may be mechanical, like turning the lights out to mark the beginning of clean-up time and turning them back on to mark the end, or having a child play a tambourine to mark the end of outdoor time.

Play stop-and-start games

Stop-and-start games include action games like "Red Light, Green Light," "Musical Chairs" (keeping the number of chairs constant so the children can concentrate on getting up when the music starts and sitting down when the music stops) and "Simon Says" (modified so that the leader says, "Simon says start jumping . . . Simon says stop. Simon says start clapping . . . Simon says stop . . ." and so on) and races of all kinds.

Many stop-and-start games can be played with musical instruments. Children can take turns being conductor, making up their own signals for when the players should start playing and when they should stop. Children can start and stop playing and marching when a record starts and stops (as long as they don't play so loud they drown out the record). Many children's records include start-and-stop singing games.

Some children enjoy games in which they must complete a simple task by the time a timer rings or runs out of sand. Games of this sort often work well at clean-up time, turning a routine clean-up task into a race against time.

Key Experience: Experiencing and describing different rates of speed

Four-year-old Ricky has made a plan to do two things in the block area: first, to make a big tower of blocks as fast as he can, and second, to build a racing car. He begins by grabbing four blocks at a time, stacking them and going back for more. He continues for about three minutes until the tower is as wide and as tall as he can make it. Next he turns to his racing car, on which he spends considerably more time and uses fewer blocks.

Later, when his racing car is finished, an adult asks, "Which took you longer to make, Ricky, the tower or the racing car?" Ricky answers that the tower took longer. "How come?" the adult asks. "Because I made it so fast and I got real tired. And I used lots of blocks in the tower and I just used these blocks in my racing car."

Like most preschoolers, Ricky does not yet understand the relation between time and rate, that building something very quickly takes less time than building something slowly. Instead he believes that since building the tower made him more tired than building the racing car, and since the tower also used more blocks than the racing car, then the tower must have taken longer to build.

Preschoolers are also confused about speed all by itself:

Kelly and an adult watch two of Kelly's friends run to the sandbox. Although Jules started ahead of Gretchen, Gretchen catches up to him, and they both arrive at the sandbox at the same time. "Kelly, who do you think ran faster, Jules or Gretchen?" the adult asks. "They both ran faster," Kelly answers promptly. "How can you tell?" "Because they got there together."

Like Kelly, preschoolers can't accurately compare the speeds of two moving people or objects because they aren't yet able to see two simultaneous rates of motion in isolation. Instead they rely on Kelly's method of judging speed on the final distance between the two people or objects. Therefore, since Jules and Gretchen ended up with no distance between them, they both ran equally fast, even though Jules had a head start on Gretchen.

Although three- and four-year-olds haven't yet developed a formally logical understanding of either speed or time or the relation between the two, they're able to recognize and describe different rates of speed. As they move, sing, build, hammer, pour, paint, dance or play the drum at different rates of speed, they're forming a solid base from which their later, more complex understanding of speed and time can emerge. Here are some ways adults can help children experience and describe different rates of speed.

Suggestions for adults

Provide materials that help children experience different rates of speed

Toys with wheels—toy vehicles, ride-on toys
Toys with legs—dolls, stuffed animals, wooden/rubber animals, dollhouse people
Things that spin—tops, pinwheels, spinners from various games, wheels on axles, lazy susans
Things that roll—balls, spools, beads, tubes, cans, jars, dowels, marbles, bearings, washers, plastic piping, pegs, stacking rings
Things that drip—water, paints, finger paints, plaster of Paris, wheat paste, glue, rubber cement
Outdoor equipment—swings, merry-go-round, seesaw, wagons, scooters, riding toys, ropes

Provide opportunities for children to experience different rates of speed with their own bodies

Playground equipment can be used by children at different rates of speed. Adults can encourage children to swing, push, twirl, seesaw, slide and climb both quickly and slowly. Adults can also

participate in these activities and thus model them for children, talking about how fast or how slow they're going.

Outdoor games—obstacle courses, follow-the-leader, tag, races, jumping, ball throwing and rolling—can be played at varying rates of speed, especially if adults are willing to participate in the games and talk about how quickly or slowly people are moving, rolling the ball, etc.

Circle games, finger plays and action songs can be played and sung at different tempos. Children enjoy deciding whether to play a game or sing a song "real fast" or "real slow."

Playing musical instruments, marching and moving to music are other enjoyable ways to experience different rates of speed. Be sure to allow children to choose how fast they should play or move. Experiment with different kinds of music to see if the children can respond to a variety of tempos.

Routine tasks like hammering nails, pouring sand, zipping a jacket, painting a box, cutting out a picture, stacking blocks, stirring button soup and wiping the table can be done at various rates of speed with a little encouragement from adults and within the bounds of safety and sense. One High/Scope teaching-team member made this observation:

The other day Troy was pouring some liquids into different containers. And all I really needed to do was add some language so he got the idea of pouring quickly and slowly. After I introduced the idea of changing the rate of speed of pouring the liquid in, he picked up on it and said, "Let's pour it slowly."

Encourage children to describe the relative speeds they are experiencing or observing

Be sure to alert children to the movement of natural phenomena and things they see outside the classroom, like the movement of clouds, birds, leaves and trees in the wind, rain, snow, water in a stream or river, shadows, insects, animals, airplanes, cars, people on the sidewalk, bicyclists, machinery, marching bands, revolving signs.

Ask children to set rates of speed for various activities and games they're involved in:

• "How shall we play the instruments this time, Ray, fast or slow?"

• "You tell us and then show us how fast or slow we should walk to the playground, Shanetra."

Key Experience:
Experiencing and comparing time intervals

Preschoolers experience and compare time intervals but not in the same way adults do. They're beginning to use the same terminology adults use—"a long time," "a short time," "a little while"—but since they haven't yet developed a concept of a uniform rate of time, their judgments of duration are entirely subjective. For example, Ricky, the child who built the tower in a few minutes and then spent the rest of work time building the racing car, believed that the time he spent building the tower was "a long time" because he worked so fast, got so tired and used so many blocks. He believed that the time he spent working on his racing car was "a short time" because he worked more slowly and used fewer blocks (and he was probably more engrossed in building the car than in building the tower).

Preschoolers also confuse duration of time with space (distance covered). For example, as they watch two rabbits hop around the classroom, three- and four-year-olds are unanimous in their belief that the rabbit who travels the longest path hops for the longest time, regardless of the two rabbits' speed or when each of them started and stopped.

Vertical distance also influences a preschooler's conception of how much time has passed. For example, a tall tree has grown for a longer time and is therefore older than a shorter tree, and by the same logic a taller person is older, has lived for a longer time than a shorter person. People (and trees) of the same height have been around for the same length of time—hence, according to preoperational logic, a child will grow up and be the exact same age as his mother or father as soon as he reaches that parent's height.

Once adults understand the preoperational logic behind preschoolers' perception of the length of time intervals, they can provide experiences that will allow children to develop their capacity to compare time intervals. Here are some suggestions.

Suggestions for adults

Establish and follow a consistent daily routine

A consistent daily routine gives children the opportunity to experience time intervals of varying lengths each day, which they can then talk about and compare.

Help children learn the name for each time period in the day so they'll be able to think and talk about, say, the length of small-group time as compared to the length of work time.

Relate the length of time periods to real actions or events

Although preschool children have no concept of a uniform rate of time like a minute or an hour, they're very concerned about time, and they often want to know "how much time until . . ." Often an adult's first response to such questions is something like, "in a few more minutes," "about an hour," "not for two more months," "in a couple of weeks." These answers are meaningless to a child who has no idea how long a minute, an hour, a month or a week actually is.

Another, more helpful, way adults can respond to "how much time until. . ." questions is by relating length of time to an actual event or an action which the child can understand, see or do. Here are some examples:

- "It will probably be clean-up time, Ricky, after you've finished building your racing car and had a chance to ride on it."
- "Before the bus comes we'll have outside time, then circle time. Then it will be time for the bus to come."
- "Right now the leaves are falling. After all the leaves fall and the first snow comes, then it will be time for your birthday, Joella."

Use sand timers

Once preschoolers have had a chance to explore sand timers, tipping them back and forth and

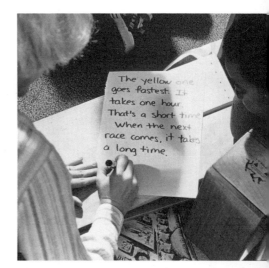

The yellow one goes fastest. It takes one hour. That's a short time. When the next race comes, it takes a long time.

watching the sand run from one end to the other, they can also begin to use them to define and mark off time periods. For example, two boys who had built a house in the block area used a sand timer in their play to tell them when it was morning. They decided that when all the sand was at the top of the timer it was nighttime, and when it had all emptied into the bottom of the timer it was morning and time to get out of bed.

Accept children's judgments about the length of time periods and ask them to explain their reasoning

Preschool-age children can't be taught to make objective judgments about the length of time intervals; therefore it's pointless for an adult to correct a child's subjective reasoning. What an adult can do is accept a child's judgment about how long something has taken and then ask him why he or she thought it took that length of time. This helps children become aware of their own reasoning and helps adults understand their preoperational viewpoint.

Key Experience:
Observing seasonal changes

Adults think of time as a process of constant movement and change—the present is forever becoming the past, the future the present. They think of individual events—sunrise, breakfast time, Labor Day, graduation—as part of a forward progression in the perpetual cycle of days and seasons. Preschoolers, on the other hand, think of individual events more as static, "still-life" situations than as part of a process of continual movement and change. Thus as a three-year-old eats the applesauce he made in class, he doesn't think of how the apples were sour before they were cut up and cinnamon was added, or how yesterday they were still hanging on the trees in the orchard. One might say that young children tend to view events as a series of slides, while adults view them as scenes in a motion picture. A preschooler, for example, is aware of how much warmer the weather is today, and how there's a robin in the play yard, but it doesn't necessarily remind him, as it is likely to remind an adult, that spring will soon be coming, followed by the leisurely days of summer. For the preschooler, it's simply a warm day. The idea of cyclical continuity—morning turning into evening, evening turning into morning, days flowing into weeks, weeks flowing into months and years—is not yet known to preschool-age children. And if they were to be told about recurrence and change and continuity, even in the simplest language, they wouldn't understand, for they are only in the process of building the mental equipment that can produce such understanding.

Observing seasonal holidays and changes and participating in activities that help make these special times memorable can contribute to a child's understanding of a year as a series of recurring events, or seasons. It was clear to the mother of one little girl that she had established her own mental calendar of seasons when she explained, "First it will be Christmas, then there will be snow for a long time, and then when it gets warm it will be my birthday."

Suggestions for adults

Talk with children about seasonal changes in everyday conversation

As adults talk with children throughout the day, they can share their observations about the current season, apparent seasonal changes and timely seasonal events:

Marla: Look, ice!
Adult: Yes, it gets so cold in the winter that water outside turns to ice.

———————

Mauricio: Here are some leaves, teacher, a whole bunch.
Adult: What beautiful red and yellow leaves, Mauricio. Where did you find them?
Mauricio: Out there on the ground.
Adult: Why do you suppose they were on the ground instead of on a tree?
Mauricio: Cause they fell down 'cause they're crumbly and make lots of noise.
Adult: That's right. In the fall, the leaves dry up and get crumbly and turn red and yellow and brown and fall to the ground. When you walk or jump in them they make lots of noise.

Focus on seasonal changes that children actually experience in their particular locale. Talking about colorful autumn leaves and winter snow to preschool-age children living in southern Florida makes little sense since these children don't experience these particular seasonal changes. More meaningful to them are the changes they see and experience for themselves—the high tides, waves and winds and the torrential rains of the hurricane season; the sight and scent of the orange groves in early spring.

Encourage children to collect and talk about objects associated with seasonal changes

Depending on the locale of the preschool, children might collect brightly colored leaves, chestnuts, dried cornstalks, acorns, walnuts, goldenrod, purple asters, apples and grapes in the fall; icicles, dried weeds and grasses in the winter; birds' eggs, pussy willows, budded branches, tadpoles, caterpillars and mud in the spring.

When talking with children about these objects, use the names of the seasons in which they're found:

"We can go to the apple orchard now and pick all the apples we want, because it's fall. Apples grow in the summer, but in the fall you can pick them and eat them."

Repeat walks and field trips at different seasons throughout the year

One way to help children focus on seasonal changes and the length of seasonal time intervals is to return to the same place periodically and look at what changed or remained the same. One teaching team, for example, took the children to the same local park once every three or four weeks throughout the fall, winter and spring.

On each trip they looked at and photographed the river, a big maple tree, a small flower garden and part of the unmowed field near the swings. At the park they examined and talked about each place on the way to the playground equipment, and back at school they compared each new set of photographs with the previous ones, noting similarities and differences. By the end of the school year, they had constructed their own calendar of seasonal changes using their photographs of the park.

Key Experience:
Observing that clocks and calendars are used to mark the passage of time

- *Upon hearing a tambourine signal, Jesse, a preschooler, looks at the wall clock and comments, "Clean-up time—it's sixty to ten."*
- *An adult is writing John's name and the date on his painting. She asks, "Does anyone happen to know today's date?" Trish, another child working in the art area, promptly responds, "It's winter 'cause it's very cold and you have to wear boots to school. But tomorrow it's going to be June 11th. That's my birthday and I'm going to have a birthday party."*

Jesse and Trish, like most preschoolers, know that clocks are connected in some way with "telling what time it is," and that adults use calendars to give days numbers and "dates." What these children don't understand is how adults use these devices to find out what time or date it is. They don't understand how clocks and calendars are used to mark or record the passage of time because the standard time units—minutes, hours, days, months, years—are too abstract and intangible for them to comprehend.

The previous descriptions of young children's understanding of time should explain why they don't understand how the passage of time can be recorded. To reiterate: First, young children don't yet comprehend time as a continuum of past, present and future. Secondly, they often confuse a given time such as work at school or bedtime at home with the space or location in which it commonly occurs; accordingly, it's not work time until they're in a work area, and it's not bedtime until they're actually in bed. Thirdly, preschoolers' view of time is subjective.

For them, time doesn't move at a uniform rate; instead it passes quickly or slowly in haphazard fashion, depending on how they feel about what they're doing. The idea of measuring time using an external, uniform motion like the hands on a clock or sand through a glass is an abstract concept most preschool-age children are only just beginning to comprehend.

The numbers on clocks and calendars which quantitatively represent the passage of time present yet another problem for young children. Thus, when they begin to grasp the notion that time can be measured, they're still faced with the problem of how to use the number system in this process.

With these limitations in mind, it should be clear to adults that drilling preschoolers in telling time and using calendars is both premature and ineffectual. What they *can* do effectively is help children become aware that clocks and calendars are tools people use to mark off time intervals; the use of these tools is a skill they'll be able to learn quite rapidly later on as their understanding of time changes and matures.

Suggestions for adults

Use conventional times and dates in conversation with children

As appropriate situations arise throughout the day, mention the time or the date to children in a natural manner:

• "It's 10 o'clock. Time for clean-up. Tiffany, would you play the tambourine to let everyone know it's clean-up time now."

• "Cletis, where on your painting would you like me to write your name and the date?"

"Right here."

"Okay. C-L-E-T-I-S. And today is Wednesday, September 8, 1976. Now we'll know that you made this picture and we'll know when you made it."

• "Hey teacher. It's my mom's birthday today. But it's not my dad's birthday till summer in July."

"My birthday's in July too, Willie, on July 2nd."

"Wow! Maybe you can come to my dad's party! But no kids can come. just grownups."

Use clocks and improvised calendars to help answer children's "how-long-until" questions

When children ask "how-long-until" questions, referring to a clock or making a calendar is an-other way adults can make their answers more concrete and meaningful:

"How many days till we come back to school, Mrs. Yanez?"

"I'll show you, Petra." *Mrs. Yanez draws the following calendar, explaining it as she draws:*

"Here's today. You came to school on the bus. Then you go home and it's nighttime so you go to bed. The next day is Saturday and you stay home again and play at home. At nighttime you go to bed, but the next day when you wake up, it's time to go to school again so you get on the bus and come to school. Let's look now. How many days are you at home?"

"One, two," Petra counts pointing to the houses.

"How many nights?"

"One, two, three," Petra counts, pointing to the beds.

"That's right, Petra. So after three nights and two days it will be time to come back to school. Do you want to take your calendar home so you can tell when it's time to come back?"

"Okay!"

Some children may enjoy their own calendars, like the one Mrs. Yanez made for Petra. With the help of a few questions or suggestions from an adult, they can find their own way of representing a day.

II   SEQUENCING EVENTS IN TIME

Key Experience: Anticipating future events

"Hi, Mom. I'm hungry," Mamie says as she arrives home from preschool. "We're going to the orchard and we have to take bags and boots so the mud won't get on us. And we can eat some and put some in the bags. More milk, please. There's the mailman. His bag sure looks heavy . . ."

While adults recall past events and project themselves into the future, young children concern themselves mainly with the events of the moment. However, their "how-long-until" questions indicate that they're beginning to be concerned about time sequences and to think and wonder now and again about what's going to happen next and when it's actually going to happen.

As adults encourage and build on children's incipient desire to anticipate events as well as experience them as they happen, they are actually helping children gain control over their environment. As children begin to anticipate future events verbally and make appropriate preparations, they're developing a rudimentary sense of control over events in their lives. They begin to see that they can have some say and make some important decisions about what those events are going to be and how they're going to occur.

Suggestions for adults

Help children anticipate and prepare for each time period of the day

For suggestions on how to establish and maintain a consistent daily routine, see chapter 2.

Once a consistent daily routine is in effect, adults can help children anticipate and prepare for each time period by 1) using signals to mark the beginning and end of time periods; 2) telling children that work time, for example, will end in five more minutes, and then it'll be time to clean up; and 3) asking children at the end of each period what comes next and what they need to do to be ready for it.

Help children prepare in advance for things they've planned to do

- "What do you need to do before you start to paint?"
- "What are you going to use to build a birdhouse?"
- "What things will you need to be an animal keeper in the house area?"
- "Which instruments do you think you'll use when you make up your song and dance?"
- "What are you going to do with the guinea pig while you're emptying out his cage and putting in new cedar shavings?"

By asking questions like these, adults can help children think about the preparations they'll need to make for a task. Adults should follow up these questions by supporting children's ideas, by helping them formulate some if they can't come up with any on their own and by assisting them in their preparations if they need help getting started. Picture "recipes" often help children remember the steps they've outlined for a task. (For sample picture "recipes" for making a birdhouse and mixing paints, see chapter 7.)

Help children anticipate problems

Often children decide to do things without any awareness of the feasibility of their ideas. A child may be inspired to build a structure in the block area without realizing that all the building materials and available space are already in use. Or a child may decide to hammer or to play a drum when all the hammers or drums are occupied. In these situations, an adult can first talk with a child about what might happen if he tried to carry out his or her idea at that particular time. The adult can help the child think about what he or she might be satisfied doing instead.

At the beginning of small-group time and circle time, talk with children about what's going to happen

Begin small-group time and circle time with a brief but clear explanation of the activity for that period. Such an explanation gives children a chance to think and talk about what's going to happen next rather than merely be guided step by step. By knowing what they're about—making playdough or making up a song about their trip to the gas station—they have a chance to see how the parts of the process relate to the whole or end product.

When possible, encourage children to help decide what's going to happen next, particularly at circle time. Ask them what they'd like to do.

Help children anticipate and prepare for changes in the schedule

Changes in the preschool routine usually occur because of field trips, special events, visitors or necessary interruptions (e.g., a nurse comes to do hearing and vision tests). Whatever the cause, adults should talk with children at the beginning of the day about what's going to be different that day, what part of the routine they'll miss and what they'll be doing instead. Sometimes this information should be conveyed in a class meeting as soon as all the children arrive, especially if the change is to occur early in the day. Otherwise, adults can talk with individuals or small groups of children during planning time.

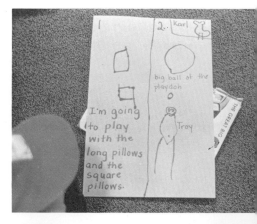

When adding pets to the classroom, include children in the plans and preparations

The addition of a pet to the classroom is a very special event children can anticipate and prepare for. Ask them what they think the pet might need to eat, to sleep in, to live in, to play with, and involve the children in making, gathering or purchasing and then assembling the necessary food and equipment. To make sure all the children know what a gerbil or rabbit or lizard is and how much space it might require, visit the pet store first. Otherwise, the children may not have a clear idea of what they're preparing for.

Key Experience:
Planning, and completing what one has planned

Perhaps the most powerful tool a child can have to affect what's going to happen next in his or her life is the ability to make a plan and carry it out. For a complete discussion of the importance of planning, its place in the plan-do-review sequence and how to help children in the planning process, see the section on planning time in chapter 2.

Key Experience:
Describing and representing past events

The other side of anticipating, preparing and planning for future events is describing and representing past events. Thinking ahead to what's going to happen next gives a child some control over time; recalling past events enables the child to establish and maintain a personal mental record of what he or she has experienced and learned. Describing and representing past events is a reflective process which allows a child to turn his or her previous actions into accessible knowledge for the future. For a complete discussion of how adults can help children describe and represent past events, see the section on recall time in chapter 2.

Key Experience:
Using conventional time units when talking about past and future events

Julius was racing around outside on the tricycle, bumping into people and things. An adult warned him that if he bumped into anything else, he would have to get off the trike for the rest of the day. A little later, Julius hit another person and had to give up the trike after being reassured that he could ride again tomorrow. The next day, Julius asked one of
the adults, "Is this tomorrow?" He carefully explained that this is "today," and the next day is "tomorrow," and Julius continued his play on the playground. Two more days passed and each day Julius asked one of the adults, "Is this tomorrow?" and each day the adult made a careful and increasingly detailed explanation of when "tomorrow" is. Finally, on Friday, Julius said, "When will it ever be tomorrow? You said I could ride the trike again tomorrow! When is tomorrow?"

Like Julius, many preschoolers are trying to come to terms with the names and meanings of the conventional time units—yesterday, today, tomorrow; day, night, morning, afternoon, evening; week, weekend; minute, hour. As they anticipate and plan future events, talk about the present and recall past events, they begin to understand that it's necessary to refer to these times in a way that will distinguish one from another. Julius, for example, knew that "tomorrow" referred to some future time, but he wasn't at all sure how much time had to elapse before tomorrow actually arrived, nor did he understand that "tomorrows" eventually become "todays"—that the future becomes the present, which in turn becomes the past.

One four-year-old girl in passing the local fire station remarked, "Oh, we went there yesterday," when in fact the class had visited the fire station several months earlier. She knew that she had been to the fire station in the past and she knew that the word "yesterday" referred to past time, so she put the two together and came up with the most accurate statement she could make. An adult who understood her reasoning was able to respond, "We did go to the fire station, Faye, a long time ago when it was still warm and there were still leaves on the trees."

The words young children use with reference to time are not always the correct or most accurate ones—"We're going to get pumpkins yesterday"—but with understanding and encouragement from adults they can begin to hear how these terms are used correctly; eventually, through experience, they'll begin to connect the right word with the right time unit.

Suggestions for adults

Use conventional time units in everyday conversation with children

- "Hi, Carry. Glad you're here today. We missed you yesterday."
- "Yesterday you didn't get to finish your plan because of the fire drill. Today you'll have a whole hour to work on it."
- "Danny, that's really a neat block structure. Maybe you'd like to leave it up so the children who come to our school before you, in the morning, can see it."
- "I saved the decorations we made yesterday at small-group time. Today we're going to paint them. After the weekend, next Monday, they'll be dry and we can put them up all around the room."

Use precise time units in conversations with children

Such phrases as "after awhile," "not yet," "in a while," "just a minute" are easy answers to young children's questions about when something will happen, but they aren't precise and therefore may confuse a child. "A little while," for example, might be two hours. Here's a more precise response:

"We'll cut open our pumpkins together in about one hour; first we'll have work time, then clean-up, then juice time and *then* we'll open them."

Accept children's attempts to use conventional time units

Even though children will use time units inaccurately in their own speech, try to understand what they're attempting to say and acknowledge their statements.

Key Experience:
Noticing, describing and representing the order of events

"Here's how I made my airplane. First I cut the wood. Then I nailed these together right here and here. Then I put on the wings and a place for the people to sit. Then I painted it red in the art area. When it's dry I'm going to carry it home."

As she tells about how she made her airplane, Miranda is describing a sequence of steps. Being able to see things in sequence—realizing that events occur in some kind of order, that some things occur before or after other things—is a critical part of a preschooler's unfolding understanding of the relations of past, present and future and of cause and effect.

Suggestions for adults

Ask children to describe the order of events they've recently experienced

As adults help children recall past events—field trips, things done during work time, the sequence of the daily routine—they can ask the children to describe what happened in terms of "first, next, next . . ."

"Who remembers what we did first on our trip this morning?"

"We all got on the bus."

"That's right. First we all got on the bus. What did we do next?"

"We drove to the store."

"Okay. We drove to the store. Next what did we do? . . ."

Depict the order of events with children

Using photographs, pictures or drawings, make up charts with children that will help them see the sequence of steps in an activity. One teaching team, for example, made a chart, using the children's signs, to depict the order of turns for passing things out at juice time. Here are their observations:

At the beginning of the year it was really chaotic. The children were frustrated because they didn't know when their turn to pass things out was going to come. We developed a chart so they could actually see when their turn was. Once they could see this they could understand and accept the order of turns. They were interested in whose turn it was going to be that day, but they were also interested in seeing the flow of turns from day to day.

Encourage children to represent the order of things

Children can draw pictures of each step in an activity, act out or pantomime each step or add a new verse to a song about each step.

Have living things in the preschool that change over time

Include plants and animals in the classroom so that children can watch them grow and change. Help them keep track of these changes by taking photographs of plants and pets periodically or encouraging them to keep their own series of pictures. Encourage children to arrange the photographs or pictures in temporal order.

Plan small-group times around activities that must be done in a particular sequence

Many cooking activities—making popcorn, jello, pudding, sandwiches, salad, applesauce—work best when a particular sequence of steps is followed. At small-group time, involve children in making some of these foods and then help them recall what they did first, next, etc.

Related films from the High/Scope Foundation

(For a complete description of each film and instructions for ordering, see appendix 4.)

Learning about Time in the Preschool Years

Learning about Time in the Preschool Years: Classroom Examples for Discussion

Temporal Relations—A Sequence of Exercises (Elementary grades)

Related reading on time

Elkind, David. "Of Time and the Child," *New York Times Magazine*, October 11, 1970.

Flavell, J. *The Developmental Psychology of Jean Piaget.* Princeton, New Jersey: Van Nostrand, 1963. pp. 275-290 and 316-326.

Ginsburg, Herbert and Sylvia Opper. *Piaget's Theory of Intellectual Development.* Englewood Cliffs, New Jersey: Prentice-Hall, 1969. pp. 98-116.

Piaget, Jean and Barbel Inhelder. *The Psychology of the Child.* New York: Basic Books, 1969. pp. 107-109.

Piaget, Jean. *Judgment and Reasoning in the Child.* New York: Harcourt Brace, 1928.

Piaget, Jean. *The Child's Conception of the World.* New York: Harcourt Brace, 1929.

Piaget, Jean. *The Child's Conception of Physical Causality.* London: Kegan Paul, 1930.

Piaget, Jean. *The Child's Conception of Time.* London: Routledge and Kegan Paul, 1969.

Research support for the curriculum

Often a new curriculum is created from ideas an individual has developed through personal experience, or from a general ethical commitment to a method or theory, or from a simple reaction to the trends of the times. Rarely does a curriculum evolve as part of a planned research and development cycle, as the Cognitively Oriented Curriculum has since 1962. A research and development context for a curriculum means that the impact of the curriculum on children can be known, and judgments can be made about its efficacy. The Cognitively Oriented Curriculum has been validated through extensive, controlled longitudinal research. What happens to children during the program, after the program while attending regular public school and in early adult life are known. Does the curriculum work? Yes, spectacularly well with diverse groups of children. Then is it claimed that the Cognitively Oriented Curriculum is the best available method for helping young children gain success in school and adult life? No, that is not the claim. We prefer to limit our assertions to demonstrable facts, one of which is that the Cognitively Oriented Curriculum has been tested in a number of longitudinal research projects and has produced outstanding results. (See marginal note.)

When Project Head Start got under way in 1965 as part of the great War on Poverty, it was heralded as one of the sure roads to equal opportunity. Then a study done by the Westinghouse Learning Corporation and Ohio University in 1969 seemed to indicate that disadvantaged children who had been enrolled in Head Start programs were only marginally better off over the long term than children who had not. The results of this study came very close to destroying Head Start and discrediting the concept of early intervention.

But recent studies, based on new data or a reanalysis of old, suggest that the Westinghouse conclusions were premature. Among the most persuasive of these is the work of David Weikart and his colleagues at the High/Scope Educational Research Foundation in Ypsilanti, Michigan, a small industrial city near Detroit. They released the findings of three studies showing that preschool education apparently gives youngsters a lasting advantage over their peers who get no special help—*when* a program has a well-managed, high-quality curriculum run by a dedicated staff. Furthermore, early intervention pays, not just in educational or intangible social benefits but in dollars and cents.

Weikart saw the connection between academic failure and the economic backgrounds of children in trouble. "Even before I administered intelligence tests," he said, "I could pretty accurately guess a child's I.Q. from his address." Boys and girls who lived in the poor sections of town nearly always scored low.

Together with his staff he sought to in-

The essay that begins on this page, originally titled "New Optimism about Preschool Education: Three Reports from Ypsilanti, Michigan" appeared in the Summer 1978 issue of the *Carnegie Quarterly* and is reprinted here (in a slightly abridged version) with the permission of that journal. It was written by Virginia Adams.

troduce curriculum changes in the schools to boost low achievers. In making his case he organized a series of meetings with school administrators to try to convince them of the close correlation between social class on the one hand and I.Q., school failure, and juvenile delinquency on the other. Most of the officials didn't mind showing what they thought of Weikart's ideas. One got up from the meeting and stood looking out a window, smoking his pipe. Others figuratively turned their backs by carrying on whispered conversations.

In frustration, Weikart and his staff, with local school system support and state special education funds, developed an educational research program of their own—one that in philosophy anticipated the Head Start idea by several years. "Since the schools would not, or could not, change," Weikart said, "we decided to focus on the preschool period." Their hope was that the program could "equip high-risk children with improved abilities to cope with the demands of schooling," making it possible for them to "wrest education from a reluctant school system." Their parallel goal was to help prevent a new crop of youthful offenders and "give these children a chance to succeed in life."

Designing the Perry Project

For the subjects of their study they chose 123 youngsters ages three and four who lived in the neighborhood of Ypsilanti's Perry School. With I.Q.s ranging from 70 to 85, the children were classified as "educable mentally retarded" (for the purpose of meeting state funding requirements). All were black, and all came from families of low socio-economic status. Most of the parents had

only an elementary school education. Nearly half of the fathers were absent from home, and of those at home more than half were jobless. Roughly half of the families were on welfare. Some lived in houses that were little more than dirt-floor garages.

Fifty-eight of the children were selected at random to be enrolled in the Ypsilanti Perry Preschool Project, while the remaining 65 were not to receive early education. The children in the experimental group entered preschool in subgroups of about a dozen each, one wave a year for five years beginning in 1962. For two school years, two-and-a-half hours a day five days a week, they took part in the preschool program. In addition, the teachers visited each mother and child at home for 90 minutes a week, not to impart wisdom but to focus the mother's interest in her child's development.

Many intervention programs compare experimental and control children only at the beginning and the end of treatment, but the High/Scope staff administered tests of intelligence and of academic achievement periodically through grade eight. Social and emotional maturity was assessed every year through grade three. And now that the subjects are leaving high school at age 19, the researchers are finding out how they are doing in the world beyond with the intention of following them all the way to age 25!

Most early intervention programs also appear to produce dramatic I.Q. gains in children only to have these "wash out" after a few years of schooling. Weikart therefore was disappointed but not surprised that the I.Q.s of his experimental subjects, which were about 11 points higher than those of the control children during preschool, differed by only 5 points during the year after preschool, and matched those of the control group by the end of grade three.

The tests of academic achievement told a strikingly different and much more encouraging story, however. Again the experimental children showed early gains—in reading, vocabulary, and arithmetic—but instead of fading with time, these gains increased significantly over the years. By grade eight, nine years after the end of the intervention program, the experimental children tested the equivalent of more than one full grade higher than the control children, and while 49 percent of the children who had attended preschool were achieving at the fifth-grade level or above, only 17 percent of those who had not gone to preschool were doing that well.

There were indications that the Perry Preschool Project did indeed lead children to "extract" a better education (as Weikart put it) as compared with the control group. By grade four only 17 percent of the experimental children had been held back a grade or referred to special education classes; for the control group the figure was 38 percent. Moreover, the teachers, without knowing which children had gone to preschool, rated the experimental children higher in social adjustment and emotional maturity. They were judged less disruptive, less resentful of criticism, more honest, more friendly.

As for the 19-year-olds, the findings are promising. Eleanor Jackson, a research assistant at High/Scope, tracked down all 28 children in the first wave, often through painstaking detective work. She interviewed them, talked to their parents and employers and, with the subjects' permission, is now checking school and court records.

Final conclusions cannot be drawn until data are complete for all five waves, but indications are that the impact of preschool has carried over into adulthood. The experimental group has fewer members on welfare than the control group. Children who went to preschool classes tended to stay in school longer and once out in the world to acquire marketable skills.

"You look at where these kids came from," Ms. Jackson said, "and it's a sign of success when they're not dead, not locked up, and are still trying to make it."

An unexpected spinoff of intervention was its apparent impact on the mothers of some preschoolers. It exposed them to a different way of life, lifted their hopes, and occasionally brought to light unsuspected abilities. One mother was hired as an aide in a High/Scope classroom and has since become a preschool teacher. Another applied for a job as a paraprofessional at the Perry School, attended workshops in how to teach remedial reading, and taught classes for more than four years.

The Curriculum Demonstration Project

The second of High/Scope's longitudinal studies, the Curriculum Demonstration Project, grew out of the main findings of the Perry Preschool Project. The purpose of the CD Project was to determine which existing educational curriculum method helps most. The researchers compared three curricula:

The Language Training Curriculum, a structured, didactic, traditional approach in which education is imposed from above, with the teacher drilling the children in language, reading, and arithmetic skills.

The Cognitively Oriented Curriculum, an "open-framework" approach in which the child chooses his activities with adult guidance. The teacher lets each child proceed at his own pace, trying to foster his mental abilities as they emerge naturally in the process of growing up.

The Unit-Based Curriculum, a child-centered approach typical of permissive nursery schools. Units of activity center around themes (farm animals, the circus, a holiday), but self-expression and the children's interests come before predetermined teaching aims, because it is assumed that children learn best by following their own inclinations.

Again, the subjects were Ypsilanti children from poor families with I.Q.s ranging from 70 to 85. Forty-one three-year-olds were divided among the three curricula in about equal numbers and went to school for the prescribed two-and-a-half hours a day, five days a week, through two school years. A teacher made a 90-minute home visit every week.

The results of the study challenge educational thought in at least three respects.

First, the researchers had expected that the three curricula would have quite distinctive effects. As it turned out, all three were effective, and "none," they report, "was more so than another." (However, the researchers emphasize that they measured chiefly aptitude and school achievement. Further study is needed to find out whether or not different educational methods lead to non-academic differences, perhaps in creativity or, ultimately, in life style.)

Second, the High/Scope staff had assumed there would be a quick wash-out of virtually all gains in I.Q. The reality was a happy surprise. At the end of the first preschool year, the I.Q.s of the children in the three programs had jumped an average of 23.5 points. Although the gain was down to 16.8 points by the end of the second year,

there was no significant falloff after that. Furthermore, all but 20 percent of the CD Project children were in the grade where they belonged. (While no clear explanations for the maintenance of I.Q. gains have emerged, it is known that the CD Project children entered grade school just at the time massive federal dollars were available to support compensatory education programs for those with learning difficulties.)

A third important finding had been anticipated by High/Scope educators. Children visited at home scored significantly higher on standardized tests of achievement than did a comparison group of children.

As a result of these two studies Weikart and his associates believe that preschool "may well be one of the few really effective means of helping educationally disadvantaged children."

Since, the researchers conclude, no one form of compensatory education is effective to the exclusion of all the others, individual school systems have a choice; they are free to design programs that reflect the values of their particular communities. "Political fights over curricula are unnecessary—and they harm children," Weikart says.

But there are requisites for the success of any program. Parents should be involved. "The combination of both classroom and home teaching was a central concept of the Perry Project and may have been the driving force behind its success," Weikart reports.

Quality in administering and operating a program is vital—and difficult to monitor. "Just opening up more Head Start centers won't help."

Caring is terribly important although it is the single ingredient that all agree is probably the hardest to export.

Assessing the cost and benefits

In the climate of taxpayer rebellion that has recently developed in the United States, the third Ypsilanti study, an economic analysis of the Perry Preschool Project, ought to be especially persuasive. Preschool programs naturally are thought of as costing money, but University of Maryland economists Carol Weber and Phillips Foster, High/Scope's cost analysts, suggest they can actually save money.

Their report explains this seeming paradox in an intricate argument that is definitely not everyday reading. The cost of running the Perry Preschool, they say, was less than the estimated dollar value of its benefits. These savings were derived mainly from the reduced overall costs of educating the preschool participants who did not require extensive special education as often as nonparticipants. Then too, the projected lifetime earnings of the experimental children (who were considered more likely to finish school and find decent jobs than the control children) were considerably higher.

The analysts figured out that money invested in a year of preschool "earned" interest in the form of benefits at the rate of 9.5 percent, although in a favorable critique of the study World Bank economist Roger Grawe calculated that the true rate was closer to 14.5 percent. If that is correct, Weikart estimates that society could pay for preschool programs and recover not only the cost of the programs but gain a return on that investment. "Since we are talking about millions of children, we are talking about huge dollar savings each year. What's good for children also appears to be of benefit to taxpayers," he says.

Thus, investment in preschool education can be justified on quantifiable economic grounds—as well as on the nonquantifiable but more important humanitarian ground of improving the quality of life of children born with a lot of strikes against them.

〜

While the Perry Preschool Project and the Curriculum Demonstration Project are the two basic studies demonstrating the long-term effectiveness of the Cognitively Oriented Curriculum, two other studies are of interest because they point up the impact of the program on other groups of children under different circumstances. The first of these is the **Planned Variation Head Start** project.

Planned Variation Head Start was initiated by the U.S. Office of Economic Opportunity in 1968 and administered by the U.S. Office of Child Development. Eight preschool "models," including the Cognitively Oriented Curriculum, were compared during the three years of the project. The curriculum developers brought their programs to Head Start centers serving a variety of ethnic groups in locations throughout the country. In all programs, children attended preschool for one school year.

The complexity and size of the Head Start project introduced problems generally not faced in intensive local experiments like the Perry and Curriculum Demonstration projects. Problems with control-group selection, testing and political pressure groups; linkages between Head Start centers and curriculum developers over distances of hundreds and in some cases thousands of miles; variations in funding levels; status of model development for dissemination (dissemination being a far different demand on a model than simply implementing it at home or producing professional articles about the theory and training base)—all of these factors conspired with the usual operational problems to make this study extraordinarily difficult to implement. Thus it was not surprising to discover that most models could not be differentiated from their control groups or from each other.

Two clear findings did emerge, however. The "programmed" (behaviorist) models achieved significantly higher scores than any of the other models or control groups on academic achievement measures such as letter naming and number recognition. And on aptitude measures at the end of a year of preschool, the children in the Cognitively Oriented program showed greater I.Q. gains than children in any other program. As Marshall Smith commented in his book, *A Preliminary Report on the Second Year of Planned Variation—1970-71* (Huron Institute, 1973):

> The High/Scope model [the Cognitively Oriented Curriculum] far outgains any of the other PV models, averaging 23.4 points in 'gains'…All of the other PV models gain between 2.5 and 5.2 points, a difference of less than ¼ of a standard deviation in individual test scores…In contrast between the observed and the 'observed-expected' gains for the PV and Comparison groups, the High/Scope models stand out as clearly different from all of the others with an advantage favoring the [High/Scope] PV group of roughly 16.5 points. None of the other [models'] measured differences exceed 3.5 points…There is only one main finding in these data—the High/Scope model *appears to be extraordinarily effective in raising Stanford-Binet scores at least in the short run.* (p. 200; author's emphasis)

While the children in the Head Start experiment were never followed up, the finding of very large immediate gains in aptitude is nonetheless significant in that it suggests the Cognitively Oriented model can be a positive force in children's lives, not just in Ypsilanti, Michigan, but in other, very different places with other, very different children.

The second study that concerns us here began in 1975 when the High/Scope Foundation was awarded a grant by the Bureau of Education for the Handicapped of the U.S. Office of Education to explore the impact of integrating, or "mainstreaming," handicapped children in a regular Cognitively Oriented classroom. This was our first systematic study of the impact of the curriculum on children with handicaps. Of special importance was the chance to study the interaction of the handicapped and non-handicapped groups and the impact of mainstreaming on the children and their families.

Thirty-one children were enrolled in the High/Scope **First Chance Preschool** project. Eleven of these children were classified as handicapped according to the guidelines of the Michigan Mandatory Special Education Act. There were ten children from low-income families who were considered "high risk" and who parallelled the children served in the Perry and Curriculum Demonstration projects. The ten nonhandicapped children were from middle-income families.

The major finding of this study was that most children made dramatic gains between pre-testing in September and post-testing in May, when the program ended, averaging 14 months gained in mental age on the standardized test used to assess their progress (the McCarthy Scales of Children's Abilities). The handicapped and nonhandicapped children gained almost equally. Surprisingly, high-ability children gained as much as low-ability children.

Findings on the High/Scope Child Observation Record (see appendix 5) complemented the McCarthy results. There were significant changes in testers' perception of children's performance in almost all areas, especially in Complexity of (Child's) Plan, Spontaneous Representation, Social Adjustment and Autonomy and Verbal Communication Skills. More important in the context of this discussion was that both handicapped and nonhandicapped children gained equally. Both groups were able to benefit from the program while attending a class which represented a wide range of socio-economic levels, ability levels and handicapping conditions.

∽

Since 1962 the Cognitively Oriented Curriculum has been tested in research projects locally, nationally and internationally and compared with other early childhood curricula. Practitioners have been consistently successful with diverse groups of children. Cognitively Oriented programs have achieved solid results with young children in terms of both short-term gains and long-term outcomes. The decision to have this program instead of some other, however, is primarily one of values: While parents and staff who choose the program for their preschool or day care center base their judgment partly on the fact that "it works," they are generally even more impressed by the fact that it reflects the way of life they want for their children as they progress through school—a way of life characterized above all by active and cooperative learning.

Related publications from the High/Scope Foundation

Longitudinal Results of the Ypsilanti Perry Preschool Project (book, 183 pp.) by D.P. Weikart, D.J. Deloria, S.A. Lawser, R. Wiegerink, 1970.

This is one of four monographs covering the High/Scope series of research projects described in this chapter, assessing the longitudinal effects of preschool education. Presented here are an overview and analysis of results from the first phase of this long-term experimental effort.

The Ypsilanti Perry Preschool Project: Preschool Years & Longitudinal Results Through Fourth Grade (book, 142 pp.) by D. P. Weikart, J. T. Bond, J. T. McNeil, 1978.

The second in a series of monographs covering the High/Scope research projects on preschool education described in this chaper, this monograph analyzes data obtained on the experimental and control groups in the Perry Preschool Project as they progressed through fourth grade.

The Ypsilanti Preschool Curriculum Demonstration Project: Preschool Years & Longitudinal Results (book, 152 pp.) by D.P. Weikart, A. Epstein, L. Schweinhart, J.T. Bond, 1978.

Another in a series of monographs covering the High/Scope research projects on preschool education described in this chapter, this monograph covers the Curriculum Demonstration Project, in which the effectiveness of three approaches to preschool curriculum was compared.

An Economic Analysis of the Ypsilanti Perry Preschool Project (book, 70 pp.) by C.U. Weber, P.W. Foster, D.P. Weikart, 1978.

Another in the monograph series on the High/Scope preschool education studies described in this chapter, this is a benefit-cost study of the social rate of return (the return to society) of public investment in the Perry Preschool Project.

Final Report of the High/Scope-BEH Demonstration Preschool Project by Bernard Banet et al., 1977.

Related reading on evaluation of early childhood programs

Abt, C.C. *The Evaluation of Social Programs.* Beverly Hills, California: Sage Publications, 1976.

Anderson, S. and S. Messick. "Social Competency in Young Children," *Developmental Psychology*, Vol. 10, No. 2, 1974. pp. 282-293.

Baker, E.L. *Evaluation of the California Early Childhood Education Program: Executive Summary.* Los Angeles: University of California, Center for the Study of Evaluation, January, 1977.

Beller, E.K. "Research on Organized Programs of Early Education," in *Second Handbook of Research on Teaching*, R.M.W. Travers, ed. Chicago: Rand McNally, 1973.

Bloom, B.S.; Hastings, J.T. and G.F. Madaus. *Handbook on Formative and Summative Evaluation of Student Learning*. New York: McGraw-Hill, 1971.

Granville, A.C.; Love, J.M.; Matz, R.D.; Schweinhart, L.J. and A.G. Smith. "The Impact of Evaluation: Lessons Drawn from the Evaluations of Five Early Childhood Education Programs," proceedings of a symposium at the annual meeting of the American Educational Research Association, Toronto, March, 1978.

Johnson, O.G. *Tests and Measurements in Child Development: Handbook II* (Vols. 1 &2). San Francisco: Jossey-Bass, 1976.

Johnson, O.G. and J.W. Bommarito. *Tests and Measurements in Child Development: A Handbook*. San Francisco: Jossey-Bass, 1971.

Love, J.M.; Nauta, M.J.; Coelen, C.J.; Hewett, K. and R.R. Ruopp. "National Home Start Evaluation: Final Report, Findings and Implications." Washington, D.C.: Home Start, ACYF, ED 134 314, March, 1976.

Love, J.M.; Nauta, M.J.; Coelen, C.J.; Hewett, K. and R.R. Ruopp. "Perspectives on the Follow Through Evaluation," *Harvard Educational Review*, May, 1978.

Morris, L.L.; Fitz-Gibbon, C.T. and M.E. Henerson. *Program Evaluation Kit*. Beverly Hills, California: Sag Publications, 1978.

Smith, M.S. *Some Short-term Effects of Project Head Start: A Preliminary Report on the Second Year of Planned Variation—1970-71*. Cambridge, Massachusetts: Huron Institute, 1973.

Thorndike, R. and E. Hagen. *Measurement and Evaluation in Psychology and Education* (4th ed.). New York: John Wiley, 1977.

Travers, R.M.W., ed. *Second Handbook of Research on Teaching: A Project of the American Educational Research Association*. Chicago: Rand McNally, 1973.

Walker, D.K. *Socioemotional Measures for Preschool and Kindergarten Children: A Handbook*. San Francisco: Jossey-Bass, 1973.

Summary of teaching methods

- Maintain a comfortable, secure environment
- Support children's actions and language
- Help children make choices and decisions
- Help children solve their own problems and do things for themselves

Maintain a comfortable, secure environment

For children to grow and prosper both socially and intellectually, they need the support of a warm, friendly environment where adults make them feel secure and appreciated, and where they can try out various ways of acting and interacting without fear of ridicule, retribution, or neglect.

- *Set limits for children and maintain them consistently.* Children need a structure within which they can be free to choose and experiment. Unlimited freedom puts too much responsibility on them and encourages them to use too much of their energy testing the limits rather than enjoying the freedom they provide.

- *Don't just say "No"* without offering a reason and an alternative. Children appreciate explanations and suggestions of other ways to act even if they appear to be ignoring them. For example, an adult might say, "Don't climb on the shelves, Hilda, because they could break or tip over. Maybe you could build stairs to climb on in the block area or climb on the climber at outside time instead."

- *Deal with difficult situations as they arise* instead of ignoring them or waiting for a more uneventful moment. Children need their energies for trying out appropriate behavior, not for worrying about past inappropriate behavior.

- *Follow up directions and commands with actions* so that children learn to believe the adults around them. If an adult reminds a child that he can cut with the scissors but not throw them, and that if he does throw them again, they'll be taken away, this "promise" should be kept if the child persists in his inappropriate behavior. The child will begin to realize that adults mean what they say and aren't making hollow statements that can be flouted again and again.

Support children's actions and language

This is something adults should do from day one to the last day of school. As adults learn more and more about the curriculum, they'll see more and more exciting dimensions to children's actions and language, but from the very first day, they can and must encourage children as they work, play, and communicate. Each child needs support at his or her particular level of development; children should never be made to feel that what they're doing isn't right or good enough. Adults must help children feel good about what they can do rather than apologetic about things they can't do.

- *Join children in their work* after observing them briefly to find out what they're doing. It takes some practice to be able to join children without disrupting them or imposing upon their train of action or thought. An adult who learns to join a child unobtrusively can be a great source of support and encouragement. In this situation the child may become the proud teacher of the adult. "Gee, Lucy," an adult might say, "you've made a very tall tower. I'm going to try to build one just like yours."

• *Keep the child's purpose in mind* when suggesting ways he might extend his activity. In other words, acknowledge and build on the child's original intention.

• *Use physical contact to support and acknowledge children's efforts.* Don't forget that touching is an important way to let children know that they are special and important. Each child and adult has his or her own way of communicating and responding nonverbally. Adults should do what they feel comfortable doing as long as it doesn't include some children and exclude others. For example, always holding Diana at circle time and never holding Ralph isn't the best situation for either child.

• *Talk with children about what they're doing* throughout the day. Speak naturally and conversationally with children. Acknowledge and describe what they're doing, but don't bombard them with language. Give them time to respond and contribute to the conversation. Be as specific as possible without being didactic or stilted. For example, instead of saying, "I see your airplane drying over there," say "I see your airplane drying on the art table." Allow children to initiate their own conversations and comments and be ready to respond supportively.

• *Help children support and talk to each other* by encouraging them to demonstrate or show to other children what they've accomplished. This can be done quite naturally within the immediate context of the children's play. Adults can also—though this is not *always* appropriate—redirect children's questions toward other children: "Joey, ask Lynnette to tell you how *she* made her book stay together."

• *Give children time* to carry out their ideas during each time period of the day. When children need more time than is available, help them plan a time for the next day when they can work on their idea or project again. Helping children find time to complete projects lets them know that what they're doing is important.

• *Save adult conversations until after the children leave.* It's demeaning to children to talk about them as if they weren't there.

Help children make choices and decisions

Allowing children to make choices and decisions is one way the curriculum helps children learn to think for themselves. Adults need to capitalize on opportunities throughout the day when children can choose, plan, and decide for themselves.

• *Provide a wide variety of materials and equipment* in each work area. Refer to the chapter on room arrangement for further details.

• *Help children explore the possibilities in the room from which they can choose.*

• *Plan activities throughout the day that include choices.* The chapter on the daily routine gives suggestions for presenting children with choices during each segment of the daily routine. Refer to this chapter frequently.

• *Acknowledge children's choices and decisions* once they've made them. Many children may not be aware that they've made a choice and thus are unmindful of the control they can exert over their own actions. A comment like, "Tommy, you've decided to use just the blue pegs" helps a child see that he's made a choice and that choosing is among the things he can do well.

- *Don't offer children a choice when there really isn't one.* "It's time to go inside now" is a far more useful and truthful statement for an adult to make at the end of outside time than, "Would you like to go in now?"

Help children solve their own problems and do things for themselves

As children learn to solve problems and take care of their own needs, they begin to approach new situations as challenges, and they gain confidence in their own ability to create and try various solutions.

- *Avoid doing things for children they can do on their own* after some trial and error. Adults who hover over children ready to bail them out at the first sign of frustration can deprive children of valuable learning and confidence-building opportunities. Instead of zipping a child's coat for him, for example, an adult can suggest some things for the child to try to facilitate zipping (like holding on to the bottom edge of the jacket) but still leave the actual zipping to the child. Adults should attempt to aid the problem-solving process without taking it over. They can do this by asking questions ("What else can you use besides a stapler to fasten your book together?") and by offering suggestions ("What about trying string or paper clips or metal fasteners?")

- *Allow children to make mistakes and learn from them* without saying, "That's wrong." Remember that the *processes* involved in any solution are where the learning occurs, even if the solution itself isn't particularly satisfactory. For example, a child trying to hold a book together with bits of clay learns something about the physical limits of clay and the requirements of objects that open and shut. With this experience, the child is ready to look for a more effective binding material. The clay didn't work, but it wasn't "wrong" either, because it led the child to try something else. Had an adult said, "Don't use clay, it won't work," the child's first idea would've been rejected, and he might have been afraid to suggest another, preferring instead the safety of waiting for an adult to tell him the "right thing."

Curriculum checklists

Arranging and equipping the classroom

The room arrangement checklist should be used at the beginning of the year, before children start school, as the teaching adults arrange and equip the classroom. They may also refer to the checklist throughout the year as they attempt to make the room as serviceable as possible to children.

1. Room is divided into several distinct areas or interest centers (house, art, block, quiet, construction, sand and water, music and movement, animal and plant).

   ☑ Boundaries are well defined by low shelves, stable screens, or walls with openings so that children and adults can see into areas.

   ☑ Each area has an adequate amount of space for children and their use of materials.

   ☑ The art area is near the sink.

   ☑ Tables are incorporated into the work areas.

   ☑ Work areas are not cluttered with unnecessary furniture or materials.

   ☑ The areas are in corners or on the edges of the room and open into a central planning or meeting area.

   ☑ The art area floor is tiled.

   ☑ The block area floor is carpeted.

   ☐ **NO** Traffic flow permits children to work without interruption.

   ☐ **NO** The house and block areas are near each other for interrelated play.

   ☑ The noisier areas are not close to the quieter areas.

   ☐ **N/A** Some work areas are set up outside in warm climates or seasons.

2. Materials are stored in the area where they are used.

   ☐ **NO** Shelves, drawers, and containers are labeled with objects, pictures, photographs or outlines of the contents.

   ☑ Identical and similar items are stored together.

   ☑ Sets of materials in different sizes are hung or stored so that size differences are apparent.

   ☑ Materials within each area are easily accessible to children.

   ☑ All materials within children's sight and reach can be used by children.

   ☐ **N/A** Planning board for an area is easily reached and seen within that area. Objects or pictures representative of the area are on the planning board.

☐ **N/A** Materials are stored so that some materials in each area are visible from where children plan.

3. There is an adequate amount and variety of materials in each area.

☐ **NO** There are unstructured materials in each area that can be used in many ways. Example: poker chips can be used for counting, stacking, matching, sorting, representing food, money.

☑ There are a variety of materials available to children to achieve their goals. Examples: papers can be put together with glue, paste, tape, stapler, paper clips, string, rubber bands; a house can be made with blocks, paper, wood at workbench, playdough, paint.

☑ There are enough materials in each area for children to work simultaneously.

☑ There are materials which can be manipulated and actively explored in each area.

☑ There are materials which can be used for pretending or making representations in each area.

☑ There are many real things (like plants, animals, real utensils, tools, and instruments) which children can explore in each area.

☐ There are culturally relevant materials in each area.

4. Space is provided for displaying and storing children's work and belongings.

☑ Display spaces are at child's eye level as much as possible.

☐ **NO** Display space is provided for children's work in each area.

☑ Individual storage (dishtubs, empty gallon containers, boxes, baskets) and coat space is provided for each child to store his or her personal belongings. These storage spaces are labeled and placed low enough so that children can use them independently.

☑ 5. Each adult familiarizes children with names and contents of areas.

6. Equipment is changed or added throughout the year.

☑ **NO** Children help decide where new materials should go.

☐ **NO** Children help make labels for new equipment.

☐ **NO** Adults talk with children about room arrangement changes.

7. The design of a new preschool facility includes the following:

☑ bathroom with child-level fixtures opening directly off each classroom.

☑ a sink in each art area.

☑ tile flooring in each art area.

☐ *covered* electrical outlets above children's reach.

☐ **NO** bulletin board covering the first 4½ feet of each wall.

☑ carpeting throughout each room except in the art area.

☑ ample storage space for supplies.

☐ *NO* a door from each room to the outside play area.

☐ *NO* a covered outdoor area.

☑ outdoor storage facility for outdoor equipment.

8. The block area includes an ample supply of the following kinds of materials:

☑ building materials.

☑ take-apart-put-together materials.

☑ materials for filling and emptying.

☑ materials for pretending.

☑ 9. Riding toys, a workbench, a sand table, table and chairs are *not* included in the block area.

10. The house area includes an ample supply of the following kinds of materials:

☑ kitchen equipment for manipulating, sorting, filling, emptying.

☑ materials for dramatic play.

☑ materials for real cooking activities (used under adult supervision).

☐ *?* 11. There is a workable clothes storage system in the house area.

☑ 12. A section of the house area is undefined, allowing for other kinds of role play.

13. The art area includes an ample supply of the following kinds of materials:

☑ paper of different sizes, textures, colors.

☑ materials for mixing and painting.

☑ materials for holding things together and taking them apart.

☑ materials for making three-dimensional representations.

☑ materials for making two-dimensional representations.

14. The art area also includes:

☑ a variety of work surfaces.

☑ workable smock storage.

☑ a place for drying pictures.

☑ a place for storing projects in progress.

☑ 15. Adults introduce art area materials gradually.

☑ 16. Adults keep the supply of expendable art area materials constant.

17. The quiet area includes an ample supply of the following kinds of materials:

☐ *NO* materials to sort and build with.

☐ *NO* materials to order and build with.

☐ *''* materials to fit together and take apart.

☐ *''* materials for decoding and pretending.

☑ books.

☑ 18. Books are stored in forward-facing racks and changed periodically.

19. The construction area includes the following:

☑ a sturdy work surface.

☑ tool and wood storage.

☑ tools.

☑ wood, cardboard, styrofoam, etc.

20. The music and movement area includes the following:

☑ space for movement.

☐ *NO* labeled instruments.

☑ a simple record player and/or tape cassette.

☑ records and/or tapes.

☑ instruments.

21. The sand and water area includes the following:

☑ an appropriate sand/water vessel.

☑ a cleanable floor surface.

☑ materials for pretending, scooping and digging, filling and emptying.

☑ additional sand-like materials for variety (beans, styrofoam bits, etc.).

☑ 22. The sand and water area is located near water and is moved outside when possible.

23. The animal and plant area includes the following:

☐ *N o* friendly animals.

☐ " easily cared-for plants.

☐ " appropriate cages and food.

24. The outdoor area includes an ample supply of the following kinds of materials:

☑ things to climb and balance on.

☑ things to swing on.

☑ things to slide on.

☑ things to get into and under.

☑ things to jump on and over.

☑ things to push, pull, and ride on.

☑ things to kick, throw, and aim for.

☑ things for sand and water play.

☑ things to build with.

25. The room arrangement accommodates visually-impaired children.

☑ Materials are maintained in consistent locations.

☑ Room arrangement changes are made gradually and visually-impaired children are acquainted with them as soon as they occur.

☐ *NO* Materials are labeled with textured labels.

☑ Consistent traffic patterns are maintained.

☑ Rugs are anchored firmly to the floor.

☑ The room includes a sand and water area and a music area.

☐ 26. The room accommodates hearing-impaired children by using sound-absorbent material and fabric wherever possible.
NO

27. The room arrangement accommodates physically-impaired children.

☑ Work surfaces are located within children's reach.

☑ Special physical arrangements are devised and maintained for individual children based on their particular needs.

28. The room arrangement accommodates mentally-impaired children.

☐ **NO** Materials are labeled with real objects.

☑ Each area includes developmentally appropriate materials.

☑ Room arrangement changes are made gradually, and children are helped to anticipate and take part in them.

Establishing a daily routine

General

☑ 1. Routine is consistent from day to day; children know what to expect.

☑ 2. The planning time/work time/clean-up time sequence is maintained.

☑ 3. Each time period has a definite name which children are helped to learn.

☑ 4. Verbal or non-verbal signals are used to mark the end of time periods.

Planning time

1. At the beginning of the year, adults help children get ready to start the planning process by helping them:

☑ learn what materials and equipment are available.

☑ learn the names of the work areas.

☑ learn the names of other people.

Ⓣ begin to make choices.

Ⓣ learn to use signs and planning boards.

☐ **N/A** 2. Planning occurs each day at the same time and in the same place.

N/A

☐ 3. Children can see the areas of the room from where they plan.

☐ 4. There is a planning board in each area **No** where children can hang their signs.

☐ 5. The planning boards are at child **No** eye-level.

☐ 6. The planning board in each area is **No** labeled with pictures or photographs of the area and/or materials from that area.

☑ 7. Each child has a sign which has his or **color** her photograph and a shape which is assigned only to this child.

☐ 8. Each child sits on the floor or at a low **NA** table to plan with an adult and a small group of children.

☐ 9. Each adult sits with a small group of children on their own level.

☐ 10. Each adult points out things to the children in her group which may be helpful during planning, such as new materials or special activities the children might like to plan for if any are to occur that day.

11. Each adult talks individually with each child in turn:

☑ asking the child what he or she would like to do.

☑ giving the child time to respond.

☑ acknowledging the choice or plan the child makes.

☑ helping the child expand his or her plan.

☑ giving suggestions if the child can't think of anything.

☐ **N/A** reminding the child of something he or she began yesterday if such is the case.

12. Depending on the needs of the child, adults help children:

☑ vary their plans from day to day.

☑ make a series of connected plans.

☑ make realistic plans.

13. Each child indicates what he is going to do during work time either by:

☐ naming an area, object, or child he's going to work with.

☑ describing *what* he's going to do.

☐ **N/A** describing *how* he's going to do something.

☐ drawing or tracing what he's going to do.

☐ dictating or writing what he's going to do.

☐ 14. Children go to the area where they have planned to work as soon as they have talked with an adult about their plan.

☐ 15. Each child hangs his or her sign on the planning board in the area where the child has planned to begin work.

☐ 16. Adults watch to see which children need assistance to get started on their plans.

☐ 17. Each adult helps children who need assistance as soon as every child in the small group has made a plan.

☐ 18. Each adult records or in some way keeps track of children's plans.

Work time

30

☑ 1. Children have approximately 45 minutes to carry out their plans and to make new ones when finished.

☑ 2. Each child is actively involved with the materials he or she has chosen.

☑ 3. Children get their own materials.

☑ 4. Each child works on his or her plan.

☑ 5. Children converse intermittently with adults or other children about what they are doing.

☑ 6. Each child attempts to solve problems he or she encounters or seeks the assistance of an adult.

☑ 7. Children clean up their own materials when they're finished with them unless another child is using them.

☑ 8. Each child makes a new plan with an adult if he or she has finished his initial plan.

☑ 9. Adults try to keep in mind what's happening in the whole room as they move from child to child throughout work time.

10. Adults assist children who:

☑ need help getting started on their plans.

☑ ask for help as they are working.

☑ don't seem to know what to do next.

☑ are making new plans.

☑ 11. Adults work with each child on his or her own level.

☑ 12. Adults talk with children about what they are doing.

13. Adults recognize and support children's work by doing one or more of the following:

☑ describing what a child seems to be doing.

☑ asking a child to tell what he or she is doing.

☑ trying out a child's ideas herself.

☑ helping children gather materials for their ideas.

☑ having a child show another child what he or she is doing.

☐ other **asking more ??**

14. Adults help children extend their plans and ideas by doing one or more of the following:

☑ helping children find additional materials.

☑ asking children open questions to help them see what they could do next with their plans.

☐ helping children relate their work to someone else's.

☑ helping children save or represent what they have done.

☑ planning experiences and/or field trips relating to children's work time pursuits.

☐ helping each child extend his or her plan along the child's own interests and at the child's own pace.

☐ taking cues from children about when their plans are complete.

☐ other **↑encouraging finish**

15. Adults help children deal with work time conflicts by doing one or more of the following:

☑ helping a grabbing child identify an alternative object to use.

☑ having the grabbing child talk to the child with the desired object.

☐ *No* helping children share by using a simple timing device.

☑ purchasing more than one of particularly desired objects when feasible.

☑ helping children solve their own space problems.

☐ *No* offering a choice of solutions to problems if children can't think of their own solutions.

☑ helping a frustrated child stop disturbing other's work, then going back to his plan to see what the real problem is.

Ⓐ helping children find alternative modes of behavior and plan more suitable activities for themselves, rather than stressing their "naughtiness" with them.

Ⓐ anticipating possible conflicts by helping children before they get into trouble.

☑ 16. Adults record observations of children throughout work time.

☑ 17. Adults encourage children to clean up throughout work time as they finish one plan and before they begin a new one.

Clean-up time

☑ 1. Children do most of clean-up work and return materials to the proper places.

☑ 2. Adults warn children about clean-up toward the end of work time and then use a consistent signal to mark the beginning of clean-up time.

☐ 3. Adults alert children to the reasons for cleaning up. *NO*

☑ 4. Adults help children define what materials they're going to put away.

☑ 5. Adults talk with children about the kinds of things they're putting away.

☑ 6. Each adult works along with the children at clean-up time.

☑ 7. Each adult uses clean-up time to implement the key experiences.

☐ 8. Adults make up clean-up games based on what the children are doing and what they enjoy. *NO*

☑ 9. Adults designate a place where children gather as they finish cleaning up.

☐ 10. Adults call group meetings to assess the progress and problems of clean-up on difficult days. *NO*

☐ 11. Adults give a child having difficulty cleaning up a choice of tasks, then leave him or her to finish the task chosen. *NO*

Recall time *NO*

☐ 1. Adults recall with children they planned with. *NO*

☐ 2. Children talk about their work time efforts. *NO*

☑ 3. Adults describe what a child did at work time or ask other children to, if the child can't do so himself.

☐ 4. Adults listen and support children as they recall. *NO*

☐ 5. Adults experiment with a variety of ways of recalling to make recall time interesting to children.

Small-group time

1. Small groups:

☑ include a cross section of the classroom population except in classrooms in which there is a very wide range of developmental levels.

☑ separate children who need a chance to work independently.

☑ are maintained long enough for children and adults to get to know one another.

☑ meet in locations suited to the activity rather than always at a table.

☐ are formed around each adult in the classroom (two groups if there are two adults, three groups if there are three adults, etc.). *NO*

☐ 2. Small groups of children (one group for each adult) are actively involved in a planned activity. *NO*

☑ 3. Each child works with his or her own set of materials.

☑ 4. Each child has enough space to work comfortably.

☑ 5. Each child uses materials in his or her own way and makes choices.

☑ 6. Each child makes discoveries on his or her own.

☑ 7. Each child talks with the adult and the other children about what he or she is doing.

☑ 8. Each child observes and responds to what others are doing.

☑ 9. Each child helps to clean up at the end of the activity.

☑ 10. *generally* Each child enjoys the activity.

☑ 11. Adults have materials ready and accessible.

☑ 12. Adults begin the activity by giving the whole group an idea about what to try with the materials.

☑ 13. Adults move from child to child to see what each child is doing, and to talk with him or her about it.

☑ 14. Adults support and work with individual approaches to the task.

☑ 15. Adults suggest ideas to children having difficulty starting.

☑ 16. Adults ask open questions to help children see new possibilities.

☑ 17. Adults respond to and acknowledge children's ideas and suggestions.

?☐ 18. Adults encourage children to share ideas with each other.

☑ 19. Adults use materials themselves to imitate and model ideas.

?☐ 20. Adults bring small-group time to a meaningful conclusion by helping

children think about and use what they've discovered.

☐ 21. *NO* Adults record small-group time observations.

22. Adults try some of the following strategies when a child causes problems at small-group time:

☑ help the child anticipate small-group time and where his or her group will meet.

☑ include materials and/or activities the child is interested in or successful with.

☑ structure the activity so that the child can have success.

☑ include a friend in the child's group with whom he or she works well.

☑ enlist the child to help other children.

☑ help the child get started.

☑ help the child find alternatives when his or her ideas don't work.

☑ support the child throughout work time so that he or she comes to small-group time in a positive frame of mind.

☑ help the child understand the limits and expectations at small-group time.

☐ other _____.

Outside time

☑ 1. Adults and children are involved in play.

☑ 2. Each child is physically active—running, walking, climbing, pushing, pulling, swinging.

☑ 3. Each child is using large motor equipment or is playing an active game.

☑ 4. Adults participate actively with children.

☑ 5. Adults talk with children about what they're doing.

☑ 6. Adults help children solve problems, find alternatives.

☑ 7. Adults encourage, support, extend children's play.

☑ 8. Adults both initiate and join games.

☑ 9. Adults structure indoor games and activities in inclement weather.

Circle time

☑ 1. There is enough space for everyone to move and sit down together.

NO – join all at once
☐ 2. Each child joins the large group activity as he finishes the previous activity.

☑ 3. Each child participates actively in the group game, song, dance, story, or planning for a special event.

☑ 4. Each child contributes his or her ideas to the activity at appropriate times, and occasionally serves as group leader.

☑ 5. Each child knows limits and expectations for circle time.

☑ 6. Children enjoy themselves.

☑ 7. Adults know the plan for circle time, the words to the song, how the game is played, etc.

☑ 8. Adults either lead or participate in the group activity, or help children finish the previous activity and then join in.

☑ 9. Adults ask children for their suggestions for the activity.   *songs, etc.*

N/A
☐ 10. Adults invite parents who arrive to pick up their children to join in the activity.

☑ 11. Adults have alternative activities in mind and can change to a favorite activity when the planned activity fails for some reason.

NO
☐ 12. Adults try to relate circle time activities to things children have been doing.

☑ 13. Adults use circle time to implement the key experiences.

Transitions

☑ 1. The daily routine has a minimum of major transitions.

☑ 2. Active times alternate with quieter times.

☐ *NO* 3. Meeting places are designated for major transition times.

☐ *NO* 4. Children help make up ways of moving from one place or activity to the next.

☑ 5. Activities begin right away without long initial waiting periods.

Planning in a team

each wk,
1. At their planning session ~~each day~~, the team goes through the following evaluative processes:

☑   reporting children's actions.

☑   assessing those actions in terms of the curriculum framework.

☑   planning strategies for supporting and extending children's actions.

2. The teaching team organizes each daily evaluation and planning session around *one* of the following topics:

☑ key experiences.

☑ the daily routine.

→ ☑ individual children.

☑ seasonal themes or holiday activities in terms of related key experiences.

☑ field trips and follow-up activities.

3. To facilitate the daily team evaluation and planning process, team members:

☑ set aside a regular time each ~~day~~ wk to meet as a team to evaluate the day and plan the next.

☑ set a specific focus for evaluation and planning.

☐ NO make up evaluation and planning forms and try out different ones—keeping the forms that work best for the team.

☑ pass the recording process around— have one member record e_valuations_, for example, while another records plans, — NO and another keeps notes about individual children.

☑ make specific statements about what individual children and adults did in relation to the focus of the evaluation and planning session.

☑ don't stop after stating a problem but go ahead and generate strategies for dealing with it.

☑ get help when necessary from the curriculum assistant, an adult more experienced in the curriculum, another teaching team, a parent.

☑ make sure every team member

contributes his or her observations and ideas.

☐ NO periodically, look at how effectively the team works together.

Active learning

1. Adults help children explore actively with all the senses by:

☑ providing materials that encourage active exploration.

☑ encouraging exploration.

☑ planning active small-group times.

☑ exploring actively outside the classroom.

2. Adults help children discover relations through direct experience by:

☑ encouraging children to do things on their own.

☑ helping children think of alternatives rather than problem-solving for them.

3. Adults help children use materials actively by:

☑ providing materials children can manipulate, transform and combine.

☑ planning activities in which children can manipulate, combine, and transform materials.

☑ supporting and extending children's use of materials.

☑ talking to children about what they are doing.

4. Adults help children choose materials, activities and purposes by:

☑ providing a consistent daily routine.

☑ helping children learn the arrangement of the room.

☑ helping children learn where materials belong.

☑ helping children work imaginatively with materials.

☑ helping children recognize that they've made choices.

☐ No providing opportunities for choosing even in "structured" small-group activities.

5. Adults help children acquire skills with tools and equipment by:

blocks

☑ setting up a construction area.

☑ supporting children's use of tools and equipment.

☐ NO making a list of tools and equipment and keeping track of each child's progress.

6. Adults help children use their large muscles by:

☑ supporting each child at his or her own level of coordination and muscular development.

☑ including physical therapy for children with special needs.

☑ providing equipment on which children can exercise their large muscles.

☑ providing space and time in the daily routine for children to be involved in vigorous indoor and outdoor activities.

7. Adults help children take care of their own needs by:

☑ providing time for children to do things for themselves.

☒ !! making self-help a part of every activity.

☑ planning activities which require children to do things for themselves.

Language

1. The classroom is arranged and equipped to facilitate language.

☑ Work areas are distinct with enough space for children to move freely and interact positively with each other. They are not cluttered with desks and tables.

☑ Boundaries for areas are low enough for children to see over.

☐ NO? An adequate supply of materials that can be used in a number of ways and which encourage children to work and talk together are available in each work area.

☑ Materials are displayed at child's eye level and available for children's use.

☑ Children's work and photographs of children are displayed at child's eye level.

☐ 2. Adults capitalize on the opportunities for
No communication among children provided by the plan-do-review sequence.

☑ 3. Adults encourage interaction and cooperation among children.

☑ 4. Adults refer one child's questions or problems to another.

☑ 5. Adults interpret and deliver messages.

☑ 6. Adults fill in the context for children's out-of-context statements.

☑ 7. Adults encourage active listening.

8. Adults show that they are available for conversation by:

☑   speaking in a natural voice.

☑   assuming the child's physical level.

☑   listening to what the child says.

☑   making physical contact with the child.

☑   remembering each child's particular interests. $ needs

9. Adults acknowledge and respect the child's role in conversations by:

☑   listening.

☑   acknowledging a child's ideas.

☑   focusing on what the child says rather than on his or her grammar.

☑   sticking to the subject.

☑ 10. Adults maintain a balance between child and adult talk throughout the day.

☑ 11. Adults converse with children who do not talk.

☐ 12. Adults find out the dominant language of each child and converse with him or her in it.
N|A

☐ 13. Adults establish non-verbal contact with children whose language they do not yet speak.
N|A

☑ 14. Adults direct children's attention to objects, events, and relations.

☑ 15. Adults ask open questions to help children describe objects, events, and relations.

☑ 16. Adults encourage children to describe things by having them try to answer their own questions.

☑ 17. Adults provide opportunities for children to describe what they are going to do, what they are doing, what they have done, and what's going to happen next throughout the day.

☐ 18. Adults make up and play describing games with children.
No

☑ 19. Adults speak precisely, describing objects, events, and relations in conversations with children.

☑ 20. Adults read stories to children.

☐ 21. Adults are aware of the role of descriptive language in the relationship areas.
?

22. Adults help children handle their feelings.

☑   Adults talk matter-of-factly with children when they bring up questions and concerns.

☑   Adults recognize and verbally acknowledge children's feelings.

☑   Adults express their own feelings in words.

☑   Adults help children find alternatives when conflicts arise.

☑   Adults help children anticipate and avoid conflicts.

☑ Adults help children find alternatives to verbal abuse and whining.

☑ Adults encourage children to think about other people's feelings.

☐ 23. Adults take dictation from children whenever possible throughout the day.
NO

☐ 24. Adults collect dictations.
NO

☑ 25. Adults respond to individual children's interest in letters, sounds, and words.
if applic

☑ 26. Adults provide a wide variety of books for children to look at and read.

☑ 27. Adults read books, stories, and poems to children.

☑ 28. Adults tell stories and recite poems, rhymes, and verses.

☑ 29. Adults sing with children.

☑ 30. Adults make up chants, rhymes and limericks with children.

☑ 31. Adults make up stories and songs with children.

32. Adults in bilingual classrooms encourage the development of skills in children's first and second languages.
N/A

☐ Adults use both languages concurrently when addressing the children as a group.

☐ Adults use both languages equally throughout the daily routine.

☐ Adults talk with other adults equally in both languages.

☐ Monolingual adults learn the second language.

☐ Adults encourage children who speak different languages to work together.

☐ Adults provide a non-pressured bilingual environment.

☐ Adults identify languages spoken.

☐ Adults answer children's questions about the other language.

☐ Adults acknowledge and support a child's second-language exploration.

☐ Adults use a child's second language in parallel situations.

☐ Adults occasionally give simple commands to the whole group in one language without translating.

☐ Adults talk to children for brief periods in their second language even before they understand it.

☐ Adults incorporate a child's second-language words into their own speech as they talk with him in his dominant language.

☐ Adults provide the "other name" for objects.

☐ Adults use second-language nouns in conversations with children when objects referred to are present.

☐ Monolingual adults learn words and phrases in the second language from children and use them in context throughout the day.

☐ Adults play "one-word" games with children.

☐ Adults keep track of children's second-language words.

☐ Adults accept a child's second-language phrases.

☐ Adults repeat a child's second-language phrases, substituting new words when possible.

☐ Adults provide opportunities for children to use their second-language phrases.

☐ Adults keep track of each child's phrases.

☐ Adults accept and respond to children's second-language sentences.

☐ Adults take dictation in children's second languages.

☐ Adults keep track of the sentences children are saying in their second languages.

☐ Adults speak to a child in his or her second language.

☐ Adults provide natural and unpressured opportunities for children to interpret and translate.

☐ Adults refrain from interpreting and translating when a child could do so.

☐ Adults include bilingual children in each small group at small-group time.

☐ Monolingual adults call upon children for translations and interpretations.

Experiencing & representing

1. The classroom is equipped with a variety of materials children can use to make representations:

☑ real objects and tools. _No_

☑ materials to taste.

☑ materials to smell.

☑ materials to listen to.

☑ materials to touch.

☑ materials for making imprints.

☑ models, pictures, and photographs of real places and things.

☑ photographs of field trips.

☑ photographs of children working and of things they have made.

☑ props and materials for role play.

☐ outdoor equipment for role play. _no_

☑ materials for making models. _Clay_

☑ materials for making paintings and drawings.

☑ picture books, storybooks, catalogs, magazines.

☑ book-making materials.

2. The classroom is arranged to allow children to represent freely.

☐ The classroom is divided into distinct work areas including an art area, house area, block area, quiet area, construction area, music area, and sand and water area.

☑ Materials are easy for children to locate, use and return on their own.

☑ Expendable art and woodworking materials are replenished frequently.

3. Children are free to generate their own representations of things.

☞ Children choose their own materials for making representations.

☑ Children construct representations from their own perceptions of things rather than from a pre-made adult model.

4. Opportunities for representation occur throughout the day at:

☐ planning time.

☑ work time.

☐ recall time.

☑ small-group time.

☑ outside time.

☑ circle time.

5. Adults encourage and support children's representational activities by:

☑ playing sensory-cue games.

☑ helping children notice and make imprints and shadows.

☑ encouraging children to imitate actions and sounds.

☑ comparing models to the objects they represent.

☑ encouraging and supporting children in their role play.

☐ *no* helping children acquire skill with tools and equipment.

☐ *no* helping children learn to prepare and use materials on their own.

☑ helping children plan and complete models of their own design.

☑ encouraging children to represent in a variety of two- and three-dimensional media.

☑ talking with children about their representations.

☐ *no* taking dictation from children about what they have made, done, seen, or experienced.

☑ encouraging children to make their own books, songs, and stories.

☑ providing real experiences directly related to things children are attempting to represent.

☑ providing opportunities for children to interpret other people's representations.

☑ following up real experiences with opportunities to represent the experiences.

Classification

1. The classroom is equipped with a variety of materials children can classify:

☑ real materials children can investigate and describe including tools, utensils, musical instruments, foods, living things, simple mechanical objects, things collected outdoors and on field trips.

☑ sets of identical materials.

☑ sets of similar materials.

☑ sets of materials that can be sorted in several different ways.

2. The classroom is arranged to give children opportunities to classify as they locate and return equipment and materials.

☑ Identical and similar materials are stored together in appropriate work areas.

☐ *no* Some classroom materials are labeled using "not" labels.

☐ *no* Some classroom materials are labeled in terms of two attributes.

3. Adults provide materials and opportunities for children to classify throughout the day:

☑ at planning time.

☑ at work time.

☑ at clean-up time.

☐ at recall time.

☑ at outside time.

☑ at circle time.

☐ on field trips.

☑ at meal and snack times.

☐ at transition times.

☑ at small-group time.

4. Adults support and encourage children as they classify materials by:

☑ talking with children, questioning them and taking dictation about things they are classifying.

☑ accepting the labels for things children generate.

☑ talking with children, questioning them and taking dictation about similarities and differences.

☐ *no* talking with children, questioning them and taking ~~dictation~~ about the multiple attributes of things.

☐ *no* using "not" statements as they talk with and question children.

☐ making observations and asking questions about the dual attributes of things.

☑ using "some" and "all" in conversations with children.

Seriation

1. The classroom is equipped with materials children can seriate:

☑ materials children can easily compare.

☑ materials that come in three or four sizes.

☑ ordered sets of materials that fit together.

2. Adults support and encourage children as they seriate by:

☑ asking questions that help children make comparisons.

☑ playing games that call for comparisons.

☐ *no* taking dictation about comparisons.

☐ talking with children and asking them questions about size relationships.

☐ *not always* using materials in three or four sizes at small-group time.

☐ *no* encouraging children to order things by size at clean-up time.

☐ *no* reading and encouraging children to represent stories that deal with size relationships.

☐ *no* encouraging children to fit ordered sets together at clean-up time.

☐ *no* talking with children about what they are doing as they fit ordered sets of objects together.

☑ including ordered sets of objects in small-group activities.

Number

1. The classroom is equipped with materials children can count:

☑ continuous materials.

☐ discontinuous materials.

☑ materials that fit together in one-to-one correspondence.

☑ sets of countable objects.

2. Adults support and encourage children as they work with number concepts by:

☑ asking children questions about amounts of things they are using throughout the day.

☐ *no* encouraging children to rearrange materials they are comparing.

☑ encouraging children to compare amounts of things they see in pictures.

☑ talking with children about what they are doing as they put things together in one-to-one correspondence.

☑ encouraging children to generate their own sets of materials in one-to-one correspondence.

☑ encouraging children to pass things out at snack and meal times.

☑ playing games that include one-to-one correspondence.

☑ encouraging children to count objects they are using.

☑ accepting children's numerical ordering.

☑ helping children who are interested to represent numbers in a way they can understand.

Spatial relations

1. Materials are provided in each work area which permit children to explore and describe spatial relations:

☑ materials which can be taken apart and put together.

☑ materials from which children can make their own fit-together-take-apart toys.

☑ simpler materials for children who can't yet fit together or take apart more complicated things.

☑ materials which can be rearranged and reshaped in space.

☑ a variety of surfaces on, around, and in which materials can be rearranged and reshaped.

☑ materials and equipment from which children can look at things from different spatial viewpoints.

☑ photographs of familiar things and places from different spatial viewpoints.

☑ materials that encourage children to explore positions, directions, and distances.

☑ photographs of children in various positions.

☑ materials that help a child learn how his body is put together.

☑ materials with which children can represent people.

☐ *no* planning boards in each work area.

☑ a wide variety of pictorial materials.

☑ a wide variety of materials with distinguishable shapes.

2. The classroom is arranged and equipped so that children can easily learn to locate things within it.

☑ The room is divided into several distinct work areas.

☑ There are a limited amount of materials in each work area at the beginning of the year.

☑ Adults provide display space for children's pictures and photographs in ~~each work area.~~

3. Adults provide opportunities throughout the day for children to explore and describe spatial concepts:

☑ at planning time.

☑ at work time.

☑ at clean-up time.

☑ at recall time.

☑ at snack and meal times.

☑ at outside time.

☑ at circle time.

☑ on field trips.

4. Adults encourage and support children's spatial learning as they work with materials and equipment throughout the day by:

☑ encouraging children to show and talk about new materials which fit together and come apart.

☑ making observations and providing suggestions about how things fit together and come apart.

☑ encouraging children to show and talk about how they are rearranging and reshaping things.

☑ describing changes for children who can't do so themselves.

☑ encouraging children to rearrange and reshape things in a variety of ways.

☐ *no* providing a series of models or picture recipes of more complex transformations.

☑ encouraging children to assume various physical positions in order to look at and describe things from various spatial viewpoints.

☑ encouraging children to represent things from different spatial viewpoints.

☑ encouraging children to describe the spatial positions, directions, and distances they are experiencing.

☑ using specific spatial terms in conversations with children.

☑ accepting children's judgments of positions, directions and distances.

☑ encouraging children to interpret spatial relations they see in pictures.

☑ providing opportunities for children to use their bodies in a variety of ways.

☑ helping children learn body part names.

☑ helping children begin to notice and feel good about how their bodies are similar to other people's and how they are unique.

☑ using the names of the work areas and the materials in them.

☑ encouraging children to compare people, objects, or scenes, with pictures or photographs of the same people, objects or scenes.

☑ encouraging children to recreate the spatial relations they see in pictures and photographs.

☑ encouraging children to make their own shapes.

☐ *no* talking with children about shapes they are using and making.

☐ *no* encouraging children to make observations about the properties of different shapes they are using.

☐ *no* refraining from asking "What shape is this?" under most circumstances.

Time

1. The classroom includes materials that allow children to experience time units and time sequences:

☑ materials children can use to signal the beginning and ending of time periods.

☑ materials that move or can be moved or played at different rates.

☑ clocks and improvised calendars.

☑ charts depicting the order of events.

☑ living things that change over time.

☑ 2. Adults signal the beginning and end of time periods within the daily routine.

☑ 3. Adults play stop-and-start games at outside and circle times.

☐ 4. Adults make up simple games that use *no* times to signal stopping and starting times.

☑ 5. Adults provide opportunities for children to experience different rates of physical movement.

☑ 6. Adults encourage children to describe the various rates of movement they are experiencing and observing.

☑ 7. Adults establish and follow a consistent daily routine.

☐ 8. Adults relate the length of time periods to *no* actual actions or events.

☐ 9. Adults help children see that sand timers *no* of different sizes take different lengths of time to empty.

☐ 10. Adults accept children's judgments about the length of time periods and ask them to explain their reasoning. *no*

11. Adults use seasonal changes as opportunities to help children understand time by:

☑ talking with children about seasonal changes in everyday conversation.

☑ focusing on seasonal changes that occur locally.

☑ encouraging children to collect and talk about objects that are the result of seasonal changes.

☑ repeating walks and field trips at different seasons throughout the year and recording them with photographs.

☑ 12. Adults help children observe longer time intervals by watching plants and animals grow.

☐ 13. Adults use conventional times and dates in conversations with children. *no*

☐ 14. Adults use clocks and improvised calendars to help answer children's "how-long-until" questions. *no*

☐ 15. Adults help children construct their own personal calendars in appropriate situations. *no*

☑ 16. Adults help children anticipate and prepare for time periods within the daily routine, for immediate processes they're about to begin, problems they may encounter, and for schedule changes.

☑ 17. Adults include children in plans and preparations for new pets.

☑ 18. Adults help children plan and complete what they've planned.

☐ 19. Adults help children describe and represent past events. *no*

☐ 20. Adults use conventional time units in everyday conversation with children. *no*

☐ 21. Adults use precise time units in conversation with children. *no*

☐ 22. Adults accept children's attempts to use conventional time units in their own conversations. *no*

☑ 23. Adults ask children to describe the order of events they've recently experienced.

☑ 24. Adults depict the order of events with children.

☑ 25. Adults encourage children to make their own representations of the order of things.

☑ 26. Adults plan small-group times around activities that must be done in a particular sequence.

APPENDIX 3
Preschool activity books: a select bibliography

("PBIP" indicates listing in Paperback Books in Print.)

Banet, Barbara *et al. The Scrap Book: A Collection of Activities for Preschoolers.* Ann Arbor, Michigan: Friends of Perry Nursery School, 1972. (Order at 1541 Washtenaw, Ann Arbor, Michigan 48104; $2.50, prepaid.)

Braley, William; Konicki, Geraldine and Catherine Leedy. *Daily Sensorimotor Training Activities: A Handbook for Teachers and Parents of Preschool Children.* Freeport, New York: Educational Activities, Inc., 1968.

Cherry, Clare. *Creative Art for the Developing Child: A Teacher's Handbook for Early Childhood Education.* Belmont, California: Fearon, 1972. PBIP

Cherry, Clare. *Creative Movement for the Developing Child: A Nursery School Handbook for Non-Musicians.* Belmont, California: Fearon, 1971. PBIP

Cole, Ann; Haas, Carolyn; Bushnell, Faith and Betty Weinberger. *I Saw a Purple Cow and 100 Other Recipes for Learning.* Boston: Little, Brown & Co., 1972. PBIP

Croft, Doreen J. and Robert D. Hess. *An Activities Handbook for Teachers of Young Children.* Boston: Houghton Mifflin, 1975. PBIP

DeFranco, Ellen B. *Learning Games for Preschool Children: A Home Teaching Handbook for Parents and Teachers.* Salt Lake City, Utah: Olympus, 1975. PBIP

Engel, Rose C. *Language Motivating Experiences for Young Children.* Van Nuys, California: DEA Publishers; 1968. (Order at 6518 Densmore, Van Nuys, California 91406.)

Flemming, Bonnie Mack; Hamilton, Darlene Softley and JoAnne Deal Hicks. *Resources for Creative Teaching in Early Childhood Education.* New York: Harcourt Brace, 1977.

Lorton, Mary Baratta. *Workjobs: Activity-Centered Learning for Early Childhood Education.* Menlo Park, California: Addison-Wesley, 1972.

Marzollo, Jean and Janice Lloyd. *Learning Through Play.* New York: Harper and Row, 1972. PBIP

Mayesky, Mary; Neuman, Donald and Raymond J. Wlodkowski. *Creative Activities for Young Children.* Albany, New York: Delmar, 1975.

Pasamanick, Judith. *Talkabout: An Early Childhood Language Development Resource.* Great Neck, New York: Center for Media Development, 1976.

Taylor, Barbara J. *A Child Goes Forth: A Curriculum Guide for Teachers of Preschool Children.* Provo, Utah: Brigham Young University Press, 1964.

Threshold Program for Early Learning. Written under the direction of Jean H. Orost. New York: Macmillan, 1970. PBIP
  Vol. 1: Eby, Carol; Kaup, Rachel and Estelle Lader. *Perceptual and Organizing Skills.*
  Vol. 2: Eby, Carol; Kaup, Rachel and Estelle Lader. *Mathematical Skills and Scientific Inquiry.*
  Vol. 3: Eby, Carol; Kaup, Rachel and Estelle Lader. *Language Skills and Social Concepts.*
  Vol. 4: Stecher, Miriam; McElherry, Hugh and Marion Greenwood. *Music and Movement Improvisation.*
  Vol. 5: Pile, Naomi F. *Art Experiences for Young Children.*
  Vol. 6: Van Tassel, Katrina and Millie Greimann. *Creative Dramatization.*

Cooking

Barrett, Isabelle. *Cooking is Easy When You Know How.* New York: Arco, 1974.

Better Homes and Gardens Junior Cookbook for Beginning Cooks of All Ages. Des Moines, Iowa: Meredith Corp., 1972. PBIP

Betty Crocker's Cookbook for Boys and Girls. New York: Western, 1975. PBIP

Burdick, Angela. *Look! I Can Cook.* New York: Crescent Books, (Octopus Books), 1972.

Kahan, Ellen House. *Cooking Activities for the Retarded Child.* New York: Abingdon Press, 1974. PBIP

Lansky, Vicki. *Feed Me! I'm Yours.* New York: Bantam, 1974. PBIP

Parents Nursery School. *Kids are Natural Cooks: Child-tested Recipes for Home and School Using Natural Foods.* Boston: Houghton Mifflin, 1972.

Audio-visual programs available from the High/Scope Foundation

The following programs are available from the High/Scope Foundation. To meet the production requirements and costs of the documentary approach, most of the materials were originally produced in either a slide-tape or one-inch black & white videotape format. Occasionally live-action 16mm footage was used. These "production" formats were then transferred to "dissemination" formats—16mm film or filmstrip with audio cassette. Thus materials originally produced as slide-tape presentations are available as 16mm films or filmstrips, and some videotape programs are also available as 16mm films. Videotape programs can be obtained in either ½" EIAJ open reel or ¾" cassette format. Contact the Foundation at 600 N. River St., Ypsilanti, Michigan 48197, (313) 485-2000 for information on rental or purchase.

Preschool Education & Child Development

Arranging the Classroom:
Case Study of the High/Scope Preschool
(color filmstrip and cassette tape; 15 min.)

A teacher from the High/Scope Preschool describes her attempts to implement principles of room arrangement and to select and organize materials to promote intellectual development—that is, to give children opportunities to exercise emerging cognitive abilities that are critical to the formation of more mature modes of thinking. She discusses the changes in her classroom structure and equipment over the course of a year. Catalog no.: PS 190

The Block Area
(color filmstrips and cassette tapes; 38.7 min. total)

A set of five filmstrips for preschool teachers who wish to establish interest areas in their classrooms. The focus is on the block area, but the information is applicable to interest areas in general and to the teacher's role as a resource and guide for active learning. Catalog no.: PS 191

1. Setting Up a Block Area (7.5 min.)
How to set up a block area and arrange it so that it is well placed and logically organized; how to equip the area initially and then add materials as the children become more familiar with the area.

2. A Place To Explore New Materials (6.5 min.)
How children explore materials by trying things out, using their senses, arranging objects, etc., and what a teacher can do to facilitate children's explorations.

3. A Place To Build All Kinds of Structures (9 min.)
How children build up, out, around—shows examples of typical structures and suggests strategies a teacher can use to encourage purposeful building.

4. A Place To Represent Things (8.7 min.)
Structures children build in the block area—roads, sidewalks, barns, garages, houses—and ways a teacher can respond to and support this important work of young children.

5. Observing a Child in the Block Area (7 min.)
Lynnette builds a large structure in the block area and a teacher observes and works with her. The narrator discusses the kinds of questions a teacher might ask in this situation and the strategies she could use to help Lynnette extend and represent her structure.

Classroom Structure and Equipment
(16mm film; color, sound; 8 min.)

This film demonstrates that the structure of the classroom and the organization of materials are crucial considerations in the design of a preschool program. It shows how to divide the classroom into work areas, or interest centers, and how to equip these areas and arrange materials in ways that will encourage children to think. *Catalog no.: PS 131*

The Cognitively Oriented Curriculum: A Framework for Education
(16mm film transfer of slide/tape presentation; color, sound; 19 min.)

An introduction to the High/Scope Cognitively Oriented Curriculum for preschool and elementary education. This film shows how the Cognitively Oriented Curriculum serves as a framework for an education in which "children are producers, not consumers, of their own learning materials and experiences," so that "academic skills are learned in the context of goals children have set for themselves." We see children of varying backgrounds and abilities learning to cooperate and communicate, to solve problems and accomplish goals, to seek out and organize information in a classroom environment that supports their self-direction and their striving toward competence. *Catalog no.: PS 136*

"El Curriculum Cognitivo"
(16mm film transfer of videotape; black & white; sound, 10 min.)

An introduction to the High/Scope Cognitively Oriented Preschool Curriculum in Spanish. Classroom scenes from the High/Scope Preschool illustrate several aspects of the curriculum: active learning through exploration and problem-solving; a chance for children to work individually and in group situations as well as one-to-one with a teacher; encouragement of children's language use; opportunities for children to plan and carry out their plans; use of field trips and a rich classroom environment to stimulate children's learning; and practice for children in representing and communicating their experiences. *Catalog no.: PS 135*

The Daily Routine
(16mm film; sound, color; 12 min.)

Discusses the organization and rationale for a consistent routine for the day that is structured to implement cognitive goals. The film documents a typical school day in a cognitively oriented preschool classroom. *Catalog no.: PS 133*

Experiencing and Representing
(16mm film transfer of slide/tape presentation; color, sound; 48 min.)

This set of four films demonstrates the importance of direct experience and representational play and shows how the preschool environment can promote both experience and representation. In each section, two teachers discuss specific activities from their classroom and demonstrate a variety of teaching strategies. *Package catalog no.: PS 110*

Part I—A Way Children Learn (12 min.)
Shows a variety of classroom activities in which children spontaneously represent things they've done or seen. Teachers discuss how children at different stages of intellectual development vary in their ability to hold details in mind and depict them in space and time. They also discuss the importance of representational play for later cognitive and academic development. *Catalog no.: PS 111*

Part II—Starting with Direct Experience (12 min.)
Some materials teachers can provide and techniques they can use to promote concrete experience in the preschool classroom as a basis for later representational activity. *Catalog no.: PS 112*

Part III—From Direct Experience to Representation (8 min.)
Teaching strategies to help children represent their experiences: sequencing activities from the concrete to the abstract; structuring the classroom in a nondirective way to encourage children to represent ideas and experiences in a variety of media. *Catalog no.: PS 113*

Part IV—Strategies for Supporting Representational Activity (16 min.)
Teaching strategies that encourage children to add detail and complexity to their representations; shows the process of taking dictation from the child to stimulate verbal representation and to help the child learn that writing is a way of representing spoken language. *Catalog no.: PS 114*

Feelings in the Cognitively Oriented Curriculum
(*videotape; black & white, sound, 42 min. total*)

Scenes from the High/Scope Preschool demonstrate how the elements of the Cognitively Oriented Curriculum contribute to a child's self-esteem. The four sets of videotape clips are intended to be used separately in discussion settings dealing with the topics listed.   *Catalog no.: PS 165*

1. Giving Positive Feedback (12 min.)
In the Cognitively Oriented Curriculum, children receive positive feedback both from teachers and peers.

2. Recognizing Children's Feelings (7 min.)
Illustrates how teachers help children express and deal with emotions, and how children's cognitive capacities affect the way they are able to understand their own and other people's feelings.

3. Interactions Between Handicapped and Nonhandicapped Children (6 min.)
Gives examples of children interacting in an integrated classroom of handicapped and nonhandicapped preschoolers and introduces strategies which help teachers deal with comments, feelings, attitudes and situations which occur in mainstreaming classrooms.

4. Resolving Conflicts (17 min.)
Classroom examples of how the Cognitively Oriented Curriculum framework helps minimize conflicts among children; introduces strategies for helping children find alternatives to aggressive behavior in their attempts to resolve conflicts.

Guidelines for Evaluating Activities
(*16mm film transfers of videotapes; black & white, sound; 58 min. total; discussion guides included*)

A set of three films, each of which demonstrates alternative ways teachers can plan and carry out activities with a group of preschool children. Each film shows two contrasting styles of structuring and leading a group activity using similar materials but different teaching methods and goals. Useful for stimulating discussion of teaching styles and educational philosophies. An accompanying observation guide offers criteria by which to evaluate and revise classroom activities. Also included is a trainer's supplement that discusses the films in terms of the criteria in the guide and offers suggestions for revising the activities.   *Package catalog no.: PS 150*

1. Contrasting Teaching Styles:
Small-Group Time (18 min.) Catalog no.: PS 151

2. Contrasting Teaching Styles:
Work Time, the Art Area (22 min.) Catalog no.: PS 152

3. Contrasting Teaching Styles:
Circle Time (18 min.) Catalog no.: PS 153

Helping Children Make Choices and Decisions
(*16mm film transfers of slide/tape presentations; color, sound; 33 min. total*)

A set of five short films that deal with aspects of the teacher's role in helping children make responsible, thoughtful, creative choices. The films were produced in several Head Start centers. Some of the dialogue is in Spanish.   *Package catalog no.: PS 100*

1. A Good Classroom is a Classroom Full of Choices (7 min.)
Children should be able to choose what they're going to do, where they're going to work, what materials they'll use, who they'll work with. This film shows how teachers can structure the classroom environment and children's activities to provide opportunities to make and carry out such critical choices.   *Catalog no.: PS 101*

2. Questions That Help Children Develop Their Ideas (7 min.)
Strategies to help young children think through the process of bringing an idea to fruition—finding materials they can use, discovering solutions to problems, and expanding their original notions to take account of new information.   *Catalog no.: PS 102*

3. Exploring the Possibilities of the Room (7 min.)
In order to make responsible and creative choices, children need to be aware of the alternatives available to them. Teachers demonstrate some ways to help young children explore the possibilities of the classroom—the many activities and materials to choose from and the many imaginative ways materials can be used.   *Catalog no.: PS 103*

4. Acknowledging Children's Choices and Decisions (6 min.)
Some ways teachers can help children recognize when they've made a decision and followed it through.

Children don't always talk about their choices or connect their actions to the choices they've made. A teacher can give a child support for his decisions by naming what the child has done, praising him, pointing out results and helping him survey his activities. *Catalog no.: PS 104*

5. *Planning Activities That Include Choices (6 min.)* Strategies for planning activities that allow children a degree of control, even when choices are limited, such as when the teacher is structuring an experience to meet certain goals or when routines and procedures are set (e.g., at lunch time or nap time). *Catalog no.: PS 105*

Integration of Handicapped and Nonhandicapped Preschool Children— Parents' Perspectives

(16mm film transfer of videotape; black & white, sound; 15 min.)

The sound portion of this film is an unrehearsed discussion among the parents of handicapped and nonhandicapped children who spent the 1974-75 school year together in the High/Scope Preschool. The parents discuss the benefits of the preschool program for their children; they mention the social and intellectual growth they have seen and discuss the aspects of the curriculum they feel have furthered this growth. They discuss some of the apprehensions they had at the beginning of the year, and how they feel at the end of the year in view of their children's experiences. They also discuss the influences they feel the children had on each other. The visual counterpoint to this dialogue is the children themselves as they work together in the preschool classroom. *Catalog no.: PS 162*

Key Experiences for Intellectual Development During the Preschool Years

(16mm film transfer of slide/tape presentation; color, sound; 19 min.)

Scenes from the High/Scope Preschool illustrate some of the major "key experiences" for the cognitive development of the preschool-age child—in active learning, language, representation, classification, seriation, number concepts, temporal relations and spatial relations. *Catalog no.: PS 137*

Learning about Time in the Preschool Years

(16mm film transfer of videotape; black & white, sound; 37.5 min.)

This two-part film shows how teachers can help children understand concepts of time; it illustrates strategies for encouraging children to recall the past, anticipate the future, and observe and represent temporal sequences and intervals. The first part shows how to help children observe the beginning and end of time periods, observe movement and change, and begin to represent the passage of time. The second part shows how young children learn to anticipate and recall events and to observe and predict the order in which events occur. *Catalog no.: PS 141*

Learning about Time in the Preschool Years: Classroom Examples for Discussion

(videotape; black & white; 18 min.)

These are unnarrated episodes of classroom interactions designed to provoke discussion or assess problem-solving or observational skills *Catalog no.: PS 142*

Observing Role Play

(16mm transfer of videotape; black & white, sound; 15 min.)

Scenes from the High/Scope Preschool are used to illustrate a sequence of role-play situations teachers can recognize and encourage in children: pretending to be someone else, sharing a pretend situation with another person, using one object to stand for another, imitating actions or sounds, using language to describe a pretend situation, using language appropriate to a role, remaining in a role-play situation for a significant amount of time. *Catalog no.: PS 144*

Home Visitor Training

(16mm film transfers of videotapes; black & white, sound)

1. *The Role of the Home Visitor (23 min.)* The key elements of a successful home-visit program, with emphasis on the roles a successful home visitor must fulfill. The importance of respecting the ideas, suggestions and beliefs of the parents is stressed, as is the need for sharing information and experiences. Various kinds of parental involvement in activities are shown, and suggestions for how a home visitor can

bring about this involvement are given. This film is particularly useful in the early stages of screening and training potential home visitors.   *Catalog no.: ID 315*

2. *Building a Relationship with Mother & Child (18 min.)*
The mother is the key person in any home-visit program. Because of her importance and influence, special care should be taken by the home visitor to establish a warm, responsive relationship with her as well as with her child. This film illustrates the kinds of things home visitors must be aware of and sensitive to in order to establish the most productive kind of relationship with the mother and child. We see the home visitor greeting all family members, showing interest in and concern for the experiences and problems of the mother and child, offering helpful suggestions when requested, simply listening when that seems most appropriate, sharing personal events and experiences with the mother—in short, being not only a teacher but a friend.   *Catalog no.: ID 316*

3. *Building a Relationship with Family Members (25 min.)*
This film stresses the importance of the home visitor's sensitivity to the people around the baby and ability to make use of their ideas, suggestions and experiences whenever possible. It demonstrates why the inclusion of father and siblings in the infant's activities is so important for the infant, and it emphasizes the sense of belonging that involvement with baby gives to the family members. Several techniques for including family members are illustrated.   *Catalog no.: ID 317*

4. *Focusing on the Baby's Actions and Development (15 min.)*
What it means in practical terms to "work with parents on development," and strategies for home visitors to use in helping parents observe and interpret their child's behavior in a developmental context. This film illustrates such strategies as noticing and describing gradual changes in the baby's interests and skills; talking about the baby's present actions and about what he's learning as he plays; tracing connections— between present and past actions, between present and possible future actions; anticipating what the baby might reasonably be expected to do with toys or materials; providing alternatives in situations where the baby's actions might be harmful or disturbing to others.   *Catalog no.: ID 318*

5. *Problems Encountered by the Home Visitor (15 min.; discussion guide included)*
A "discussion starter" designed to supply home-visit trainees with examples of situations and problems they might encounter in the home, such as the following:
- The teacher arrives late without contacting the mother. The mother is very angry because she had a doctor's appointment.
- The teacher finds she cannot discuss the infant's development or make arrangements for visits with the mother because the father interrupts the mother's answers and makes all the arrangements himself. The father also puts the teacher "on trial."
- The teacher arrives to find that the mother is not home. It is obvious from the teacher's remark, "Oh no, not again!" that the mother is often not at home.   *Catalog no.: ID 319*

6. *A Home Visit with Julie—12 Weeks Old (33 min.)*
An actual home visit from beginning to end, unedited and unnarrated. This is the first home visit with Julie and her mother. During the half hour, the High/Scope home visitor and the mother observe and discuss Julie's ability to follow moving objects with her eyes, grasp a rattle, respond to the sound of a bell by looking to see where it's coming from. Since it is not a dramatization of a "perfect" home visit but a record of a real one, this film can serve as the basis for discussion of the realities of parent-infant education as well as for evaluation of initial home visits.   *Catalog no.: ID 320*

Small Group Time: An Illustrated Checklist
(*videotape, black & white, sound; 11.5 min.*)

Intended as a springboard for discussion in teacher training workshops, this set of film clips presents some examples of preschool teachers conducting small-group activities, and offers a set of questions for teachers to use in planning and evaluating small-group activities with young children.   *Catalog no.: PS 154*

Spatial Learning in the Preschool Years
(*16mm film transfer of videotape; black & white, sound; 22 min.*)

A view of the preoperational child's understanding of the way things relate to one another in three-dimensional space—the look and feel of objects, their shapes, contours and edges, and the way some things fit next to or inside of one another. This film shows children gaining spatial understanding through exploration and manipulation of objects. Scenes from the High/Scope Preschool suggests ways of providing appropriate classroom materials and experiences for spatial problem solving. There are also scenes showing the development of spatial understanding in infancy. *Catalog no.: PS 143*

Supporting Children's Intellectual & Physical Development

(16mm film transfer of videotape; black & white, sound; 59 min.; discussion guide included)

This film shows several teachers conducting typical day care or preschool activities in a variety of teaching styles and situations. Designed for use in the training of teachers and curriculum assistants, the film has eight unnarrated sections, which show the following scenes for discussion: a flashcard activity at sharing time; a "mystery bag" game; two children making fish in the art area and describing their activity to the teacher; a teacher using a hand puppet to discuss the day's weather; a teacher passing a pineapple around for the children to see, feel, smell and eat; a teacher helping children make individual portions of playdough; children planting seeds and talking with a teacher about their "gardens"; a teacher reading a story about robins to the children and asking them questions about it. An accompanying training guide provides questions and learning activities for each section. *Catalog no.: PS 161*

Supporting Communication Among Preschoolers

(16mm film transfer of videotape; black & white, sound; 3 reels, 78 min. total)

This seven-part film deals with the cognitive, social and linguistic aspects of communication and illustrates a wide variety of teaching strategies for stimulating communication among preschoolers. Parts I and II are narrated films. Parts II-VI illustrate teaching strategies and show unnarrated classroom episodes which viewers are asked to analyze; part VII is in a question-answer format with breaks for discussion. *Catalog no.: PS 145*

Part I—An Important Opportunity
Examples of verbal communication in the classroom; the ways children use language and the benefits they gain from it.

Part II—Opportunities in the Classroom
How the daily routine can provide children with opportunities to communicte with one another. How teachers can support children as givers and receivers of information.

Part III—Encouraging Interaction and Cooperation
A presentation of teaching strategies to promote interaction and cooperation among children.

Part IV—Referring One Child's Questions or Problems to Another
Often children can help each other with problems that arise in the course of their activities. In asking and answering questions and helping each other to solve problems, they use language in important and meaningful ways. This film shows what teachers can do to encourage this type of interaction.

Part V—Interpreting or "Delivering" Messages
Sometimes a teacher needs to be a "go between" for children, helping one child understand what another is trying to say, helping the other find ways to say what he means. Often the teacher may have to "deliver" messages that weren't received or acknowledged. This film illustrates several such situations.

Part VI—Encouraging Active Listening
Ways in which teachers can help children listen to, think about and act upon each other's statements, questions or suggestions.

Part VII—Examples for Discussion

Team Planning in the Cognitively Oriented Curriculum

(16mm film transfer of videotape; black & white, 18 min.)

This film documents the activities of two preschool teachers at various times of the school day. It shows them planning, considering ways to support both the children and each other, sharing observations of the children, and evaluating the effectiveness of the activities they had planned for the day. *Catalog no.: PS 160*

Thinking and Reasoning in Preschool Children
(16mm film transfer of videotape; black & white, sound; 23 min.)

An overview of the characteristics of children's thinking in the "preoperational" stage of development. The film illustrates some of the important concepts and reasoning abilities that children develop during the preschool years. It shows how the child's understanding of the world affects his behavior and problem-solving methods. A concise introduction to a complex subject.   *Catalog no.: PS 138*

This Is the Way We Go to School
(16mm film; color, sound; 28 min.)

A documentary on the Ypsilanti Preschool Curriculum Demonstration Project (1968-71), with "voice-over" commentary by the project's director, David P. Weikart. Scenes from the Language Training (Bereiter-Engelmann), Unit-Based and Cognitive classrooms provide vivid illustrations of the philosophies and methods of these contrasting approaches to preschool education and point up the major conclusions of the study.   *Catalog no.: PS 134*

Working with Teachers and Parents
(videotape, 30 min. total)

1. *Leading Group Discussions*
2. *Inservice Training*

These film clips show dramatizations of typical situations encountered by early childhood curriculum specialists. Viewers are asked to analyze the interactions and suggest strategies for dealing with the situations. These are targeted for individuals in leadership and training roles in early childhood programs.   *Catalog no.: PS 163*

Elementary Education & Child Development

Cognitive Development Series
(16mm film transfers of slide/tape presentations with live action; color, sound)

Each film in this series deals with a different kind of thinking process—classifying, seriating, temporal thinking, spatial understanding—and shows a sequence of curriculum goals and corresponding key experiences for elementary-age students. Each goal and experience is described briefly and illustrated with classroom examples.

1. *Classification—a Sequence of Exercises (25 min.)* Children gradually develop the ability to group things on the basis of similarities and differences in attributes and use; they learn to make and identify connections.   *Catalog no.: EE 211*

2. *Seriation—a Sequence of Exercises (25 min.)* Children learn to order objects along a dimension—for example, saying which of two objects is bigger, or lining people up according to height.   *Catalog no.: EE 212*

3. *Spatial Relations—a Sequence of Exercises (20 min.)* Children orient themselves and objects in space and mentally organize their experience of the physical world.   *Catalog no.: EE 213*

4. *Temporal Relations—a Sequence of Exercises (on 2 reels)* Aspects of the development of the child's orientation in time—ways children learn to understand and function within time.   *Catalog no.: Part I—EE 214, Part II—EE 215*

The Daily Routine
(16mm film transfer of slide/tape presentation; color, sound; 30 min.)

A typical day in a cognitively oriented elementary classroom, with scenes from the High/Scope Elementary School. This film shows how a consistent routine can help children take a more self-directed, active approach to learning. The film documents the major components of the daily routine—planning and work time, clean-up, small-group and juice time, activity time and circle time—and discusses the purposes of each.   *Catalog no.: EE 201*

Representation
(16mm film transfers of slide/tape presentations with live action; color, sound)

Children portray, or "represent," their thoughts in many ways—for example, they draw and paint, tell or write stories, make models, enact familiar scenes. Representation enriches experience and helps to clarify thought— it is a crucial factor in development, as these two films demonstrate.

1. *Children Make Representations for Many Reasons (16 min.)*
An overview of representation—why it is important in an educational setting, what kinds of representation are likely to occur throughout the children's day. The film pinpoints the role of representational activity in stimulating and clarifying thinking and in developing a more detailed and accurate conception of reality.   *Catalog no.: EE 202*

2. *Teachers Make Representing a Thinking Process (17 min.)*
This film depicts the role of the teacher in implementing representation as a formal curriculum component. It demonstrates that representation is a creative process, satisfying both for teacher and child, and stresses the role of the teacher as a facilitator and observer of children's representations. It also shows some ways teachers can use questions, participation in children's activities, and additional materials to help children expand their representational activities and thus their thinking.   *Catalog no.: EE 203*

Understanding and Using the Concept of Number (K-3)

(color filmstrips and cassette tapes; 58 min. total)

The first in a series of filmstrip sets dealing with the mathematical reasoning abilities of children during different stages of intellectual development. The presentations use scenes of the classroom and teacher-planning sessions to show that children's math experience can and should be integrated with their everyday activities. They demonstrate how teachers can use various child-initiated situations to help children think mathematically and use mathematics to solve problems they encounter in their work. The three parts of the filmstrip set deal with the preoperational child, the "transitional" child, and the concrete operational child, respectively.   *Catalog no.: EE 220*

Parent-Infant Education

Parents as Volunteers

(color filmstrip and cassette tape, 25 min.)

An introduction to the Cognitively Oriented Curriculum for bilingual parents, this film follows two parent volunteers, one Spanish-speaking, one English-speaking, through a typical classroom day. The film depicts specific examples of children's activities in the Cognitively Oriented classroom and the ways parent volunteers can fit into them.   *Catalog no.: PS 192*

Infant Development

(16mm film transfers of videotape; black & white; sound)

1. *Early Learning: An Introduction to the Stages of Development in Infancy (26 min.)*
An overview of cognitive development during infancy. This film illustrates the six stages of the sensory-motor period of development in a form that is easily understood. Through selections from home visits showing babies involved in various activities, the film offers a practical view of things babies generally do and learn at each step.   *Catalog no.: ID 302*

2. *Learning to Talk: An Introduction to Language Development in Infancy (25 min.)*
The language of infants is traced from very early attempts to make sounds through the successive steps that finally result in the use of words and phrases. There are four sections, corresponding to the phases of language development in infancy. Each section has examples of infants' speech. The first section deals with the beginning sounds babies make, and with their attentiveness to sounds around them. The second section focuses on imitation—babies imitating first their own sounds, then the sounds of other people and objects. Next, the child's imitation of words and phrases is shown in a variety of situations. The final section deals with the baby's use of words to express needs and ask questions.
Catalog no.: ID 303

3. *Visual Pursuit and Object Permanence (27 min.)*
The viewer is taken through the four major steps in the development of the infant's ability to recognize and distinguish objects: visual search, partial disappearance, complete disappearance and

invisible displacement. Concrete examples and everyday language are used to illustrate these four steps. There are also several examples of home-teaching techniques.   *Catalog no.: ID 304*

4. *Toot 'n Tub—Object Concepts During Sensory-Motor Stage 3 (19 min.)*
This film illustrates the different ways a child can play with and learn about a toy, and it documents in nontechnical terms the infant's development of the object concept during one of the stages of the sensory-motor period of development. It focuses on one infant, Toot, and his play with a particular toy, called "Three Men in a Tub." The viewer is able to observe how the infant's approach to playing with the toy changes as his sensory-motor skills develop.
Catalog no.: ID 305

5. *Development of Means for Achieving Desired Ends (20 min.)*
Through scenes of actual home visits, this film shows how babies develop the ability to control their environment—to make things happen their way. The film illustrates the five stages through which this development proceeds: (1) accidental discoveries about objects, (2) purposeful handling of objects, (3) choosing appropriate actions, (4) using objects as tools and (5) inventing new ways to use objects.
Catalog no.: ID 306

6. *Causing Events To Occur—Development of Causality (23 min.)*
Highlights the learning involved in the infant's development of the concept of causality. This film has three parts, each of which shows babies in a different phase of the development of causality.   *Catalog no.: ID 307*

Part I—Noticing and Responding to Interesting Events
We see the baby observing movements and objects around him, turning towards sounds, beginning to react to facial expressions and becoming more and more active in responding to things in his environment.

Part II—Making Things Happen
How babies learn that they can manipulate objects to get a result: they can bang on a xylophone, hit a noise-making clown and produce sounds, push a block to knock it over.

Part III—Understanding What Makes Things Happen
The baby now understands indirect action; for

example, he can push a button to release a jack-in-the-box. He also learns that he can get other people to make things happen—he understands interpersonal causality as well as object causality.

Parental Support of Early Learning
(16mm film transfers of videotape; black & white; sound)

1. *Opportunities for Learning (27 min.)*
This film is designed to stimulate discussion among parents and infant-caregivers. It illustrates the process of exploration and discovery that is characteristic of most one- and two-year-olds by following the activities of one child through a series of play situations. In order to learn from his environment, the child needs *materials* for playing and learning, *time* to try things out, *people* to help him and to have fun with, *freedom* to learn on his own. Each section of the film focuses on one of these elements and gives suggestions to parents on how they can provide opportunities for learning in the home.   *Catalog no.: ID 308*

2. *Babies Like Attention (13 min.)*
Several clips from home visits chosen to stimulate discussion of the use of praise and encouragement with infants. Includes the spontaneous reactions of a group of mothers who watched themselves on videotape interacting with their children. Each mother gives a summary of her views on praise and encouragement and suggests things she feels are important to remember when interacting with a child. A good introduction for parents to the home-visit situation.   *Catalog no.: ID 309.*

3. *A Special Kind of Mother (15 min.)*
This film features and is narrated by a mother from High/Scope's Infant Videotaping Project. It focuses on some of the special skills a mother can learn. Interactions between this mother and her baby point up her ability to understand, interpret and act upon her child's needs. Throughout the film she comments on her actions with the child and how she thought the baby felt at the time.   *Catalog no.: ID 310*

4. *Learning through Problems: A Baby's Point of View (10 min.)*
Often a problem that's easy for an adult, such as holding two rattles at the same time, is very difficult for a baby. This film asks viewers to observe events from

the baby's point of view. It shows how complex reaching, holding, moving and pulling can be for an infant and how babies' sensory-motor explorations and difficulties can be turned into learning experiences which are fun for both baby and parent. *Catalog no.: ID 311*

5. *Cans: Toys for Learning (17 min.)*
A practical demonstration of how a simple household object, a can, can be used as an educational toy. Infants are shown progressing from simple manipulation, to recognition of objects inside a can, to putting objects back inside the can. The film shows how activities can be made more complex once the infant becomes aware of the variety of the can's uses— for example, by adding a lid for the baby to remove and replace and by putting a hole in the lid through which the baby can drop objects. There are suggestions for using other household objects—e.g., pots and pans, Bandaid boxes—in a similar manner. *Catalog no.: ID 312*

6. *Responding to a Baby's Actions (24 min.; discussion guide included)*
Babies have special ways of letting adults know their participation is wanted. Adults' responses can take many forms. Some of the possible adult responses are illustrated in this film: imitating the baby's sounds, exploring objects and toys with the baby, joining in a game the baby has started. Following a summary of these responses, three unnarrated examples of adult-child interactions are presented for use in group discussions, for which a discussion guide is included. *Catalog no.: ID 313*

APPENDIX 5
The High/Scope Child Observation Record

Preschool & Kindergarten

The complete Child Observation Record may be obtained at a nominal charge from the High/Scope Foundation. Address inquiries to:
High/Scope Foundation
Administration Dept.
600 North River Street
Ypsilanti, Michigan 48197

—Sample—

Child's Name_____

Teacher's Name_____

Date of Observation Period _____
                                        week/month/year

I. INTENSIVE FIVE-DAY OBSERVATION

PLANNING TIME

Item 1: Expression of Choices and Plans

0. Child gives *no* indication of having choices or *plans* in mind, stands around idly or follows the teacher around, not making any decision of his own 0

1. Child *looks at or touches materials* in the room and/or moves toward an area or material. However, there is no other communication to the teacher of a plan 1

2. Child *intentionally communicates* choice to the teacher by pointing to, walking over to, or naming an area, material, or child, but the teacher *has to "recognize"* the plan 2   CIRCLE ONE

3. *With* a lot of prompting from teacher, child communicates *what* he is going to do 3

4. *Without* a lot of prompting from teacher, child communicates *what* he is going to do 4

5. *With* a lot of prompting from teacher, child communicates *how* he will carry out his plan 5

6. *Without* a lot of prompting from teacher, child communicates *how* he will carry out his plan 6

WORK TIME

Item 2: Following Initial Plan

0. Child *does not make* initial plan, so this item is inapplicable 0

1. Child *does not follow* initial plan 1

2. Child *follows* initial plan *one or two days* out of five 2

3. Child *follows* initial plan at least *three days* out of five, but sticks to it for *less than ten minutes* 3   CIRCLE ONE

4. *One or two days* out of five, child *follows* initial plan for *at least ten minutes*, sticking with the original goal even when introducing slight modifications, such as moving to a different area of the room 4

5. At least *three days* out of five, child *follows* initial plan for *ten or more minutes*, sticking with the original goal even when introducing slight modifications 5

Item 3: Long-Term Projects

0. Child never engages in long-term projects .. 0
1. Child engages in *long-term projects* 1   CIRCLE ONE

Item 4: Problem-Solving with Materials

0. Child seems to *never or seldom perceive* problems 0

1. Child *perceives* problems, but *seldom confronts* them 1

2. Child makes *one attempt* to solve a problem, but gives up if she does not succeed 2   CIRCLE ONE

3. Child tries to solve a problem in a *second*, different *way* if her first attempt is unsuccessful 3

4. Child makes *more than two attempts* to solve a problem 4

Item 5: Focused Activity

Child focuses on one activity for:

1. less than two minutes at a time 1
2. less than five minutes at a time 2
3. less than ten minutes at a time 3   CIRCLE ONE
4. ten to thirty minutes at a time 4
5. thirty minutes or more at a time 5

Item 6: Diversity of Activities and Contacts

Over the course of a week, the child:

1. incorporates a number of different *materials* in her activities 1

2. works in two or more *areas* of the classroom 2

3. interacts with three or more *children* 3   CIRCLE ALL
4. accepts interactions with more than one regular classroom *staff* person 4   THAT APPLY

Item 7: Spontaneous Representation Using Materials

1. Child engages only in *object level play* 1

2. Child's structures and/or drawings always take the form of simple towers or dots and lines that have no apparent organization. They are sometimes named by the child, but are *not recognizable as representations* to the observer even after the child has explained them 2

3. The child creates structures and/or drawings with shapes or forms that are *recognizable as representations after the child has explained them* 3   CIRCLE ONE

4. Structures and/or drawings include shapes or forms that are *recognizable representations without any explanation* 4

5. The child's representations are of level 4 type, but in addition, include *3 or more details representing specific attributes of the things being represented* 5

Item 8: Spontaneous Representation in Dramatic Play

0. Not observed 0
1. Child uses *one object to stand for another* ... 1
2. Child uses *actions or sounds to pretend* to be doing something 2
3. Child uses *words to set stage* 3
4. Child *assumes role of someone else* (5+ minutes) 4   CIRCLE ALL THAT APPLY
5. *Inanimate objects used as characters* in child's dramatic play 5
6. Child talks in *language appropriate to role* .. 6
7. Child *coordinates role play* with peers (5+ minutes) 7

Item 9: Representation Through Art Media

0. Child *does not* use art media to *represent* what she did 0

1. Child *sometimes* creates *representations*, but with *two or fewer details* 1   CIRCLE ONE

2. Child *usually* creates *representations* with *two or fewer details* 1

Parent Interview & Assessment Schedule

Parent's Name_____

Child's Name_____

Date_____

I. PARENT ORIENTATIONS TOWARD PRESCHOOL & CHILD REARING

1. Give me your first reason for enrolling _____ in the preschool.

2. Do you prefer that your child speak in class the same way he or she does at home or do you want the teacher to correct the child?

3. Answer **yes** or **no** if you think children should learn the following:

	Yes	No
a) to interact with people from their own cultural background		
b) to enjoy activities (songs, games) and materials (construction materials, clothes, food) typical of their own cultural backgrounds		
c) to enjoy activities and materials typical of other cultures		
d) to make choices and to follow through on their decisions		
e) to learn by being active (by exploring with all their senses, using their large and small muscles, using tools, experimenting with materials)		
f) to role play (pretend they're someone else)		
g) to draw pictures and make things out of clay and blocks		
h) to learn the alphabet and how to count to 20		
i) to work together		
j) to speak properly		

4. **If there is something you want** _____ to learn in the preschool above all else, what would that be?

5. Do you prefer that your child learn it on his/her own or that the teacher teach it to him/her?

6. Can you name at least three things you don't want your child ever to forget?

7. What do you do at home to make sure she/he does not forget these things?

8. Name at least three places where you usually take your child with you.

9. Name one place where you usually take your child to have a nice time and learn.

II. PARENT NEEDS AND INTERESTS

1. Would you like to work with the children in the classroom?

2. What would you prefer doing in the classroom if you were to come?

3. Name something special that you can do or make or something you know about that you would be willing to share with the children.

4. I'm going to read a list of items to you. Tell me if you have ever felt a need to know more about any of these areas by answering either yes or no.
    (Interviewer: Please check appropriate category.)

	Yes	No
a. How to teach my preschool children		
b. Whether my child is developing appropriately		
c. Services provided by community agencies to which I have a right		
d. How to communicate better with my children		
e. How to help my children interact better with others		
f. How to discipline my children		
g. How to make toys and other things for my children		
h. How to tell whether my child is progressing in school		
i. What to do when my children do things that I do not consider proper (temper tantrums, thumb sucking, bad manners)		
j. How to play with my children		
k. Where to take my children so they can have a nice time and learn		
l. How to get my children to retain their cultural heritage		
m. How to use and develop the talents and skills that I know I have		
n. How to refrain from hitting my child		
o. How to guarantee that my child will succeed in school		
p. How to talk to teachers		
q. How to help my child learn a second language when I don't speak a second language		

	Yes	No
r. How to extend language learning		
s. How to use my home environment as a learning experience for my children		

5. What is your opinion about the idea of preschool parents coming together at least once a month to talk and learn more about the areas to which you answered "yes"?

6. If you felt that this parent meeting is a good idea, how can we make sure that the meetings are worthwhile for parents?

7. Would you be willing to help organize the first parent meeting?

8. Are there other ways you might be willing to help with the parent meetings?

9. Name something special that you can do, make or know about that you would be willing to share with other parents.

Subject Index